SO ONCE WAS I

Warren Farrell, from Inchicore, Dublin, is a first-time author with a passion for social history. A Maynooth University graduate in Politics and History, he furthered his education with a Masters in Secondary School Education. He has since shared his love of history and politics with many students in Dublin as a secondary school teacher. Warren is now a coordinator for Trinity Access Programmes at Trinity College, where he works with students from disadvantaged backgrounds to help them achieve their college aspirations and to try to ensure greater equity in access to higher education. Since January 2016, Warren has also worked as a tour guide in Glasnevin Cemetery, where he takes great pride in being able to share the stories of people who have shaped Ireland's history over the last two centuries.

SO ONCE WAS I

Forgotten Tales from Glasnevin Cemetery

Warren Farrell

MERRION PRESS

First published in 2024 by
Merrion Press
10 George's Street
Newbridge
Co. Kildare
Ireland
www.merrionpress.ie

978 1 78537 512 5 (Paper)
978 1 78537 513 2 (Ebook)

A CIP catalogue record for this book is
available from the British Library.

Typeset in Minion Pro 11/15 pt

Cover design by kvaughan.com

Merrion Press is a member of Publishing Ireland.

For Leo Farrell
(1932–2023)

Contents

Author's Note

This publication is a personal one to me, independent of my role as a tour guide in Glasnevin Cemetery and Dublin Cemeteries Trust. It began as a passion project to keep myself busy during Covid-19 lockdowns and to help me personally learn more about this historic site. It has led me to collect some of the lesser-told stories from the cemetery and to present them in this book. Some of the legacies included have been previously included in tours of the cemetery, such as the former 'Dead Interesting' and 'Women in History' tours. I would like to thank all within Dublin Cemeteries Trust for their original internal research that brought some of these stories to my attention in the first instance. Staff members both past and present in Glasnevin have provided me with a good foundation to help retell the stories in this book. Many former guides and Dublin Cemeteries Trust staff passionately kept the hidden legacies in the cemetery alive before my time working as a guide. I would like to acknowledge their efforts. Their names can be found referenced within the endnotes and in the acknowledgments section. This book seeks to expand on these neglected narratives and to record a selection of them in one place.

Here, you'll find numerous grave references and locations in Glasnevin Cemetery. To navigate your way around, you need to understand that the cemetery is organised into sections A to Z, with each section running alphabetically and then numerically. For instance, William J. Fitzpatrick (1830–95), a historian mentioned in this book, is buried in TA 75 in the Chapel Circle. This means his grave is in Row T of section A, seventy-five graves along. The Chapel Circle indicates the broader section. Consult the maps on pages x and 10 for section locations. While there are some exceptions, for example with the St Paul's section, this short guide should help you in your search for the graves featured in the book.

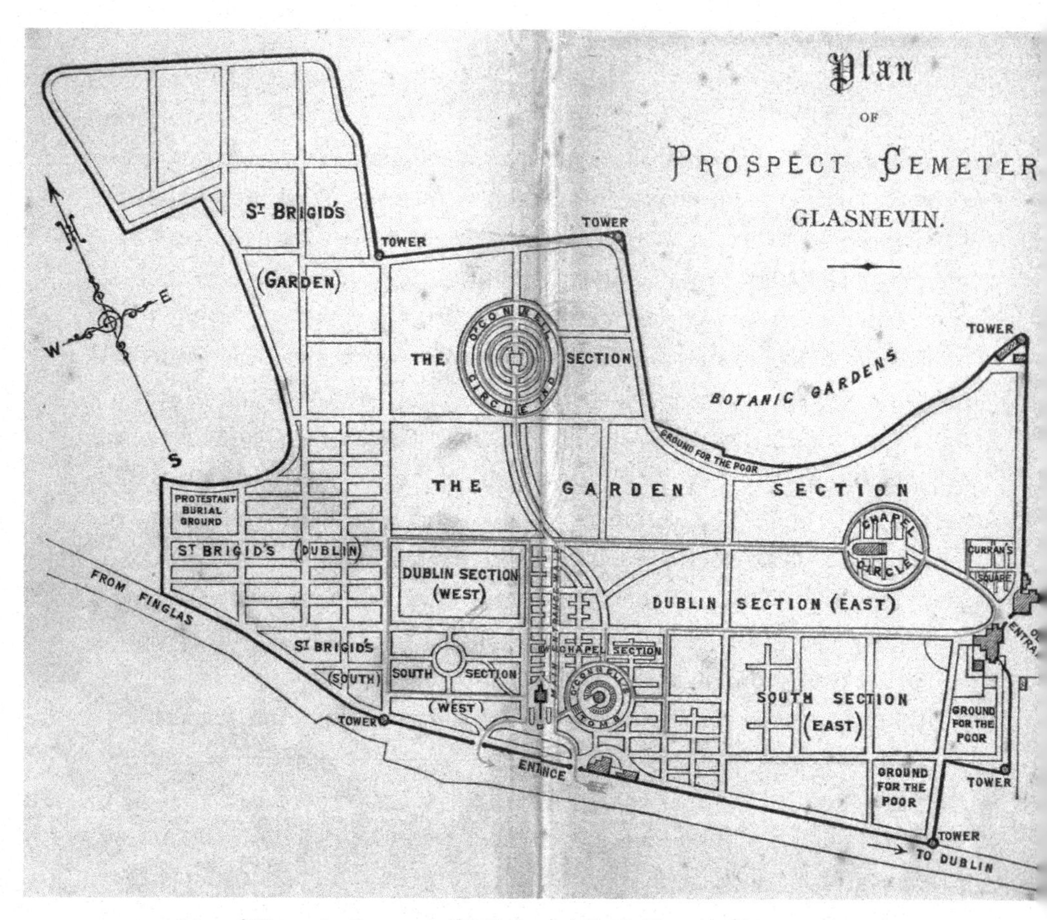

Map of Glasnevin Cemetery (1879) from *A Guide Through Glasnevin Cemetery.* (Courtesy of the National Library of Ireland)

Foreword

James Joyce's character in *Ulysses*, Leopold Bloom, attending Paddy Dignam's funeral in Glasnevin Cemetery, pondered, 'How many! All these here once walked round Dublin. Faithful departed. As you are now so once were we.' Glasnevin Cemetery (a graveyard is too coarse a word for it) is the resting place of a million and more souls from every part of Dublin and beyond. It has been said there are more people buried in the cemetery than living in Dublin and certainly there is no greater concentration of people from all sectors of Irish society lying in their plots, patiently waiting for a passer-by to stop, possibly remember them or read their epitaph and consider their life for a moment. Personally, Glasnevin is growing on me with each passing year. I'm not dying to get into it, but lately it has become my favourite part of Dublin – no doubt an attempt by my subconscious mind to get used to my future and long-term accommodation.

My good friend Shane MacThomáis worked with me on the *1916 Walking Tour of Dublin* for many years and became the most well-known guide in the cemetery. He wrote a couple of wonderful books and although he wasn't the first person to write about Glasnevin, he was the first to write in an appealing, humorous and accessible manner about a subject that many people prefer to treat as taboo: death. Shane took thousands of visitors on tours around the necropolis and not only made them cry but made them laugh as well. Shane is now resting with his equally famous father, Éamonn MacThomáis, and they are buried right beside Frank Ryan, who led the Irish Brigade in the fight against fascism in Spain. Within a hundred yards of Shane's grave, there are hundreds more equally important Irish republicans and socialists keeping each other company.

Every generation worries that the next generation may be careless with certain traditions and stories. Perhaps there is some truth in this. Modern-day life sometimes has little room for older ways. However, the younger generation of guides in Glasnevin Cemetery are as good if not better than the previous generation. Added to this there is a new generation of young historians in Ireland continuing to research and write about our wonderful nation, bursting at the seams with poets, writers, artists, musicians, sporting and revolutionary heroes. Joining that illustrious list of young historians is Warren Farrell, who has researched and written this wonderful and important new volume, *So Once Was I: Forgotten Tales from Glasnevin Cemetery*. Warren's approach is commendable in that he chooses to write on characters who were in great danger of being forgotten. The people are related to subjects as far apart as Dublin Zoo and Sydney Harbour Bridge and as diverse as Jimmy O'Dea and Thomas Addis Emmet.

As one of the outstanding guides in Glasnevin for many years, he has written this book as a personal endeavour. Warren knows how to tell a great story, what details people are interested in, what is moving and what is amusing, which essentially makes a perfect writer; and you now have in your hand a book that will be around for many years to come. Shane loved the little rhyme that Warren has borrowed for the book's title. So did James Joyce. So did the unknown monk who first penned it centuries ago and when you're in Glasnevin, you can hear this being whispered as you read a headstone:

Remember now as you walk by
As you are now, so once was I.

Lorcan Collins

Introduction

Glasnevin Cemetery, or Prospect Cemetery as it was originally called, has often been described as the final resting place of a veritable who's who in Irish history spanning nearly two centuries. Tour guides regularly joke that it is the 'dead centre of Dublin' and that there are more people buried on the land than there are alive in Dublin city. Many books have been written on the history of the cemetery, its founder – the legendary Daniel O'Connell – and the many significant political, religious and cultural figures buried there. However, amongst these many famous figures, from Michael Collins to Éamon de Valera, Countess Constance Markievicz to Maud Gonne MacBride, Daniel O'Connell to Charles Stewart Parnell, and Brendan Behan to Luke Kelly, lie many others with incredible stories. Some of these have become forgotten, neglected and lost amongst the forest of monuments, sculptures and headstones in an area that today covers approximately 140 acres.

As a tour guide in Glasnevin over the past eight years, I have developed a passion for trying to retell these forgotten tales; not only the stories that tell us the history of the island of Ireland over the past two centuries but also the social, quirky, strange and unbelievable tales of many who have become lost within a set of records containing over 1.5 million people. I have had the

---

Glasnevin Cemetery *c.* 1865–1914. (Reproduced courtesy of the National Library of Ireland)

privilege to work alongside many wonderful staff members who have helped to unearth a lot of the stories in this book. I am indebted to their unending curiosity about Ireland's necropolis. My hope is that this book will encourage more people to explore the grounds for themselves and to begin to retell the stories of those who are now simply forgotten about in this, the national cemetery of Ireland.

At a site like Glasnevin it is impossible to know everything. What the visitor sees today when strolling around is a far cry from what the cemetery looked like before 2006. Before that the cemetery had fallen into a state of disrepair and a lot of work has since been undertaken to try and get it back to its former glory as a fully functioning Victorian-style garden cemetery. Work is still ongoing to ensure headstones are upstanding and legible. Being a not-for-profit organisation and a registered charity, the cemetery began to lose the power to preserve and maintain such a large space during the mid- to late twentieth century. The year 2006 was, therefore, an important turning point. Glasnevin Trust (formerly the Dublin Cemeteries Committee and today the Dublin Cemeteries Trust) petitioned the then Taoiseach, Bertie Ahern, for funding from government to allow for the restoration of the grounds and monuments. This was to help ensure that the cemetery could act in a number of capacities: first, to become a prime tourist attraction where people could visit a new museum and avail of public tours to learn about Ireland's great necropolis; second, to allow for the site to act as a centre of national pride for the centenary of the Easter Rising. All this was done in preparation for the larger Decade of Centenaries programme (1913–23). It also helped to restore dignity to those buried in Glasnevin Cemetery and allowed families to mourn in a more suitable setting.

Many of the events for the Decade of Centenaries had strong links to the cemetery, making it even more important for restoration to take place. The government included the cemetery in the National Development Plan as an Office of Public Works (OPW) project in June 2006, and the OPW has since made very important contributions towards restoring this great cemetery. Their most recent contribution can be seen in the restored staircase inside the O'Connell Round Tower. This now allows visitors to climb 198 steps to a height of 55 metres, and experience wonderful views of the wider Dublin area. These works were completed in 2018.

In addition, burials and, since 1982, cremation services continue to take place in the cemetery from Monday to Saturday. This is a non-denominational space for people from all walks of life to have their dead laid to rest. Dublin Cemeteries Trust strives to provide for all to have their loved ones buried or cremated in a respectful, dignified and peaceful way. By upholding these original ideals, the Trust is maintaining one of the first mission statements of its founder, Daniel O'Connell.

I remember sitting down in the café beside the visitor centre with my friend and former colleague Alan Cleary in January 2020. We began to chat about the number of stories we had uncovered and learned about since beginning our work as guides. Out of interest, we wrote down a list of people we felt had not received the attention they deserved in the daily storytelling of Glasnevin. We began to realise that the list could easily surpass 100 names. Lynn Brady, a close friend and then resident genealogist, agreed to look up their locations. Each morning before opening time, Alan and I ventured down out of general interest to one or two of these graves. In many cases it was the first time anyone had paid a visit in over a hundred years. Some had small grave markers, some had impressive funerary monuments, but most had no marker whatsoever.

Then, in March 2020 the world was engulfed by the Covid-19 pandemic and with that came the closure of the cemetery's visitor centre. Instead, Glasnevin turned its focus back to its primary function: burying the dead. Another chapter of history was thus added. Some of those who sadly passed away due to Covid-19 now lie at rest inside. We remember them all, and especially the families who had to grieve in such strange and challenging circumstances. It was in this context that I began to use the list of forgotten graves to write the stories of those on it and that project has since become the book you are now reading.

The notable dead in Glasnevin are voluminous in nature and lie side by side, with impressive monuments above their graves; they receive countless visitors each day. While I do not wish to discount their national importance, to visit just these graves only scratches the surface of Glasnevin Cemetery's history. For thousands at rest, their contributions and achievements are forgotten. In compiling this collection, I hope that more people will pay a visit to the less well-known gravesides. In searching for them, it is impossible not to notice the art, architecture, symbolism, vanity and, in some cases, the sadness and the simplicity of the cemetery's grave markers. Every story is unique to its time and place. Some people's stories overlap and show that in Glasnevin at least, there are certainly less than six degrees of separation.

This book seeks to tell some of the overlooked stories associated with Glasnevin and I have greatly enjoyed the challenge of researching them. Much inspiration for this book came from reading Shane MacThomáis' earlier publications on the notable dead of the cemetery. His words from *Glasnevin: Ireland's Necropolis* stick with me each time I walk the grounds: 'rest assured for every poet noted, we may be sure there are another hundred. For every patriot, statesperson, scholar, hundreds more. For every ordinary citizen of Dublin pointed out, tens of thousands more.'[1]

Shane dedicated much of his life to bringing people to the final resting places of many of Ireland's famous and not so famous figures in Glasnevin. In *Dead Interesting* (2012), he suggested that to make a good tour guide you needed four things: 'one … to tell people something they already know; two, to tell them something they don't; three, be able to make them laugh; and four, to make them cry'.[2] As a guide I have tried to achieve these elements in my own tours, admittedly with varying levels of success! I hope this book achieves what Shane believed were the ingredients for a good tour – to give the reader a collection of stories that will provide added insight into, as James Joyce calls them, our 'faithful departed'.

The title chosen for my work may already be familiar to readers, as the epitaph from which it came was recited by the late Martin Galligan, former Restoration Project Manager at Glasnevin, in the award-winning documentary *One Million Dubliners*: 'Remember now as you go by, as you are now so once was I; and as I am now so you shall be, so prepare for death and follow me.'[3] It is a fitting reminder that one day someone may be telling our stories long after we are gone.

A Brief History

Prospect Cemetery opened its gates for the first time on 21 February 1832. The repressive Penal Laws of the eighteenth century, with their roots in the Reformation, had placed harsh restrictions on the Catholic population in Ireland. Restrictions on the public performance of Catholic services at funerals was of particular significance, and it was as a result of these restrictions that Daniel O'Connell adopted burial rights as a key area in highlighting the discrimination that Catholics faced. Lisa Marie Griffith and Ciarán Wallace refer to this as 'a forgotten feature of death and burial up to the 1820s in Ireland'.[4] The Reformation had seen the wholesale exchange of

Catholic churchyards and churches in Ireland to the Established Church: the Anglican Church of Ireland. The burial of Catholics by clergy on land that was now deemed unfit for their beliefs became a major issue. Catholics at the time were also expected to pay added funeral charges to the parson for the right to be buried on these lands. This was on top of already existing taxes (tithes) paid by the Catholic population.

It was a burial in a local Church of Ireland graveyard called St Kevin's on 9 September 1823 that led O'Connell into a series of burial disputes. The deceased, Arthur D'Arcy, had been a well-known businessman, politically active and a supporter of O'Connell's Catholic Association. As the mourners encircled the grave in order to recite the 'De Profundis' and other prayers led by Michael Blake (the Catholic archdeacon of the Dublin diocese), they were interrupted by the sexton of the parish, William B. Dunn. He insisted that they desist in accordance with the law and, after a tense exchange, everyone departed the scene. Claims later emerged in an anonymous letter from 'A Protestant who was present' to the editor of the *Dublin Evening Post* that the sexton was acting under the orders of the Protestant Archbishop of Dublin, William Magee. Michael Blake, in response, wrote his own letter, insisting that 'I did nothing which any layman might not lawfully do …'[5] O'Connell gave his legal opinion that there was no statute law preventing a Catholic priest from praying for a deceased Catholic in a churchyard. This, in fact, was not completely true, but it was the beginning of a protracted burial dispute that culminated with a campaign to open a new burial ground where people of different religions could be buried alongside each other.

Legislation soon followed in Westminster to address the matter, with the Act of Easement of Burial Bill (1824). It repealed certain parts of a previous act going back to the ninth century related to the burial of individuals in Ireland at suppressed monasteries, abbeys or convents. But the amended act caused more problems than it gave solutions, as it put in place a law where none had previously existed. The bill dealt with the rights of Catholics but was also designed to protect Protestants from Catholic funerals. Furthermore, it formally introduced a requirement for Catholics and dissenters to give notice and to obtain formal permission to carry out funeral rites in Protestant churchyards. Many Catholics saw it as demeaning and O'Connell described it as a 'rascally bill'.[6] However, with the suppression of the Catholic Association in 1825, O'Connell's mission to establish a non-denominational burial ground was halted.

Things would change after the funeral of Thomas Rooney of Moore Street in August 1827. He had been a member of O'Connell's Catholic Association. When his remains were brought for burial to the churchyard in Howth, a priest in attendance began to recite prayers as the coffin was lowered. The rector, a son-in-law of Archbishop Magee, interrupted and stated that he couldn't allow this. This incident proved to be the turning point for O'Connell. At a meeting on 15 September 1827 of the new Catholic Association (formed to get around the suppression of the old one), a motion was formally raised for the establishment of a committee to work towards establishing a non-denominational burial place.[7] This committee in time became the Dublin Cemeteries Committee (Dublin Cemeteries Trust today) which opened Goldenbridge Cemetery in 1829 and later Prospect (Glasnevin) Cemetery in 1832.

From the outset, Prospect, in accordance with O'Connell's wishes, was open to people of all and no religions. The first burial took place on 22 February 1832 in what is today the Garden section (O 43). It was of a young boy, Michael Carey, from the inner city of Dublin who died of tuberculosis. He had lived on Francis Street and was just 11 years old. From this first burial Glasnevin has expanded from its original 9 acres to its present size of 140, with over 1.5 million people at rest. The cemetery was not the only non-denominational one in Dublin. Officially Mount Jerome in Harold's Cross on the southside of Dublin, established in 1836, also catered for those of all and no religions. Local beliefs about these cemeteries in the Victorian era in Dublin held, however, that 'Glasnevin was commonly seen as non-denominational but really for Catholics and Mount Jerome as non-denominational but meant for Protestants'.[8] This does not diminish the fact that Glasnevin has gone through the last two centuries of history burying people of all religions, from capitalists to socialists, the clergy and the agnostic, Catholic next to Protestant, and even Irish rebels next to contemporaneous members of the British military from the same period. Today the cemetery is the final resting place for people of over twenty-five different beliefs and faiths, as well as those of none.

The Garden Cemetery

Glasnevin, established as a Victorian garden-style cemetery, acts as the best example of the changing funerary landscapes and customs at the turn of the nineteenth century in Ireland. Its design was heavily influenced by the landscape gardener and cemetery reformist John Claudius Loudon (1783–1843). Significant population increases throughout Europe and the United Kingdom in the mid- to late eighteenth century resulted in massive problems for local churches and cathedrals in the task of burying their dead. Traditionally the higher classes or nobility were buried in vaults beneath the church, but as over-crowding became a problem, this was extended to graves outside the church and we begin to see the idea of the local 'churchyard' or 'graveyard' take hold. The issue of space, or lack of it, continued to worsen throughout the nineteenth century as the other two sections of society, the middle and lower or pauper class, now sought the right to be buried within these churchyards or graveyards.

This led to awful burial conditions, particularly for those on the lower end of the societal spectrum. Carmel Connell references the great Christopher Wren, the man responsible for the design of the structure of St Paul's Cathedral in London, who remarked that '50,000 dead bodies were putrefying, rotting, giving out exhalations, darkening the air with vapours' and that this was commonplace in London's 150 local graveyards.[9]

Such conditions persisted for a long time, until people like J.C. Loudon began to take notice of developments on the continent. The French had begun to question the Church's attitude towards death and burial, and gradually writers and reformers, with their arguments on egalitarianism, began to push for a shift away from the crowded scenes in local churchyards. Instead, there was a move towards a garden setting outside urban areas for cemeteries. Napoleon Bonaparte decreed in 1804 that all burials in churches were to stop at once. From that point onwards a cemetery was to be established in each local community. This led to very fine examples of garden cemeteries, such as Père Lachaise in Paris. This cemetery in Paris acted as the prototype for changing ideas of how a cemetery should be arranged, structured and organised. Cemetery reformers from near and far would visit Père Lachaise, including J.C. Loudon.

Loudon had a great influence on the design of what became known as the Victorian garden cemetery. The influence of his work can still be seen in Glasnevin. It features many aspects of what Loudon wrote about in his 1843 publication, *On the Laying Out, Planting, and Managing of Cemeteries; and on the Improvement of Churchyards.* When you walk the grounds, you can see for yourself an ordered space, with high stone border walls, watchtowers for added security, organised plants and shrubbery and a detailed system of graves, that has allowed for extremely good record keeping and allows for a relaxed atmosphere away from the bustling city centre. Most important was the idea that Glasnevin was not just a burial site but a place where historical records could be amassed and stored. As Loudon stated:

> The country churchyard was formerly the country labourer's only library, and it has limited his knowledge of history, chronology, and biography; every grave was to him a page, and every headstone or tomb a picture or an engraving. With the progress of education and refinement, this part of the uses of churchyards, is not superseded, but only extended and improved.[10]

He also said:

> A Garden Cemetery and monumental decoration our eloquent author observes afford the most convincing tokens of a nation's progress in civilisation and in the arts which are its result. We have seen with what pains the most celebrated nations of which history speaks have adorned their places of sepulture, and it is from their funeral monuments that we gather much that is known of their civil progress and of their advancements in taste.[11]

It is another man, however, who has left the biggest legacy for Glasnevin as a garden cemetery. The 'naturalist' Matthias Joseph O'Kelly (1786–1868) was instrumental in devising the grid system that the cemetery uses. He originally mapped out the smaller cemetery at Goldenbridge, before using a similar system in Glasnevin. From east to west Glasnevin Cemetery was laid out in sections A–Z, with numbers south to north. In effect he created a massive grid system where you can cross-reference the letters (rows and sections) with the numbers (position of a grave along each row) to pinpoint every burial. Even for people who are today in unmarked plots, it is relatively easy to find the precise location of their grave.

O'Kelly was a supporter of O'Connell and his campaign for Catholic Emancipation, and he accompanied O'Connell's body home to Ireland for burial at Glasnevin in 1847, yet he is largely forgotten about today.[12] He was buried in the Old O'Connell Circle (C 62.5) in 1868, where his headstone describes in great detail his dedication to Daniel O'Connell.

Glasnevin Cemetery *c.* 1865–1914. (Reproduced courtesy of the National Library of Ireland)

The cemetery grounds were later further divided into a number of distinct sections. As extra land was acquired, new sections were created. They include the Garden, St Patrick's, St Bridget's, St Mobhi's and St Paul's section, the South section, New Chapel Circle, Dublin section east and west, Old Chapel Circle, Curran Square, Old O'Connell Circle, O'Connell Tower Circle and Old Chapel Circle. Each one has been mapped out in a series of 'map-books', which has facilitated detailed record keeping. When walking the grounds, the words of the Dublin Cemeteries Committee from their 1879 publication still resonate:

> It will not be without pleasure that for a while the shady alleys may be traversed, and the exquisite shrubs so carefully and judiciously planted under the careful supervision of some members of the committee, may be observed with satisfaction. In many and many a spot the chaplet of Immortelles, the wreath or cross of flowers, the tasteful decoration, the little statue or crucifix laid upon the earth, or the jealous removal of weeds and nurturing of flowers or grass will tell the touching tale of love constant, living, abiding for some of whom nought but memory remains for those bereaved. … Lessons soothing and comforting may be learned in a walk through Glasnevin Cemetery.[13]

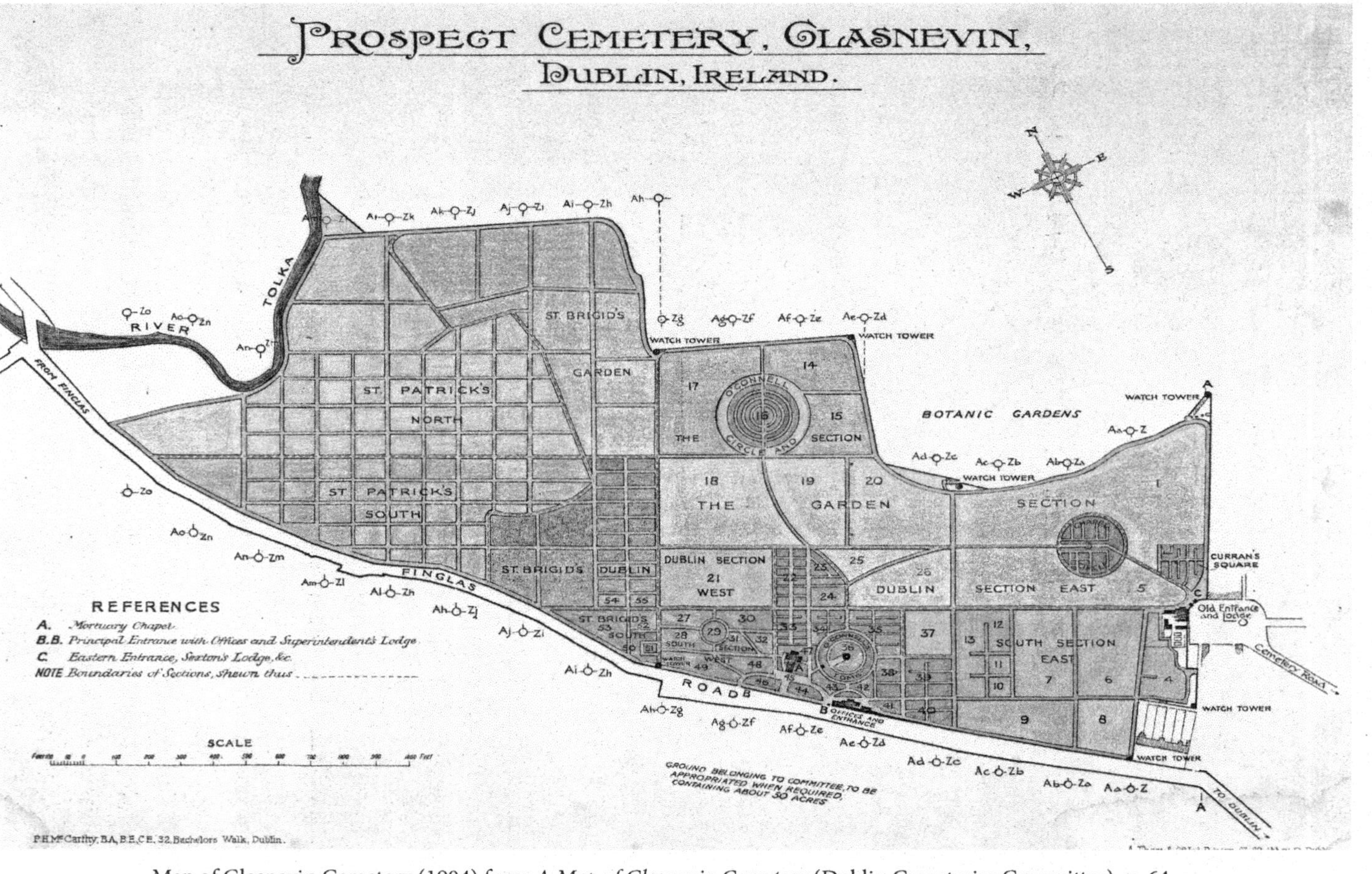

Map of Glasnevin Cemetery (1904) from *A Map of Glasnevin Cemetery* (Dublin Cemeteries Committee), p. 64.
Used with the kind permission of Dublin Cemeteries Trust.

Strange Things

Dublin's Zoological Gardens

The Zoological Gardens were first opened to the public on 1 September 1831. Around that same time the 9 acres of land where Glasnevin Cemetery was set up was being consecrated by the Very Reverend Monsignor Yore. Five months later the first burial took place. Both the zoo and Glasnevin have lived through the Famine years (1845–52), the Easter Rising of 1916, the Irish War of Independence (1919–21) and the Irish Civil War (1921–23). On a global scale they have lived through both world wars and seen forty presidents of the United States of America and nine British monarchs, and counting. The fact both have endured for nearly two centuries is a remarkable feat. What they share in common is that they were both, in many respects, ahead of their time. Dublin Zoo, as Catherine De Courcy explains, was established at a time when 'cruelty to animals was commonplace' and 'they wanted to promote greater respect for all living creatures'.[1]

Three men buried in Glasnevin have strong links with the zoo. Their names are John Supple, Thomas Flood and James McNally. All worked for the Zoological Gardens and died in strange circumstances. A walk through the cemetery towards the adjoining gates that link the National Botanical

---

Glasnevin Cemetery *c.* 1865–1914. (Reproduced courtesy of the National Library of Ireland)

Gardens to Glasnevin takes you into the Garden section. It is here that the three men are buried in unmarked plots. During their lives they cared for the animals in the zoo and helped provide entertainment for many people who entered its grounds.

The Freeman's Journal has a small piece relating to John Supple, dated 8 November 1867. The piece states: 'Death from the Bite of a Python – A man named John Supple, of 6 West Liffey Street, who had been employed in the Zoological Gardens in care of the reptiles, was bitten on Tuesday by a python, and was removed to Steevens' Hospital, where he died yesterday. The body awaits an inquest to be held this day.'[2]

John Supple was born in Dublin sometime in 1812. We know that he married a woman named Catherine Plunkett on 1 April 1839 in the parish of St Paul's in Dublin's Arran Quay district. He took up employment with the zoo shortly after it opened in 1831, where he was put in charge of the reptile house. In November 1867 John was bitten by a reticulated python in one of its enclosures. This type of python can reach up to 10 metres in length, but it is not venomous – its chosen method of killing is by strangulation. This led to much confusion when investigating John's death. It became the 'case of the mysterious snake bite'. He had definitely been bitten by the python and had died while in Dr Steevens' Hospital in Kilmainham. The Zoological Society of Ireland contacted London Zoo, which had similar pythons. They wanted to find out whether it was possible to die from a reticulated python's bite. London Zoo responded that in their opinion it was unlikely. In their zoo some keepers had been frequently bitten by these pythons but had only experienced a 'smarting, unpleasant sensation'.[3] It was agreed, however, that it was entirely possible to die from shock as a result of being bitten by a snake.

The record for John Supple does not contain a cause of death. However, the case has led tour guides to sometimes suggest that he died as a result of snake fright and not snake bite. Supple was buried in the Garden section (G 155) and his wife, Catherine, was interred in the same grave two years later, in 1869. Her husband was just 48 according to Glasnevin's records. The council of the Zoological Society of Ireland paid for the funeral expenses and then employed John's son Patrick. Up until his father's death he had been working in Middle Abbey Street as a lithographer.[4] Patrick worked as a keeper at the zoo up until his own death in 1913. Patrick, whose last address was 19 St David's Terrace, North Circular Road, Dublin, was also buried in Glasnevin, in the St Paul's section (SB 48). He was 65 years old and died as a result

John (Jack Supple) with orangutans. (Courtesy of the Board of Trinity College Dublin)

of an 'enlarged prostrate'. The Supple family continued their legacy at the zoo through Patrick's son Jack (John), who became one of its most famous keepers. He was the zookeeper in charge of the chimpanzee tea parties. Jack retired in 1961 and was buried with his father Patrick in the St Paul's section after his death on 31 January 1974.

Thomas Flood worked with John Supple in the earlier days of the zoo. On one occasion, both John and Thomas were recorded in the Royal Zoological Society of Ireland visitors notebooks as staying overnight to look after an extremely ill rhinoceros in 1865.[5] Sadly it died, but this shows the level of devotion the men must have felt towards the animals. Thomas was born sometime in the year 1835 and took up employment at the zoo in 1858. He had built up twenty-two years of service and was a very experienced employee. However, tragedy struck on 2 November 1880 as he was finishing cleaning the enclosure of a red deer stag and it attacked him. The animal, feeling territorially threatened, inflicted terrible injuries on Thomas, who sustained a fractured skull, seven broken ribs and badly lacerated hands.[6] Not realising at the time how bad his injuries were, Thomas managed to push the stag back into its enclosure and shut the gate. At that point the superintendent of the zoo, Edward Snow, and another keeper, George Bristow, approached. Thomas looked up at them as they approached, barely conscious and in considerable pain. The two men lifted him to his feet and then into their arms. He muttered, 'I think I'll walk', but died shortly afterwards. He was removed to Steevens' Hospital in Kilmainham.[7]

Thomas was 45 years old and his death certificate states that he died as a result of being 'accidentally killed by a wild animal at the Zoological Gardens'. He was a married man living at 18 Barracks Street, Dublin. His grave is unmarked in the Garden section (AD 70.5), quite close to that of John Supple. An investigation into what happened was launched by the Zoological Society of Ireland, but it proved to be inconclusive. Thomas Flood's son, Christopher, was later employed by the zoo in his early twenties.

Thomas Flood with a lion cub, *c.* 1869. (Courtesy of the Board of Trinity College Dublin)

He went on to become another of the zoo's famous head keepers and was a well-known face in the carnivores' house for over fifty years. He died of natural causes in 1933, aged 64, and is buried in the St Patrick's section (BN 155). Christopher's sons John and Charles also worked as keepers at the zoo. John sadly died of influenza in 1918 during the Spanish flu pandemic. He was 32 years old and is buried with his father in Glasnevin.

Tragedy struck the zoo again on 9 June 1903. James McNally was another experienced keeper and was heavily involved with the care of the elephants. He had been a keeper in the zoo since 1873 and had built up a relationship with the elephant Sita. That evening, he went in to dress Sita's foot. When he entered the enclosure, he found that she had an ingrown toenail and was in some pain. He began to apply the recommended lotion to the foot under the

Sita and James McNally *c.* 1902. (Courtesy of the RCSI)

supervision of a vet on site. Usually Sita, under his instruction, would kneel at his command. This time, however, as the keeper's 20-year-old son, John, looked on, Sita turned on her keeper. She knocked him to the ground and onto his side using her trunk. She then crushed his head with her right foot. James' son called for the elephant to fall back and release his father's head from under her foot. The whole thing was over in a matter of seconds. James McNally was dead.

The coroner's report into James' death stated 'the animal had met the fate usually meted out to animals guilty of deeds of this character. It had been destroyed that morning.'[8] What the coroner meant was that Sita was killed with a special rifle that had been sent from London. *The Irish Times*, on 12 June 1903, led with the headline 'The Elephant Shot'.[9] On hand were five members of the Royal Irish Constabulary (RIC), who had been given instructions to fire at Sita's shoulders. At the same time, using his 'large-bore games rifle', Colonel Neville Chamberlain fired two bullets: one between her eyes and the other under her ear. The original plan had been to poison Sita using potassium cyanide disguised inside an apple for her to eat. However, Sita spat the apple out.[10]

Once the elephant had been killed, a new problem arose. How would they remove the 5-tonne elephant from the enclosure? Forty members of the RIC, with two giant tug-of-war ropes, had to drag the animal into an

Hollowed-out foot of Sita. (Courtesy of Dublin Zoo)

outer enclosure where she could be dissected. Sita's foot, the same one that had killed James McNally, was hollowed out and preserved. It was given to the RIC as a thank you in recognition of their hard work in killing and removing the animal from the inner enclosure. The foot remained within the RIC sergeant's mess in the Phoenix Park depot until 1922.[11] It must be noted that it was common practice at the time for animals to be killed following an accident like the one that led to James McNally's death.

Sita had previously tested the patience of the zoo officials prior to the tragic death of her keeper. In February 1897 it was noted that she had headbutted the side of her enclosure house repeatedly. The walls had to be strengthened and rebuilt. A few months later, a large crowd in the zoo were throwing pennies towards her. This was the custom at the time and in exchange for the pennies, Sita would pass people out a biscuit or bun using her trunk. On this day, Sita became overly excited and in her anxious state managed to push James McNally backwards with her trunk. James slipped and fell onto the metallic railings, severely cutting his head. Although hurt, he insisted no further action be taken. After James' death, a subscription was opened for his widow and family. His son, John, was also given a permanent job as a keeper.[12]

Today James McNally lies close to the other two zookeepers in the Garden section (Z 129). He too is buried in an unmarked grave. He lived at 19 Ross Street, Stoneybatter, Dublin, was 60 years of age and his recorded cause of death in the Glasnevin records is 'head crushed by an elephant'. While it is true that there are some strange causes of death on the record books of Glasnevin, this one ranks high amongst them. On the whole affair of James McNally and Sita, *The Irish Times* said that during the night after the event she 'kept the other denizens of the gardens awake with shrill trumpetings'.[13]

The Fraudulent Burial Case

At the old Prospect entrance, not far from where the three zookeepers are buried, a funeral approached on 31 July 1858. Over the gates in gold Latin lettering the words *Beati Morti Qui in Domino Mortiuntur* or 'Blessed are those who die in the name of the Lord' can still be read today. A hearse drawn by four black horses with black plumes on their heads entered under its arch. The modest cortege made its way slowly along the main pathway flanked on both sides by yew trees. The funeral reached its final destination at the Garden section (WG 233.5). Trees surrounded the freshly dug grave. The coffin was placed beside the open grave as gravediggers positioned themselves to lower the remains into the plot.

Beside the grave a small gathering had taken shape. The husband of the deceased, Charles Higgins, stood closest. It was the burial of his dearly beloved wife, Maria. The coffin featured a small breastplate inscribed with the words 'Maria Higgins, aged 54, died 29th July 1858'.[14] Next to Charles stood his brother John. Beside them stood Charles' brother-in-law and close friend Henry William Devereux. The coffin of Maria was lowered into the plot. Some soil was thrown into the grave, pattering on the wooden coffin below as members of the procession slowly departed.

Two years later, in 1860, a woman, supposedly Maria Higgins, entered the solicitor's office of J.D. Rosenthal just off Nassau Street. She wanted to make a complaint relating to some previous business conducted at the office in 1858. The matter related to the signing of her will. She said that she was unhappy about how it had been distributed. A Mr Hamilton dealt with the woman supposedly back from the dead and brought her into Rosenthal's office. Rosenthal recalled how:

> She was brought into my office by Mr. Hamilton; she told me she was Mrs Higgins; I was very much struck; she told me all about the affairs of the Higginses; I got her to write her name, and compared it with the handwriting in the mortgage: I did not believe her, and got her identified; I asked her did she know all about what her husband [Charles Higgins] had done; she said she did, but that she did not care what was done to him; I consulted counsel, and issued summonses against the parties for conspiracy, and for obtaining money under false pretences.[15]

What transpired was the biggest fraud ever to hit Glasnevin. The first burial was all part of a highly intricate insurance scam. It rested on a series of family wills. The first will was signed by all the main players in the story: Charles and Maria Higgins and Mr Devereux (Charles' brother-in-law). It was witnessed by Rosenthal, the solicitor, and his employee Peter Edwards. It was made up of a sum of money and property that had been bequeathed to Maria Higgins by a relative called Francis Foster, dating back to 1843. The will was made up of two properties owned by members of this part of Mrs Higgins' family. It totalled £500. All the arrangements had been put in place that in the event of her sudden death where no children had been born, the money would be released and allocated in accordance with her last will. Once Maria had blown her cover, rumours quickly began to circulate about the fraudulent burial case. Her 'remains' were exhumed from the plot. It revealed bags of sand and no corpse. A full court case at Greenstreet Courthouse followed. The judge stated at the time, 'this is a case which from the very nature of it, should be sifted from top to bottom'.[16]

Maria, in 1856, two years before her first burial, made out a mortgage on the properties with a J.P. Byrne, solicitor, to ensure everything was secure and safe. Sometime later, she made out her first signed and witnessed will. In it she made provisions for the £500 to be given to her husband in the event of her death. Her husband, Charles, joined this arrangement by agreeing to leave whatever money he had at the time of his death to his wife in the event he died first. J.D. Rosenthal of Nassau Street agreed to witness the signing of the will and to take care of the money until the right time came. For security, and to assure the Higgins family that their life interest was secure, Rosenthal added some of his own money to the sum.

Maria, however, was unhappy. She believed her own brother, William Devereux (who by chance was a non-practising attorney at law), and her husband had conspired against her in presenting a second will supposedly all agreed to by herself before her 'death'. It stated that all of the money should be left to her brother-in-law (John Higgins) and not her husband. This had the effect of cutting Maria out of the picture and left little of the £500 for herself to make use of in her new second life. Maria had been living under self-imposed house-arrest in the basement of a house on Haddington Road Terrace close to Kingstown (now Dún Laoghaire). Fed up with the way the whole affair had been handled, she went to see Rosenthal to bring the case to light. This set in motion a chain of events in both Dublin and London that saw a fascinating court case evolve.

The elaborate plan had begun with Charles calling to the office of the son of Rosenthal. Charles appeared in deep mourning and stated that he was very sorry to say that his wife had died. He told him that she had made a second will and that they could disregard the first. He produced a certificate of her burial and stated that a Dr Thorne, a physician, had attended to her. Dr Thorne, it was stated, was paid £10 for his attendance and a 'wake' was held for three days after which the body was interred in Glasnevin.[17] The solicitors were not convinced. Rosenthal threatened to challenge the will.

Devereux, the brother of his beloved 'dead sister Maria', stepped in as a 'man of the law' and negotiated. Eventually it was agreed that they would set aside £90 for the solicitor if he agreed not to challenge the will and to allow for proceedings to begin by confirming the relevant details and to present a petition to the Court of Chancery in England where the money was being held in credit for the relevant claimant.

The Freeman's Journal reported on this 'strange and interesting case' both in London and Dublin.[18] In trying to make head or tail of the intricate and complex case, what follows is a summation of the court case from start to finish. At times it is amusing, sometimes sad and tragic, but in the main, it is truly baffling. The *Belfast News-Letter* covered the beginnings of proceedings on 15 May 1861. It revealed:

> [N]o suspicion was entertained of the matter until very recently, when it was discovered that the supposed testatrix was alive, and enjoying the fruits of her legacy. The coffin was exhumed in the presence of the Surgeon Porter and Mr Andrews (Crown solicitor) and found to contain nothing but stones and rags ... Mr Andrews deposed that within the last three weeks he searched in the principal registry of the Court of Probate, and investigated a document purporting to be the last will and testament of Maria Higgins, of No.1 Haddington Terrace. Bequeathing to her brother-in-law John Higgins, the sum of £500, or thereabouts ...[19]

The Irish Times and the *Kerry Evening Post* on 18 May 1861 also covered the story. The article from the *Belfast News-Letter* went into the greatest detail:

> Mr. Sweeney, the proprietor of the funeral establishment, No. 5 Camden Street ... on the 29th of July, 1858 ... Mr. Devereux had purchased a coffin there, and that the following inscription was directed to be put on the plate of the lid, 'Mrs Maria Higgins, aged 54 years, died on the 29th July 1858.' That same coffin was then ordered to be sent to No. 28 Bishop Street. A Mr. O'Neill was the undertaker given the task of organising the other arrangements. What followed was the fictitious burial of Maria Higgins on the 31st July 1858. When the grave was opened two years later all that was found was a large amount of sand in two rotting bags.[20]

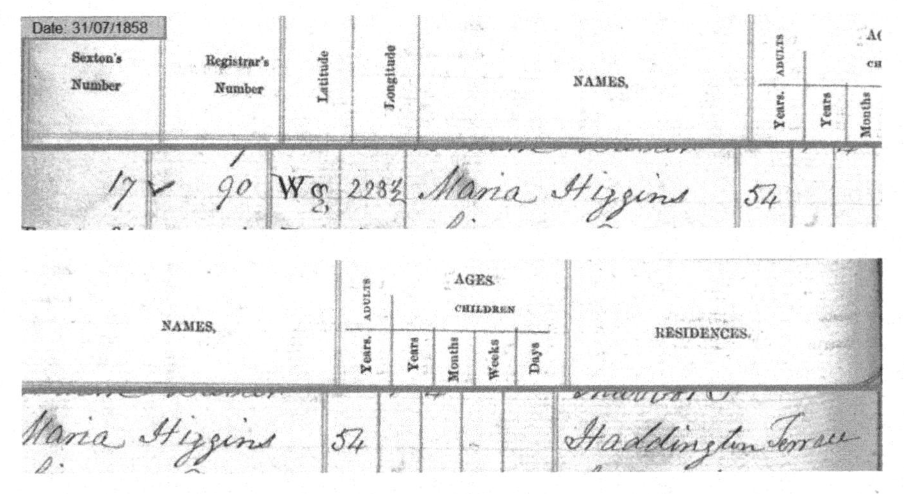

Date: 31/07/1858

Sexton's Number	Registrar's Number	Latitude	Longitude	NAMES.	AGES Adults Years.	Children Years	Months
17	90	W g	228½	Maria Higgins	54		

NAMES.	AGES. Adults Years.	Children Years	Months	Weeks	Days	RESIDENCES.
Maria Higgins	54					Haddington Terrace

Burial record for Maria Higgins in Glasnevin Cemetery from 1858. (Reproduced with the kind permission of Dublin Cemeteries Trust)

The court case that followed introduces a large cast of characters. They include residents of the house where the staged wake took place, supposed friends of the Higgins family and general acquaintances. Thomas McKenna, an employee of James Sweeney of Camden Street and hearse driver on the day said:

> I drove the hearse with Mrs Higgins supposed corpse in it, from 28 Bishop Street to Glasnevin … there were some gentlemen present in carriages … I think I saw Devereux and Higgins there; they did not appear to be in much grief; they appeared to be in a fuss; the hearse had four horses; I was told by one of the gentlemen to go to 31 Dame Street for my fare; I got no money, however.[21]

Sweeney also took the stand and stated he had not been paid either. He had supplied the coffin that had been filled with the large bags of sand.

The plate from the coffin was shown to the full courtroom. *The Irish Times* reported this was done 'amidst much laughter'. Mr Phelan, the superintendent of Glasnevin, later said:

> He knew nothing of his own knowledge of the supposed funeral of Maria Higgins; but he produced a book, in the handwriting of a man named Reid, in which there was an entry of the burial of Maria

> Higgins; the grave in which was supposed Maria Higgins was interred was opened the other day in his presence … To Mr. McDermott (judge) the coffin was opened, contained a bag of sand (laughter).[22]

People who were present at the wake then presented to the court. First up was Catherine Codd:

> I live at 13 Digges Street, I was at the wake of Mrs Higgins, I was invited by Eliza Duffy, the sister-in-law of Mr Devereux; she asked me to go to my husband, to procure a room for the wake; I did so; it took place at 28 Bishop Street; Mrs Devereux and Mr Higgins, and Eliza Duffy were present; I purchased the candles; Miss Duffy told me that her brother-in-law (Mr Devereux) was to get some money on the death of the deceased.[23]

Clara Conway, another person at the wake, said, 'she remained half an hour', in which time she had found a mysterious doctor named Thorne. She also revealed that the same doctor had died since the wake and due to the fact there was an absence of drink at the wake she had left it early. Ms Pearson, the caretaker of the house on Bishop Street, told the court that she 'never saw such a wake before'.[24] The courtroom apparently erupted into a fit of laughter after her remarks. Charles Higgins was then heard for the first time. He argued that 'my lord … I have been swindled out of my property in a few days; I had a carriage, a car, and every comfort, but I have been deprived of all by a band of swindlers; I will prove this at a future day'.[25]

As more evidence from Rosenthal was read to the court, Mr Higgins continued to argue his claims that he had been 'swindled'. The bench had to stop him and after some consultation remanded the case until he agreed to stop. *The Freeman's Journal*, *The Leinster Express*, *The Cork Examiner* and *The Munster Express* all detail the rest of the trial. *The Cork Examiner* tells that on 29 May 1861 a Miss Anne O'Loughlin was examined in the case. She lived on Charlemont Street and was an acquaintance of the Higgins family. She told the court: 'I knew Mr and Mrs Higgins for five years, and first saw Mr Devereux about two years ago; I remembered the time when Mrs Higgins was supposed to have been buried; I went to the house where they were stopping in Haddington Road-Terrace, with clothes I had been washing for Mr Higgins; they were in great want …'[26]

One thing that Charles Higgins asked her to do was to bring him a bit of clay. This was to help with the mock funeral. O'Loughlin said to the court that she 'had never heard of such a thing before'. Nevertheless, she brought the clay to the house where she unloaded half a stone weight of clay from her apron and went home. She returned later that night and was brought upstairs by Miss Duffield to take some tea. She stayed until two or three o'clock in the morning. Mrs Devereux, Miss Duffield, Mr Higgins and several lodgers were also there but the coffin was in a room below stairs. *The Leinster Express* put the final nail in the coffin on 22 June 1861 as it reported with a couple of sentences: 'Fraudulent Burial – At the Commission Court, Greenstreet, Dublin, Monday, Charles Higgins and William Henry Devereux were found guilty of conspiring to obtain money by falsely representing that Maria Higgins, wife of the former, was dead and buried. They were sentenced to two years imprisonment each.'[27]

Dr Thorne, who had signed the initial death certificate, had died before judgment was passed on the case, apparently from liver poisoning. For Maria, the court ruled she had nothing to do with the whole affair. The guilty parties were her husband and brother. Charles Higgins and William Devereux saw out their respective sentences and Maria, while maintaining her marriage, kept her scheming husband at arm's length. She died for a second time on 24 July 1871. Her death certificate from 1871 tells us she was 62 years old. Glasnevin's records provide us with more details. Her last known address was 31 Grenville Street and she was buried on 28 July. She is listed as still being married at her time of death and living with Charles Higgins. Her occupation is listed as a 'Lady'. She is the only person to hold two separate burial records in the cemetery and today lies in an unmarked plot in the Garden section (WF 18.5). At the opposite end of the same pathway you can find the unmarked plot where her empty coffin was laid to rest in 1858 (WG 233.5).

The Grand Ceremonial Opening of Sydney Harbour Bridge

It was 19 March 1932 and crowds had gathered in their thousands in Sydney for the grand ceremonial opening of Sydney Harbour Bridge. It is estimated that up to 500,000 people were present. Newspapers and reporters from around the world were there to witness the occasion. Work had begun on the bridge in 1927. To this day it is viewed as an engineering marvel. Spanning

1,149 metres, with an arch span of 503 metres, it remains the world's largest steel-arch bridge. Built at a time of great poverty for many Australians struggling through the Great Depression, it was remarkable that the project took just six years to complete. For context, the bridge would cover the entire length of Dublin's O'Connell Street.[28] Newsreel footage from the grand opening shows jubilant and expectant crowds. They awaited the arrival of the Premier of New South Wales, J.T. Lang, whose job was symbolic – to cut the ribbon and declare the engineering marvel open to the public. One Irishman had other ideas.

Mounted on horseback, Francis Edward De Groot from Dublin had managed to sneak his way into the vice-regal entourage. He waited for the opportune moment to strike. He emerged from the entourage, his ceremonial First World War sword in hand, and proceeded to cut the ribbon himself in front of thousands of onlookers. He declared the bridge to be open 'in the name of the decent and respectable people of New South Wales'.[29] Back in Ireland the *Irish Independent* covered the events in an article by reporter James Hilton:

> The Australians have every reason to be proud of their new bridge over Sydney Harbour … It is in many ways the most ambitious bridge in the world, and we over here may take perhaps a slightly extra interest in it because it has just been 'opened' by a Dublin man. Unofficially, however … Afterwards it was discovered that the impetuous swordsman was named De Groot, that he was a native of Dublin … He dressed in a showy uniform and allowed the crowds to admire him and wonder who he was. They all, including the officials themselves, quite naturally assumed he must be part of 'the show' … Anyhow, this Mr. De Groot, formerly of Dublin, seems to be a lively fellow, and

Francis De Groot, *c.* 1915.

> though it was undoubtedly very naughty of him to 'open' the greatest bridge in the world without permission, one may as well admit that swords have often been used for worse purposes than cutting tapes.[30]

Francis (Frank) Edward De Groot was born on 24 October 1888, into a comfortable family with modest wealth and good social standing. He was the youngest child of four to Cornelius De Groot, a sculptor of Dutch Huguenot descent, and Mary Butler from Clonmel. His birth certificate states that he was born at 23 Upper Liffey Street in Dublin, but Frank later in life recalled that he had been told he had been born in their family house called 'Lakefield' overlooking Dublin Bay.[31] The family name originated in Antwerp, and although the family did retain links to Flanders, by the time Frank was born they were, as he said in his autobiography, 'more Irish than many others living in Ireland'.[32]

As a young boy he had a rather privileged childhood, unlike many others in the Dublin of the late nineteenth century. His father, Cornelius, had a notable Dublin carving and sculpting business, and had even been represented amongst the medal-winning wood carvers at the 1851 Great Exhibition of All Nations in London. After a brief but unhappy time at the elite Blackrock and Belvedere colleges in Dublin, Francis pursued his dreams of soldiering and joined the Merchant Navy aged just 13 in 1910. He wrote in his autobiography: 'I had better draw a veil … school and I did not get along well together … I preferred the National Art Gallery and Museum.'[33] It was to be later in his life, while living in Australia, that his talent for antiques would come to be an important part of his life. Sport, however, was ever-present.

Frank was a familiar figure on the skiffs at Islandbridge, Ireland's premier rowing centre, beside the Phoenix Park in Dublin. He was a noted sportsperson involved in athletics, rugby union, rowing and horse riding. Riding horses was a particular passion that he later put to good use on Sydney Harbour Bridge. He was described as being adventurous, but rather slight in build and not especially tall, at 10 stone in weight and 5 foot 8 inches tall.[34] He completed a five-year apprenticeship with his uncle Michael Butler, an antique dealer, before emigrating to Australia in 1910.[35] He arrived in Sydney with his apprenticeship in the family business, the Butler Firm, behind him. His reasons for emigrating, although unclear, could relate to his uncle's Butler Firm getting into some serious financial difficulties. This, and the fact that Frank was the youngest son of the family, meant he would have understood that inheriting much of the family estate or business was not likely to happen.

His siblings had already made many of their life choices. His eldest brother, Cornelius, had established himself as one of Dublin's most respected antique dealers. Cornelius' career was very much in line with a similar business run by his mother's family, the Butlers, in Dublin and London. His other brother, Harry, had become the proprietor of a general store in Dublin.[36] For a while Frank followed a different path in the Merchant Navy, but while handling heavy wire in bitterly cold weather near Antwerp, he broke his wrist. An Antwerp surgeon uncaringly set the break with some plaster, but it did not heal properly and required Frank to return to Dublin, where it had to be painfully rebroken and reset. It was at this time that Frank's father asked him to reconsider his career choice. He agreed to learn more about his family's business in fine arts. Learning the antiques trade in Dublin made a lot of sense to young Frank before emigrating to Australia.

On arrival in Sydney he was very fortunate to meet a publisher called George Robertson and his associate, Fred Wynmark. In 1910 both were struggling to open an art gallery on Castlereagh Street in the city. De Groot's knowledge and connections with the antiquities trade in Dublin and London proved invaluable. He was advanced £10,000 by Robertson to purchase antiques for resale in Sydney.[37] De Groot, it was agreed, would cable his brother Cornelius in Dublin to see if he was in a position to dispatch an initial consignment of valuable goods to Sydney, together with regular monthly shipments. Cornelius agreed. While waiting on this initial shipment, a minor remodelling of the Castlereagh Street premises took place. With De Groot's direction, the art gallery quickly became a very classy venue and he quickly became a minor celebrity as a purveyor of fine antique furniture.[38]

His autobiography provides no details of his private life outside his work in Sydney apart from the fact that he lived at Astor Boarding House in Macquarie Street and later at Rose Bay. Before leaving Dublin in 1910, Frank had met Mary Elizabeth Byrne (nicknamed 'Bessie') of Portumna, County Galway. They maintained contact between 1910 and 1914, and their relationship eventually prompted Frank to leave what was a good commercial career to return to Dublin in April 1914. It was a relationship full of opposites. Firstly, Bessie's family were from a lower-class under-privileged Protestant background. Her father was a British soldier, who had died while stationed in Birr, County Offaly. This left just her mother and eldest brother, Ned, to raise a family of six children. She worked at Switzer's (now Brown Thomas on Grafton Street). Although this gave her some financial independence, it did not disguise the fact that in the eyes of an upper-middle-class Irish family like the De Groots, her social background was not considered good enough for their youngest son.[39] More significant for the De Groots was the religious divide. They were Catholic and in the society of early twentieth-century Ireland, mixed marriages were often frowned upon. Neither the De Groots nor the Byrnes approved of the marriage. The Catholic Church only gave permission to any marriage between such a couple if the Protestant partner was prepared to convert to Catholicism and agree that all their children would be raised as Catholic. Andrew Moore, in his biography of Francis De Groot, states that: '1914 was indubitably a traumatic time for the young Irish-man, returning to Dublin to see how such practical and social obstacles intruded upon the wishes of his heart.'[40]

Despite these difficulties, his return to Dublin as a more confident businessman was a happy one. With the outbreak of the First World War, Bessie and Frank agreed to put their marriage plans on hold. For Bessie this conflict would take three of her brothers, who had emigrated to New Zealand where they joined the Hauraki Regiment. One was killed in France two months before the end of hostilities, while another died from the effects of mustard gas poisoning. For Bessie's fiancé, however, military service proved a surprisingly positive experience. Frank survived the carnage of France without sustaining a single injury. Soldiering had always been a passion of De Groot's – by 1907 he had joined the South of Ireland Imperial Yeomanry and in 1909 spent six months in barracks with the 5th Dragoon Guards.

In 1914 he enlisted in the 15th Hussars. He served with distinction on the Western Front. He was posted to the Somme on 28 June 1916. From August to November 1917, he was at the centre of the Third Battle of Ypres, more commonly known as the Battle of Passchendaele. He was later transferred to the 15th Tank Battalion with the rank of acting captain.[41] His commanding officer described him as: 'A very capable Officer … good all round. Excellent disciplinarian and leader of men, a very determined Officer with plenty of dash. I consider this Officer eminently fit for Staff Employment and strongly recommend him for promotion.'[42]

De Groot's account of his war experiences is very matter of fact and unreflective in his autobiography. Like many who survived the conflict, he preferred not to look back on that time in too much detail. Soldiering remained a big part of his life, however. There is some evidence that early in April 1919 he volunteered to serve in Russia to help fight against the Bolsheviks.[43] His only experience of war-time illness was succumbing to influenza for three days as part of the Spanish flu pandemic of 1918–19.[44] This caused a minor delay in submitting his resignation papers. It was during this delay that Frank spotted a report in a Cologne newspaper. It was about a War Office decision to repatriate soldiers to the Dominions by providing free passage. Bessie and Frank decided to emigrate to Australia. The couple had married on 25 October 1919 at the Star of the Sea Catholic church in Donnybrook, Dublin, a day after Frank's 31st birthday. Bessie had converted to Catholicism to facilitate the marriage. They arrived in Sydney in May 1920. Frank opened a business that designed, manufactured and marketed reproduction furniture to a very high standard. This, according to Andrew Moore, was his most profound contribution to the city of Sydney.[45] By 1927 he claimed to employ a staff of 200 artisans at his factory at Rushcutters Bay. He had established himself in Sydney as both employer and craftsman.

As a young man Frank had felt some connection to the ideals of the conservative Irish nationalist John Redmond. His father's unionist views almost certainly influenced him as a boy and they instilled in him a loyalty to the British Empire and the Crown. If you had to sum up Frank De Groot's politics, he could be described as an Empire loyalist. The year 1929 saw the Great Depression hit Australia and Frank became increasingly worried about those in power in New South Wales and their politics. He was most concerned with the Labour Premier J.T. Lang, a left-leaning politician, whom Frank regarded as a communist and a threat to the people of New South Wales. Ultimately, he decided to join the proto-fascist New Guard party led by Eric Campbell in September 1931. Just five months later he was a zone commander and senior member of the council of action. Campbell saw him as a trusted intermediary in dealing with the Commonwealth attorney general, Sir John Latham, in disputes.[46] By 1929, Frank had been back to Ireland, before returning to Sydney to make preparations to close his business. His decision to close was one based on running costs. It was a business decision that made sense for his family.

In the economic uncertainties of 1929–31, Frank and Bessie moved to a rented seaside location at a place called Pittwater. Today it is part of the wider cityscape in Sydney, but in 1930 they were far away from city life. The milkman had to arrive in a rowing boat and they reported that there were days when not a single person passed by their cottage.[47] Ironically this was the same period that Frank became most politically active in Australia. The New Guard gained significant footholds in the working-class communities of Sydney through the offices of some trade unions, including the Railway Services Association (RSA), whose membership had more than doubled from 1930 to 1933 due to the Depression.[48] Eric Campbell was the founder of the party that became the most significant fascist organisation in Australian history from 1931 to 1935.[49]

The party tried to embrace a number of the working class that had been attracted to the New Guard because of the economic chaos caused by the Great Depression. It cannot, however, be described as a party with its roots in working-class constituencies. In times of political and economic uncertainties people tend to turn to extremes. Sydney was no different. After months of waiting for an expected 'Red Revolution' to justify the New Guard's mobilisation, it was decided around the time that Frank De Groot joined the organisation in October 1931 that they should adopt a more militant policy. This militant policy meant force, riots and violence.

The local divisional commander of the New Guard said that 'the best reply to force, was greater force … and seeing that we could command the greater force, I saw no reason why it should not be employed'.[50] These were the words of Francis Edward De Groot in his autobiography. Throughout December 1931 he organised strong-arm groups of up to 1,000 New Guardsmen to attack leftist meetings in waves of about 200. These would then double up and return to the end of a queue to give the impression of an even larger and more irresistible force. Innocent bystanders were caught up in many of these tactics. One of the most extreme examples, in which De Groot was heavily involved, was at Darlinghurst on 11 December 1931, when three policemen were injured in a fight between New Guardsmen and Communists.[51]

It was in this context that Frank went down in Australian history at Sydney Harbour Bridge. Arrested shortly after the bridge incident, he was taken to a detention centre on the premise that he was insane. A Dr Hillier carried out an initial examination on De Groot. Shortly after 9 a.m. on Monday, 21 March 1932, dressed in a beautifully tailored brown suit and looking 'as cool as a cucumber', Frank appeared before Mr McDougall, stipendiary magistrate at a specially convened Lunacy Court at the reception centre.[52] A crowd gathered outside the court and proceedings were brief. Dr Hillier gave his judgment that De Groot was sane and recommended his discharge from the reception centre, and McDougall, the stipendiary magistrate, ordered that this should happen immediately. He would not be sent to an asylum – something that must have come as a relief to Bessie, looking on from the gallery.

Shortly afterwards, several large policemen asked De Groot to accompany them next door to the Darlinghurst police station. Inside the police station, he was rearrested and charged. He was to appear on trial on three counts: maliciously damaging a ribbon which was the property of the New South Wales government (damages amounting to £2); behaving in an offensive manner at the junction of Bradfield Highway; and using threatening words to Inspector Stuart Robson as follows: 'I am a King's Officer; Stand Back; don't you interfere with me.'[53]

He ended up facing a trial at the Central Police Court in Sydney before the Chief Stipendiary Magistrate of New South Wales, J.W. Laidlaw. Bail was set at £10. A preliminary hearing was scheduled for 22 March, with the main trial set for the date of 1 April, April Fool's Day. The process was over in a matter of minutes. He was defended by the legal team of C.A. Hardwick and the in-house New Guard barrister, Ernest Lamb KG. In summing up his defence, Lamb made the following statement: 'All his life Captain De Groot will cherish his gesture of loyalty. By his deed he has shown the world that there are people in Australia loyal to the King and the Constitution. When the name of Lang is lost in obscurity the name of De Groot will stand out as the name of a hero.'[54]

Ultimately, De Groot was found innocent of the charges against him and managed to secure a tidy out-of-court settlement. The Irish newspapers reported on proceedings. According to *The Irish Press*, 'batons had to be used by the Sydney police outside the court as an angry mob had gathered to protest at the charges levelled against him'.[55] The *Offaly Independent* even sarcastically likened his antics to the Boston Tea Party in terms of their significance.[56] The *Irish Independent* reported on the out-of-court settlement and that Frank had secured a 'claim of 5,000 [Australian dollars] damages'.[57]

The Lang government detested by De Groot and the New Guard was dismissed on 13 May 1932. Shortly afterwards, the Labour government was defeated in elections and took with it any momentum the New Guard had built around a proposed seizure of power. The defeat of J.T. Lang and the

Labour movement, coupled with improving economic conditions, meant the New Guard became politically unimportant. Fascism became an embodiment of 'foreignness' in Australia and the result was a total collapse of the movement.[58] Neither Campbell nor De Groot remained politically active after 1935. The bridge incident became the New Guard's most significant achievement. Beyond its leader's bragging and bravado, according to Andrew Moore, the New Guard was, in reality, 'slightly pathetic'.[59]

On 2 April 1942, Frank was appointed commandant of the Greta army camp. This was located north of Sydney in the heart of the Hunter Valley coalfields around the city of Newcastle. His military service in the Second World War was a long way from the front lines. It was, however, a highly significant operation. In 1942 records show that there were no fewer than 8,900 troops based there. At that time he was also in charge of the Singleton army camp, made up of 4,800 troops, and a smaller camp at Branxton where 200 troops were based.[60] The Greta army camp, Frank recorded in his autobiography, 'was a City in itself ... and I was Mayor, Corporation, surveyor, Chief Magistrate, and Police Force all in one'.[61] Major De Groot's fascist past, however, became the subject of many controversies in this period. His name and associations made his job a difficult one. His final roles within the army were at Tamworth and later at the Sydney showground, where he was put in charge of courts of inquiry into any escapes from detention.[62] Before that he spent six months attached to the United States Army in the South Pacific Area Command.[63] He was placed on the Retired List in January 1944.

Away from the army, he spent most of his spare time finalising a remarkable house and grounds that he and Bessie had purchased in 1938–39. But for the De Groots, the house of their dreams came with a problem. The house and land were not a package deal. The house they purchased was an imposing stone structure located at the corner of Old South Head Road and Bellevue Hill Road named 'Llandudno'.[64] Frank and Bessie's land was 35 miles (60 kilometres) away. The house had been scheduled for demolition. A group of builders eagerly awaited the chance to use the vacant site for the construction of a block of flats. The couple wanted to set the house high on a ridge off Castle Hill Road, with a 250-foot frontage and an 850-foot drop. The land was part of an orchard and had stunning views. As Brian Wright contends, only someone 'as headstrong, tenacious, determined and aesthetically committed as Frank De Groot could have seen through such a mammoth project'.[65] Frank's friend, the architect B.I. Waterhouse, detailed a draftsman to take measured drawings of the house with photographs taken from every angle. Each stone was numbered and De Groot's workers got down to the task at hand of disassembling the house.[66]

The house was originally built in 1864 for the Stephen family by skilled stonemasons in ashlar dimension sandstone from the Pyrmont quarry and featured red cedar woodwork. By 1938 the Montefiore Society was using it as a nursing home for elderly Jewish men. They were planning to relocate to more suitable premises.[67] The 120 square foot house was reassembled brick by brick on its new site and renamed 'Dunrath' after the Irish castle in the south of Dublin. The project was completed by 1946 but sadly the couple did not get to enjoy it for long. Frank faced difficulties in reviving his furniture business in Sydney and his brother Cornelius died in Dublin on 28 November 1946, leaving behind a widow and a young family of five sons ranging in age from six to fourteen. Frank, with no children of his own, returned to Ireland to help his sister-in-law. He later said, 'I felt it was up to me to return home and take an interest in them.'[68]

Frank and his wife returned to Dublin in 1950. He continued to work in antiques and was active in the Irish Australian Society.[69] For the last two years of his life he lived in a Dublin nursing home. He died aptly on April Fool's Day 1969. Frank never had any children. His wife, Bessie, lived until 1981. She was not buried in Glasnevin like her husband. Instead, she was buried with her family, the Byrnes, at Powerscourt church on the hill above Enniskerry overlooking the Wicklow hills.[70]

Frank's death was reported in *The Irish Press* on 2 April 1969:

> A Dublin man who held the headlines of the world's press for an exploit in Australia 37 years ago died quietly yesterday in a city nursing home, aged 78. He was Major F. E. de Groot, late of 68 Terenure Road, East, Dublin, who in 1932 'opened' the newly-constructed Sydney Harbour Bridge rather than let the then socialist prime minister of Australia open it.[71]

An obituary also appeared on page three of *The Daily Telegraph* on 16 April 1969 under the headline 'De Groot of Bridge fame dead'.[72] Following 10 a.m. mass at St Joseph's church in Terenure, Francis Edward De Groot's remains were brought to Glasnevin for burial in the St Patrick's section (D1 158). His headstone today is a small white rectangular stone low to the ground with a small cross etched on top. There is no mention of his involvement in the Bridge incident. To this day in New South Wales pranksters often say they are 'doing a De Groot' when pulling a prank or making a joke. Re-enactors on the bridge have also become commonplace and what happened remains a talking point among Sydneysiders.[73]

The Lion Tamer

Glasnevin is made up of many sections. Most of the land used for burials is located on the side of the Finglas Road where the O'Connell Tower can be found. Behind the housing estate on the other side of the road, however, is a smaller section called St Paul's. In this section you can trace the graves of some of the relatives of those zookeepers at rest in the Garden section. It is also the final resting place for another fascinating individual associated with animals. If you had picked up *The Irish Times* newspaper on the evening of 12 November 1951, you would have been confronted with the front-page headline: 'Lioness Escapes in Dublin and Mauls Two'.[74]

The lioness of the self-taught lion tamer William 'Bill' Stephens had escaped its enclosure located on Merville Avenue in Fairview. The lioness, called Zalinka, escaped around 5.15 p.m. on Sunday 11 November and proceeded to make its way around the local area. She left behind another lioness, Sultan, and a lion called Finn in the cage. The three had been taken off the road for the winter period. Their owner made his living as a professional lion tamer and worked for both Duffy's and Fossett's circuses. His act captivated audiences as he sometimes placed his head inside the lion and lioness' mouths. In time his act incorporated his wife, Mai, and was entitled: 'Jungle Capers, Bill Stephens and Lovely Partner'. It included a number of death-defying feats with his troupe of lions, Alsatian dogs, sometimes some monkeys and even snakes.[75] It was designed to thrill and terrify. Dressed in an explorer's safari khaki suit and pith helmet, he cracked his whip around. He modelled himself on the famed Clyde Beatty who was the star of America's Ringling Brothers and Barnum and Bailey Circus.[76]

On 11 November 1951, as people left the Fairview Strand cinema (today a Tesco Express), they were met with the strange sight of a lioness meandering through the traffic on the street outside. Coincidentally the film that evening was *Jungle Stampede*. In an award-winning documentary made by Joe Lee and Bill Whelan entitled *Fortune's Wheel: The Life and Legacy of the Fairview*

Lion Tamer, Pam Fox, who was there, recalled what she saw: 'The Lioness came down Merville Avenue and she stuck her head into the little dairy ... now that particular day there was only Ms Macken there and she just stood, I should imagine, terrified out of her wits, but the lioness did not fully go in, she backed out again.'[77]

Radio Éireann announced that: 'At 5.30 on the evening of the 11th of November the Dublin Suburb of Fairview was startled by a sound that may have come from the African jungle ...'[78] The radio broadcast continued:

> A lioness had escaped from her trainer's cage from the yard of a garage beside the local cinema. It was dark at the time ... In front of the garage an Apprentice mechanic named Andy Massey rolled a spare wheel out onto the pathway and bent down to blow it up; that was the scene of a normal suburban moment when down the lane beside the garage came the Big Yellow Cat. She saw Andy in front of her and sprang ...[79]

Bill Stephens at this point had been made aware of the fact that his lioness had escaped and was getting ready to give chase to save his livelihood. The Radio Éireann broadcast interviewed Stephens, who, speaking in a relaxed, nonplussed Dublin accent, said:

> Just then I heard the shout from the garage for help. The boys in the garage shouted through the sliding gate for me to come down quick and that the lion was out. I dashed around and she seemed to be lying with Andy with one paw on his chest. Well, I came up quietly behind her and he was calling for me all this time and I could hear him shouting, 'Billy, Billy, Billy ...'[80]

The young mechanic had been going about his daily business in the garage when he was struck. In the broadcast, the voice of a young, innocent boy begins to recount his experience: 'I was putting the wheel down on the path to pump it up, something hit me in the back and I saw a big paw go over my shoulder ...'[81]

The interviewer asked: 'Did you know what it was?'

Andy Massey replied: 'I thought it was a dog at first but when I saw the big paw I knew it was a lion.'

The interviewer responded, 'Was it not a lioness?'

The young mechanic made the point: 'Listen Mister if you were pumping up a wheel and something hit you, you wouldn't worry if it was a lion or a lioness … I didn't feel any pain at all until it was gone … I didn't hear him approaching; it was very quiet coming …'[82]

He was taken to Jervis Street Hospital. Zalinka in the meantime had run up Merville Avenue. Stephens actually managed to corner her and sent for a rope to make a noose to help recapture the animal. A big crowd had gathered to witness the bizarre sight. At this point a squad car from Dublin Castle arrived. Inside were gardaí armed with .303 rifles. Stephens convinced the guards to give him a chance to capture the lioness without killing her. He recounted in the interview how he managed to corner her between two walls. He was about to grab her when some local school children began to mess about on the wall looking down at the spectacle. Startled, the lioness reacted. Bill recounted how:

> [As she] lifted herself into the air … I threw my noose over her head and shoulders and I went to rush in to tie her up when she lifted herself in a second spring. She grabbed me by the arm, knocked me onto the grass and she actually carried me at least 8 feet in her mouth. My legs trailing along the ground, I kept quiet in her grip and she took her teeth out and it was only then I felt the pain. It really was a terrific pain. A sudden surge of pain as I chased her over to the wall where the police were and I shouted to the sergeant: 'For God's sake shoot her quick I can do nothing more my arm is crippled.'

The radio report concluded: 'That was the end … a .303 rang out and Fairview's wild beast fell dead among the nettles and old bicycle frames.'[83]

Stephens was also sent to Jervis Street Hospital. The mechanic was in worse shape, but both made full recoveries. For William the event had rocked his career and livelihood. One lioness was now dead. His other two prized possessions, Finn and Sultan, had been transferred to Dublin Zoo in their cage via CIÉ lorry.[84] While Stephens was in hospital, Dr Flood, superintendant at the zoo, went to visit him to keep him up to date about his two lions. A reporter on a visit asked Dr Flood, 'What is the proper thing to do if you meet a lion or lioness on the street?' He replied, 'Ignore it. If you show fear, they know and they get afraid and they pounce.'[85]

As he recovered, Bill was very conscious about the well-being of the young mechanic. He said to reporters, 'Please say in your paper that I am sorry about Andy Massey and that I am so glad he is recovering. And say that I wouldn't have had those kids scared for anything.'[86]

William 'Bill' Stephens was born in 1923 to parents Robert and Matilda. He grew up as the youngest child of nine and lived at 23 Fairview Green. The family previously lived at 35 Rutland Street before settling in the new Dublin Corporation housing estate in Marino. His father, Robert, worked as a bicycle mechanic. Sadly, as a young boy, William lost his sister Elizabeth aged just 16. She died on 10 February 1926 when he was only 3. She was buried in the St Paul's section (DB 13). The family plot in Glasnevin was originally purchased for the burial of his parents' firstborn, Robert. He died aged just 5 on 13 September 1911. Another sister, Margaret (also known as Rita), died at the young age of 17 on 8 March 1932. She was buried in the same plot.

As a young man, Bill trained as a welder. He abandoned this career, however, and instead went to play drums in Billy Carter's swing band.[87] He performed mainly on weekends at places like the Arcadia in Bray, the Metropole and the Gresham on Dublin's O'Connell Street. Around this time Bill married the love of his life, Margaret (Mai) Carton, on 19 October 1942. He was also working as a welder in the Inchicore works and was living at 59 Stephens Road. After John Duffy's circus pitched up beside the Arcadia ballroom in Bray, he decided it was time to pursue his dream and join the circus.

Mai decided they should run away with the circus. Initially Bill played in the circus band. Later he acquired a small lion cub that he called Sultan from a performer who was leaving the show. With no experience in training lions, he trained the animal as if it were a dog. He went on to develop a unique act. In its infancy his act mixed the lion with Alsatians, while Mai walked around the ring draped with snakes.[88] Bill had developed his love for animals from the Ash family, who were his neighbours on Fairview Green as a child. The family was well known in the area for taking in stray animals and being members of the ISPCA.[89]

Despite owning a small cottage on Annesley Bridge (where the current fire station stands), the couple had a passion for travelling. They purchased a caravan and travelled from place to place. Mai was viewed as exotic and from the 'East'. This was due to her dark hair, sallow skin and passion for reptiles. In actual fact she was from the East Wall Road in Dublin.[90]

In the circus, Bill's act became more ambitious. Stunts included feeding a lion from his own mouth, a lion leaping through a hoop above Mai's head and a 'bouncing lions' routine. The 'bouncing lion' was performed in a small wagon pushed into the big top by a tractor. Inside it he got lions to frantically run in circles around him causing the wagon to shake violently. The end of it saw him give a command for them to stop. The lions would immediately obey.[91] When the circus went into the winter season, they took their lions to rest in the shed behind the garage at Fairview on Merville Avenue. It was from there that Zalinka made her great escape.

After Bill's recovery, he became more determined to make an international name for himself. The escaped lioness made his name instantly recognisable to many in Dublin and he wanted to try and cash in on his newfound fame. The incident with Zalinka had made headlines around the world and led to the couple playing a Christmas season with Chipperfield's Circus in Dublin. The *Irish Independent* on 8 January 1952 reported on their act saying: 'Still fearless as ever, he puts his head into the mouth of his Dublin Zoo-bred Lion …'[92]

The Fairview incident not only paved the way for employment, but it also posed serious financial difficulties for Mai and Bill. Andrew Massey, the mechanic who had been mauled, sued.[93] Despite this Bill decided he would need a new lion. He bought himself an unpredictable animal from Dublin Zoo called Albert. Albert had originally lived in Antwerp Zoo and had been named after the Belgian king. Allegedly it had killed before, and the zoo in Belgium was happy to send it to Dublin. Stephens believed strongly that he needed a real risk of danger to make his act more popular and daring. Despite Dublin Zoo's initial refusal to sell him the lion, he persisted. The zoo finally agreed to sell Albert, whom he renamed Pasha.[94] The purchase of Pasha restored his compliment of three big cats. Most circus acts involving lions had five animals so they could form a perfect pyramid in the ring as a finale. Financially this was impossible for Bill. Instead, he hoped that the unreliable and dangerous Pasha would compensate.

During the period 1951–53, Bill performed during the off season in many Dublin venues including the Olympia and the Theatre Royal. His act was made up of a cage on stage with his three lions. He finished by putting his head inside one of the lions' mouths. It was a captivating experience for the audience. It was also highly dangerous, and to some of his friends and family, extremely reckless, but to Bill it served as good publicity. He sustained multiple injuries, mainly scratches, but during one of his acts with Fossett's Circus in September 1952, in Rathkeale, Limerick, he had a

Bill Stephens feeding his lion with his mouth during a performance with Fossett's Circus in Rathkeale, Limerick, 1952. (Image from the *Limerick Leader*, 6 September 1952, used with the kind permission of Irish Newspaper Archives)

near-death experience. One of the lions closed its jaws while his head was inside. Reports said he could be heard 'roaring down the lion's throat for a full minute before the audience guessed anything was wrong'. He managed to free himself with a powerful hand-wrench at the lion's jaws. Bill was badly cut and bleeding from several chin and throat wounds. But the next day he performed the same act twice in Newcastle West. His mother died that same weekend, on 30 August 1952 at the age of 70, and was buried in the family plot in Glasnevin with her deceased children.[95] She was joining her husband, Robert, who had died in 1946 aged 64.

Bill dreamed constantly of making it big in the United States. He wrote many letters to Clyde Beatty, the famed star of America's Ringling Brothers and Barnum & Bailey Circus, asking if the circus would be interested in funding his passage to America to tour with them.[96]

Bill had moved his big cats towards Finglas in the off season to avoid any crowded settings. However, another of the lions attempted to escape on 24 November 1952. *The Cork Examiner* reported:

> It was after this episode that An Garda Síochána notified Bill that if his Lions escaped anymore that they would be confiscated and sent

> to Dublin Zoo or shot dead. He turned to Fossett's who had been employing him with his act to take custody of the animals at St. Margaret's in the farmlands at Dunsoughley during off-season times.

They agreed to his proposal and gave him a season to perform with them. One of the Fossetts – Herta – recalled how Bill would cycle out from the city every evening with meat to feed his lions. She also recalled how the Fossetts were not big fans of Pasha. Her father told Bill, 'He's a killer.'[97]

In late January 1953, Bill was approached by an American talent scout called June Badger, who worked for the Ringling Brothers.[98] It was her job to scout out new acts for their circus. She was accompanied on 28 January 1953 to St Margaret's by the head superintendent of Dublin Zoo, Cecil S. Webb. The circus crew had been insistent that Stephens should not perform alone in the cages with the lions, but that evening he entered the large cage alone and began his act. The trap doors opened to let the animals leave their small cage to come into the larger one. Pasha did not budge. Bill made the decision to climb into the small carriage cage to coax him out and in that small space Pasha pounced. The lion inflicted horrific injuries. The circus crew ran to try to get Bill out of the cage, but the lion continued to maul the body for some time.

Cecil S. Webb gave evidence at the inquest into Bill's death:

> The moment the accident happened there was a loud shout of alarm behind me and within seconds a number of circus employees arrived with poles and iron bars. We all pounded the lion with no effect. I got the crowbar into the lion's mouth, but he would not release his grip. After what seemed a very long period, but may have been only five minutes, we beat off the lion and during this time we had great difficulty in keeping back the second lion, Finn, who also wanted to attack. Pasha, whom we beat back, dashed at Mr. Stephens again, caught him by the chest and dragged him across the cage. We hammered the lion again in the head and again he let go his grip and appeared to be dazed. At this stage I shouted to Mrs. Badger to phone for an ambulance. Immediately after we raised the flap both lions stood with their backs to it and their eyes on the prostrated Mr. Stephens, and we had great difficulty in getting them to enter the other section. Eventually Finn saw the open flap and dashed in

> followed by Pasha. We then entered the cage and removed the body of Mr. Stephens which was lifeless ...[99]

Herta Lordini was to be married on 11 February 1953 to Edward Fossett. There was a planned ceremony at St Margaret's church before a large reception in Dublin's Gresham Hotel.[100] Bill had gone to R. Coyle Hatter and Outfitters at 8 Aungier Street to buy a new suit for the wedding. He decided to wear it during the ill-fated performance. Herta believed that:

> When you work with animals they know your scent. Bill wanted to impress them so he put the new suit on that he bought for my wedding and of course the animals had a completely different smell ... And I think that had a lot to do with it ... And for me it was dramatic because it was the suit he bought to go to my wedding.[101]

He was just 29 years old. His recorded cause of death in Glasnevin is 'as a result of being mauled to death by a lion'. He left behind his young wife, Mai, who later married again and started a second life with Joe Tracy, who worked for the seed and grain merchants Dardis & Dunne. They married in 1959 and lived in a corporation house at 1 East Wall Road.[102] She never spoke about her time in the circus or of her first husband, Bill. Mai died in 2015 aged 91.

Bill's funeral to Glasnevin was attended by Lord Mayor of Dublin Alfie Byrne and much of the Irish showbusiness family. It was also widely attended by members of Duffy's and Fossett's circuses. He was buried in the family plot in the St Paul's section (DB 13). The grave today is marked by a small shield and flat slab. Beneath his parents' names reads, 'And their beloved son Bill, killed by a Lion.' Pasha was put down after the incident and the other big cats were sent to Dublin Zoo.[103] Herta Fossett was married as planned, two weeks after Bill's death. As one Dublin newspaper described Bill Stephens while he was alive, he was: 'The most bitten man in showbusiness.'

A Dublin Woman and the Belgian Resistance

In the remembrance garden and cremation section of Glasnevin Cemetery (Wall 7 Row D 30), next to the car park and Mortuary Chapel, there are a number of columbarium (cremation) walls. Along the lower section of one of these walls you can read the name: Mary O'Kelly de Galway. Her cremated remains were laid to rest in 1999, aged 94. Not many stop to read her name. She was born on 24 April 1905 in Dublin and was one of ten children of Thomas Patrick Cummins, a plumber, and his wife, Ellen Black. Later, she attended the Dominican College in Eccles Street, Dublin, where she excelled at languages and French. Deciding to use her talents, she travelled to Brussels where she got a job as a governess for a Belgian countess and her twelve children.[104] Mary then worked as a translator for the Canadian embassy and during the Nazi invasion of May 1940 she became heavily involved with the Belgian resistance. Due to the fact she had an Irish passport, she was able to move more freely around and acted as a courier, passing messages through Belgium and Europe. She also worked as a translator and smuggled weapons.[105] Eventually she was betrayed, arrested by the Gestapo and taken to Berlin, where she was to witness the horrors of the Holocaust and the Nazi concentration camps.

She was held in camps in Bremen, Dresden, Essen and Bergen-Belsen among others. In a radio documentary for RTÉ in 1993, Mary reflected on how she witnessed prisoners being forced to drink water laced with crushed glass, men being dipped into boiling water, cannibalism and people drinking urine, while she was subjected to brutal beatings and torture. In the radio documentary she also described how she was 'trussed up naked while "every orifice"' of her body was explored.[106] As April 1945 progressed she was selected for extermination at Auschwitz, but luckily the train she was on derailed and never made it. The camp was liberated shortly afterwards, on 25 April. She weighed just 4 stone when American troops found her and had decalcification of the spine as well as many other illnesses.[107] After months recovering in hospitals in Switzerland, she received decorations from King Leopold and General Eisenhower.[108]

After the war Mary underwent an assessment in Belgium to receive compensation for her efforts. It was during that time in 1946 that she met her future husband, Count Guy O'Kelly de Galway. He was a barrister, and his descendants could trace their ancestry back to the Wild Geese of the seventeenth century who had left Ireland to fight in European armies. They married in 1949 and spent fifteen happily married years together. In 1964 she drove him to the airport for a business trip to England, where they said their goodbyes. Little did she know that was the last time she would see him. Despite efforts to trace him for the rest of her life, nobody is certain about what became of him.[109] A theory exists that he may have been an undercover agent for the British, but the mystery remains today – who was the real Guy O'Kelly de Galway?

Despite the hardships, horrors and loss during her life, Mary continued to live life to the full and without bitterness up until her death on 20 June 1999. She lived in Clontarf and even in her nineties continued to go for regular walks on Howth pier, taking great care of her appearance; she loved parties and social occasions. *The Irish Times* reported on 3 July that she often said to her nieces and nephews: 'Aren't I marvellous for my age? They'll have to shoot me.'[110] Her funeral took place on 23 June at St Anthony's Church, Clontarf, before she made her final journey to Glasnevin for cremation.[111]

I can take no credit for unearthing her story. I am indebted to the curiosity of colleagues Daniel Eglington-Carey, Dr Caitlin White and Lynn Brady for this remarkable tale. Mary admirably reflected on her life in 1993:

> The body is not made to last forever and the physical state has to deteriorate, that is the normal run of things … well I accept that and I do what I can to help myself on the way; I remain optimistic and grateful that I am alive … I appreciate looking at the moon and the stars … the smell of new cut grass and joy of drinking water …[112]

Glasnevin Cemetery *c.* 1865–1914. (Reproduced courtesy of the National Library of Ireland)

Sport

Val Harris: 'Never Mark a Man, Mark the Ball!'

Windsor Park, Belfast, Saturday, 15 February 1913. Ireland were preparing to take to the pitch to face the old enemy England in an International Home Nations Championship soccer fixture. Kick-off was scheduled for 3.30 p.m. This pre-match build-up description in the *Saturday Herald* captures some of the anticipation at the time:

> [The match saw] the moves of all followers of sport in the North and special train after special deposited its load in the Northern capital. All bent with the one intention of witnessing the thirty-second classic between what is considered the elite of Ireland and England … as tram and taxi deposited its load after load at the gates, to say nothing of those that joined on their own feet for getting to the scene of the encounter, with the result that when the teams appeared to a great salve of applause it was estimated that there was fully 30,000 present.[1]

For Valentine 'Val' Harris the sense of anticipation would have been much the same in the dressing room as he prepared himself to captain the Irish side against England. This Irish team was representative of the whole island of Ireland – this was before the split between the Irish Football Association (IFA) in the North of Ireland and the Football Association of Ireland (FAI) of the Free State, created in 1921 in the South. Harris was, by this stage in his career, a very well-known player. He had started his professional soccer career with Shelbourne FC before making the move to Everton FC in 1908. He had previously played Gaelic football with the Dublin side 'Isles of the Sea' and was regarded as what the *Irish Independent* described as a 'maker not a taker of goals'.[2] Now, as captain of the Irish side, he hoped to provide the fans with a belated Belfast Valentine's gift against an England side the Irish had never defeated before in their history.

Out of thirty-one previous meetings, dating as far back as 1889, the English had beaten the Irish twenty-eight times. The other three results were draws. The most recent match between the sides had been played in Dublin in 1912 and had ended with a 6–0 defeat. The year 1910 was the last time the Irish had managed to record any kind of result against the English, in a spirited display in Belfast that ended 1–1.[3] The *Saturday Herald,* in its extensive write-up of the occasion, described the scenes as both sets of players took to the field:

> Great satisfaction was given at the appointment of the old Shelbourne player, Val Harris, as captain of the Irish side. At 3.25 it was estimated there were over 25,000 present, when Val Harris led out the Irishmen to the strains of St. Patrick's Day. Crompton (the English captain) a moment later leading out the Englishmen. Harris won the toss and defended the hill goal, but there was no advantage.[4]

The game itself featured some of the best players in Ireland and England at the time. The starting eleven for Ireland included 'Billy' Scott (Leeds United) in goal. William O'Connell and Peter Warren (Shelbourne) were at full back. Instead of traditional midfielders, the teams featured a mix of 'half-backs' and 'forwards' who occupied different positions from outside left, centre and outside right on the pitch. For Ireland the three half-backs were Val Harris (Everton), who played inside centre, with Harry Hampton (Bradford City) and Andrews (Grimsby Town) either side of him. The forwards were made up of Johnny Houston (who played with Harris at Everton), outside right; Dennis Hannon (Bohemians), inside right; Billy

Gillespie (also of Grimsby Town) centre forward; and Jim Macauley (Huddersfield Town and later Rangers), along with Frank Thompson (Bradford City and ex-Everton).

Harris had been part of the Irish side that lost 6–0 in Dublin versus the 'Saxon connoisseurs' as the *Herald* described them.[5] They lined up with their goalkeeper Tim Williamson (Middlesborough). Their captain, William 'Bob' Crompton (Blackburn Rovers), was at right full back, with Benson (Sheffield United) at left full. Cuggy (Sunderland), Boyle (Burnley) and Uttley (Barnsley) made up the half back line, with their forward line-up of Mordue (Sunderland) at outside right, Buchan (Sunderland) inside right, George Elliott (Middlesborough) centre forward, Joe Smith (Bolton Wanderers) at inside left forward and Wall (Manchester United) at outside left forward. The Irish had made the Imperial Hotel in Belfast their residence the day before the match. The English had made Newcastle in County Down their temporary headquarters. The *Herald* reported that 'as usual, every prominent official in football circles in the British Isles was present at the match' the following day.[6]

The match itself did not disappoint. Early chances by the English forced decent saves from Billy Scott. Later the Irish began to test Williamson at the opposite end. The reports of the action give a colourful account of proceedings. It was fast-paced and end to end. A good delivery by the Sunderland player Mordue saw the ball meet the head of his teammate Buchan, who directed the ball under the crossbar and into the back of the net. It was 1–0 to the visitors. Just before half-time, and against the run of play, the Irish struck. From a corner to Ireland the ball ended up in the back of the English net through an own goal by Sheffield United's Benson. Ireland were gifted a way back into the match.

In the second half it was clear the Irish felt that this was their chance. It was reported the crowd grew noisier and more vocal in support of the team:

> Harris now was cheered for stopping Wall after Benson and Mordue had been prominent, and then, as Smith returned, Thompson got a grand pass from Harris, and, making headway, he sent dead across to the goal-mouth, and the English defence, getting mixed up, Gillespie got on and after twelve minutes play in this [second] half scored the leading goal amidst an indescribable outburst of cheers. It was a splendid performance, and the cheering lasted for some time, and

> considering that Ireland were one short [no subs available to replace their injured Macauley] mesmerised all.[7]

The Irish, with no substitutes available, were reduced to ten men. It was a tense final period. The match finally came to an end with the ten Irishmen holding on to claim an historic victory. Val Harris had captained the first ever Irish victory over an English side.

Years later, Harris' beloved Shelbourne drew their cup match against Glenavon in Belfast on 7 March 1921. They had presumed that any scheduled replay would then be held in Dublin and Shelbourne given home advantage. This was not to be the case. The IFA's 'Protests and Appeals Committee' deemed the game unsafe to be played in Dublin due to the ongoing War of Independence. Shelbourne were asked to return to Belfast to play the replay. They refused. This, as Cormac Moore says, 'was the catalyst that led to the secession of the Leinster Football Association from the IFA and the formation of the FAI a few months later.'[8]

It was the straw that broke the camel's back. In Ireland, soccer had its roots in Ulster, and the IFA had come to prefer selecting international players from that province. They further liked staging nearly all international matches in Windsor Park as opposed to Dublin. A power struggle emerged that resulted in two Irish soccer teams on the one island, but the newly created Irish Free State were unable to play England until 1946 due to lack of recognition by the British home nation associations. This meant that players could play for both Ireland selections if they chose to up until 1950. The newly created Irish Free State team did succeed in its application to compete in the 1924 Olympics but had to wear blue jerseys with a white shielded crest covered in shamrocks as their emblem. The first time that the Republic of Ireland and Northern Ireland faced each other was in 1978. For Val Harris and his teammates in early 1913, however, an all-island Ireland selection had made history. Some of those players later opted for the IFA, while Harris opted for the Irish Free State as both player and coach.

Harris was born at 12 Clarence Place, Dublin on 23 June 1884 to Thomas Harris and Mary Fulham. His father worked as a 'boiler maker'. As a young boy, both soccer and GAA were sports he enjoyed equally. His boyhood junior soccer teams were Beaumont and Pembroke, and later Emeralds. He played in the centre-forward position and competed in matches every Saturday. On Sundays GAA would have taken centre stage for him. He played regularly up until he was a young man. He played at club and county level and won an All-Ireland medal in Gaelic football with the famous 'Isles of the Sea' in 1903 at Jones Road.[9] A few weeks earlier he had helped claim victory for the same team in Tipperary on 5 July 1903 for the 'home final'. They beat the Cork Nils team by 1–2 to 0–4 and it was noted the victors had a 'young lad called Harris who played top of the left'.[10] Most prized for Harris was his All-Ireland winner's medal for the Dublin team of 1901. However, due to the GAA ban on players who were found to be playing foreign sports (such as soccer), he left the world of GAA after his 1903 win and instead went to play for Shelbourne FC. He established himself as one of the greatest figures in what many refer to as a 'golden era of Irish soccer'.

Harris played with Shelbourne from 1903 to 1908 and again from 1914 to 1927. The first of these periods saw the team reach four successive Irish Cup finals. Out of the four finals, they won just one, in 1906 against Belfast Celtic. The life of a soccer player in Harris' time was a precarious one. The Irish soccer scene, especially in Leinster, was not as thriving as in Ulster, where the game had its roots. Career-ending injuries were a major concern. Players had to be careful to look out for themselves on the field. For Val this threat nearly became a reality. During a match against Bellevue in 1901 it was reported that he turned on his ankle and fractured it. Anecdotally, he later recalled that he had heard the doctors say he would never play again.[11] Thankfully he recovered.

With Shelbourne Harris became a fan favourite. In a Shelbourne v. Bohemians League match on 25 September 1905 the *Irish Independent* reported: 'a match that was neither magnificent, grand, rousing nor exhilarating, and, truth to tell, it was the attitude of the crowd that made it even exciting … There was no better forward on the field than Valentine Harris, who in the centre played well up to his fine reputation.'[12] It ended in a disappointing 0–0 draw.

In April 1908 Val moved to Everton on Merseyside, a decision made to progress his professional career. The club paid Shelbourne the sum of £350 for him, which was the maximum fee permitted to sign a player at the time.[13] He made his Everton debut away to Woolwich Arsenal on 18 April 1908. 'The Arsenal' played at the Manor Ground in Plumstead in those days.[14] Woolwich Arsenal won the game 2–1. Harris' debut came with just three games of the season remaining; he played in all three and made an impression.

He established himself as a regular in the starting eleven and only missed two games throughout the 1908–9 season as Everton finished runners-up in the First Division table behind Newcastle United. In the 1909–10 campaign, he featured in every game and Everton reached the semi-finals in the FA Cup. By the end of the 1911–12 season Harris had played 153 games for Everton. Despite his many appearances, he still hadn't scored a goal. It is still one of the longest goalless runs in the club's history. It came to an end though on his 155th appearance in their third match of the 1912–13 season, when Harris finally found the net against Notts County. Much was made in the Liverpool papers of the goal. The *Liverpool Echo* had a cartoon depiction of all classes of its city's citizens in apparent shock at the news that Harris, the Everton player, had scored a goal. Under the cartoon a caption read, 'A thrill of horror shook the civilised football world last Saturday when the fact was published that Val Harris had scored his first goal in five seasons at Everton. Experts in history declared that nothing has excited the populace so much since the sinking of the Spanish Armada.'[15] Val kept a copy of that cartoon framed in his house in Dublin. The *Liverpool Echo* even presented him with a small gold medal and the club presented Harris with a piano to mark the occasion.[16] It showed the level of his fame at the time and level of regard in which the supporters at Goodison held him.

His last season at Everton was in 1913–14. The team struggled to find any sort of form and finished a disappointing fifteenth in the First Division. They also suffered a shock FA Cup first-round exit to Second Division Glossop. That was the only time Harris ever lost in the opening round of a cup competition. He played his final game for Everton on Saturday, 25 April 1914, in a 2–0 defeat against Chelsea at Stamford Bridge. That year brought with it the outbreak of the First World War and the return of Harris to Dublin. He had married Elizabeth Walsh in 1908 while in England. He returned to Dublin with Elizabeth and his 4-year-old son to play once more for Shelbourne FC. He left behind an Everton career made up of 213 games and two goals.

The soccer star's return to the red jersey of Shelbourne was reported in *The Freeman's Journal* on 5 May 1914 and was captioned: 'Shelbourne's Clever Capture.'[17] With the Ireland International team, he was part of the squad that won the British Home International Championship for the very first time in 1914. He secured twenty caps from 1906 to 1914 with some memorable highlights. His Shelbourne career was also far from over. The club transitioned from being part of the IFA set-up on an all-island basis to being members of the new FAI of the Free State in 1921. In total, Harris played eighteen seasons with his beloved Shelbourne. He helped the team reach two FAI Cup finals. Its first appearance came in the 1922–23 season but did not go to plan. He later spoke of how 'Shels' were awarded a penalty on the day of the final. Arguments on the pitch over who should take it resulted in a player called Harvey claiming the ball and taking the spot kick. He missed. The goalkeeper cleared the ball away and minutes later McSherry got the only goal of the game for Alton United in what ended as a 1–0 defeat for Harris and his team.[18]

They returned to the final in 1925 against Shamrock Rovers, which was staged at Dalymount Park. It was reported on the day that the gates of the stadium had to be closed thirty minutes before kick-off due to the size of the crowd. Some 23,000 people packed in to witness another defeat for Harris and Shelbourne.[19] Rovers won 2–1 on the day. By the end of the 1924–25 season Harris was nearly 40 years of age.

In 1925–26 Shelbourne won the League of Ireland for the first time in the club's history. They finished two points clear of Shamrock Rovers. Harris by this point was getting less game time. He was living at 14 Rosehill, Carysfort Avenue, Blackrock, County Dublin. He and Elizabeth by then had three sons – Valentine, Kevin and Vincent – and two daughters, Maura and Kathleen. Kathleen died in 2013 and is buried in the family plot in Glasnevin with her father, mother, brother Vincent and sister Maura. Val's son Kevin became a player and coach himself.[20]

Following his retirement from the game as a player, Val became a coach with the new Irish Free State International team and, shortly afterwards, head coach of Shelbourne in 1933. His coaching career had some notable high points. With Shelbourne he finally tasted cup glory in 1939. As the teams coach or 'advisor' he led them to their first FAI Cup victory. In a pre-match interview, Harris was asked what he thought of his team's chance of success. He said, 'I think they'll win. They are not a great side, but they have fine team spirit, and they are getting that little bit of fortune without which it is impossible to win the Cup. No club ever won the Cup without a bit of luck in some round and Shelbourne are getting this season what's long overdue to them.'[21] They defeated Sligo Rovers 1–0 at Dalymount Park in the replayed final.[22]

Another high point of Harris' coaching career was leading the Irish Free State team to a memorable 2–0 away victory over the Netherlands in Amsterdam in 1932. The FAI of the Irish Free State, still in its infancy, struggled

Everton X1 with director, trainer, chairman and secretary. Harris is third from left, back row.
(Images courtesy of Everton FC Heritage Society and Billy Smith)

for international recognition in its early days against the competing IFA. In 1934 the Football Association of the Irish Free State (FAIFS) competed in their first qualifying campaign for the 1934 World Cup – a campaign that recorded a remarkable 4–4 draw with Belgium. Paddy Moore became the first player in the world to score four goals in a World Cup match when he netted all four Ireland goals at Dalymount. That result was followed by a 5–2 revenge demolition by Holland in Amsterdam.

In the last two decades of his life Harris took a step back from soccer but did maintain his links with Shelbourne FC. Newspaper articles reflecting on the 'golden era' of Irish soccer regularly featured his name. One interview conducted with Harris in 1956 ended with the lines:

> Before I parted from this great sportsman, still alert and one of the greatest of the many great gentlemen I have met in my journeying into soccer history, I asked him for a simple word of advice that I could pass on to the footballers of today. 'There is one golden rule' he says. 'It is often quoted but not always adhered to. Never mark a man, mark the ball! It is the secret of football success.'[23]

In an interview from the *Sunday Independent* in 1905 he was asked about the progression of soccer in Ireland: 'you know long ago there was no such thing as training a team, but now it is different and even the junior clubs are most careful to train ... I neither drink nor smoke and am rarely ill ... Well, I must be off to the training ground now as I am a little late already ...'[24]

He died, as a result of heart failure, on 9 November 1963 aged 79, while in St Columcille's Hospital in Loughlinstown. He left behind his wife, Elizabeth, who died in 1968. He was buried in the family plot that he had purchased to bury his young son Vincent in 1930. He was buried at 11.05 on the morning of 12 November in the St Patrick's section (LL 197.5). Many newspapers reported on the sad occasion of his death, with *The Irish Press* stating, 'Fans mourn soccer Star ... A "natural" footballer, he also made the top grade as a Gaelic player ...'[25] Perhaps most fittingly, the *Irish Independent*, which had covered some of his greatest successes on the football field, reported, 'Val Harris was one of the greats, one of the greats of Irish Football both Gaelic and Soccer ...'[26]

The Golden Age of Irish Tennis

Next to the St Patrick's section where Harris lies is the St Bridget's section, where other forgotten sporting legends can be found. A walk from Harris' grave towards the Tolka River leads you to a fork in the pathway. In its centre lies a small island of graves. One of these graves helps to tell the story of Ireland's 'Golden Age' of tennis in the 1890s.

Names like Willoughby Hamilton, Joshua Pim, Helena Bertha Grace Rice and Harold Mahony are not well known today, but they all won singles titles at Wimbledon in the 1890s. In the doubles, the legendary partnership of Frank Owen Stoker and Joshua Pim won twice at Wimbledon. In the July 1895 edition of *Pastime* magazine, a poem called 'A Lament from Wimbledon' recalled the sad occasion when the Irish players did not make the journey to play at the All-England Tennis Club. The reasons they did not are not entirely clear. The poem reads:

> Mr. Pim, Mr. Mahony, Mr. Stoker,
> Do you hear the sighs upon the classic green?
> Do you hear us saying what a sorry joke a
> Week at Wimbledon, with you left out, has been?

Are your triumphs so insipid that, escaping,
You forego your English laurels for a whim?
Come back again and set us all a-gaping,
Mr. Stoker, Mr. Mahony, Mr. Pim!

Mr. Pim, Mr. Stoker, Mr. Mahony,
The play was very brilliant now and then;
But, frankly, and without a bit of blarney,
'Twas not Wimbledon without the Irishmen.
Some there be who follow closely in your traces
But the champion of All England, what of him?
Come back again and put them in their places,
Mr. Mahony, Mr. Stoker. Mr. Pim![27]

The 1890s were truly the summit of Irish tennis. Willoughby Hamilton, from County Kildare, became the first Irishman to win the singles title in 1890. He was able to go one step further than that of his fellow countryman, Vere Thomas 'St Leger' Goold, who had managed to reach the All-Comers Final in 1879.[28] Goold later earned an unenviable reputation as the only Wimbledon player ever to be convicted of murder. Dr Joshua Pim had followed hot on the heels of Hamilton's success and lifted the singles trophy in 1893 and 1894. Alongside the Dublin-born Frank Stoker, Pim also prevailed in the doubles championship in 1890 and 1893. Harold Mahony of County Kerry completed the hat-trick of Irish champions in the gentlemen's singles event, defeating Wilfred Baddeley in five sets in 1896.[29] Lena Rice was also crowned

Frank Owen Stoker.

ladies champion of the All-England Lawn Tennis Championship in 1890. As Turtle Bunbury tells us: 'during the Golden Age of the 1890s and early 20th century Ireland's tennis players racked up nine Wimbledon titles (4 x men's, 1 x ladies, 2 x men's doubles and 2 x mixed doubles) as well as two Olympic Golds, the Australian Open, the US Open and effectively, the Davis Cup that we would know today'.[30]

Of particular interest for Glasnevin is the name of Francis (Frank) Owen Stoker, the man who won the men's doubles alongside the great Joshua Pim in 1890 and 1893. They were also runners up in 1891. Stoker is buried a short walk away from Val Harris and a handful of graves away from Francis Edward De Groot. He was born to a surgeon, Edward Aloysius Alexander Stoker, and Henrietta (née Wisdom) on 29 May 1866 in Dublin and was baptised in St Mary's church. Their address is listed as 46 Rutland Square (today Parnell Square). His older brother's name (born in 1860) is Graves Stoker – a strange choice considering the family's connections to Bram Stoker, the world-renowned Irish Gothic author. The brothers were second cousins to Bram.

Frank's father Edward died in 1898. Shortly afterwards Frank married Margaret Maunsell, on 29 June 1899 in Naas at the Catholic chapel of St Eustace, and moved to 23 Westland Row. His occupation is listed as a 'surgeon dentist'. He was a graduate of the Royal College of Surgeons and qualified with a license in Dental Surgery. Frank and Margaret had seven children, with five surviving. All were daughters: May, Norma, Joan, Ruth and Monica.

Although a dentist, sport was a constant in his life. Lawn tennis had grown steadily in Ireland during the 1870s and 1880s. Clubs were 'fairly abundant in the 1880s, especially on the outskirts and in suburban areas of cities and county towns'.[31] The address where Frank lived was very close to Fitzwilliam Square. This is where you would have found the Fitzwilliam Lawn Tennis club and not far away was the Lansdowne Lawn Tennis Club, of which Frank was a member. The 'Irish Championship' took root at Fitzwilliam Square and rivalled if not out-did the All-England Lawn Tennis Club at Wimbledon in its early days. In the words of Eaves and Higgins, the Fitzwilliam club 'can perhaps claim to have been the most significant catalyst for the game's development in Ireland'.[32]

The 'Fitzwilliam' in particular gained a big reputation both in Ireland and internationally and became the place where the inaugural 'Irish Championship' (1879) took place just two years after the All-England Lawn tennis Club at Wimbledon had held its first championships (1877). The location of the Irish Championship at Fitzwilliam Square was a spectacle: not only a sporting occasion but a fashion and societal event for the upper-class elite. It was described as the 'Wimbledon of Ireland' and the magazine *Pastime* (1886) describes the setting of the tournament:

> The houses surrounding the enclosed space are large and uniformly built … tenanted by Dublin 'fashionables' … In the centre of the enclosure is a splendid piece of turf, something over a hundred yards in length, and about fifty in width. This is surrounded by shrubs and trees now in their full spring foliage, their varied tints leading an additional charm to an already picturesque scene. A gravel path skirts around the edge of the turf, while another, with rustic grace, winds in and out of the well-kept shrubberies … The courts – six in number – are arranged side by side, with military precision. A slight barrier surrounds the whole, the spectators viewing the play from the ends of each court, except those at each extremity, which also offer a side view. On the outer side of the gravel path … is a strong barrier, evidently erected to prevent the spectators, who crowd here in their thousands, from injuring the flower-beds, etc.; and against it are raised tiers of footboards, from which a capital view of the play can be obtained. Tents for competitors and officials are pitched in convenient positions.[33]

Frank was also an accomplished international rugby player. He played for Wanderers Rugby Club and was capped five times for the Irish international rugby union team between 1886 and 1891. These included his first cap against Scotland in Edinburgh on 20 February 1886 at Raeburn Place. The match ended in defeat for the Irish team. Frank had played as a forward.

He played three more Home Nations matches. His last was against Wales in Llanelli on 7 March 1889. He also competed against a New Zealand Natives selection in a test match at Lansdowne Road on 1 December 1888 but was on the losing side.[34] The only victory for Frank during his time as a player was against Wales at Lansdowne Road on 3 March 1888. At the same time, he was an active member of the Lansdowne Lawn Tennis club. This was the same club where his playing partner Pim honed his skills. From 1890 to 1894 Stoker played two singles matches at Wimbledon. He was victorious

1887–88 Wanderers starting XV. Frank Owen Stoker is in the back row, third from the left. Also featured are Frank's two brothers: Graves, middle row, third from the left, and Edward, beside Frank in the back row. Graves was captain of this starting XV. (Used with kind permission of Wanderers Rugby Club)

in the first round in 1893, beating Herbert Baddeley of Great Britain in four sets. He suffered defeat to Wilberforce Eaves of Great Britain in the second round and that was the end of Stoker's participation in the singles event. His doubles career was much more rewarding.

Pim and Stoker's highly successful partnership was replicated on Irish soil. In the Irish Championship at Fitzwilliam Square, the duo secured victories in the doubles tournament in both 1890 and 1891. In 1893 they secured both the Wimbledon doubles title and the Irish Championship one. This had never been done before.[35] Due to this Irish dominance, places like Wimbledon and the Irish Championship began to call for an international challenge match or series against England. This had taken place once before in 1881. Tensions ran high between the English and Irish tennis bodies, particularly when it came to the selection of players to represent both sides. The Irish wanted to select a professional player – a member of the Fitzwilliam Club, George Kerr. The Lawn Tennis Association and the All-England Lawn Tennis Club objected on the grounds that it went against the amateur nature of competitions.[36] In the end it took the efforts of players like Frank Stoker to liaise with other players in Ireland and England to organise an official challenge match, as a benefit for the Masonic Female Orphan School of Ireland. Once the English associations and bodies received assurance that the leading Irish clubs had sanctioned the event, it was game on. The first match was held just before the Irish Championships in May 1892, and ended in an Irish victory, 5–4.[37]

The later years of Frank's life were dominated by dentistry, golf and horse-racing, for which he developed a passion. His links to tennis were maintained as he was made both an honorary member of the Lansdowne Lawn Tennis Club and an umpire at the Fitzwilliam. He moved from Westland Row to 6 Eglington Park, Dún Laoghaire, and died on 8 January 1939 at 72 years of age. His daughter Monica died a year later and was buried in the same plot. Joan, one of his other daughters, then died two years later aged just 34 in 1942, while his wife Rita was buried in the same grave in 1976. The Stoker family dealt with their fair share of tragedy during Frank's life. He lost his 14-year-old daughter Ruth to heart failure in 1923 while on her first term at Kylemore Abbey, where she is buried in the nuns' cemetery today. Frank had previously lost his 50-year-old brother, Ernest, on Christmas Eve 1914 from diabetes. Ernest is buried in the Stoker vault of St Patrick's Cathedral in Dublin.

Frank Stoker's recorded cause of death, like that of his brother Ernest, was 'Diabetes'. His obituary in *The Irish Times* says, 'Irishmen in many branches of sport will learn with deep regret of the death of Mr Frank Owen Stoker, LDS, RCSI, who was an extremely popular figure at Lansdowne Road, Fitzwilliam, Dollymount and on the race courses around Dublin …'[38]

The funeral took place on the morning of 10 January 1939, just months before the outbreak of the Second World War. He was laid to rest in Glasnevin at 10 a.m. in the St Bridget's Section (AI 162.5). To this day he remains the only rugby international to have won Wimbledon. One of his four daughters, Norma, followed in his sporting shoes and was a runner-up singles player at Wimbledon in 1931 and 1933. *The Freeman's Journal* at the end of the nineteenth century reported that 'Tennis no longer possesses the magnetic power of attracting all the world and its wife to Fitzwilliam Square as it used to.'[39]

Ally Sloper and the Aintree Grand National

Back at the O'Connell Tower Circle, beside the impressive sequoia redwood tree there is a circle of numbered doors. Number 29 is the family vault of the Nelsons, home to a forgotten set of stories. Next to their headstone stands the chapel of the Boland family, who once owned Boland's Mills. Many people walk to the nearby Republican Plot, located feet away from the Nelson and Boland vaults, to see the famed names of O'Donovan Rossa, Countess Markievicz, Harry Boland, Cathal Brugha, Helena Molony, Erskine Childers and many more. Hardly anyone pays attention to the marker for the Nelson family, but it is a vault with a sporting tale to tell.

Margaret Hope was baptised on 19 July 1857 in the parish of Mayne, County Westmeath. Her parents were Michael Hope, a 'gentleman farmer', and Mary Heffernan, both hailing from Gartlandstown. At the age of 21, Margaret married 25-year-old 'Gentleman' William Nelson from Liverpool. William was born in Cooldrinagh in County Kildare.[40] Their marriage took place on 16 July 1879 in the chapel of Whitehall in Delvin, County Westmeath. John Pinfold, the author of *Aintree: The History of the Racecourse*, has put together some invaluable research on the lives of both Lady Margaret and William Nelson. He kindly shared much of it with me and has helped greatly in the telling of another of Glasnevin's forgotten lives. Lady Margaret went on to become the first woman to own a winner of the Grand National at Aintree with her horse Ally Sloper (1915).

Lady Margaret's husband William was the son of James Nelson, an Irish cattle trader who had set up James Nelson & Sons Ltd in Liverpool, where they owned around twenty butcher's shops. He had been educated at St Edward's College in Liverpool.[41] An idea of the size and wealth obtained by the Nelson family comes with this account of their firm from 1893:

> Theirs [is] the largest European firm in cattle and dead meat. They are large consignees of cattle from the States, Canada, Portugal and Ireland, and their clients are in all parts of the United Kingdom, Spain, Portugal, and both South and North America. They have a branch

> in West Smithfield, London, besides about 200 others throughout the kingdom, and every butcher is familiar with their name. No small portion of the work done at the Birkenhead Lairages is theirs while their freezing establishment at Bramley Moore Dock will store close on 50,000 carcasses of mutton. They also have a freezing establishment at Buenos Ayres, freezing 1,000 per diem, and an oleomargarine works in Bridge Street, Birkenhead, turning out 50 tons weekly.[42]

Margaret had done well for herself. William had helped his family expand and diversify their business when he set up the highly successful Nelson shipping line. He was later made a baronet on 5 February 1912. The Nelson family, through William and his brother Hugh, even set up a direct shipping line between River Plate in Argentina and Merseyside in Liverpool in 1897. By 1910 they had over seventeen ships for both haulage and passenger accommodation.[43] To give a good sense of the wealth accumulated by Sir William throughout his life, his obituary in *The Cork Examiner* leads with the title 'Sir William Nelson's Fortune' and states that he had 'left an estate of the gross value of £992,751, of which the net personality has been sworn at £831,499. The duties will amount to about £285,000 …'[44] His estate today would be valued somewhere in the region of over €51,000,000.

William and Margaret lived at a number of addresses both in England and Ireland. Notably they had a house in London at 16 Hill Street, Berkeley Square, Mayfair, and also owned Acton Park in Denbighshire, Wales. In Ireland they had a horse stud at Clonbarron, Athboy, in County Meath, and had horses in training at Lambourn in England. They had eight children – five daughters and three sons: Josephine Mary and Mary Elizabeth (1880), James (1883), who as their eldest son assumed his father's title in 1922, William (1885), Hugh (1886), Leonie (1889), Gladys Mary (1890) and Violet Mary (1891). The Nelson Shipping Line between Liverpool and River Plate was taken over by the Royal Mail group (or the Royal Mail Steam Packet Company) in 1913. This would have been the Nelson's principal rival on the route. It was decided that the name would be retained for the existing fleet of ships owned by the Nelsons.

Sir William retired from commercial life after 1913. The reasons why are unclear, but there are reports of a hostile takeover by rivals and a series of court cases against how the company was run. This allowed him to pursue another of his great passions: horse racing.[45] Both Lady Margaret and Sir

Lady Margaret Nelson. (Courtesy John Pinfold)

William shared in this passion. Sir William's chosen colours from 1909 onwards were red and white with a blue sash and scarlet cap. They were based on the house colours of the Nelson shipping line.[46] The couple spent a lot of time at their stud in Meath and were regular visitors to Lambourn to see their horses train.

One of the few ways for women to get involved in racing at this time was through the ownership of horses. Lady Margaret's husband's highly successful shipping exploits to Argentina allowed her to indulge her love for the turf. The couple enjoyed their own successes. Her husband's best-known horse was Tangiers, a bay horse by Cylgad out of Orange Girl. Tangiers had success at the Ascot Gold Cup, the Newbury Summers Cup and the Jubilee Handicap. Tangiers, in his racing career, had won stakes to the tune of £8,258. Sir William owned other horses including Bachelor's Wedding, who won the Irish Derby for him in 1913. Another horse called Atilius won the Wales Stakes in 1920 while Veneedor won the Flying Handicap at Newmarket with '10st 7lb in the saddle'. When Sir William Nelson died in July 1922 at the age of 71, he still had a number of horses in training at Penrith in Wales and at the family's stud in Athboy in County Meath.[47]

Sir William was initially buried at Kensal Green Cemetery in London. Two years later a decision was made by his widow, Lady Nelson, to exhume his remains and have them repatriated to Ireland. She chose Glasnevin. The reason why Glasnevin was chosen is not clear, but Lady Nelson purchased vault 29 on the O'Connell Tower Circle. It is next to the founder of the cemetery and his impressive Round Tower. This is where you will find some of the wealthiest individuals at rest in the cemetery. Sir William was placed into vault 29 at 9 a.m. on 10 June 1924, the delay partly due to the Irish Civil War.

Lady Margaret Nelson went on to succeed where her husband had failed in the world of horse racing. She came into the ownership of a horse called Ally Sloper. The horse was named after the famous comic strip character who made his debut in a magazine called *Judy*, a rival of *Punch* dating back to the mid-1860s. *The Scotsman* in its sporting news section recounted the events that led to her owning the horse:

> Lady Nelson became the owner of Ally Sloper in rather unusual circumstances. He was as good as sold to the late Frank Bibby for 700gns, but just before the transaction was completed the gelding was rejected by Bibby's agent because he turned one of his toes out. The Lambourn trainer Gwilt who at that time had charge of Lady Nelson's horses then stepped in and purchased Ally Sloper and his judgement was vindicated when the gelding won the Grand National shortly afterwards.[48]

The 1915 Grand National was unusual in that it occurred during wartime. On a cold and icy 26 March, it was reported that the nature of the crowd was very different from normal. Many were away doing their duty in the First World War. Others had stayed away to continue in their jobs at offices or in factories to support the war effort. Not everyone stayed away, though. The professional classes and businessmen of Liverpool turned out in large numbers. Separately it was recorded that a large number of wounded servicemen in their khaki uniforms being treated in local hospitals were given free entry to the County Stand, the most exclusive stand on the course. The *Belfast News-Letter* accounted that 'out of 20 starters only 9 completed the course …'[49]

Ally Sloper was just six years old as the competitors readied themselves for the steeplechase. The jockey was the famous 21-year-old Jack Anthony, who had previously won the Grand National on the one-eyed horse Glenside in 1911. The horse was trained by the very well-respected Aubrey Hastings of the Nelson stud in Athboy. *Tatler* magazine featured a set of images including the horse, its jockey and its trainer, Mr Hastings, in April 1915. The race itself was recounted in later years by the jockey:

> Ally Sloper … made two bad blunders which might easily have been fatal. At the second fence it was the nearest thing in the world that he didn't come to grief, and I shall always think that the reason my horse kept up was that he leaned over towards Ilaton, who … was ridden by my brother Ivor [who helped pull Jack back into the saddle]. Ally

> Sloper's mistake was caused through jumping on to the top of the fence, and the same thing happened at the Canal Turn. He took off too soon, got to the top of the fence, and was all but down. As a matter of fact I lost both irons and my reins. But when I got him going again he jumped perfectly and did not make a similar mistake. When we had completed one circuit of the course we were no better off than having eighth place and coming onto the racecourse for the first [I think he means second here] time there were still five horses in front of us. Then I began to move up. It was now or never, and I am sure that Ally Sloper realised that this was so. He had taken on something better than second wind; he was full of pep and go. When we had come to the last fence but one, Ally was second to Jacques, the mount of Newey, and what exercised my mind was not whether he could beat any of the survivors in the run in, but whether he, the impetuous, the bustling fellow that he was, would make another blunder at these final fences. Was it going to be a case of 'So near, and yet so far'? And now we were at the last jump of all. I put Ally Sloper to it with all the impudence, all the assurance that was in me. And Ally did what I shall always believe was the best jump in that long and jagged journey. He flew over it, it seemed to me. The joy I felt as he landed fair and square was indescribable. That jump had given him the lead for the first time in the race. I knew we were winning. There was Jacobus battling it out stoutly, but Ally seemed to know. I could feel the gallant fellow straining and pulling and tugging at his heart. He never quaked nor winced. Two lengths in front of Jacobus we sailed past the post.[50]

According to John Pinfold, author of *Aintree: The History of a Racecourse*, this is one of the best descriptions of what it is like to ride the winner of the Grand National that he has ever come across. Other accounts can be read in newspapers like the *British Mail*.

Lady Nelson was not at Aintree to see her horse win; she had not in truth expected it to. The odds before the race had placed Ally Sloper and his jockey at 100–8.[51] When she discovered the historic news back in London, she immediately set out on a journey to Liverpool. She arrived the following day to congratulate both her horse and the jockey. In her absence, Lady Nelson's daughter 'made a flying descent' from the top of the County Stand, delighted

ALLY SLOPER AND HIS TRAINER

A Pictorial Re-echo of the Grand National, 1915.

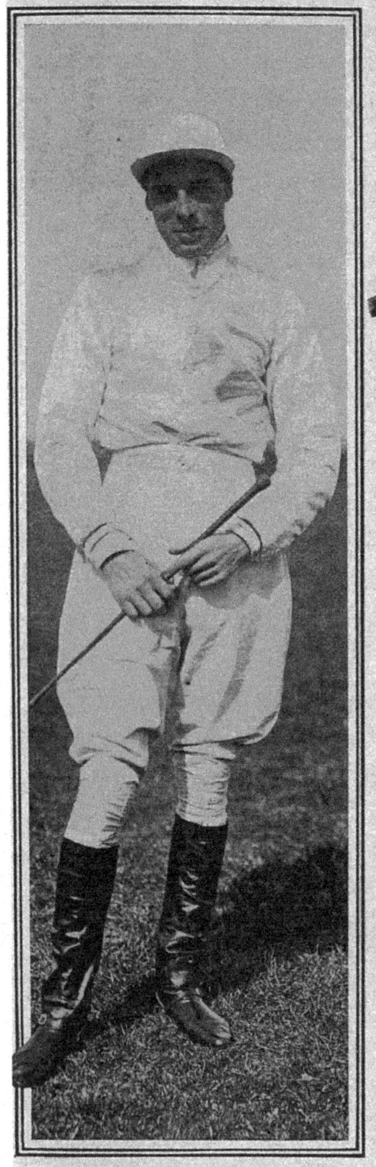

LADY NELSON'S ALLY SLOPER

(Mr. Jack Anthony up), winner of the Grand National, with the Hon. Aubrey Hastings, who trained the horse

Photographs by Rouch

MR. JACK ANTHONY

The most famous amateur "jock" of the day. He has had the unique distinction of winning two Grand Nationals. He also rode the winner of the Champion Steeplechase at Liverpool

THE HON. AUBREY AND MRS. HASTINGS

With their Sealyham terriers. Mr. Hastings is the youngest brother of Lord Huntingdon, and has had a successful training career. His stables are at Wroughton, Swindon. Mrs. Hastings was before her marriage a Miss Forsyth-Forrest

The *Tatler*, Wednesday, 14 April 1915, p. 19.

with the spectacle. She had just witnessed history. She hoped to help lead the horse in on her mother's behalf. In the madness of the moment, however, she took a wrong turn across the asphalt pavement and was too late.[52] The crowds and cheers were electric as Sir William Nelson (son of Lady Nelson), along with his sister, managed to get to the horse. In the bustling crowds they both managed to give it a congratulatory slap on the neck. A reporter managed to interview Jack Anthony immediately afterwards: 'I never expected him to show such wonderful speed as he did for the last fence after such a tiring journey. You must remember he is only a six-year-old, and it proves that horses when they are six-year-olds are capable of staying the distance …'[53]

Lady Nelson decided after the historic victory at Aintree to give a quarter of the winning stakes to funds for soldiers and sailors. Family relatives accounted that she donated her full winnings to the Red Cross and said, 'it was not only a pleasure to give it but also her duty'.[54] The value of the race was about £3,515.[55] Her 'excitable horse, always squealing and making a fuss' became a roaring success.[56]

She assumed full control of the family stud at Clonbarron in Athboy afterwards and devoted much of her time to her trainers' and horses' needs. In 1929 she made the decision to step back and began to sell most of her thoroughbred mares, foals and yearlings. She held onto one or two horses and had them in training with the brother of Jack Anthony, Ivor at Wroughton.[57] The last horse that won a race for her was at Lingfield and was called Grim Warrior. This was just days before her death on 6 April 1932 aged 75, while living on Berkeley Square in London. *The Irish Times* reported on the sad news with the headline 'Margaret Lady Nelson Dead, First Woman to Win the Grand National'.[58] Her death was also reported in lesser-known newspapers such as *The Courier and the Adventurer*, which ran with the headline: 'Death of Famous Woman Racehorse Owner'.[59]

Her remains were brought back to Ireland where the funeral mass took place on 11 April 1932 at 9 a.m. in Dublin's Pro-Cathedral on Marlborough Street. After the service the procession made its way to the gates of Glasnevin, where she was buried in the same vault as her husband. Her cause of death was 'pneumonia'. The vault was used again in subsequent years and today it is the family vault for the Nelsons. Ally Sloper outlived his owners. In June 1932 The *Drogheda Independent* reported that he was 'amongst the most distinguished arrivals for the International Horse Show in London … now 23 years old, he belonged to the late Lady (Margaret) Nelson and now belongs to Sir James Nelson, of Clonbarron'.[60] I was unable to trace when exactly Ally Sloper died. It must be assumed that he lived out the rest of his days with a happy retirement at the paddocks near Wantage, England. It was not until 1977 that Charlotte Brew would become the first woman to compete at the Grand National. In 2021 Rachael Blackmore became the first female jockey to win it.[61] It all began with Lady Nelson from Westmeath.

Murder and Mystery

Many tales of murder and mystery are at rest in Glasnevin Cemetery, some of which have been the subject of much study and attention in recent times, while others have remained just that – a mystery. An example of one event that has received greater attention in recent times is the Phoenix Park Murders. The cemetery is the final resting place of one of the victims from 6 May 1882 – Thomas Henry Burke, who was buried in his father's grave in the South section (ZB 74). He was born in Tuam, County Galway in 1829 and went on to work for the British establishment as head of the civil service. He was closely associated with the British coercion policy during the Land Wars of 1879–82 in Ireland. Despite the fact that he was a Roman Catholic, many Irish republican organisations of the period saw him as a traitor and nicknamed him the 'castle rat'. An organisation called the National Invincibles decided to take action, resulting in the deaths of both Burke and Lord Frederick Cavendish, the newly appointed Chief Secretary for Ireland. Five executions followed in Kilmainham Gaol and it became one of the most dramatic episodes in nineteenth-century Ireland.

Glasnevin Cemetery, Old O'Connell Circle, *c.* 1865–1914. (Reproduced courtesy of the National Library of Ireland)

A large memorial to Burke stands directly opposite his grave today. He is the only person buried in the cemetery with two headstones. Both memorials unusually feature how he died with the words 'murdered in the Phoenix Park' clearly visible on both.[1] The grave is a short walk from Michael Collins'. This is a tale which has received much attention thanks to the late historian Shane Kenna and his book *The Invincibles: The Phoenix Park Assassinations and the Conspiracy that Shook an Empire* (2019), and more recently the podcast *The Invincibles: Park Assassins* (2020) by Róisín Jones, which takes the listener through each twist and turn of the planning, murder and aftermath in a true-crime-style series. Other people have received less attention.

Boy Killed by his Mother

It was 8 a.m. on Saturday, 16 May 1896. A young Patrick Lacken, 16 years old had come into the kitchen of his family residence at No. 15 Balls Lane, East Arran Street, Dublin. His belly rumbling, his mother, Mary, agreed to put on two boiled eggs for him. She was busy cleaning and gutting fish for his father, John, to sell later at the markets nearby. The family had a number of addresses and were constantly on the move. This was quite common for the time. We first see John and Mary Lacken living at 3 Cathedral Lane, close to Kevin Street Police Station in 1859. By 1880 they had moved to 5 Patrick's Close in Dublin. It is there that Patrick was born. There also exist records of the family living in Bray, County Wicklow at Tillystown around 1886. By 1896, however, the family were living on Balls Lane, on the northside of Dublin City.

Patrick had retired to the drawing room to wait for his breakfast to be cooked. His mother brought the boiled eggs to him and he began to eat. Shortly afterwards he began to complain that they were not cooked right. Mary, not best pleased, tried to ignore him as she went to the adjoining yard to carry on with her work. Patrick finished his eggs. Despite clearing his plate, the moaning continued. In a fit of anger and frustration Mary picked up a large pair of fish gutting scissors and threw them in the direction of her son. To her surprise, the force she had used was enough for them to lodge in his back close to his left shoulder blade.

Mary ran towards her son, who was now in a state of shock and removed them from his back. Patrick bolted for the front door and out onto the road outside. He was bleeding significantly from his back, and blood was flowing from his mouth. As he gripped the walls on the street and continued along in agony, he tried desperately to catch his breath. At this point Patrick began to vomit blood. As he approached the junction of North King Street and 15 North Anne Street he collapsed. A passing member of the Dublin Metropolitan Police (DMP) Constable Henry Dixon (103D) attended the scene and had the boy removed to Richmond Hospital on a car. Before reaching the hospital, Patrick was pronounced dead. Glasnevin records note that he died as a result of a 'haemorrhage caused by a wound to the lung'. His official death certificate tells a similar tale, stating that he died as a result of a 'haemorrhage lasting about ten minutes due to a penetrating wound of his left lung accidentally inflicted'.

The Irish Times ran a story on the tragedy on Saturday, 23 May 1896. The headline of the article stated: 'Domestic Tragedy in Dublin: A boy killed by his mother.'[2] It described the scene that Constable Dixon saw as he approached North Anne Street: 'There was a wound under the blade of the left shoulder, the clothes were soaked with blood, and the mouth was filled with blood.' Other newspapers that covered the story included *The Ballinrobe Chronicle* and *The Nenagh Guardian*.[3]

Mary Lacken was arrested and at her trial in Green Street Courthouse the scissors used were produced. It was reported that she exclaimed, 'these were the unlucky scissors' and that 'no punishment would be too much'.[4] An inquest was carried out. *The Freeman's Journal* covered the story on 19 May 1896. It reported on the words of Dr Kenny, the city coroner, who gave his statement: 'The case was a pitiable one. It showed the danger of taking up a weapon, dangerous or not against any person.'[5] Patrick was buried on 18 May. It is hard to imagine the emotions that his mother must have felt. The funeral was a small affair. John, his father, made the appropriate arrangements for the internment. Today he lies in the Garden section (DC 66).

Mary was sentenced to six months' hard labour at Grangegorman. The charge she was found guilty of was manslaughter. Her sentence began on 10 June 1896. For her husband and family this must have been a bizarre time. It was part of a sad pattern for Mary, who was in fact quite the regular with the constables in Kevin Street police station. If you look at her criminal record, a pattern of unstable behaviour emerges. From 1886 to 1895 six previous convictions can be found. The convictions include 'drunk and threatening behaviour', 'assault', 'malicious damage' and '8 times for drunkenness and sentenced to short periods'.[6] Alcoholism and violent outbursts were an issue for Mary.

If you search for all births for John and Mary Lacken in this time frame there is a sizeable list. First, we have the birth of Hanna on 9 March 1860 (who sadly died aged just two). Next there is a Thomas, born in 1862, who sadly died just ten months later. Both Hanna and Thomas are buried in the same unmarked plot as Patrick. In February 1868, Matthew was born, followed by James (1873) Eliza (1875), an unknown male child (1877) and Patrick at Patrick's Close (1880). While they were living in Wicklow, she gave birth to Bridget (1887). Alcohol may have been one of the few remedies for getting Mary through each day in a family situation that highlights the nature of life in Dublin at the turn of the twentieth century. A hard life.

The General Register of Prisoners for Grangegorman provides us with the best description of what she looked like. Mary had brown hair, brown eyes and a fair complexion. On admission to the prison, she was weighed at 128lbs, while on discharge she had in fact gained weight and was 132lbs, an indication on the nature of the hardship of life outside prison. The release date is listed as 6 December 1896.[7] Financially, the family struggled. John and Mary both entered the North Dublin workhouse and their names can be found on its indoor relief registers. Mary died in the infirmary of the workhouse on 10 May 1901 aged 50. Her occupation is recorded as unknown. John died one month later in the same infirmary on 7 June. He was 54 years of age with an occupation of 'Dealer'. Mary's cause of death is recorded as 'Hemiplegia' (a stroke) while her husband John's cause of death is listed as 'Bright's Disease'. John was buried in what was at that time a poor ground section of the cemetery, St Patrick's (CJ 28.5), while his wife was buried in the same section (YI 28.5). It proved extremely difficult to locate these graves. However, Lynn Brady, the then resident genealogist at Glasnevin, succeeded in tracking down both. Human error meant that Mary had been recorded as 'Larkin' and not 'Lacken' on her death certificate, while her burial record was mistakenly recorded with her age as 80 instead of 50. Her maiden name was Larkin, so perhaps the confusion arose from there. It tells us that she was buried on 14 May 1901, forty-eight hours before the fifth anniversary of the death of her son Patrick.

Today, Patrick, Mary and John Lacken all lie in unmarked graves and for over 100 years their story lay hidden and forgotten. Mary, as it turns out, is my great-great-great grandmother. My grandmother confirmed to me that as a child she was often told to watch what she said to her own grandfather, James Lacken – the brother of Patrick – when visiting. My grandmother has since organised for a small plaque to remember this side of the family. She is not alone in finding that her ancestors (and indeed my own) lie in unmarked plots. Due to the size of the cemetery, there are many other similarly forgotten stories.

Murder on Ireland's Eye

Close to the back of the O'Connell Tower as you walk along a pathway of impressive Celtic crosses and Gothic pointed obelisks arcing to the left, take the small path to the right. In amongst the old and aged rectangular stones, there is a small wooden cross made from garden decking and painted black marking a grave in the Garden section (XD 39). It reads: 'Died Tragically, Ireland's Eye.' A small image of a young woman is attached. This is the grave of Maria Kirwan. Her story is another that until recently has not received the attention it deserves.

On 6 September 1852, Sarah Maria Crowe, the wife of Irish artist and illustrator William Bourke Kirwan, was murdered a short distance north of Howth on a small uninhabited island mostly made up of rocky terrain called Ireland's Eye. Maria, the name by which she was usually known, and her husband had rented accommodation in Howth near Dublin for their summer holidays in June 1852. He was very interested in sketching seascapes, and she enjoyed the newly fashionable recreation of sea bathing. It was a Monday morning, and the Kirwans asked a boatman named Patrick Nagle to row them to Ireland's Eye with some provisions to spend the day there. The boatman left with instructions to return at 8 o'clock that evening.

Before the boatman and his cousin Michael Nagle left from Howth to collect the Kirwans, three local residents reported hearing loud cries coming across the water from the island. When the boatmen arrived back at Ireland's Eye they caught a glimpse of something strange. It was the body of Mrs Kirwan. William Kirwan arrived on the scene and began to throw himself on top of his wife's body crying 'Maria! Maria!' He turned to one of the boatmen and told him to find his wife's clothes. After some time, the boatman returned. Her clothes could not be found. William Kirwan said the clothes were on a rock close at hand and he would get them himself. And so he did. The boatman later reflected that he had looked in the same spot where William seemingly found them, but no clothes were to be seen when the boatman looked.

The body of Sarah Maria Kirwan was rowed back to Howth, where a medical student was on hand. He pronounced that she had died by drowning. Rumours quickly began to spread in Dublin that Mrs Kirwan had been murdered by her own husband. It later transpired that William had a second family with a Miss Kenny, by whom he had seven children. The Kirwans' residence was at 11 Merrion Street, Dublin. The Kenny residence was only one mile away. William Kirwan had been living a double life, with one wife living up the road from the other. This new information came to the ears of the authorities, who arrived at the not unreasonable assumption that Kirwan had a motive to kill one of his wives.

He was arrested and put on trial. It was a sensation. A newspaper reported that 'Long before the arrival of the judges, the avenues leading to the court were thronged by a vast number of gentry seeking admission.' Kirwan was sentenced to death by hanging. This was later commuted to life imprisonment. He spent twenty-seven years in the notorious Spike Island prison in Cobh before being released on condition he settle nowhere in the British Empire. It is believed he went to America, but little is known of what became of him after leaving Ireland.

To this day opinions are divided as to whether he did or didn't kill his wife. The trial was largely based on circumstantial evidence. The jury had to be locked in the courtroom overnight by orders of the judge to reach a verdict. They simply could not agree. Although Kirwan was a bigamist, many argued that it did not make him a murderer. We will likely never know the true facts of the murder of Maria on Ireland's Eye. If you visit the cemetery today, you will find Maria Kirwan's lawn-covered grave. Dean Ruxton, who has recently published a book on the whole story, reflected on his own visit to her grave and stated:

> Returning to the grave from my tour among the celebrity headstones, I examine the proud, ornate structures neighbouring Maria's plot, the material remnants of the effort and expense of families and friends in mourning. Maria, after her death was likely one of the most spoken-about people in the country. That in mind, there's a very real, physical

inequality that's hard to escape. It's common to hear people say there is undue focus on the criminal when it comes to writing about crimes. It's not incorrect ...[8]

Lissard House and the More O'Ferralls

Behind the France–Ireland memorial, remembering all Irish people who lost their lives in the British military defending France in both world wars and in the earlier Franco-Prussian conflict of 1870–71, a sea of Celtic crosses emerges. One of the crosses on the main pathway remembers Gerald Richard More O'Ferrall, who was mortally wounded on 9 February 1935 during a dinner party at Lissard House in County Longford. It marks the family plot in the St Bridget's section (AH 30.5). The side of the cross reads 'Died 20th February 1935 from wounds received when gallantly defending his father from assailants.'

The More O'Ferrall family were aristocrats who held proud Longford connections.[9] Descended from chiefs known as the Lords of Annaly, they had acquired the Lissard property in the nineteenth century thanks to John Lewis More O'Ferrall. It was his grandson Gerald More O'Ferrall who came to inherit the property in 1914. In 1934 Gerald was appointed as land agent for the Sanderson estate, which included properties for 120 families.

The 1930s were times of desperation and economic hardship for many in the fledgling Irish Free State. The More O'Ferralls were one of the few remaining landlord gentry families in the State. Many big houses had been burned during the Civil War and the owners of those that remained by the 1930s knew that many were eager to see them removed. Tenants refused to pay their outstanding rents to the More O'Ferrall family and eleven were served with eviction notices. For many the rents were simply too high and they could not afford to pay. In response the Edgeworthstown Tenants Association was formed to resist any forced evictions and in time they asked the local IRA for help. The fact that Gerald lived in Lissard and not in Edgeworthstown did little to help his case. Many branded him as the archetypal absentee landlord demanding high rents from tenants.

On the night of 9 February, he was hosting a dinner party to try and smooth relations with his son Gerald Richard More O'Ferrall, who had married, without family approval, a woman called Moya Brady. At about 9 p.m. that evening four IRA men dressed as members of An Garda Síochána called at the house. They pushed their way into the party to try and kidnap Gerald. His son, in the chaos, tried to help pull his father out of the hands of the assailants. The disguised men opened fire, shooting Gerald Richard in the back and Gerald his father in the chest. Miraculously Gerald senior was not seriously injured. A gold cigarette case in his breast pocket had saved him. His son, however, died of his injuries in hospital eleven days later, at just twenty years old.[10]

The men responsible were never tried or convicted, but the killing did result in a clampdown on the IRA by de Valera in the 1930s. It also saw the establishment of a Special Criminal Court with no jury for future cases and the use of military courts for such matters. The family later relocated to County Kildare and Lissard House was demolished in the 1950s. Its lands were acquired by the Forestry Department. A full account of this fascinating story of murder in the new Irish Free State has been researched and written by the historian from Gowna, Frank Columb. Gerald Richard's murder contributed to the eventual banning of the IRA by the State and, in later years, the execution of several prominent IRA men either by firing squad or hanging during the Emergency Period.

In retelling the stories of Patrick Lacken, Maria Kirwan and Gerald Richard More O'Ferrall, we should not forget the gruesome ways in which all met their end. When visiting their graves, the inequalities in their monuments and how their stories have been remembered or forgotten are very evident.

The Case of Count Jottka

For some buried in the cemetery, not all their details are known. They remain a mystery. One example is 'a man supposed to be William Jottka'. On the morning of 8 July 1884, Count William Jottka was in his lodgings at 39 Lower Sheriff Street. He was a 'well-built man of medium height, rather slight in build … his complexion was dark and his eyes light blue'.[11] He was reading when he heard a knock on his door. In walked Miss Polly (Mary) Inglis, his fiancée. She was described as being 'slight' in build, 'fair haired … extremely prepossessing and barely 19 years of age'.[12] They were to be married later that afternoon.

The Count had yet to prove his noble credentials to his proposed in-laws. He had arrived in Dublin around 11 February 1884 and had taken up lodgings with the Inglis family on Lower Sheriff Street shortly afterwards. He had told Polly's mother that he was the owner of many farms and properties. Not much other background information is available to us. Polly's mother had seen some correspondence of his from Edinburgh addressed to 'Count William Jottka', but that is as much context as we have on the man.[13] We are not completely certain if 'Count Jottka' was even his name. In some accounts he is described as a journeyman, an adventurer traveller, a commercial silk dealer, a 'mobs-man' and a pickpocket. One thing is certain – he was an elusive character.

The 'nobleman' had been splitting his time between Lower Sheriff Street and the Shelbourne Hotel in the city centre. Polly wondered what he might fancy for his last breakfast as a bachelor. On entering his room, the Count asked if she could go to his valise and bring over some papers for the marriage. She walked towards the case and opened it up. The Count had been very cautious and secretive in sharing information about his family in the lead-up to the engagement and Polly's mother had her suspicions about his background. It had led to minor arguments between the couple in the past and on the morning of their proposed marriage, things came to a head. Inside his valise Polly found a framed photo of herself and her fiancé; she had previously been assured that it had been sent to his brother in Hamburg as proof of their engagement. Her mind began to race with doubts. She wanted to know why he had lied about sending the photograph. Instead of calmly trying to explain the situation, the Count became visibly agitated and a heated argument broke out. Polly later recounted that 'his manner grew wild and strange … I had never seen such a look in his eyes'.[14] Shocked and scared, she backed away from her husband-to-be. Before she could get out of the room the Count had bolted for his valise. From within the bag, he produced a revolver. He grabbed the young woman by the arm and pressed the muzzle into her left side towards her abdomen. He began to whisper and mutter what she described as 'half-intelligible words' before, to her shock, he pulled the trigger.[15] She waited for the pain of the bullet and to feel herself go limp. She was frozen with fear. As she looked down, she noticed that a scorched hole was visible through her dress – the bullet had taken a large chunk of the clothing but had completely missed her body and lodged in the bedframe behind.

The Count's grip loosened on Polly as he staggered back a little with the unexpected shock of the gunshot. Polly barely had the strength to make it to the door, but she dashed out onto the landing. As she began to scream and cry, she heard another shot ring out inside the room. She did not know whether it was meant for her or for her fiancé. As the commotion continued, her mother and aunts ran up the stairs. Mrs Inglis got to the top as a final gunshot rang out. A policeman was called for.

The first constable on the scene was one Patrick Travers (20 C). As they all entered the drawing room they found: 'The room filled with smoke; on the floor near the fireplace lay the man in a pool of blood; the smoking revolver still in his hand; the police and some persons from the street ran in and he was placed on a car and conveyed to Jervis Street hospital, where he subsequently died.'[16]

Count William Jottka, before dying in the hospital, was asked by police to account for his actions. He refused to give any information and refused to speak to a member of the clergy. He was buried in Glasnevin four days later. Most of the fields in the register for his burial are today marked as 'Unknown'. He lies in the Garden section (VA 147) and was recorded as being 35 years old. When asked why he did it, he 'shook his head, and then commenced to ramble about Miss Polly Inglis. He regretted he had not killed himself and sank soon afterwards.'[17] The strange events relating to the Count were widely covered in newspapers. Lengthy full-page articles can be found in both *The Irish Times* and *The Freeman's Journal*, the latter leading on 10 July 1884 with the headline 'Tragic Occurrence in Dublin, Attempted Murder and Suicide by a German Count.'

On the Wednesday following the death of Jottka, an inquest was held at Jervis Street Hospital by the city coroner, Dr N.C. Whyte. The body was described to the coroner as being 'Count William Jottka'. A surgeon aptly named Doctor Chance also examined the body. A man named Louis Kohrs, a German native who had been living in Dublin for over seventeen years and who owned a cook-shop (a place to eat) along the Quays, was called on to give some insight into the nature of the 'Count'. Kohrs provided some of the most interesting details available to us today. Out of everyone examined at the inquest, he had the most to say. He told the jury:

> I keep a little cook-shop on the Quays. About 11 months ago I found on coming home the deceased getting some meat supper. I don't sell drink. My missus said to me it was a country man of yours. I spoke to him in German but he could not speak German and answered in

> Dutch. I speak that language as well as German. He told me that he had just come from Glasgow that morning, he also said that he was a silk commercial traveller and had been travelling three or four years in the country. On that occasion deceased was very plainly dressed. Next day … saw deceased and he was dressed like a gentleman with diamonds and rings. [He] used to call two and three times every week and once in a while dined. He used to remain hours talking to me and whenever he came back from Scotland or Hamburg he used first to call … nothing of importance occurred in the conversations. He gave me his name as 'William Jottka'. I believed what he used to tell me. He informed me that he was a poor man. He used to talk to me about his home and he said that he was an only son and that at his father's death he would have £1,200 a year. He said that he had fallen in love with a girl in Dublin and that he had taken a house and engaged two servants, and that when he was married he would invite me to the house. He refused to tell me where the house [was] … On one occasion he came to my house on horseback.[18]

A Detective Officer Graham also stated at the inquest that 'He was not a pickpocket in Dublin. Seeing that he had no business in Dublin. He had no company in Dublin and I have made enquiries about him and procured this card from him.'[19] The coroner held the business card up to the jury. It had the simple inscription, 'Count William Jottka'. Whyte, with the card in his hand said, 'If a commercial traveller presented such a card at a business establishment he would be kicked out …'[20]

At the inquest the supposed 'Count' had been accused of being a pickpocket, a 'mobs man', a Jack-in-the-box and a commercial silk traveller. The coroner even made the suggestion that he was an undercover London detective. A jury man was quick to put an end to such suggestions: 'We really don't care what his rank or name was.'[21] Everyone in the room eventually came to the conclusion that they may never get to the bottom of the man's identity. The jury returned a verdict that a man 'unknown calling himself Count William Jottka committed suicide by shooting himself through the chest at 39 Lower Sheriff Street on the 8th of July 1884 and that his death took place on the same date at Jervis Street Hospital'.[22]

As the case was brought to a close, one final intriguing detail was revealed to the room. Months before Jottka's death on Lower Sheriff Street, Detective

Officer Graham had interviewed an unnamed witness who had provided some information about the supposed Count to the police. He said that: 'The deceased man supposedly travelled under the name of "Smyth" or "Schmidt" as being a name familiar and common in the United Kingdom and that he was actually a German Count and his family resided near Berlin.'[23]

Two questions arise here: why were the police conducting interviews with witnesses relating to the Count in the first place and who was this 'unnamed witness' whom the detective was 'not at liberty' to reveal? These are questions that we will likely never know the answers to.

Charlotte Inglis, the landlady, appears to have moved away from her house on Sheriff Street to Amiens Street. Her daughter Polly, who so nearly died that morning, does not appear on any records – census, marriage or death – between 1884 and 1901. Like the man she was involved with, much of her story remains a mystery to this day.

TV, Movies and Stage

The cemetery has many famed performers buried within its walls. Jimmy O'Dea is one of the more remembered names, yet hardly anyone stops at his graveside anymore. He made his name as an actor and comedian on the stages of the Abbey, the Empire (Olympia), the Queen's Theatre (which once stood on Pearse Street but was later demolished), the Theatre Royal and, later, London's Coliseum. He became a central part of the Irish comedy scene both on stage and screen in the 1950s and 1960s.[1] His biggest legacy for some was his depiction of 'King Brian' in Walt Disney's *Darby O'Gill and the Little People* (1959). To others it was on the stage, as his leading female character persona: 'Biddy Mulligan, the Pride of the Coombe'. At the graveside in the Garden section (MF 57) on the day of his funeral, floral tributes were piled around the plot. One tribute read, 'He gave me great pleasure all down through the years. God rest his noble soul.' It was from the Senator Margaret Pearse.[2] O'Dea's life story, although forgotten by many, has been chronicled by the author Philip B. Ryan in *Jimmy O'Dea: The Pride of the Coombe* (1990). The cemetery also houses many other forgotten stories of lives spent on stage and on screen. Many are lost and undervalued female voices and presences.

Glasnevin Cemetery *c.* 1900 with monument by Sir Thomas Farrell to actor Barry Sullivan (1821–91). (Reproduced courtesy of the National Library of Ireland)

The Grand Old Lady of the Abbey

Saturday, 26 January 1907 – the opening night and world premiere at the Abbey Theatre of John Millington Synge's *The Playboy of the Western World.* It was to result in what today is called the Playboy Riots. The play depicted the controversial story of a local village 'loon' who splits his father's head open with a spade before running away and boasting about what he has done only to become a hero (of sorts) to some excitable women and drunken men. The topic of patricide and lines about ladies' underwear offended most in the auditorium that night. Many in the nationalist community, meanwhile, were not prepared to see Irish society depicted in such a way on the national stage. The *Evening Echo* reported on the aftermath of the opening night using the words of William Butler Yeats, who described the scenes:

> From the first rise of the curtain there was an obviously organised attempt to prevent the play being heard … The noise consisted of shouting and booing and stamping of feet. I did not hear six consecutive lines of the play last night owing to the noise. The section that caused the disturbance was not part of the regular audience. The conduct of the section was riotous and offensive, and disturbed and annoyed the audience …[3]

On stage that night was the 18-year-old Mary 'May' Craig. She was playing the part of 'Honor Blake', one of the giggling girls keen to hear the stories from the son in the play boasting about what he had done to his own father. Fr Eugene MacCarthy (often misspelled McCarthy), the parish priest from James's Street, had played a part in bringing her talents to light. May Craig reflected how:

> The school excursion, in the lovely summer of 1906, was to Killiney. In charge of us was Father Eugene McCarthy … and I was looking after the younger girls … None of us knew that Father McCarthy was a great friend of William Fay [a friend of the Abbey's looking for female actresses to fill roles for Synge's *Playboy*] until that evening in 1907, when he called to ask if he might bring me to the Abbey Theatre to see Mr Fay … It appeared that Mr Fay had told Father McCarthy he had

> not enough girls in the company for the parts which the play required. My mother gave me permission, and so I went to the Abbey …[4]

Mary Craig, better known as 'May', was born in Dublin in 1889 to parents David Joseph Craig and Emma Redmond. Her father worked as a 'fitter' and engineer. She had one elder sister.[5] In her life she forged an impressive acting career at the Abbey. Between 1907 and 1968 she appeared on stage in over 950 productions and toured North America six times with different Abbey companies. Productions she was involved with included works by Synge, Shaw, O'Casey, Robinson, St John Gogarty, Lady Gregory, W.B. Yeats, Oscar Wilde and William Shakespeare.

As a child she enjoyed many trips to see plays and operas with her mother Emma.[6] The census of 1901 shows that the family was living in Kilmainham at 5 Woodfield Place. Although May had appeared on the Abbey stage in 1907, it was not until December 1915 that her big break came with a performance of *The Colleen Bawn* at the St Francis Xavier Hall. She spent time on the stage of the Workingmen's Club and St Francis Xavier Hall in Dublin learning her trade.[7] In the production of *The Colleen Bawn* she played the part of a young woman called Ellen Hanley. The play was based on the true story of her murder. Luckily for May, the manager of the Abbey, Mr Keogh, was in the audience for one of her performances. That resulted in her appearing at the Abbey again in 1916, in a performance playing Raina Petkoff in *Arms and the Man* by G.B. Shaw.[8]

This led to a number of appearances in the Abbey playing 'Miss O'Neill' in the comedy *Nic* by William Boyle on 26 October 1916, 'Jane' in *The White-headed Boy* on 13 December 1916 and a much-praised performance for her role as 'Jude' in T.C. Murray's *Spring* in 1918.[9] She married Vincent Power-Vardy at St Andrew's church on 22 August 1916. They had met on the Abbey stage. Although she had a great love for acting, it did not support her family and in the 1911 census her occupation was listed as working in a 'boot factory' with her sister. By 1916, at the time of her marriage, she had moved to Clonliffe Road. Her husband was originally from New York. The couple had four surviving children. One of them, Vincent, was buried on 30 April 1928 in the St Bridget's section of Glasnevin (KH 174.5). His recorded cause of death is listed as a result of 'convulsions'.

As her career progressed, May found herself at the centre of another series of disturbances with the first production of Seán O'Casey's *The Plough and the Stars* (February 1926). She played the part of 'Mrs Gogan'. This was after another actress, Eileen Crowe, had refused to deliver some of her lines on political grounds.[10] Although the riots did not match those that had marred the opening performance of Synge's *Playboy*, the crowd did not take kindly to the political undertones in O'Casey's play. May recollected later in life:

> I found it very exciting [speaking about the *Playboy* riots of 1907], but I hardly knew at the time what it was about. Nor did I think then that in years to come I would be in the middle of another theatre riot, in O'Casey's *The Plough and the Stars* ... Looking back on it now, the *Playboy* row was much bigger and certainly much more noisy than the row over *The Plough*. There was the difference, too, that the first was on moral grounds and the second on political ones.[11]

She travelled to North America in 1931 with the Abbey Company.[12] That was the first of six North American Tours that she embarked on. In 1927 she made her maiden appearance in broadcasting with her voice on 2RN. The unexpected death of her husband aged just 41 on the 28 June 1933, however, cast a shadow over this period of her life. He was buried with his young son in Glasnevin (KH 174.5). Despite these tragedies, her acting life continued. In a play written by W.B. Yeats, *The Words Upon the Window Pane* (1930), she played the part of the medium Mrs Henderson summoning the spirit of Jonathan Swift in a one-act play. Yeats was full of praise for her: 'After the curtain he bowed and kissed her hand: of her performances he said: "When May Craig leaves her dressing room she locks the door and leaves May Craig inside and becomes Mrs Henderson."'[13]

Her favourite parts to play were 'Mrs Grigson' from O'Casey's *The Shadow of a Gunman* and 'Mrs Tancred' in *Juno and the Paycock*. Some other highlights in her career included her depiction of 'Nona' in Yeats' *The Player Queen* (1919), as 'Mrs Anderson' in Shaw's *The Devil's Disciple* (1920), the title role in Brinsley McNamara's *Margaret Gillan* (1933) and as 'Miss Prosperine Garnett' in *Candida* by Shaw (1935).

Her career took many forms and included appearances on stage, radio and in films. From 1952 onwards she starred on screen in films like the famed *Quiet Man* (1952), *The Rising of the Moon* (1957), *Johnny Nobody* (1960) and *A Pair of Green Eyes* (1964). RTÉ asked May to portray one of her favourite roles on television in the 1966 depiction of O'Casey's *Juno and the Paycock*.[14] The 1960s also saw her travel to London to perform alongside fellow Abbey veterans in another production of *Juno* at the Aldwych Theatre. This was part of the World Theatre Season of 1964. *The Irish Press* in 1963 reported on her forty-seven years at the Abbey:

> the longest serving member of the Abbey Theatre Co. … was last night presented with an illuminated address, a cheque and life membership by the Irish Actors Equity Association in the Metropole … This is the first time that Equity has conferred such an honour on one of its members, and last night its president Mr Edward Golden, paid tribute to Miss Craig's outstanding career …[15]

Her final performance at the Abbey was in 1968 when she played the part of 'Miss Eliza Draper' in *The Last Eleven* by Jack White. The final few months of her life were spent in a nursing home in Dalkey, County Dublin. She died aged 83 on 8 February 1972. News of her death was widely reported in the media, both in Ireland and abroad. Both *The Irish Press* and *The New York Times* printed lengthy obituaries on her achievements.[16] Her funeral took place two days after her death. She was laid to rest in the Garden section (MG 186.5) and is buried with her older sister, Margaret. About a five-minute walk away lies her husband, Vincent, her father, David, and her young child who died in infancy in 1928. De Valera was represented at the funeral and 'many people' from the theatrical profession were there.[17] *The Irish Times* stated: 'Grand Old Lady of Abbey dies …'[18]

Publicity photograph of May Craig for an Abbey Theatre American tour (1931–32). (Courtesy of Abbey Theatre Archive)

Her career had begun when the Abbey was still in its infancy. John Slemon, the then manager of the Abbey, reflected:

> What impressed me most about May Craig was not so much that she was a link with the founders but that despite the many tragic events in her personal life, she retained a youthful charm and dignity which

> made us all look on her with affection, as a grand old lady of the theatre: she was indeed ageless in this respect.[19]

May Craig was a true professional, who helped bring to life the words of some of Ireland's greatest playwrights of the twentieth century. Her portrait hangs today on the wall of the stairs in the Abbey.

'Peg O' My Heart'

Another forgotten name of the stage is Margaret Tisdall, better known as Peggy Dell. The popular singer, pianist and entertainer was born on 8 January 1906 at the Rotunda Hospital, Dublin to her mother, Margaret Gibbons, and father, William Tisdall. The census of 1911 tells us that she was raised in one of the artisans' dwellings at 44 Manor Place along the North Circular Road. An only child, she became known as Peggy. Both of her parents were also only children, creating a small familial circle.[20] Her career spanned the same time frame as that of May Craig, but the two appeared on very different stages.

Her father had helped to give Peggy her stage debut at the young age of 9 on the Empire stage.[21] By the age of just 13, Peggy had developed a talent for playing the piano. Despite her father's objections, she played in Woolworth's department store on Dublin's Grafton Street to help promote the sale of sheet music.[22] In time she came to perform on the stages of many of the capital's most famed auditoriums: The Capitol (formerly La Scala Theatre), the Theatre Royal and the Queen's Theatre. She appeared alongside names like Noel Purcell, Jimmy O'Dea and Jack Cruise and helped to form the backbone of a highly popular Dublin vaudevillian generation. Sadly, her father, who was a talented pit musician at the Empire Theatre (today the Olympia), died at the age of 51 on 30 October 1926. He was buried at Glasnevin in the St Patrick's section (SL 280.5).

Before her father died, Peggy managed to set up her own band with four male musicians.[23] Her performances became noted for their enthusiasm and high energy. With her newly formed band, she played in Dublin's smaller venues, such as Fuller's restaurant on Grafton Street.[24] These early experiences led to stints at the Capitol Theatre from 1930 to 1932.[25] It was through appearances at the Capitol that a Paramount booking agent called Charlie Munster from London spotted her and asked her to travel to London.

By the early 1930s she had joined Roy Fox's band in London and became his first female singer. For visual appeal on posters the stage name 'Peggy Dell' was adopted.[26] Peggy later said that: 'In London I played at all the Paramount Astorias ... Then Roy Fox heard me, asked me to audition and I joined his band ... We played in the Kit Rat, a very fashionable nightclub in the Café Anglais and the Café de Paris between 1932 and 1935.'[27] In July 1935, the *Irish Independent* noted the appearance of both Peggy Dell and Roy Fox in Dublin at Clery's Department Store. They were there to promote sales for gramophones.[28] Recordings of Peggy's singing voice can be heard to this day online; a powerful low jazzy voice singing a popular tune of the time: 'Some of these Days'. She later went on to tour the USA with the famed Jack Hylton Orchestra. In an interview with Gus Smith of the *Sunday Independent* in 1975, Peggy said:

> Jack Hylton was a marvellous man and a great professional. He presented fabulous stage shows ... I mean if we were doing a number like 'Horsey, Horsey' we had two real horses back stage running on rollers ... And how can I ever forget those European tours in the early thirties with the Hylton band. We had glittering audiences in Vienna and Budapest ...[29]

Peggy returned to Dublin on the eve of the Second World War. She had actually turned down the BBC, which had offered her a place in Tommy Handley's new *It's That Man Again* (ITMA) radio show that ran from 1939 to 1949. The series, in time, became part of the history of British entertainment.[30] During the 'Emergency' in Ireland, she spent most of her performing time at the Theatre Royal supporting her contemporaries Purcell and Cruise. She also spent some months in the North of Ireland with what was called the Entertainments National Service Association (ENSA), an organisation for the entertainment of the troops, and performed at many army camps based there to boost their morale.[31] Another of her talents that emerged during these war years was her knack for pantomime and vaudeville. She was to spend nearly thirteen months in the Queen's Theatre on Pearse Street acting as principal boy in pantomimes. Work was scarce at this time, and she happily took any job that could be found.

The post-war climate for entertainers was tougher. Peggy's style of performance became less fashionable as the times moved on. On 4 January 1954 her mother Margaret died, aged 74, while still living at Manor Place.

Irish pianist Peggy Dell, pictured in October 1966. (Courtesy of RTÉ Stills Library)

She was buried in Glasnevin with her husband in the St Patrick's section (SL 280.5). Peggy's family had been small to begin with and as a single woman, unmarried and now without any parents left, it must have been an isolating time.

The 1960s saw the demise of many music and entertainment halls in Ireland. The Theatre Royal was demolished in 1962, the Queen's Theatre followed in the late 1960s, with the Capitol demolished in 1974. The establishment of RTÉ and the advent of television replaced these venues. Economic development and progress saw office blocks replace the once glittering bills and facades of many music halls and theatres. Peggy Dell performed for the final week of shows on the stage of the Theatre Royal in 1962 before it was demolished. The final show finished at 10.40 p.m. on Saturday 30 June and it was reported by the *Evening Herald* that it 'was far from being the greatest … but it was throat catching and heart-tugging as a host of familiar performers trooped onto the stage briefly did their spot and then bid farewell to Jimmy Campbell and his orchestra, and the vast audience'.[32] Peggy sang 'A Little Sprig of Shamrock', a song that she had first performed on the Theatre Royal stage twenty-six years earlier with Roy Fox and his band in London.[33] The final two songs, 'No Business Like Show Business' and 'Auld Lang Syne' played out and the curtain came down one last time. It signalled the end for many in an industry that was in serious decline.

For Peggy, her musical career continued with her piano at Cavendishes' shop up until 1967 and she was also a member of Eamonn Andrews' performing group called the Dolphin Troupe at the Dolphin Hotel. By 1970 things had become so bad that when the Dolphin Hotel also closed its doors, she was effectively unemployed.[34] In 1970 she suffered serious head injuries in a taxi accident after leaving the Dolphin Hotel: 'About quarter to one, the taxi turned up Cathal Brugha street, and a car coming down O'Connell Street ran into us … I was thrown out and woke up in Jervis St hospital having my head stitched and a priest standing by to anoint me …'[35]

The accident was to have long-lasting impacts. Later, she would suffer from blackouts, recurrent fainting spells and weakness. This temporarily ended her career. As her name faded from memory, some people believed she had died.[36] However, 1971 saw her win Show Business Personality of the Year from the Variety Club of Ireland at the Gresham Hotel. She was reported in the *Evening Herald* as having received a cut-glass vase in recognition of her 'outstanding show business personality'.[37] This award was in fact her first public appearance following her accident.

She would have faded from public memory completely except for an invitation from Gay Byrne on 22 December 1973 to appear on RTÉ's flagship *Late Late Show* to celebrate the career of Noel Purcell. The public reaction was so good that it led to many return appearances. RTÉ even gave her a television series called *Peg O' My Heart*. The show resulted in an album, *Among My Souvenirs*. Despite continual medical challenges because of the accident, Peggy's comeback television series saw her win a Jacob's award in 1974 and she continued to entertain on Mediterranean cruises up until 1975.[38] The famous Derry singer, Josef Locke, even featured on her television show. His ashes today lie in the cremation section of Glasnevin, beside Parnell's graveside, and are a ten-minute walk away from Peggy's.

Peggy Dell died on 30 April 1979. Following a stroke that affected the use of her left arm, she had spent much of 1978 in St Mary's Hospital in the Phoenix Park.[39] Her funeral service took place at Aughrim Street church and was attended by many of her old friends and colleagues, including Maureen Potter, Griff Cashman, Paddy Crosbie, Noel Purcell, Jack Cruise and Cecil Sheridan. Her death was widely reported in the newspapers. The *Irish Independent* reported on 'The death of Dublin's Queen of the music hall'.[40] *The Irish Times* recalled her career and songs at the piano as 'the very stuff of individual artistry'.[41] In the *Evening Press* Peggy's friend Cecil Nash reflected on her life: 'Working with Peggy Dell was working with an international artist who would charm the highest and the lowest from Dublin, to London. You instantly knew you were in the presence of a brilliant star …'[42]

A photograph taken at her funeral in the *Evening Press* and *Herald* featured Sheridan, Harry Bailey, Dermot Doolan, Purcell and Cruise. Four days after her burial, Cruise also died and followed her to Glasnevin. He was laid to rest close to the O'Connell Round Tower in the South New Chapel section (SE 31.5). He had been unwell and suffering from pneumonia for months before Peggy's funeral but seems in rather jovial spirits in the image below.[43] The *Evening Herald* reporter John Finnegan said, 'His sudden death came as a shock to the theatrical profession. Only on Wednesday I was talking to him at the funeral of another great entertainer Peggy Dell.'[44]

Since her burial in Glasnevin, Peggy's story has faded from public consciousness and, except for a local historical society's Facebook post looking to raise money for a small headstone on her grave, it would never have come to my attention. Her grave remained unmarked until 2021. A GoFundMe page was set up by musician Rob Twamley and today a black marble headstone proudly marks her grave. It features the inscription: 'The

Cecil Sheridan, Jack Cruise (second from left who died just four days later), Harry Bailey, Dermot Doolan (Gen Sec Irish Actors Equity) and Noel Purcell pictured at Peggy Dell's funeral service. (*Evening Press*, 2.05.1979, used with kind permission of Irish Newspaper Archives)

song is ended but the melody lives on … Peg O' My Heart' with a section of her famed song of that same name inscribed on a musical stave. Peggy herself had no family and often joked throughout her career that she 'had not got the time'.[45] This is likely why her grave fell into such a state of neglect. To end her story in her own words, in an interview when asked about her beloved city and its changing nature she said, 'I love Dublin. I regret the changes and the pulling down of the buildings, but I am a Dubliner out and out. I am so much a Dubliner that though I don't follow Gaelic football I am still enough a Dubliner to be upset when Dublin loses …'[46]

Maggie from Mayo

On 17 April 1958 a performance of Puccini's *Manon Lescaut*, at which then Taoiseach Éamon de Valera was present, was interrupted and the Italian Ambassador to Ireland, Signore Mazio, took to the stage of the Gaiety Theatre to announce to the audience the death of an Irishwoman from Castlebar in County Mayo. He said:

> She was a great friend of my country … Italy admired and loved her. She was more than a prima donna. She was literally the first great Lady of the Opera house of Rome, Milan and Naples. Toscanini and Puccini will ever be linked with her name. My countrymen cherish the memory of the years she spent with us. She made us the gift not only of her golden voice but of her generous, warm Irish heart. It is fitting that tonight's performance should be of a Puccini opera, Margherita Sheridan was his greatest interpreter.[47]

Margaret Burke Sheridan was born on 15 October 1889 at The Mall, Castlebar, County Mayo to John Burke Sheridan (the local postmaster) and Mary Ellen Cooley. She was the fifth surviving child of ten with three brothers and a sister (her parents had lost three infant children, a 3-year-old son, Richard, and a 2-year-old daughter, Ellen).[48] Much of what I have come to learn about Margaret and her career in becoming one of Ireland's most enduring legends of the operatic scene comes from the biography written by Anne Chambers: *La Sheridan, Adorable Diva: Margaret Burke Sheridan, Irish Prima-donna, 1889–1958*.

The Sheridan family came from moderate wealth and could boast that they were related to the famed novelist Joseph Le Fanu Sheridan. Margaret's father, John, as postmaster of Castlebar, was well connected. He was noted for having a particularly good singing voice and encouraged his children to take up music and study it in school. Her mother was the daughter of a building contractor, Tomás Cooley. Her childhood, although comfortable, was traumatic. When she was just 5 years old, her mother died on 21 April 1895, aged just 41, after complications with influenza. Her death certificate records that she died of exhaustion due to a diagnosis of pneumonia. Margaret's father, John, was left behind to act as lone parent to a large family with five children ranging from 5 to 19 years old. He used alcohol as a way of coping, which ultimately proved fatal. In 1901, he was diagnosed with carcinoma of the liver and entered the Mater Private Hospital in Dublin for whatever treatment they could give him. He died on 8 February and was buried in Castlebar.

Her father's years of drinking had led to a fractious familial situation. Her oldest brother, John Charles, effectively disowned the family. Her sister Hester and brother Thomas both emigrated to England. The youngest of the children, Paddy and 'Maggie', were left £630 between them from the sale of the family house in Castlebar. This was to be used for their education and maintenance.[49]

By age 11, Margaret had been orphaned and placed in the care of the Dominican nuns on Dublin's Eccles Street. It was in the convent that she received her first singing lessons from a Mother Clement, who was a music teacher.[50] In 1908 she competed at the Feis Ceol in the mezzo-soprano class and won the gold medal.[51] Music lessons progressed from just the convent to lessons with the respected Dr Vincent O'Brien. Dr O'Brien was famed for discovering the talent of the young John McCormack and for having trained James Joyce briefly.[52] The young, untried mezzo-soprano took to the stage at the Rotunda rooms in North Dublin in 1908. Arranged by Dr O'Brien, this was a chance to showcase her talent. In attendance at the concert was the English Lord Lieutenant of Ireland and heading the performance bill was none other than the famed Count John McCormack. Last on the performance bill was Margaret Burke Sheridan. This was to be the only time that Ireland's two most famous singers and exports of the time were to share the same platform.[53]

Afterwards she was accepted as a student at the Royal Academy of Music in London. Dr O'Brien helped to organise a benefit concert for her at the

Theatre Royal in Dublin on 20 May 1909. It was a great success and managed to raise over £600. This set her up in London with the tutorship of a vocal trainer with a catchy name: William Shakespeare. On 21 December 1910 she sang at another of Dublin's great venues, the Gaiety, as the soprano lead in *The Messiah*, conducted by her teacher Dr O'Brien.[54]

Through her beneficiaries in Dublin, Margaret got a place to stay in the Convent of Les Filles de Marie, in Kensington, London. This accommodation was designed to give private hostel-type quarters to young Catholic women alone in the city of London.[55] As a young woman in London she met many influential figures. These included the likes of Howard de Walden, Lady Millicent Palmer and T.P. O'Connor, the Irish politician. Her studies were financed through the generosity of Lady Palmer, whom she had met in Rush, County Dublin at a local concert.[56] Lady Palmer had properties in Wales, where Margaret holidayed and also attended many dinner parties. At one of these occasions the singer met Lord and Lady de Walden.

Lady de Walden and her husband were both patrons of music. Sheridan's singing so impressed them that they arranged for lessons with Olga Lynn who, according to Anne Chambers, was to have a big impact on Margaret's career.[57] The next few years saw her mainly sing at private parties to those of particular wealth and status. While these types of performances gained her some powerful patrons, her career was not moving in the direction she hoped. That was until she met and the great inventor Guglielmo Marconi at a dinner party, who would play a major role in bringing young Margaret's voice to prominence. He told the singer that her voice was what he had been 'waiting to hear all his life'.[58] It was Marconi who advised the singer to go to Italy to realise her true potential, and it was under his patronage and guidance that she made her way there in 1916, as the First World War raged.

The journey was a dangerous one by boat, with many close encounters with German U-boats, and by land, travelling through war-torn France. Her decision to go to Italy had been a hard one. The choice, as she told a schoolfriend, was 'between love and ambition'.[59] She had been romantically involved for a number of years with the nationalist MP for North County Galway, Richard Hazelton. He was 35, living in Blackrock, County Dublin, and was a regular visitor to Eccles Street when Margaret was on her trips home to Mother Clement. Their relationship could have developed into marriage were it not for Marconi in 1916. With the move to Italy, she left Hazelton behind. This was to be the first of two complicated love stories in her life.[60]

Margaret eventually reached Milan. Outside the Stazione Centrale di Milano, crowds had gathered to see the inventor of the wireless telegraph, Marconi. As the people jockeyed for position to get a glimpse of him, according to a programme on RTÉ in 1958 called *The Silenced Voice*, Margaret recounted how he smiled at her and said, 'It's nice to be famous, Margherita, some day you must be famous too.'[61]

Through Marconi and the Italian composer Tosti she was introduced to Alfredo Martino, who further coached her voice. He was of the opinion that her voice was good, but she didn't know how to use it properly.[62] At the age of 29 she was summoned and asked if she could learn the role of Mimi in Puccini's *La Bohéme* in just four days.[63] She was to replace the contracted singer, who had fallen ill for the production. On 3 February 1918, in the Costanzi Opera House, 'Maggie from Mayo' made her dramatic international debut and became a star. Both the public and critics gave her a wonderful reception and her success led to several additional performances.

In the following year, 1919, she fulfilled her long-standing ambition to sing at Covent Garden, London. Here she appeared in *La Bohème*, *Madama Butterfly* and then in a Covent Garden premiere of Mascagni's *Iris*.[64] It was around this time that she met Eustace Blois. He was a retired army officer and managing director of the London Opera Syndicate. Though Blois was married, they began a passionate friendship that had a deep effect on both her life and career. It developed from a friendship into a love affair, with both exchanging many letters. Her devoutly Catholic upbringing was at odds with the idea of this relationship, however, and the strains of frequent protracted separations because of work and the discretion that they had to exercise at all times eventually proved too much; after a decade, their association came to an end.[65]

Her achievements in London set her up with a twelve-year run at La Scala and at Covent Garden intermittently. She secured a five-year contract for the international seasons in London's Covent Garden and eight seasons at La Scala.[66] In 1920 the Italian Arturo Toscanini was appointed as director of La Scala in Milan and with her blonde hair, blue eyes and, as he described it, 'Boticelli' looks, Margaret matched his vision for physical beauty on stage. After an initial performance given by the Mayo woman at Teatro San Carlo, her performance on 6 April 1922 at La Scala persuaded Toscanini to invite her to return the following year for the world premiere of Respighi's

Belfagor.[67] This was to be the beginning of a tough but productive working relationship between 1922 and 1924.

In 1923 Puccini personally stepped in and coached her for the role of Manon in *Manon Lescaut*. He would later say of her voice that 'she was full of charismatic intensity and childlike appeal.'[68] Puccini witnessed her make the role of Manon her own and she became well respected for her masterful performances in his *Madama Butterfly*. Margaret became one of the supreme exponents of Puccini's work and he was known to regard her as 'the outstanding butterfly of all.'[69] Puccini died a year later, and she took part in many commemorative events to remember his life. She became such a sensation in Italy that she was even chosen to sing at the wedding of the Italian Crown Prince, Umberto, in February 1930.[70]

Her final performance at La Scala came in 1924 with her role as Maddalena in *Andrea Chénier*, for which she received high praise for her challenging duets alongside noted Italian operatic star Gigli.[71] However, tensions between Toscanini and the 'Empress of Ireland', as he called the singer, brought to an end her time in Milan. The tensions were rooted in a number of factors, but of most significance was his outright rejection of the rise of Mussolini in his country and the passive way in which the Mayo prima-donna socialised with many pro-fascist benefactors and patrons. As an Irishwoman in Italy, she kept her opinions to herself, and this was a source of irritation for the dictatorial director of La Scala. In 1950, however, when Toscanini stopped over at Shannon Airport he asked, 'Dóve La Sheridan?' She turned up at the airport to greet him and mend their fractious relationship.[72]

Between 1925 and 1926, Covent Garden was the location of most of Margaret's engagements. She rarely performed in Ireland during her career, but she did sing to a captivated audience at the Theatre Royal on Hawkins Street in November 1922 during the Civil War. She later spoke of the occasion: 'It's always nice to come back to this lovely theatre.'[73] This was to be the only performance during her operatic career in Ireland. In the 1926 season at Covent Garden the conductor Vincenzo Belazza recalled after a performance of *La Bohéme* that the company were summoned to the Royal Box to be congratulated by King George V, Queen Mary and the Princess Royal. Belazza recalled how:

> They were extremely kind and cordial to all of us. Peggie [Margaret], in the simple dress of Mimi, was enchanting. The King who had spoken

> to us in English and heard us reply with obvious Italian accents turning to Peggie said, 'With you there is no language difficulty as you are English.' At these words, she impulsively, but decisively replied, 'Sire, I beg your pardon, I am Irish' and the King smiled, amused. Peggie was Irish truly, profoundly Irish, and she loved her country passionately.[74]

While perhaps not politically vocal during the revolutionary period, this account by Belazza paints a picture of a quietly patriotic singer eager to hold on to her Castlebar roots.

At the height of her career, Margaret was offered the title of Papal Countess by Pope Pius XI, but she refused. Between 1918 and 1930 she captured the hearts of both the Italian and British operatic public. She signed her first recording contract in these years and made a number of recordings of operatic arias and of Irish songs for HMV. Her recording of *Madama Butterfly* was considered *the* recording until the 1950s. It was even transferred to both LP and CD such was its popularity.[75] Constant bouts of throat complaints and her diva reputation in recording studios resulted in no full recordings between 1930 and 1944. She continually rejected offers to go

Margaret Burke Sheridan with soprano Vincenzo Bellezza, London, 1938.

to America and sing with the Metropolitan in New York and Chicago Opera in the early 1940s.[76]

In a later live broadcast of *Madama Butterfly* on 10 June 1930 for the BBC, illness was to strike again. After the first act, in which Margaret's throat caused a cracked note, Maggie Teyte took over the rest of the performance.[77] A combination of throat difficulties, gynaecological problems and ongoing complications with Eustace Blois saw her self-confidence diminish and, although no one knew at the time, her career was at the beginning of the end. A performance of *La Bohéme* at Covent Garden on 24 June 1929 was to be her last in the role that had become most associated with her success.[78]

Her final Italian performance came in Turin in 1930, but her very last major operatic performance took place on the Covent Garden stage that same year alongside the Chilean tenor Zanelli in *Otello*, in the rôle of Desdemona. Officially she did not retire until 1936 but appearances became a rarity.[79] She became increasingly self-conscious and her finances began to decline. A combination of a luxurious lifestyle spent in many fine European hotels coupled with heavy medical bills forced her to make use of what she termed her 'nest egg' in London. Essentially this was a securities account in London and her friends' kindness.

She returned to Ireland in 1937 and made a brief stop in Dublin to see Mother Clement and presented her with a complete set of her *Butterfly* recording inscribed: 'To my very best and most careful teacher in memory of my very young and happy days in the Dominican Convent, Eccles Street, Gratefully and lovingly, Margaret Sheridan.'[80] Much of her time back in Ireland was spent in Connemara and she stayed at the hotel home of Oliver St John Gogarty called Renvyle House.[81] The house had been burned out by the anti-Treaty side of the Civil War in reprisal for him accepting a seat in the Senate of the Irish Free State. Determined to stay in Ireland, he had rebuilt the house and opened it as a hotel in 1930. This was a vivid reminder of the country she had returned to in 1922 compared to the one she now visited in 1937.

Throughout the Second World War she remained in Ireland and was regularly requested at various embassies in Dublin including the German, Italian and British, not to sing but to entertain with stories. In 1946 she was hit with the sad news that her beloved Mother Clement had died.

Margaret stayed at the Gresham and Shelbourne hotels and held a residence on Fitzwilliam Street. She was regularly seen walking around

Dublin's streets and made time to attend the annual Feis Ceoil. A trophy today known as the 'Margaret Burke Sheridan Cup' was later presented in her memory by her friend Prince Ferdinando d'Ardia Caracciolo to the Feis organisers. To this day it is awarded annually to the most promising female vocalist in the competition.

After the Second World War, she returned to London on a number of visits before accepting an invitation from the director of the American National Arts Foundation, Carlton Smith, to travel to New York.[82] While there she befriended Ruth and Emerson Axe. Financial experts and founders of E.W. Axe & Co., they managed around $400 million in mutual funds by 1964 and were big supporters of the arts. They gave her the use of an apartment on Fifth Avenue and a box at the opera.[83] In New York she was also diagnosed with cancer. Months later she entered the Pembroke Nursing home attached to St Vincent's Hospital in Dublin. Ruth Axe arranged for the best suite to look after her good friend in her final months. The suite had previously been occupied by Arthur Griffith in 1922 after his brain haemorrhage, and Margaret revelled in the sense of significance around her. Every time she went to the loo, she said she felt a great sense of history about the place![84]

She died on 16 April 1958 aged 69. Before her death she had made final arrangements for her grave at Glasnevin. In conversation with Cyril Cusack, she exclaimed, 'I'll be tippy toes with Dev's secretary, Kathleen O'Connell.'[85] They had been close friends and today both are buried feet away from each other; Kathleen O'Connell is buried in the South New Chapel section (YD 16).

In Italy news of Margaret's death was received at La Scala as being like a 'veil of sorrow'.[86] *The Nenagh Guardian* reported: 'With the death of Margaret Burke Sheridan there has gone from us a remarkable woman who set a headline for all Irish artistes and it is fitting that we should all remember her in some little way.'[87] The *Irish Independent*, reporting on her funeral, stated, 'The Taoiseach, Mr de Valera, many public representatives and persons prominent in musical and theatrical circles attended the funeral of Miss Margaret Burke Sheridan ...'[88]

She was buried in the South New Chapel section of the cemetery (XD 16). Today her grave is surrounded by many of those who stood in sadness at her graveside, including Seán Francis MacEntee and his wife, Phyllis, Éamon and Sinead de Valera, Dr Pádraig de Brun, and the executor of her will, John

Fagan. Her headstone reads simply, in gold lettering, 'Margherita Sheridan, Prima Donna'. Countless guided tours stop at the graveside of statesman de Valera, but little attention is given to this remarkable Mayo woman. As her one-time colleague Maria Caniglia reflected, 'New Butterflys come and go here [in Italy] but people say we heard La Sheridan.'[89]

A Forgotten Hollywood Actor

A handful of graves away there is another forgotten star. Marked by an impressive white marble statue of the Virgin Mary, it is the final resting place of Kathleen Ryan, buried in the same South New Chapel section (TD 18). She was the star of the 1947 film noir classic *The Odd Man Out* starring James Mason. It was a role that defined Mason's career for many. Opposite him, Ryan played the part of Kathleen Sullivan. She was viewed as a rising star in Hollywood, but Mason and Ryan's careers were to take very different paths.

Kathleen Ryan was born on 8 September 1922 above her family's shop in Camden Street, Dublin. Her parents were Agnes Harding and Séamus Ryan, both from Tipperary. Her family set up the highly successful 'Monument Creamery' chain. Séamus was a long-time friend of Éamon de Valera and founding member of Fianna Fáil before becoming a senator in Seanad Éireann.[90] During the Irish War of Independence, the family regularly aided the IRA. Many of their shops were used as safe houses and meeting places. The family were also friends with the likes of Dan Breen, Seán Treacy, Sean Hogan and Séumus Robinson. They were largely safe from reprisal or action by the authorities at the time due to the protection of Michael Collins, who appreciated the kindness of the Ryans financially.[91]

Kathleen was one of eight children and grew up in a wealthy family environment in Rathgar and Sandyford. Her education is indicative of a family with money. At the age of six she was sent to Bruff boarding school in County Limerick. Later she attended Mount Anville college in Dublin before being sent to Paris to a finishing school. As the Second World War gripped the European continent, Kathleen travelled home to Ireland where she studied at UCD. Regarded as quite beautiful, she became the subject of a portrait by Louis Le Brocquy in 1941, which today is held in the National Museum of Northern Ireland.[92] She later acted opposite leading Hollywood men of the time, such as James Mason, Rock Hudson, Dirk Bogarde and Stewart Granger. Her acting career had started on the Peacock Stage of the

Abbey Theatre in the UCD Players' production of Thomas Dekker's *The Shoemaker's Holiday*.[93]

She fell in love with Dermod Devane while acting with the troupe at the Abbey. He was a medical student from Limerick. Kathleen lost interest in her studies and failed to graduate from UCD, but the couple were considered the most attractive on campus.[94] They married on 18 July 1944 at Foxrock, had three children together and lived in Ballinacurra, County Limerick. At the wedding ceremony it was reported that she was dressed in a 'cloth of gold' and at a lavish reception afterwards attendees included Tánaiste Seán T. O'Kelly and Ministers Eoin Ryan, Frank Aiken, Seán MacEntee and P.J. Ruttledge and their wives.[95]

Her father, Séamus, died on 30 July 1933 unexpectedly. He had only recently been appointed as a Senator in the Seanad when Fianna Fáil came to power. His funeral was a large affair and Fianna Fáil managed the State funeral. Dan Breen acted as coffin bearer, and it was seen as a show of strength from those within Fianna Fáil, who had recently risen to political prominence.[96] He was buried in the same grave where Kathleen lies today, close to the Republican Plot. It is directly opposite many high-ranking Fianna Fáil politicians including Éamon de Valera, James O'Mara, Seán MacEntee and P.J. Ruttledge. Following her father's death, her mother, Agnes, decided to move the family in 1938 to a thirty-room mansion and a 100-acre demesne called Burton Hall at Sandyford.[97] The family business went from strength to strength with twenty-six shops, two bakeries, two tearooms, a pub and over 500 employees, mainly young women.[98] John Ryan, Kathleen's brother, helped to organise the first Bloomsday event in 1954 with novelist Flann O'Brien. He also purchased The Bailey pub in Dublin in 1957, which became a literary haunt in the city.

In 1946 Kathleen was chosen on Dan O'Herlihy's recommendation (whom she had acted with on the Abbey stages) as the female lead in the film *Odd Man Out,* directed by Carol Reed. This was her first film appearance. James Mason, in his autobiography, later reflected: 'There was a girl who played Kathleen in whose performance the same quality of truth, simply expressed, could be seen. Kathleen Ryan was this actress.'[99]

For Kathleen it signalled the beginning of a career that can be summarised as 'what if'. From 1947 to 1957 she appeared in a further eleven British and American films. These included *Captain Boycott* (1947), *Captain Lightfoot* (1955) and *Jacqueline* (1956), all based on Irish themes.[100] She signed with a Hollywood studio and was contracted to make seven films in 1952, but ultimately only produced two. A combination of bad directing and superfluous details made them unsuccessful.[101] Her final movie was *Sail into Danger* in 1957 with Dennis O'Keeffe.

Kathleen Ryan Devane, *The Los Angeles Times*, 21 May 1950.

Bad directing and sub-standard films were not the only cause of tragedy for Kathleen. In 1954 she was the driver involved in an alleged hit-and-run incident near Ballinacurra. A travelling salesman, Peter Kelliher, lost his leg and a compensation claim in the civil courts followed.[102] These legal proceedings involved a charge of dangerous driving at Limerick City Court. The proceedings were adjourned to allow her to shoot her role in *Captain Lightfoot*. When the case resumed on 4 September 1954, she sat and listened to the verdict. Press reporters and public interest were high due to the nature of her status in Hollywood. The case came to an end the following year in 1955 when Mr Kelliher was awarded damages of £7,000.

Ten years later Kathleen found herself dealing with another large compensation claim through the civil courts for a separate car accident. Her film career was, by that time, finished.[103] Her marriage also deteriorated in the 1950s, and at the time of the second car accident she was back living with her family in Dublin. The marriage was annulled in 1958.[104] Constant battles with ill health plagued the final years of her life and she never acted again. Liam Collins, in an *Irish Independent* article said: 'The once celebrated beauty seems to have been haunted by "what might have been" – what one of her sisters called the "tragedy" of her promising Hollywood career, a "hit-and-run" accident in which a man lost his leg and the break-up of her marriage to a leading Limerick doctor.'[105]

The family business went into liquidation in 1961 and ten years later her mother died on 5 May 1971. She was buried in the same grave as her husband. Kathleen later moved to Killiney with Niall Desmond Lawlor. He was an Old Belvedere boy, a teacher, army man and a journalist with the

Irish Independent.[106] They were familiar faces in many Dublin pubs around the Grafton Street area, particularly The Bailey pub, owned by John Ryan. She followed her mother and father into the same grave fourteen years later, on 11 December 1985. Her death certificate records that she died as a result of lung cancer. Luck had not been on her side. Liam O'Leary in *The Irish Times* wrote: 'another Irish film personality has passed away, and with it a charming and gentle person ... As long as Carol Reed's masterpiece "Odd Man Out" continues to be revived again and again and is preserved in many film archives throughout the world, her beauty will live forever.'[107]

Unlike her father's State funeral, there was no such occasion for Kathleen's burial. Her name is inscribed on the side of the rectangular headstone with a white statue of the Virgin Mary on top. It was built as a remembrance to the Ryan family as merchants, politicians and nationalists. She lives on today not as Kathleen Ryan, but as Kathleen Sullivan from the gritty thriller *Odd Man Out.*

The Oscars and the Emmys

Sticking with the theme of cinema and Hollywood, and a short distance away from Kathleen Ryan's grave, opposite Michael Collins' grave, is the final resting place of a famous art director and set designer.

In the opening scene of Michael Anderson's 1959 film *Shake Hands with the Devil*, filmed at Glasnevin, the opening titles feature the name Josie McAvin – the first of many film credits. Her film and television career stretched across six decades and included many cinema greats. She received Oscar nominations twice in the 1960s for her work on the films *Tom Jones* and *The Spy Who Came in from the Cold.* In 1986 she received an Academy Award for Best Art Direction–Set Decoration, for Sydney Pollack's epic romance *Out of Africa*, while in 1995 she won an Emmy Award for *Scarlett*, a mini-series sequel to *Gone with the Wind.* Many of the films Josie worked on have strong Irish links, including *Ryan's Daughter* (1970), *Michael Collins* (1996), Jim Sheridan's *The Field* (1990) and *The Butcher Boy* (1997). Josie believed her work with John Huston on *The Dead* and Neil Jordan on *Michael Collins* ranked as her two favourite productions from the many on which she worked.[108]

Josephine McAvin was born on 23 April 1919 on Mount Street in Dublin. She was one of six children born to John McAvin, a cattle exporter and last

High Sheriff of Dublin, and his wife, Mary Josephine Callaghan. Originally, Josie trained as a teacher and was a member of the teaching staff at Marino College.[109] Ultimately a life in education was not for her, and through her cousins, Maureen and Ronald Ibbs, with their touring theatrical company, her career in the arts was ignited. She became stage manager at the Gate Theatre in the 1950s and her work took her to some adventurous and challenging locations. In 1969, for example, she found herself working in the Alps with director Michael Winner, actor Oliver Reed and an actual elephant in *Hannibal Brooks.*[110]

Her father sadly did not live to see any of his daughter's successes. John Patrick died on 20 December 1938 aged 57. He was buried in Glasnevin, a short distance from Michael Collins in the South New Chapel section (HD 75). Later in life Josie reflected on the loss of her father, saying: 'He died when I was quite young ... And I think he might have been horrified to learn that I went to work in the film industry.'[111] Her mother on the other hand lived until 1992 and witnessed many of her achievements, dying aged 101 on 20 March 1992; she is buried with her husband in the family plot.

To this day Josie is the only Irish woman with the distinction of winning both an Oscar and an Emmy award.[112] Throughout her career she continued to work on stage as well as screen. As late as 1994 she was still working on the stage for Shivaun O'Casey's production of *The Plough and the Stars*. Josie was a key player in promoting Irish films and acted as a mentor for many young set designers later in life. The last film she worked on was *Evelyn* (2002), directed by Bruce Beresford and starring Pierce Brosnan. She never married and had no children. She died peacefully in Blackrock Hospice on 26 January 2005 aged 85. The funeral mass was held at 10 a.m. in St Patrick's Church, Monkstown, County Dublin, followed by her removal to Glasnevin. She is buried in the grave beside her parents (HD 74) with her sister Sunny Mulligan, whom she had often worked with throughout her career as a props buyer. The grave features a notable Celtic cross and its location is likely due to her father's close relationship with W.T. Cosgrave and his role in the War of Independence.

Both Josephine McAvin's and Kathleen Ryan's graves are marked by impressive monuments. Their contributions to stage and screen, however, are not recorded. Their headstones were erected to remember their families' status rather than their own.

Pioneers and Innovators

Some overlooked pioneers and innovators buried in the cemetery include Giuseppe Cervi from Picinisco, who set up the first fish and chip shop in Dublin on Great Brunswick (now Pearse) Street.[1] When people entered they would point to what they wanted and Giuseppe would put his finger up to make sure it was one portion. Usually, customers would point to one fish and one portion of chips. Dublin lore has it that it is due to the broken English of Giuseppe and his wife that 'the wan and wan' was born.[2] Giuseppe, like many Italian migrants, altered his name over time to a more anglicised version – in his case 'Joseph'. The father of the Irish chipper died on 3 January 1927 and was buried in the St Patrick's section (TK 262.5).

Another pioneer was the 'Father of Irish Railways' William Dargan, who is buried beside the Republican Plot alongside well-known names such as James Stephens, John O'Leary, Harry Boland and Countess Constance Markievicz, beneath a large stone sarcophagus (TD 40). Fergus Mulligan, who has held a lifelong fascination with the life of Dargan, published *William Dargan: An Honourable Life 1799–1867* in 2014. He believes 'Dargan is arguably the greatest Irishman of the 19th century. His name is often recognised yet his life achievements are still only vaguely acknowledged …'[3] During his life,

Glasnevin Cemetery *c.* 1865–1914. (Reproduced courtesy of the National Library of Ireland)

Dargan built roads, railways, canals and reservoirs. He developed hotels and resort coastal towns, such as Bray in County Wicklow and Portrush in County Antrim, and he laid out Belfast port. He was the sole funder of the great 1853 Art-Industry Exhibition on Dublin's Merrion Square to aid an island struggling to recover from the legacy of the Famine. This would lead to the foundation of what is today the National Gallery of Ireland. Dargan has his own wing in the Gallery today and his statue stands outside the main entrance on Merrion Square.[4] It is the only statue in Dublin to have been erected for a person while they were still alive and signifies the status he held during his lifetime.

Before the existence of any railways in London, Dargan had built the first public passenger railway in Ireland in 1834 – the Dublin to Kingstown line – and by the time of his death he had helped to build around 830 miles (1,335 km) of railway line in Ireland.[5] He also built the Howth to Dublin road, the Kilbeggan Branch of the Grand Canal, and the Ulster Canal, which connected Lough Neagh to Lough Erne. Dargan invested in many hotels, including the Royal Marine in Dún Laoghaire, and ran a threadmill in Chapelizod, which at its height employed some 900 people.[6] With such a successful career, he was offered a seat as MP for Newry in Westminster on multiple occasions but refused. Queen Victoria even visited Dargan at Mount Anville, the family home, in 1853 for afternoon tea, but he later refused a baronetcy from her. In the later years of his life, he lived at No. 2 Fitzwilliam Square and a plaque commemorating him can be seen on the house today.

The day of Dargan's funeral, 11 February 1868, was described as a cloudy but fine day with some breeze.[7] Four black horses pulled the hearse from Fitzwilliam Square, with two for each of the three mourning coaches.[8] *The Irish Times* described it as 'the largest public funeral which has taken place in the city for many years'.[9] Estimates in attendance, according to *Saunder's News-Letter* and *The Irish Times*, ranged from 150–250 carriages.[10]

Close to the grave of Dargan, an impressive Celtic cross at the front of the O'Connell Tower marks the resting place of another forgotten pioneer.

The Grand Nephew of Robert Emmet and Gynaecological Advancement

Robert Emmet was executed outside St Catherine's Church on Thomas Street on 20 September 1803. After his abortive rebellion ended in failure, he was led to a specially erected gallows outside the church before being hanged and beheaded. Where his remains are today is still one of the biggest mysteries in Irish history and many theories exist. One man who became obsessed with tracing this grave was his own grand-nephew, Thomas Addis Emmet. He was the grandson of the exiled Thomas Addis Emmet, Robert Emmet's brother. Thomas Addis Emmet Senior was highly respected in the world of medicine, law, politics and in railroad promotions. He arrived in New York City in 1804 in an effort to try and escape the aftermath of his brother's failed rebellion. He did not travel alone. With him was his wife and three of his children. One of those children was John Patten Emmet, a 10-year-old boy at the time. John Patten Emmet would go on to become the father of Thomas Addis Emmet Junior, who spent a good deal of his adult life searching for the remains of his relative.

Thomas Addis Emmet Junior was born on 28 May 1828 in Charlottesville, Virginia. His father attended West Point for cadet training but his time there was brief due to tuberculosis.[11] By 1828 he was Professor of Chemistry and Materia Medica at the University of Virginia. This was a new university at the time and he was appointed to the position by Thomas Jefferson.[12] As a result he spent time winning a degree as a physician at Columbia University College of Physicians. Thomas Addis's childhood was thus spent on his father's 100-acre farm and house called 'Morea' near the university. His father had built this house to his own designs and planted a wide array of botanical specimens in the grounds.[13] His mother, Mary Byrd Farely Tucker, was interestingly of English descent but had been raised in Bermuda.

Thomas Addis spent some time at an elementary school in Charlottesville but with no suitable schools in Northern Virginia, he later attended St Thomas's Hall at Long Island to study.[14] He did not settle well at this school in Flushing, Long Island. It was during that same time his father died of tuberculosis on 13 August 1842 at the country home of one of his brothers near New York; he was buried in the New York City Marble Cemetery.[15] Today both a major thoroughfare next to the University of Virginia and a twentieth-century residence hall use his name.[16]

His father's death left the family without any financial security and a return to school was put on hold. Instead, Thomas spent several hours a day in the library of his uncle, Mr George Tucker, who was the Professor of Political Economy and Belles-Lettres at the University in Virginia. He later reflected: 'I keenly felt the death of my father and his loss seemed irreparable, as I could see no future for myself, and my life became an aimless drift until I would be old enough to enter the University as a student.'[17] His teenage years were filled with jobs he hated. He rejected an appointment at West Point to follow in the footsteps of his father. Then, a letter to Dr Dunglison, who had assisted in his own birth, sparked his interest in the medical profession. In the letter he explained his difficulties and asked what his opinion was on going to study medicine. The doctor replied with advice. It was simple and inspired: to attend as many medical lectures as possible and to remember what he could but not to sit down and study at all.[18]

After graduating from the Jefferson Medical College, Thomas Addis was offered an impressive job as doctor on an expedition being outfitted to build a railroad in Chile with a salary of $3,000 per year in gold with all living expenses catered for.[19] He declined. Instead, he opted to become the New York resident physician to the Emigrant Refugee Hospital on Ward's Island. The hospital had been established to aid Irish refugees from the Great Famine. The work at the Emigrant Refugee Hospital proved to be exhausting, but he threw himself into the job to such an extent that ten days after starting he contracted typhus, which almost killed him. He recovered only to get the disease again thirteen months later.[20] He had as many as 3–4,000 patients under his care at any one time and remained in this job for over three years.

He cared for patients with a wide range of needs and conditions including fevers, over 1,900 cases of typhus, a considerable number of operations, approximately five obstetric deliveries per day and 1,000 post-mortem examinations.[21] It was a place where he experienced a lot and it prepared him well for the future. His record was so impeccable that he was appointed visiting physician to the hospital due to his untiring work.

In 1855 he had an unexpected encounter with the physician Dr J. Marion Sims, which would alter his career forever. Thomas Addis recorded this chance meeting:

> In the early spring of 1855, I was engaged late one night with my case-book in tabulating all the features of each typhus-fever case I had treated at Ward's Island, so as to obtain as it were the natural history of the disease. It had been snowing all day and the quiet was conducive to continued work, when I was startled by a loud rap on my window. On opening the door I admitted Dr Marion Sims, whom I had met before, but I did not recognize him until he introduced himself. He

> stated that his [street]car had gotten off the track almost opposite my house and seeing my light burning he had come in to warm himself, as he had become chilled from standing so long outside. After he had revived, seeing my table covered with papers, he asked what work I was at. On explaining the system and what I expected to accomplish, he suddenly said; 'Well, doctor, you are just the man I am looking for, and if you will come up to the hospital tomorrow morning at nine o'clock I will show you something you have never seen before. I have been all the evening engaged with the board of governors in organizing a new hospital ...'[22]

Dr J. Marion Sims had invited the young physician to attend The Woman's Hospital Association building at 93 Madison Avenue to observe one of his own operations for a serious birth injury. It was something new to Thomas. The Woman's Hospital was founded primarily to give Dr Sims a space to perform the operation which he had managed to perfect for vesicovaginal fistulas. For women, this condition could become a very upsetting after-effect of childbirth in the nineteenth century. It is still a problem today in parts of the world where access to medical care is not readily available. Only a handful of gynaecological surgeons in industrialised countries have even seen an obstetric fistula. This was not the case for Dr Sims. It was a condition with which Thomas Addis was to become very familiar.[23]

In the 1850s a vesicovaginal fistula usually followed a hysterectomy. The results of such a procedure usually caused infections to develop, with incomplete healing of the tissue and the development of a small vesicovaginal fistula, usually at the vaginal cuff. Another form of fistula both doctors dealt with was the obstetric fistula resulting from prolonged or obstructed childbirth. This could result in death for the mother and/or child. In cases where the mother survived, she would often be left with a massive vascular injury to the soft tissues of her pelvis that caused widespread damage, as well as possible asphyxiation of her young child. The amount of injured tissue that developed after these cases often saw a complete destruction of the urethra, the loss of the entire base of the woman's bladder and the destruction of her cervix.

The hospital quickly became full to capacity and Dr Sims found himself operating on at least one of these conditions per day. He was in need of an assistant.[24] The Board of Governors agreed. They instructed him to find a female physician but Dr Sims refused and instead persuaded Thomas Addis Emmet to step in for a period of six months. He was to spend five and a half years assisting Sims. In time he came to master his technique for the closure of fistulas and began to apply what he had learned by performing many of the operations himself. In fact, he was doing up to two-thirds of all the operations at the hospital by 1859. Additionally, he took an active role in taking care of all of the hospital's routine affairs, recording in shorthand all patients admitted, full clinical histories of the patients and detailed descriptions and drawings of procedures.[25] Thomas Addis Emmet published his book, *Vesico-Vaginal Fistula*, in 1868.[26] It was a collection of descriptions of the consequences of these types of complications. In reviewing 161 cases, Emmet found that the average length of time women were spending in labour was a staggering 58.6 hours.[27]

Both Thomas Addis and Sims worked extremely closely together from 1855 to 1861. They came to perfect medical procedures to help women survive, recover and live their lives again after childbirth. Howard Kelly, another pioneering American gynaecological surgeon, left a description of Emmet in the operating room:

> In his fistula operations at the Woman's Hospital he sat by a simple table in a small room with the patient in the semi-prone position … with visitors crowded about him and trying now and then to catch a glimpse of what was going on. The early operations were without an anaesthetic. While operating, he was testy and complaining much of his awkward assistants, as he advanced slowly but with deliberation and painstaking accuracy towards the goal, the closure of a large rent in the vesical septum, first denuding the edges with scissors, his own innovation, and continually sponging away the blood, and then leading the silver wire sutures through with a needle and silk thread carrier, shouldering and adjusting the wires with wonderful skill … In the consciousness of the visitors there was a sense of the dawn of a new era in surgery and the anticipation of the relief coming to an army of sufferers, and his criticisms of the instruments and querulousness made no bad impression, for all felt that they were in the presence of a great leader.[28]

In time Thomas Addis dealt with all types of fistulas and through the mastery of Dr Sims' earlier procedures forged his own forty-year career. Today he is remembered as one of the most outstanding pioneers of modern gynaecology and vaginal reconstructive operations. Many of the techniques used by Thomas Addis seem very simplistic and matter of fact to us today but in the 1850s they were pioneering and life-changing. His operative results were extraordinarily good. Patients would come from all over America to get help and were willing to put up with a great deal of discomfort simply because they knew the operation had a good chance of being a successful one.

Operations were performed with patients in a knee-chest or semi-prone position on a plain wooden table. The Sims speculum was held by an assistant and used to expose the part of the body where surgery was needed.[29] With little to no knowledge of the bacterial origin of infections, surgeons depended solely on cleanliness and detailed cleaning of wounds to prevent post-operative infections. Clean linen was used to drape over the patient afterwards. Operating time had to be brief to keep within the physical endurance of a patient. There was no handbook, and instruments had to be made from scratch and used with the assistance of poorly trained domestic servants.[30]

By 1861, the year the American Civil War broke out, Thomas Addis Emmet had been married for seven years to Catherine R. Duncan. They married on Valentine's Day and had seven children. The war proved to be a massive challenge for the Women's Hospital and practice. Emmet left the hospital briefly and set out for Montgomery, Alabama to offer his services to Jefferson Davis as an army surgeon. He was sympathetic to the Confederate side, as was Dr Sims. His offer was rejected and so he returned to his practice in New York. The Civil War saw Dr Sims leave the hospital for good. As a supporter of the Confederate side of the conflict, he fell out of favour with the medical profession as a whole. He left for Europe in 1861 but beforehand asked T. Gaillard Thomas to run the outpatient clinic for him in the hospital and to help Thomas Addis.

In 1862 Thomas Addis was appointed chief surgeon, when he was just 33 years old.[31] According to Albert H. Aldridge MD in his 1961 address to the annual meeting of the American Gynecological Society, 'When Emmet assumed his duties as Chief Surgeon (1862) he was well on the way to becoming a master at vaginal plastic surgery.'[32] In time he focused solely on hospital governance. He established two clinics per week where members of the medical profession could learn his techniques. Later he developed a plastic procedure for constructing a new urethra in women after theirs had been damaged through birthing injuries.[33] He also improved on Sims' surgical procedure for dealing with uterine prolapses. Future surgeons would develop on these pioneering techniques. Many obstetricians, however, resented the work by Emmet in their field. They saw him as a meddling gynaecological surgeon.

By 1867 the American Civil War had ended and the hospital was doing so well that a new building was opened at Fiftieth Street and Park Avenue on the same plot of ground which is now occupied by the Waldorf Astoria Hotel.[34] In this new building a forty-bed ward was reserved for the treatment of vaginal fistulas alone. Thomas Addis continued to work as the sole surgeon at the Woman's Hospital until 1872. The hospital expanded again in 1877, with a new building called the Baldwin Pavilion providing for sixty-nine additional patients and three cottages to provide more operating spaces and recovery rooms for postoperative patients. During his time at the Women's Hospital there are records of Emmet delivering some 1,100 babies. One of the babies he delivered was none other than the future President of America, Theodore Roosevelt.[35]

Thomas Addis retired in 1900, at the age of 72, and later committed himself to becoming a writer. He was a renowned collector of American historical documents, newspapers, currency, autographs and memorabilia. His collection comprised over 30,000 portraits of famous American people.[36] It was during this time that he began to search for his lost ancestor, Robert Emmet. He came to Ireland in 1903 to try to find his remains for the 100th anniversary of Robert's execution. He visited St Peter's Church on Aungier Street (since demolished) and St Michan's but was unsuccessful. In 1905, his wife died aged 78 in New York. *The Tribune* newspaper reported: 'Mrs Catherine Emmet, wife of Dr. Thomas Addis Emmet died yesterday at her home, No. 89 Madison Ave. Mrs Emmet was over seventy years old, and had not been ill very long …'[37]

Six years after the death of his wife he sold his house on Madison Avenue to make way for a fifteen-storey office building. He lived at the top of it, and his massive historical collection of books and documents was kept there until his death. By 1911 he lived the life of a recluse. He was suffering from deafness and poor healing of a fracture of one leg. Still mentally agile, he continued to read and write. Amongst his many publications, of particular note is *The Principles and Practice of Gynaecology* (1884).[38] His autobiography, *Incidents of My Life; Professional, Literary, Social, with Services in the Cause of Ireland* (1911) and his *Ireland under English Rule: A Plea for the Plaintiff* (1903; republished in 1909) are also noted works.

Thomas Addis Emmet died on 1 March 1919 aged 91 at his residence on Madison Avenue. *The Daily Progress* reported on his life achievements on 8 March 1919: 'Death of Noted Physician.'[39] His obituary, written by Dr J. Riddle Goffe in *Surgery, Gynecology and Obstetrics*, said:

> Dr Emmet exploited every field of plastic work within the range of the gynaecologist, studied its pathology, devised operative procedures, proved their efficiency, and described them with perfection of detail that made them acceptable to every skilled operator. For all time all operators who do plastic gynaecological surgery will be under permanent obligation [to] Dr Emmet. Undoubtedly, he did more than any one man to put it on a scientific basis. All succeeding operations have been an evolution of his work. He founded a school of pathology, of treatment, and of operative technique that was individually his, and he clung to its underlying principles to the end of his career.[40]

Following his death, he was buried temporarily in the family vault in White Plains until arrangements were made for his reburial at Glasnevin. He had expressed a wish to be buried in the country where his ancestors were from. These wishes were fulfilled on 15 September 1922. Difficulties with the ongoing Irish War of Independence delayed his return to Ireland. *The Freeman's Journal* reported: 'The event forges a remarkable and enduring link with Ireland's storied past …'[41] The *Irish Independent* reported meanwhile on the day that his remains were laid to rest in Glasnevin that: 'A large number of people attended at the reception of the remains at the Pro-Cathedral … He has succeeded in obtaining a suitable place in the O'Connell Circle where the burial will take place today …'[42]

Today as you walk in the main gates of the cemetery one of the first things you see is the Round Tower for Daniel O'Connell. It is surrounded by many beautiful funerary monuments. The tallest of these is Thomas Addis Emmet's (A 7.5 O'Connell Tower Circle). Some tourists like to take a snap of the phrase 'founder of plastic surgery' on his epitaph, not realising the context. The plastic surgery that Emmet pioneered changed the lives of thousands of women around the world. His work in reconstructive surgery for women after childbirth undoubtedly changed the medical landscape in the field of gynaecology forever. Operations that developed after his death are an 'evolution of his work.'[43] His grave is one of the finest in the cemetery, yet his story is rarely told in full.

Fluid of Magnesia

When discussing medical pioneers in Glasnevin, another can be found next to the original entrance gates close to where the zookeepers are buried and where the staged funeral of Maria Higgins took place in 1858. There you can see the final resting place of Sir James Murray – a man who, during his lifetime, made many significant contributions to science and medicine. His interests lay in the field of electrotherapy, infectious diseases and epidemics. His legacy today is one usually attributed to the American John Callen and Englishman Charles Henry Phillips. Both became the first people to patent 'milk of magnesia' in 1873. It became an extremely popular antacid and laxative and is still used today. It is Sir James Murray and his 'fluid of magnesia', however, who deserves much more credit.

Born in County Derry, near Maghera, in 1788, James was the eldest son of Edward Murray and Belinda Powell. Raised as a Catholic, he had at least two siblings we know about. As a 19-year-old man he studied medicine in both Dublin and Edinburgh. He obtained the Royal College Surgeons of Edinburgh Diploma on 21 April 1807, a respected and recognised medical qualification used as an addition or alternative to a university medical degree.[44] In Dublin he was licensed by the Royal College of Surgeons in Ireland in 1808.[45] Around that time he became apothecary to Belfast dispensary from 1807, and in 1808 set up his own practice on High Street, in Belfast.[46] As his medical career took shape he married Margaret Sherlock in 1809. They had at least five children together.

Pharmaceutical products were of great interest to the young physician. He conducted a lot of experiments with the substance then known as magnesia (MgO). He experimented on its use as a purge or laxative for the human body. Around 1812 he developed a way of making magnesia into a fluid form that allowed for easier administration to patients. It had a very similar make-up to what we know today as 'milk of magnesia'. Today it is one of the world's best-selling medicaments and most households keep a bottle of the solution in their medicine cabinet.

He wrote about his discovery in a pamphlet published in 1817 called: *The danger of using solid magnesia and on its great value in a fluid state for internal use. The Freeman's Journal*, in December 1871, stated that the 'most valuable discovery of concentrating magnesia in solution spread his fame far and near amongst men interested in medical chemistry ...'[47] James used this discovery to establish a family business in Belfast on York Street. It produced large quantities of fluid magnesia for medicinal use and it was branded 'fluid magnesia'. Decades later he expanded the business to Dublin with his son Edward. They set up a manufacturing base for it at Temple Street.[48] There are numerous advertisements for 'Murray's Fluid Magnesia' in newspapers from the 1860s onwards.

Lord Anglesey or Henry William Paget, the Irish viceroy who was an old Waterloo hero, went to see Dr Murray in 1831. He was prescribed the new fluid magnesia. It was said that Lord Anglesey received so much relief from the new treatment that Murray remained his medical adviser for years afterwards.[49] In 1835 he was given a similar role under Lord Normanby (Constantine Phipps) and in 1839 became physician to Viscount Ebrington (Hugh Fortescue).[50] Both men were lord lieutenants of Ireland. By 1840 he had established a successful private practice in Dublin, was appointed physician to two Dublin hospitals (the Anglesey and Netterville) and in 1833 was knighted by the lord lieutenant.[51]

In 1834 James was appointed the first Inspector of Anatomy for Ireland under the 1832 Anatomy Act. In this position he saw to it that the practice of desecrating the dead by 'Resurrectionists' and graverobbers was greatly reduced in Ireland. Glasnevin had tall stone walls, watchtowers with armed watchmen, Cuban bloodhounds and portable wooden watchtowers installed to protect those buried from being stolen and sold to medical schools. Some of these structures can still be seen today. People had for generations hated the idea that their bodies would not be safe after death. James fulfilled this role passionately for forty years.

His wife, Margaret, died on 1 September 1841 in Belfast. He was later married again, to a woman called Mary Allen in 1848, and had three more children, with one surviving. Aside from his fluid magnesia factory in Belfast, he was highly engaged in the manufacture of superphosphates. In May 1842 his son Edward applied for Scottish and English patents to protect his father's process of making powdered superphosphate fertilisers for farming. He established a company for this business in Dublin and carried out many experiments on land in Terenure.[52] A fertiliser manufacturing rival called Sir John Bennet Lawes in 1846 managed to buy out the Murrays patent and went on to develop chemical fertilisers as a major industrialist. It was to be Bennet Lawes who was given the credit for the discovery of superphosphates, despite the fact that Sir James Murray had made discoveries about them as early as 1808.

John Fisher Murray, the eldest son of James, died on 21 October 1865 aged 54 while living at 70 Capel Street. He was buried in the South section of Glasnevin (NC 44). He had made a career as a journalist and had been very interested in Irish nationalism. His father was in attendance at the funeral alongside John's widow, Hannah Service, who later erected a monument above his grave.[53] Six years later Sir James died on 8 December 1871 at his residence at 19 Upper Temple Street Dublin, aged 83. His recorded profession in Glasnevin is listed as a 'Knight and Medical Doctor'. He was buried on 11 December 1871 in Curran Square (D 42) close to the original arched entrance gates. His headstone resembles a table with six thick columnesque legs with a flat slab on top. *The Freeman's Journal* reported that he was:

> an earnest and practical worker, he illustrated through his long and honoured career how competent it is for a man to promote his own wealth and enduring interest whilst advancing the public welfare and consulting the general good … In private and public life Sir James Murray was a man of rare excellence, upright in all his dealings, humane and charitable to the poor, an earnest and a practical patriot, kind and considerate, to all differing from him, and, above all, a good Christian, R.I.P.[54]

W.J. Fitzpatrick in his *History of the Dublin Catholic Cemeteries* (1900) reflected on the life of Murray, stating that his discovery of fluid magnesia allowed 'scores of pharmacologists' to go on and make fortunes for themselves.[55] Sadly, Callen and Phillips took the credit with their later patent, which is often referenced as the starting point for the popular laxative. Equally, while Sir John Bennet Lawes took the credit for his industrialisation of superphosphates and their use for fertiliser, it was Sir James' research that paved the way for him. James Murray is one of Ireland's greatest scientific minds but his name, sadly, is another forgotten one in the cemetery. The *Dundalk Democrat* rightly remembered him as: 'a man of no ordinary note'.[56]

The Pioneering Aviator

Many are familiar with stories of the pioneering Wright brothers and Amelia Earhart, but few know of Glasnevin Cemetery's own pioneer of the skies – James Fitzmaurice. His grave is a modest white weathered headstone featuring his parents' names, his own and those of his sisters. It is hidden away in the St Patrick's section (VJ 158.5) and rarely visited. What made him famous all began at 5.40 a.m. on 12 April 1928 on board the *Bremen*, a Junkers W33 single-engine monoplane. It took off from Baldonnel Aerodrome, County Dublin. On board was the crew – two Germans and an Irishman. They were Commandant James Fitzmaurice, OC Irish Army Air Force, Captain Herman Koehl and Baron von Huenefeld. They were attempting something that had never been done before – to cross the Atlantic Ocean on an aircraft travelling from east to west.

In 1919 Alcock and Brown had successfully flown from Newfoundland to Clifden, Galway. Of the seven flights that attempted to repeat the feat in 1927, four succeeded but three failed, with eight lives lost.[57] This three-person crew, however, wanted to accomplish the dangerous journey in the opposite direction. Looking on as the aircraft laboured to take off with the weight of the large quantities of fuel on board was President of the Executive Council of the Irish Free State W.T. Cosgrave and his son, Liam. Other dignitaries and members of the government made up the crowd who had turned out to witness history.

Their plan was to fly a 'dead' course for Newfoundland for approximately thirty hours. If at the end of that time they found that their supplies of petrol were short, they proposed to turn north-west. They had calculated that as the mainland would be in that direction this was the safest plan.[58] In the hours following their take-off, reports filtered in to Baldonnel. They managed to reach the mid-Atlantic by flying low and avoiding any headwinds. Conditions, although good when leaving Baldonnel, worsened as darkness descended over the Atlantic.[59] Their instrument lights began to fail and darkness engulfed the monoplane.

Later in the mission James Fitzmaurice discovered oil leaking from the aircraft. There was no other option but to change course. Just before dawn, they flew over Labrador and landed on frozen ice at a place called Greenly Island in the Gulf of St Lawrence on the evening of 13 April 1928.[60] The men had just completed the first ever east–west transatlantic flight.[61] The distance to Greenly Island from Ireland is approximately 2,000 miles. The journey had taken the men 38.5 hours. After the *Bremen* had landed on frozen ice it was impossible for them to take off again to make it to New York. Rescue attempts were made by a Canadian steamer to cut her way through the ice but in the end the aviators were rescued by air. The famous

American airman Floyd Bennett had been preparing for his own aviation expedition to the South Pole but had become ill with what was believed to be a bad cold. When word reached Bennett that the three pilots were in need of rescue he decided to help. He reached Quebec City where his condition worsened considerably and despite the best efforts of another pilot Charles Lindbergh to try and get a life-saving serum to Bennett; it was too late, he died of pneumonia on 25 April 1928.[62] The rescue effort he had started was a success, however, and the news began to break slowly around the world that Fitzmaurice, Baron von Huenefeld and Captain Herman Koehl had conquered the Atlantic Ocean by air. Bennett was buried at Arlington National Cemetery.[63]

Parades and receptions were held in New York, Washington, Bremen and Berlin. As the aviators' fame grew they decided to visit the exiled German emperor, Wilhelm II, at Doorn in the Netherlands. On 30 June 1928 they all received the freedom of the city of Dublin and while he was still abroad, Fitzmaurice was promoted to major retrospectively and later became colonel in July 1928. The aircraft that had made the journey was rescued and brought to Bremen, where he went to see it in October 1928.[64]

James Christopher Fitzmaurice was born on 6 January 1898 at 35 Mountjoy Prison Cottages, North Circular Road, Dublin. His parents were Michael Fitzmaurice, a prison warder, and Mary Agnes Riordan. Both of them were from County Limerick. The census of 1911 shows us that he had three siblings and that the family lived for a time at a house in Portlaoise. His parents had moved there in 1902 to facilitate his father's work as a prison warder. He attended the local school St Mary's CBS and later boarded at St

James Fitzmaurice in Berlin. (Courtesy of Bundesarchiv, Bild 102-06095 / CC-BY-SA 3.0)

Joseph's College (Holy Ghost Fathers) in Rockwell, Cashel, County Tipperary until 1913.[65]

He worked as a trainee salesman as a 15-year-old at a store called Hearn's drapery but hated it. James became highly influenced by the Irish Parliamentary Party (IPP) and by John Redmond. Following the establishment of the Irish Volunteers in 1913, he joined its Waterford Battalion. If needed, he was ready to fight against any aggression by the newly created Ulster Volunteer Force, which was opposed to the ideals of Home Rule. James answered the call from Redmond to enlist in the British Army at the beginning of the First World War; he was just 16 years old. He joined the cadet company of the 7th Battalion, Leinster Regiment secretly. When his parents discovered what he had done his father made him leave immediately.

He returned, however, just three months later, the second time enlisting in the 17th Lancers cavalry regiment.[66] It was dispatched to France in early 1915 and James arrived at the front lines before trench warfare had set in. Eighteen months later he was seriously wounded; after recovering he was transferred to the 7th Battalion, Queen's Royal (West Surrey) Regiment.[67] By 1917 his experience of warfare on horseback was obsolete. He survived both the Somme and later Arras in 1917.[68] Due to his services in both battles, he was awarded a commission in the 8th Irish (King's) Liverpool Regiment.[69] Early in 1918 he answered a call for junior officers to begin training as pilots in the Royal Flying Corps (RFC).

A year after the end of the conflict he joined the newly formed RAF and was commissioned.[70] It was at this time that he began a secret relationship with Violet 'Bill' Clarke, a young woman from Kilburn in North London. She had served as part of the female ground staff at Eastbourne training base during the conflict. They had to keep their relationship secret due to strict military regulations, but on 6 January 1919, on his 21st birthday, they married. Their only daughter, Patricia, was born on 21 June 1921. As his training with the RAF came to an end, James was selected to pilot the first night mail flight from Folkestone to Cologne.[71] He then received command of the working party of 6 Wing and was based at Lympne in Kent. Afterwards he went onto the reserve list and was demobilised.

James returned to Ireland after the signing of the Anglo-Irish Treaty in 1921. With the formal creation of the twenty-six-county Irish Free State in 1922, the 24-year-old joined the newly created Irish Free State Army

Air Service just as the Civil War broke out. He became a lieutenant in the newly created Irish Air Corps and flew missions during the Civil War, including leaflet-dropping flights to try to persuade anti-Treaty IRA men in the mountains of Cork and Kerry to surrender.[72] His base was at the former British aerodrome in Fermoy, Cork, where he lived with his family. Baldonnel Aerodrome in Dublin later became his base. By 1924 he had been promoted to the rank of captain and he commanded No. 1 Squadron with an acting commandant's rank.[73] The officer commanding until 1927 was Colonel Charles Russell; James was given that position in 1927.

He had tried once before to enter aviation history by crossing the Atlantic on board the *Princess Xenia*, but the mission had ended in failure.[74] A disappointed captain, he didn't have to wait too long for his second opportunity.

Shortly after he had made history on the *Bremen*, James lost his mother Mary on 11 November 1929. Then, in the aftermath of his groundbreaking flight in 1928, he decided to retire. His attentions turned to trying to promote commercial air travel from Ireland to Germany. His marriage failed in 1931 and he buried his father in Glasnevin in June 1932. Emigration to New York followed in the 1930s, where he remained for nearly ten years.[75] He later moved to London, where he tried his hand at other aviation ventures and even ran a wartime servicemen's club. He returned to Dublin in 1951 where his once well-known name had faded into obscurity. His name in Germany on the other hand was still relatively well known. He was by that time the only survivor of the *Bremen* crew and was given a medal in Munich on 26 September 1965. Just three weeks later, on 26 September 1965, he died at the City of Dublin Hospital on Baggot Street.[76] The general manager of Aer Lingus at the time, J.F. Dempsey, said:

> His contribution to ... [the advance of aviation] in its pioneer years was of great importance to this country and his part in the successful flight of the *Bremen* was an inspiration to those who worked to establish the national airline, particularly one with a transatlantic arm ... Each time I cross the Atlantic, I never fail to think of him and of those other pioneers who risked so much to conquer that great ocean. I know from my close association with him how deeply interested he was in the progress of our national airline and how greatly he admired our efforts to hold a position in the world of civil aviation, I and all

> those who work with me, in the airline, will forever hold in grateful remembrance all that this fine Irish airman achieved ...[77]

The *Irish Independent* wrote an extensive obituary on James' life, as did many other newspapers. The obituary was printed in Ireland, America and Germany. *The Evening Herald* reported:

> [He] was laid to rest in the family burial plot, following Requiem Mass in St Mary's Church Haddington Road ... The coffin, draped with the Tricolour, bearing Col. Fitzmaurice's sword and cap, was borne on a gun-carriage from the Church to the cemetery, where three volleys were fired over the grave. The Last Post and Reveille were sounded by a Corps of Buglers and Drummers from the Army No. 1 Band ... a Guard of Honour of officers, N.C.O.s and men of the Air Corps, under Capt. P. Nugent, rendered honours while the Army No 1. band, under Comdt. J. O'Doherty, played requiem music. Ten pilots from the Air Corps acted as pall bearers, under Lieut.-Col. O'Higgins, and Military Police formed the bearer party ...[78]

His achievement on the *Bremen* came at a time when the Irish Free State was trying to establish itself on an international stage. His contribution cannot be understated. He wore his Irish Air Corps uniform on all the receptions after the successful flight and carried a tricolour with him everywhere. He was given the Distinguished Flying Cross by then president of the USA, Calvin Coolidge. He and his German co-pilots were the first non-American citizens to be given that honour, and he undoubtedly helped put Ireland onto the international aviation map.[79] The crew members even wrote a book about their adventure: *The Three Musketeers of the Air*.[80] The aviation school at Baldonnel was renamed after him and postage stamps were issued in his memory in both 1978 and 1998 on the anniversary of the historic flight.[81] Despite all of this, James Fitzmaurice lies largely forgotten in Glasnevin.

Chisel and Hammer

Recently some of the cemetery's forgotten architects and sculptors have begun to receive the recognition that they deserved during their lifetime. Albert Power is one of them. Until recently, his grave was unmarked and much of his work under-appreciated, but his legacy has now been fully remembered in Síghle Bhreathnach-Lynch's *Expressions of Nationhood in Bronze and Stone.* The cemetery today acts as an outdoor gallery to some of his works. A short walk around the grounds reveals a number of these, such as the impressive lying figure of Archbishop of Dublin William Walsh in the St Lawrence section of the cemetery (C 45.5) and his Celtic cross for the second president of Ireland, Seán T. O'Kelly, and his wives Cáit (died 1934) and Philomena Frances Ní Ríain (1983) in the St Bridget's section (AH 54.5).[1]

Through his firm on 18 Geraldine Street and its later expansion to 15 Berkeley Street in Dublin, Power produced a wide range of sculptures, monuments, busts and plaster casts. Close to Seán T. O'Kelly's grave is the final resting place of Fr Patrick Dineen (CH 83.5). He was the editor of the first ever Irish–English dictionary in 1904 and Power viewed him as being

---

Archbishop Edward McCabe's Mausoleum by Ashlin, Glasnevin Cemetery *c.* 1900. (Reproduced courtesy of the National Library of Ireland)

important to the nationalist cause. In 1934 Power unveiled a plaster cast of his hand in recognition of Dineen's services to Irish nationalism. The grave of noted sculptor Joshua Clarke, the father of famed stained-glass artist Harry, is on a small pathway to the left past Michael Collins' resting place. Joshua died in 1921 and it was a sign of Power's status that Clarke asked him to design this memorial, completed in 1925.[2]

Some of Power's most notable non-funerary works include reliefs over the main entrance to the Grand Central Bar on the junction of O'Connell Street and Abbey Street; much of the stone carving for Wynn's Hotel on Middle Abbey Street;[3] the Robert Emmet bronze relief bust on the Robert Emmet Bridge leading into Harold's Cross (1937);[4] statues and busts to Thomas Kettle, the First World War poet (1919); and a limestone bench in St Stephen's Green to Anna Maria and Thomas Haslam, who fought for women's rights in the late nineteenth and early twentieth centuries.[5]

Between 1922 and 1931 the Irish Free State government also availed of his talents, commissioning sculptures of Arthur Griffith (1922), Michael Collins (1936) and Austin Stack (1939).[6] Power created the two portrait medallions of Collins and Griffith that surmounted a memorial that formed the Cenotaph on Leinster Lawn. It was unveiled on the first anniversary of both men's deaths in 1923.[7] This memorial no longer stands, but the medallions are set into the ground below a large obelisk. St John Gogarty asked Power to make plaster casts of the faces of both Collins and Griffith before their remains were laid out in state.[8] Power also completed a cast for Cathal Brugha, at the request of Brugha's wife,[9] and completed a bust of Hugh Lane for the Municipal Gallery of Modern Art.[10]

His famous Pádraic Ó Conaire statue was unveiled in 1935 at Eyre Square, in Galway.[11] Power's monument to W.B. Yeats (1939) at Sandymount Green in Dublin is another example of his enduring legacy.[12] Outside Dublin some of his most notable memorials include the Pikemen in Tralee (1939) and a memorial to the leaders of 1916 in Limerick, which was his last completed work.[13] His final commission came in County Donegal for the design of four statues to compliment the dome of the Church of the Sacred Heart at Carndonagh.

He died on 10 July 1945 aged 62 and was buried in the Dublin New Chapel section (DF 22.5). *The Irish Times* featured a fitting obituary: 'As time goes on his work will be more appreciated as that of the outstanding native sculptor of his time'.[14] His funeral to Glasnevin was reported by the *Irish*

Independent, which said, 'It is a tragedy that Albert Power has died before some national recognition of his genius was paid to him ...'[15]

Power has had his works and story brought back to life, but for others in Glasnevin this is not the case. An example of someone who has not yet been the subject of a biography is the architect John Joseph O'Callaghan. He is buried in the Old O'Connell Circle of vaults on Row D: Number 34. The plot is sadly unmarked. In the absence of major church-building projects, he used his talents to construct municipal and domestic buildings. On Dame Street you can view his Callaghan buildings completed in 1879 opposite the Olympia Theatre. At 27 Dame Street, the Trinity City Bar and Hotel were also designed by O'Callaghan. If you have ever sipped a pint at Bruxelles pub then you were in one of O'Callaghan's Gothic-designed buildings (1886). The rebuilt red-brick Dolphin Hotel at 33–34 Essex Street is another example of his work. Many of the red-brick buildings on Suffolk Street also bear his mark from the late 1880s, but his best work is located at the Westmoreland and D'Olier Street junction, now part of the National Wax Museum. It was described by his contemporaries as his 'big chance'.[16]

Plagued by illness in the final few years of his life, O'Callaghan died on 2 November 1905 at the age of 67. *The Irish Times* summed up the life and death of this forgotten architect: 'An artist of exceptional ability, he has passed away more a disappointed man than a successful man, from a monetary point of view at least. Later on, undoubtedly, his fine works will be better appreciated as those of a master of architectural designs and construction.'[17]

Amongst the thousands of funerary monuments in Glasnevin lie a host of forgotten sculptors and architects, whose stories remain untold. During their lives they helped to shape Ireland's major cities and towns and most of their work can still be seen.

George Coppinger Ashlin and the Gothic Revival

During his life, George Coppinger Ashlin was one of Cork's best-known architects and designed a multitude of different churches and religious buildings, including Cork's SS Peter and Paul church, Cobh's impressive cathedral and the McCabe memorial in Glasnevin. Ashlin was born on 28 May 1837 at a house called 'Carrigrenane' in Little Island, Cork and was the third son of John Musson Ashlin, JP, of Rush Hill, Wandsworth in Surrey, and Dorinda Coppinger.[18] His mother's family were well established, and this afforded him an education in Belgium at the College of St Servais, Liège, and later in Birmingham at Oscott. He went to London at the age of 17, where he became an articled pupil of the great revivalist of Gothic architect, Augustus Welby Pugin.[19] This was the beginning of a life-long partnership with the Pugin family, who are referenced in the *Irish Independent* in 1923 as 'A great family of Architects … The Wonderful Pugins.'[20] George became a student of A.W. Pugin (1812–52) up until his death and forged a close working relationship with Pugin's eldest son, Edward (or E.W. for short). He was later given responsibility for Pugin's commissions in Ireland, setting up a Dublin branch in the family name. Emmet O'Brien, in an essay, describes the Pugin and Ashlin partnership as the 'Catholic High Gothic Circle' in Ireland.[21]

Ashlin worked closely with Pugin up until the early 1880s. One of the earliest commissions he secured was the large SS Peter and Paul church in Cork. He also worked on the construction of some bank buildings, a good example being the old Munster and Leinster bank building in Midleton, County Cork, and the asylum at Portrane, County Dublin. In 1867 he married Mary Pugin, the younger sister of E.W. Pugin.[22] The Pugins believed firmly in building churches in the Gothic style. This was all part of a wider Gothic Revival in church building in nineteenth-century Ireland. This style, so noticeable today across the skylines of many Irish towns and cities, became the staple design for much of Ashlin's work. It achieved 'ascendancy in Catholic church building in the 1860s', starting with James Joseph McCarthy's Saint Saviour's church in Dominick Street (1858), and being used by Pugin and Ashlin for SS Augustine and St John, Thomas Street in 1862.[23] These dominating Gothic structures became religious skyscrapers and helped to put the Catholic Church on the map following the emancipation achieved by O'Connell in the 1830s. Funding for these buildings came from years of fundraising from local parishes, and for this reason nineteenth-century ecclesiastical patrons were usually in a strong position to exert a form of 'architectural dictatorship over his architect'.[24] The only architects strong enough to go against the expressed wishes of a patron were the Pugins.

Ashlin's work culminated in 1868 with his role in the building of the impressive Cobh Cathedral. After 1870 he became the sole architect of the cathedral, a role he kept until 1902. In the 1880s he decided to go it alone and by 1907 had set up his own business in Dawson Street working as Ashlin &

Coleman. Thomas Aloysius Coleman was one of his former pupils and was his office manager in the Dawson Street office until his death.

In Ashlin's *Irish Times* obituary there is a long list of major churches and buildings in which he played a role. It includes the Augustinian church, Thomas Street, the Redemptoristine convent in Drumcondra and the Church of Mary Immaculate on Tyrconnell Road, Inchicore.[25] A brief scan through the online *Dictionary of Irish Architects* reveals a striking CV. It includes other churches like Clonakilty's Church of the Immaculate Conception (1869–80), Dundrum Main Street, Church of the Holy Cross (1876–80), Emly Church of St Ailbhe, Tipperary (1880–82) and the Church of All Saint's, Dublin Howth Road (1885–90).[26] He also worked on the Boys' Chapel at Clongowes Wood College and a private chapel for Sir Christopher Palles at his house at No. 28 Fitzwilliam Place, Dublin. Palles was the last Chief Baron of the Exchequer in Ireland, a title that dated back to the twelfth century and was abolished when the Irish Free State was set up in 1922.

The O'Connell Memorial Roman Catholic Chapel in Cahirciveen, the only chapel in Ireland to be named after a layperson, was designed by Ashlin in O'Connell's honour. Its cornerstone was a gift from the pope in late 1888 in recognition of O'Connell's final request to be buried in Ireland but to have his heart sent to Rome. The chapel is still open to parishioners and visitors today. A link between Ashlin and Glasnevin can be seen beside the cemetery offices. It is the mausoleum marking the final resting place of Archbishop Edward McCabe. Following McCabe's death in 1885, a competition was opened to design the mausoleum. The winning design was by Sir Thomas Drew, but he later withdrew and the commission was given instead to Ashlin. It is an ornate piece complete with disciples' heads mounted on columns that surround a prone marble figure of McCabe (sculpted by Sir Thomas Farrell at a cost of £500). It is styled in the shape of a chapel replicating the shape of the cross. It stands in direct competition with the cemetery's mortuary chapel. This was deliberate.

Ashlin's Biggest Rival

Ashlin's biggest architectural rival in Dublin was James Joseph McCarthy, who built the mortuary chapel. The archbishop's mausoleum gave Ashlin the perfect opportunity to upstage his rival's work in Glasnevin. The two monuments still compete for architectural dominance at the front gates of the cemetery today. McCarthy was from Listowel, County Kerry (1817–82) and became known during his life as the 'Irish Pugin'. He is buried just a five-minute walk from Ashlin. Among his most notable works are St Kevin's church at Glendalough, County Wicklow (1851), All Hallows Missionary College in Drumcondra (1860), St Saviour's church in Dominick Street, Dublin (1852–61), St Patrick's College chapel at Maynooth (1875) and the church of St Mary of the Angels on Church Street, Dublin (1881).[27] McCarthy was also a professor of ecclesiastical architecture at All Hallows in Drumcondra, professor of architecture at the Catholic University of Ireland (an unpaid position) and later professor of architecture at the Royal Hibernian Academy (RHA).[28] He died on 6 February 1882 from heart disease, aged 65. He was buried behind his Romanesque Mortuary Chapel in the Garden section (JF 24).

George Coppinger Ashlin meanwhile went on to become a prominent member of the Architectural Association of Ireland (AAI), both in its older and newer forms, and became a member of the London Architectural Association, where he spent a good deal of time travelling and sketching in the UK. He also assessed many competitions for commissions here in Ireland and was an active member of the Royal Irish Academy (RIA), becoming its president between the years 1902 and 1904.

He died on 10 December 1921 at the age of 84 and was buried on the morning of 13 December in the St Bridget's section (TH 30). His obituarist in the Royal Institute of Architects Ireland (RIAI) journal wrote that 'he continued in active energy until a short while before his death' and 'preserved his comparatively youthful bearing almost to the end of his active career'.[29] He was one of a group that would come to be known as a generation of 'Catholic' architects, alongside J.J. McCarthy, William H. Byrne, Patrick Byrne, William Hague and the Pugins, all of whom contributed greatly to church building in Ireland.[30]

Patrick Byrne: Master Church Builder

Patrick Byrne was the once resident architect for Glasnevin during his life and also oversaw the building of a large number of Dublin churches in the nineteenth century, including St Paul's on Arran Quay (1835); St Audoen's, High Street (1841); St John the Baptist, Blackrock (1842); St James's on James's Street (1844); Our Lady of the Visitation, Fairview Strand (1847); St Pappin's,

Ballymun (1848); Our Lady of Refuge, Rathmines (1850); SS Alphonsus and Columba, Ballybrack, County Dublin (1854); St Assam's, Raheny (1859); and the Three Patrons, Rathgar (1860). He is another forgotten architect from the nineteenth century at rest in Glasnevin.[31]

The period 1830–80 was a time of unprecedented Catholic church building in Ireland. Brian Crowley states that such was the need for churches to be built in this period that there 'was a church built every week of the nineteenth century'.[32] Brendan Grimes contends that between 1835 until his death in 1864 Patrick Byrne would come to hold a near monopoly on the design of Catholic churches around Dublin.[33] His first church, St Paul's, can be seen along the Quays today (construction began in 1835).

Patrick Byrne's name is rarely mentioned in the story of Ireland's church-building boom of the nineteenth century, as he was largely eclipsed by the Pugins. However, many of his works still punctuate the Dublin cityscape. Grimes notes that 'little is known for certain of Byrne's family background'.[34] Likewise, C.P. Curran wrote of him in 1944 that 'his origin is unknown and his personality only to be guessed at'.[35] We know his father, John, was an architect and this is where he likely got much of his inspiration. The young Patrick grew up around Dublin in a time before many of Dublin's most prominent buildings and monuments, such as the GPO, Nelson's Pillar or the Four Courts, had been completed.

At the age of 13 he enrolled at Dublin's Society of Architectural Drawing, where he was taught by the well-respected Henry Aaron Baker, who had been a past student to the great Neoclassicist architect James Gandon.[36] Byrne excelled in his studies and earned two medals at the society between 1797 and 1798.[37] He got some work with the Wide Street Commissioners for a period from 1820 to 1848 and can be found referred to as the 'Boards Architect', although no such position actually existed on the board's list of paying jobs.[38] He also worked on the new Royal Exchange building (City Hall today) but little else is known of his early works.

In 1835 he was given his first major commission, for St Paul's church on Arran Quay. Grimes makes the case that it is likely he worked with architect Francis Johnston on projects including Saint George's on Hardwicke Place (1813), the Chapel Royal Dublin Castle (1814), King's Inns (1816) and the General Post Office (1818). Francis Johnston died in 1829 and his protégé was Patrick Byrne's teacher, Henry Aaron Baker.[39]

For Glasnevin, Patrick Byrne was an important architectural voice; he became the de facto resident architect for the cemetery. His name litters the minute books. He helped with everything from the planting of trees and the laying out of pathways to the erection of walls, watchtowers and chapels. Carmel Connell states that 'Patrick Byrne was the architect most associated with the cemetery from its foundation in 1832 until his death in 1864.'[40] The cemetery officials sent him a request on 7 April 1834 to put together a set of plans along with examples of appropriate monuments to be displayed for the public at the Committee's Head offices on Ormond Quay. He accepted. The committee said this was necessary to ensure that only the 'best of taste could be witnessed in the cemetery'.[41] The overall design and development for Glasnevin as a space was never properly mapped out. It evolved and changed over time. As the cemetery increased in size, additions were suggested and it was Byrne who was usually called on to help.[42]

By the 1830s he had his office at 8 Mabbot Street (today James Joyce Street). Before the cemetery opened, Byrne had submitted designs for the entrance lodge and the original entrance gates on 14 November 1831.[43] The designs were accepted and you can still walk through them today. With their completion the cemetery opened an office on site. Previously the head office had been at 4 Rutland (Parnell) Square. Once you passed through these gates in the 1830s the cemetery was symmetrically laid out. From the entrance there would have been a main thoroughfare that ran east–west to the back boundary wall at the westerly end. Off this main pathway existed smaller gravel paths in keeping with the Victorian ideals of a planned garden cemetery. All that remains of this original cemetery are the gates and lodge by Byrne.

As demand grew for burials the cemetery grew in size. Original walls that had been erected by 1838 at the westerly end of the cemetery featuring stone towers for security and seats at appropriate spaces needed to be altered. Byrne oversaw this job. From 1838 to 1844 four of the eight towers that can be seen surrounding the grounds on the Ordnance Survey map of 1867 had been finished.[44] The four completed towers were all built along the perimeter of the so-called 'New Ground'. One of the first towers completed was the Finglas road tower closest to Dublin, finished in September 1841. It can be seen in its entirety today beside the Holy Angels Plot. Byrne recommended that the towers and walls be finished with hammered stone. He also used cut stone for the battlements on the towers.[45] There exists to this day a break in the north boundary wall, filled instead with railings. This was deliberate, to provide a better view into the botanical gardens in order to create a more tranquil space. The railings remain but not the terrace, of which Byrne stated in 1842: 'The general view obtained of the burial ground and of the beautiful scenery of the adjoining neighbourhood on the north side by ascending this terrace is doubtlessly calculated to afford considerable recreation to many persons visiting the cemetery …'[46]

While working for the cemetery, Byrne's church of St Paul's on Arran Quay was completed in 1837. The church had been the idea of Dr Canon William Yore, who had consecrated the cemetery in September 1831. After this commission, Byrne was given almost all ecclesiastical work for Catholic church building in Dublin until his death in 1864.[47] Previously, in 1834, he had worked on the Church of St Francis (Adam and Eve) on Merchant's Quay, notable for its irregular entrances. The nave of this church today displays some of his earliest church work.[48]

Unlike Ashlin and McCarthy, Byrne was trained in the classical language of architecture. The use of Romanesque pillars and Greek Revivalist elements became his trademarks. His versatility, however, allowed him to adapt to the new Gothic styles that emerged in the 1850s. The foundation stone for his Gothic Saint James's Catholic church on James's Street was laid in 1844 by Daniel O'Connell. It was completed in 1854. When walking past you can see the sculpted heads of O'Connell and Fr Canavan (its patron) at the entrance door. The Famine years, 1845–52, and the economic depression that followed in its wake meant that his work on St Audoen's on High Street was left unfinished for many years and without many of the ornamental features you see today. The structure was actually completed by Stephen Ashlin, the son of George Coppinger Ashlin, and W.H. Byrne, the son of Patrick Byrne, in the 1890s, many years after Patrick's death.

As Byrne's church-building monopoly went from strength to strength, his duties with Glasnevin continued. It is suggested by Grimes that there may have been some familial relationship with Edward Byrne, who was a rich Dublin merchant and chairman of the Catholic Committee at the time. These connections, along with his reliability, made him a prolific figure in the period 1835–64.[49] His work for the cemetery was wide-ranging. Originally the cemetery featured a temple in its centre built by Byrne. Today in Goldenbridge cemetery a similar one can be seen; Goldenbridge acted as a blueprint for Glasnevin. The temple that once stood in Glasnevin would have featured columns, a roof canopy with granite and an ornamental chimney on top. A series of granite steps would have led up to its floor covered in sheet lead surrounded by an iron-gated railing in the shape of a large circle.[50] As early as 14 March 1839 Byrne was asked by the board to prepare plans for a new Gothic-style entrance to the cemetery on the Finglas Road.[51] It was not until 1845, however, that concrete plans were requested from Byrne, plans that never materialised in his lifetime. It was not until 1878 that the new entrance, its gates and lodge were completed by the architect J.J. McCarthy.

Byrne's other major works for the cemetery included plans for a new chapel close to the site of the original temple, which had become obsolete with the addition of extra land. On 7 September 1840 he received the request to prepare plans and an estimate for a new chapel on a budget of just £800.[52] He replied that it was not possible. Instead, he was asked to examine the possibility of building a chapel as an extension to the already existing temple. He managed to complete this project by the end of 1842 at a cost of just £475.[53] It would be another thirty-six years until this hastily erected mortuary chapel completed by Byrne was replaced by the current cemetery chapel by J.J McCarthy.

After Daniel O'Connell's death in 1847, his remains were returned to Ireland from Italy for burial. He was temporarily laid to rest in a section of the cemetery known today as the Old O'Connell Circle. This northern part of the cemetery was considered New Ground in the 1840s and was highly sought after. O'Connell was buried at its centre while a more fitting memorial to the 'Liberator' was decided on. Both this circle of vaults and the future O'Connell Round Tower were built and designed by Patrick Byrne. The circle itself was artificially created by digging a deep trench around a circular piece of earth. He then had a wall built around the circumference of this patch of earth and vaults were cut out of the sides of the circle just below ground level. These works were conducted throughout 1841 and completed in January 1842.[54] This circle consists of an outer circle of doored vaults measuring 8 feet by 8 feet and two bridges to its centre which has three inner concentric circles of ground vaults and horizontal tombs. Byrne laid down strict rules about what type of monuments were to be permitted in each section of this circle. Headstones were excluded entirely. No heavy monuments or columns were to be erected on top of the outer circle of doored vaults. Spiral monuments were permitted only in the second circle.[55] This was to be the centrepiece of the cemetery as it continued to expand. A walk around this section today, however, shows that his rules were not followed. After O'Connell's burial in the circle its name was changed to the 'O'Connell Circle'.

Byrne's biggest legacy for the cemetery is the O'Connell Tower that keeps watchful guard over the graves. A special 'O'Connell Monuments Committee' was set up shortly after his burial in the circle. Original plans were considered by the great Irish antiquarian George Petrie, who envisioned a replica early Christian-style monastic site complete with a small chapel and a miniature round tower. Work began with the tower, which eventually came to measure an impressive 180 feet (55 metres). It included steps to the top with a wrought-iron spiral staircase and hand-carved wooden steps, six landing platforms and four windows at the top. The solid granite cross on top measures 2½ metres and weighs 3 tonnes; it was hoisted by hand with a system of pulleys under the supervision of Byrne.

The tower is still one of the highest structures in Dublin. Construction took just sixteen months and it was completed by 1856. It took hundreds of skilled tradespeople and labourers to finish it at a cost of £18,000 (approximately 12–15 million euro today). Its size and cost meant the remainder of Petrie's vision for an ancient Christian monastic site never materialised. The tower came to act as the singular memorial to O'Connell. O'Connell's remains were moved into the adjoining altar-tomb in its crypt under the tower on 14 May 1869. By this time Patrick Byrne had died. Despite the tower being finished by 1856, the surrounding area consisting of a circle of newer vaults still needed to be added and this process took considerably longer to complete.

Outside of Dublin Byrne's work stretched to Tipperary, with his design for the Catholic church in Drangan (1853) and a Catholic church in Arklow (1859).[56] By 1860 his monopoly on church building was in decline. His last completed work was the Church of the Three Patrons in Rathgar (1860) when he was 77 years old.[57] Both his St John the Baptist church in Blackrock and St James's Catholic church on James's Street make him 'a pioneer of the Gothic Revival in Dublin'. His designs predate the emergence of Ashlin, Pugin and J.J. McCarthy as masters of the Gothic style.[58]

Using the burial records of Glasnevin, you can find a Mary Byrne listed as the wife of Patrick Byrne from Talbot Street. Her date of death is recorded as 10 March 1856. Patrick buried his wife in the same section where he had erected his temple and chapel twenty years previously. Mary was 72 and was buried in the Chapel Circle (XA 34.5). Patrick was granted this grave as a family plot by the Dublin Cemeteries Committee in 1841. It was 'in order to mark their high sense of the services rendered by Mr. Byrne as architect to the cemeteries.'[59] There is a letter sent by Byrne to thank the committee for this gesture:

> Allow me most respectfully to thank you for your very liberal grant … for a piece of ground eight feet by eight feet square within the Circle of the Temple at your Prospect Cemetery as a place of sepulchre for myself and my family. To receive so unexpected a mark of your kindness I feel to be a compliment of no ordinary character and for which I again beg to make my most sincere and grateful acknowledgement.[60]

Also at rest in this grave are his two sons and a daughter-in-law: John Byrne, Hugh Byrne and Frances Byrne. His sons followed in their father's footsteps and became architects.

Byrne was elected vice-president of the RIAI from 1854. This would be a post that he held until his death in 1864 and was the highest honour architects of the time could award him.[61] In his elder years he also became a founding member of the Society of Irish Artists and in 1860 became a member of the RHA.[62] Dr William Meagher, one of his greatest patrons, said:

> Of this gifted man whose talents and disinterested care have laid us under such obligations, of him who designed the portico of St. Paul's, and erected the majestic shrine of St. Audoen's, and the solemn cathedral like pile of St. James and the bold and beauteous dome of Our Lady of Refuge, of the accomplished and good and generous Patrick Byrne how truly may it not be said that he regarded the beauties of classical and medieval art with equal reverence, studied their several excellencies with equal assiduity and wrought upon the principles of both with equal supereminent success.[63]

He died at his residence, 41 Lower Gardiner Street, on 10 January 1864 aged 81 and was buried a day later in the cemetery that he had helped to shape into what visitors see today. His grave, however, is unmarked and nobody remembers his name. His work for the city of Dublin and the cemetery place him highly in the pantheon of Ireland's nineteenth-century architects. It should not be forgotten that while Pugin, Ashlin and J.J. McCarthy became masters of the Gothic Revivalist period in Ireland, it was Byrne who, through his Gothic experiments, paved the way for them to follow. If you do wish to sit and think about his legacy today, take a walk towards his original entrance gates beside Kavanagh's pub. Along the wall you will find an enclave in the form of a seat. Byrne was asked to design a plan for a 'covered seat at the termination of the long walk from the old entrance gate to the wall on the west side.'[64] One of these recesses in the east wall can still be enjoyed. Sit here and look out over the cemetery and you will be able to make out his epitaph – his gate lodge and arched entrance to your left and his Round Tower straight ahead.

James Pearse: 'English, Puritan and Mechanical'

James Pearse was a stonemason with many links to the churches of Byrne, Ashlin, the Pugins and J.J. McCarthy, as well as to Glasnevin. He was one of the most famed ecclesiastical sculptors of the nineteenth century in Ireland and was father to the 1916 Rising leader, Patrick. His son said of his father: 'If ever in an Irish Church you find, amid a wilderness of bad sculpture, something good and true and lovingly finished, you may be sure that it was carved by my father or by one of his pupils.'[65] He also described him as being 'English, Puritan and Mechanical.'[66] Brian Crowley, the curator of the Pearse Museum and Kilmainham Gaol, has written extensively on the background of Pearse. He believes that it can at times be commonplace within the republican narrative to 'see things in black or white, or, to be more precise, green and orange.'[67] James Pearse's English heritage may be one of the reasons why most people know so little about his life.

Pearse was born on 8 December 1839 in Bloomsbury, Middlesex, London. His parents were James Pearse, a composition-maker and picture framer, and Mary Thompson, a Unitarian. The area he was born into was described as being 'a comfortable working-class area.'[68] They moved to Birmingham in order to better their circumstances. While James was young, he was sent out to work with his two brothers. His older brother, William, worked in a gun factory, while his younger brother managed to get a job at a picture framing company.[69] James worked in a chain factory in a dangerous manual labour position.[70] During his formative years he is recorded as having a restless mind but a lack of formal education; he was enrolled in the local Sunday school for a time, but this was cut short. Apparently, the young child's questions, according

James Pearse. (Courtesy of the Pearse Museum and Brian Crowley)

to the leader of the school, bordered on atheism. This was a trait that James carried with him throughout his adult life – not openly atheist, but a person who questioned the world around him. His next job as a printer's devil (an apprentice in a printing office) also ended abruptly when he was accused of having a run-in with his boss's son and got the sack. Despite all of this he had an insatiable appetite for knowledge, reading and learning. As Ruth Dudley Edwards tells us in her biography of Patrick Pearse, 'he [James] never ceased to read and question and the library he built up in his more prosperous years betrayed a wide interest in comparative religions, as well as literature, history and politics, the more usual diet of the self-educated'.[71]

Birmingham had become a centre for a movement labelled the 'earnest minority' and the city itself had become known as the 'city of trades' in the nineteenth century. It saw people of the same socio-economic background as James challenge old ideas that only those at the top of society could have access to literature and learning.[72] James became influenced by the first republican club to be set up in Great Britain. He particularly liked the 'earnest minority' movement for its 'secularist' ideals and for its 'freethought' wing that disputed the central role of Judaeo-Christianity.[73] The unpublished autobiography of Patrick Pearse described James as: 'Working in the daytime and in the Art School every evening, he read books by night and came to know most of English Literature well and some of it better than most men who have lived in universities.'[74]

He also became heavily influenced by the Gothic Revival. He 'rode the wave', as Ruth Dudley Edwards describes it, to become a stone carver.[75] This was the main reason that he made his way to Ireland, which was in the middle of a church-building boom; no church was complete without its set of ornate statues and monuments. Once he had completed his stonemason's apprenticeship in Birmingham, James became part of a wide group of English craftsmen who made the move to Dublin in search of work.[76] By 1857 18-year-old James was in Dublin plying his trade. He maintained close links with Birmingham in these early days. Regular visits home led to marriage with Emily Suzanna Fox in St Thomas' church in Birmingham on 28 April 1863.

Up until the 1870s, James continued to work as a journeyman mason in Dublin.[77] The first firm he worked for was Hardman and Co. of Birmingham. It had strong links to the Pugins and had just opened a Dublin branch with Early and Powell's. James became part of a community of English craftsmen around the Great Brunswick Street area (today Pearse Street). He joined the company of the Pugin school of thought. A lot of his work has sadly been forgotten due to the fact he worked for different firms before establishing his own, but it can be ranked alongside the Gothic architectural names of Pugin, McCarthy and the sculptor and artist Sir Thomas Farrell.

With Early and Powell's, he carved the twelve saints on the spire of the church of SS Augustine and John on Thomas Street.[78] In 1867 Patrick Maume noted that James also worked with the Hardman and Co. firm on their commission to decorate the newly constructed House of Lords in London. He worked particularly on the designs of the carved princesses that adorned the Lords robing room.[79] By 1873 he had set up a small firm of his own in partnership with another English stonemason by the name of P.J. Neill.[80]

Emily gave birth to their first child in 1864 – a daughter called Mary Emily. They had three more children together, James Vincent (1866), Agnes Maud (1869) and Amy Catherine (1871). Sadly both Agnes Maud and Amy Catherine died in infancy. The family lived in a small, terraced house close to Great Brunswick Street, today's Macken Street. Agnes Maud and Amy Catherine were both buried in Glasnevin, a five-minute walk from their father's grave today. James purchased the plot in the Garden section (CE 59.5) in 1872 to bury his young 3-year-old daughter on 22 October 1872. Amy, their second daughter, was the next to be buried there, on 20 November 1872. James later reflected on this sad time of his life and claimed that both his daughters' deaths were a direct result of neglect by their mother.[81] There is no proof to support these claims, but it is certain that the marriage was an unhappy one after 1872.[82]

Despite being a radical thinker, James was received into the Catholic Church around 1870.[83] This decision likely dealt with the practicalities of eking out a better living for himself. Brian Crowley believes that this was a 'prudent' move to make 'for an ambitious ecclesiastical sculptor ... while working in an overwhelmingly Catholic country'.[84]

Emily, his wife, died in 1876 aged just 30. On her burial record it states she died as a result of 'congestion of the lungs'. She was buried in the same grave (CE 59.5) as her two young daughters. James Vincent, Pearse's surviving son, and Mary Emily, his daughter, moved into the house of a friend, John McLoughlin.[85] As a tradesman and artisan, James' daily work life depended on him finding a new wife to help raise his children. His wages would not cover a housekeeper, childminder or nurse. By this time his partnership with P.J. Neill had come to an end and he had taken out a lease on his premises at 27 Great Brunswick Street. Around the corner there was a local shop where be bought his daily newspaper. This is where he met a young woman called Margaret Brady. He had met her some time before his wife's death in 1876.

Margaret was much younger than James and from a different familial background. She was the daughter of a coal-factory worker and her grandfather was a native Irish speaker from County Meath who had been evicted in the Great Hunger of 1845–52. At least two of her family had fought during the 1798 rebellion. She was a 'traditional, pious, well-mannered girl with limited education'.[86] On the one hand there was James – a reserved, clever, ambitious, unspiritual and refined man. On the other hand there was Margaret – young, bright and impulsive, with a simplistic but devout Catholic outlook on life. Their correspondence reveals that despite these differences there was genuine attraction. In one letter Margaret gushingly wrote to him, 'My Dearest Mr Pearse ... I do be watching every post during the day to see if you are thinking of me ... I would like you to write ... more affectionately. I don't know if you are so anxious to see me as I am you ... I think every day a week thinking when I shall see you.'[87]

James replied in a much more reserved manner: 'It strikes me I have not the power of writing so affectionately as you have but you know you must take the will for the deed sometimes. Anyhow I think you must know that I love you dearly and sincerely and I tell you, that you must not be doubting and fancying all sorts of things.'[88] He married Margaret fifteen months later, on 24 October 1877. With her, he had four more children: Margaret (1878), Patrick (1879), William (1881) and Mary Brigid (1884). All four were born at 27–28 Great Brunswick Street above his workshop. None of the four children went on to have any children and so there are no direct descendants of the Pearse genealogical line today. James, although not overtly affectionate, was loving

William Pearse stands on the bench beside his father James, Mary Brigid sits on her mother's knee, while Margaret sits to their left. Patrick is standing to his father's right.
(Courtesy of the Pearse Museum and Brian Crowley)

and generous in his own way. He often brought home gifts to his children including a rocking horse he had made himself called 'Dobbin' for Patrick.[89]

In the period 1880–91 James flourished as an ecclesiastical sculptor and worked on and off with a man called Edmund Sharp from Birmingham. During this time he produced some of his finest work. With his fellow Englishman by his side, he produced many altars, pulpits, railings and expensive features for churches all over the country. James was doing well financially and moved to number 3 Newbridge Avenue in Sandymount.[90] The year 1882 saw Pearse and Sharp awarded a first-class award at the Dublin Exhibition for their work on a high altar in statuary and coloured marbles.[91] In 1889 he completed one of his finest pieces of work, his *Erin go Breagh* for the National Bank on College Green. This piece can still be seen today on top of 34 College Green, where the bank once operated. Other particularly notable works from this time, still visible today, include his work on Enniscorthy Cathedral and on the Church of St Michael in Tipperary.[92]

Between 1880 and 1890 he also worked a lot with his son from his first marriage, James Vincent. Initially he travelled home with him to visit his aging father and to attend to business matters in London. This resulted in him taking out a lease on a premises at 83 Bristol Street, Birmingham to try to expand his Pearse & Sons firm into a British market. There is the possibility that he might have been considering a full relocation of his family to Birmingham away from Catholic Dublin, where his free-thinking and bohemian ideals made him somewhat of an outcast.[93] This poses the intriguing question of 'what if?' If James had decided to make this move back to England, what then would have become of Patrick Pearse's future at the turn of the twentieth century?

James Vincent, his son from his first marriage, joined the family business in 1890, but due to disagreements with Margaret, his stepmother, it did not work out. He died in 1912 at the age of 44 and was buried in the same plot as his young siblings and mother (CE 59.5). Later, William (Willie) Pearse, joined the family firm while studying part time at the Metropolitan School of Art. Patrick, although not a sculptor, also helped the family firm in administrative matters while studying for his Bachelor of Arts degree.[94] At its height, Pearse & Sons boasted a workforce of some forty men from its premises at 27–28 Brunswick Street. By the end of 1900 Pearse and Sons was 'the largest stonemasons yard in Ireland, employing forty workmen and leasing as business premises three properties on Townsend Street adjacent to the family residence on Brunswick Street.'[95] The company motto was *Labor Omina Vincit* (work conquers all).[96]

Beside the Round Tower in Glasnevin, a short walk around the circle leads to an example of James Pearse's skilled work. Beside the graveside of Roger Casement (1864–1916) there is a fine Celtic cross in the revivalist tradition. The cross was erected to the memory of the Burke family at rest behind one of the doored vaults surrounding O'Connell's Round Tower. Their cross contains some of the finest stone carved panels in the cemetery.[97] They depict the story of St Patrick. This work was all completed by James under the firm name 'Pearse and Sharp'.[98] The panelling completed by James Pearse on this monument is an excellent example of 'the vogue for the Celtic in art'.[99]

Other sculpture work that we know is directly attributed to him in the cemetery includes the heads of the ancient kings and queens of Ireland beneath the awning of the mortuary chapel. All the fixed carvings for the mortuary chapel were also completed by the firm of James Pearse and Sons of Great Brunswick Street.[100] They elaborately carved the arches and shafts made of Portland and Wicklow granite.[101]

Much of James Pearse's work has today been lost or removed from certain churches due to changes in liturgy introduced by Vatican II reforms. It is true to say that 'Pearse's artistic achievement is difficult to assess because much of his work was anonymous, attributed to firms which employed him rather than individually, or executed to other's designs'.[102] Two of his most obvious works still visible today are the group of figures with the motif 'Erin-go-bragh' above the National Bank building in College Green and the high altar in the Carmelite church of Clarendon Street.[103] Despite the difficulty in identifying what works are his, you get a sense of his success from the jealousy felt by his contemporaries. One of his former partners, P.J. Neill, began a smear campaign against James while he was working with Sharp. James defended himself forcefully in a letter to the Archdeacon of Fethard in January of 1883 stating, 'I am bound to admit that we are both guilty of being Englishmen but as God in his wisdom thought fit to call us into existence upon the other side of the water, and as His will was done in this matter, and not ours, we think there needs no apology from us on that head.'[104]

During his life he accumulated a sizeable library. Much of this went on to form the foundation of the library in the school his son Patrick set up at St Enda's, Rathfarnham. His library came to include everything from books on the plight of the Native American populations, classics, legal texts and even an English copy of the Qur'an that is still in St Enda's today.

James was a Parnellite and supported Home Rule during the 1880s, but in a more general sense he can be viewed as a non-conformist. Certainly no revolutionary, he was conscious of the fact that he was not an Irishman and also of his Lancashire accent. Patrick Pearse later recalled that the polar opposite traditions of his parents made him the 'strange thing I am'.[105] James published his one and only piece of accredited and signed literary work in 1866 – a pamphlet that can be seen today at the Pearse Museum at St Enda's. Its title – 'England's Duty to Ireland as it appears to an Englishman' – is indicative of the politics and beliefs of the man. It was a defence of the ideals of Home Rule and was written in response to a piece written by a Catholic fellow of Trinity College, Thomas Maguire, who was Professor of Moral Philosophy. James was so angry with what the professor had written that he decided to respond with his own set of arguments through the eyes of an Englishman living in Dublin.[106]

James travelled home to Birmingham to visit his relations in early September 1900. While staying with his brother, he suffered a fatal cerebral haemorrhage and died suddenly at the age of 60. His family in Ireland were keen at the time to make it known that he had died in accordance with the rites of the Catholic Church. His death notice in *The Freeman's Journal* tells us he died 'fortified by the rites of the Roman Catholic Faith'.[107] He died without a will and so it fell to Patrick to administer his estate. James left behind an estate valued at £1,470 17s and 6d.[108] His monumental workshop continued after his death. William finished some of his father's last commissions, notably the Pulpit of the Four Masters for the Cathedral of St Eunan in Letterkenny and the mortuary chapel of St Andrew's church on Westland Row. By 1908 the firm was liquidated and the money used to set up the all-boys school at St Enda's in 1910.

Obituaries for James can be found in *The Freeman's Journal*, *The Irish Times* and the *Irish Independent*.[109] One reported that 'He rapidly rose to the foremost place amongst the ecclesiastical sculptors of the Three Kingdoms. His works may be seen in practically every church throughout the country helping to form beautiful and enduring memorials to the skill of the chisel.'[110] *The Freeman's Journal* reported on his funeral, which took place on the morning of 8 September 1900. He was buried in a grave that was purchased by his wife, Margaret, in the St Bridget's section of the cemetery

(OH 10).[111] The grave is not far from Parnell's. His occupation was registered as 'Monumental Builder'. Today it is hidden amongst a sea of Celtic crosses.

Margaret died on 26 April 1932 and was buried in the same grave. She witnessed the executions of her two sons, William and Patrick, for their roles in the Rising of 1916. Her two daughters, Mary Brigid and Margaret Mary, joined their parents in the plot in later years. A short walk away lies James' first family – his wife, Emily Suzanna Fox, is buried with his two young daughters and son James Vincent. The only members of the Pearse family not buried in Glasnevin are William and Patrick, who instead lie in Arbour Hill military cemetery. The Brady family also have family plots in the Garden section.

Today the Pearse Museum possesses some of James' most noteworthy pieces, including the original maquette of his 'Erin go Bragh' design for the National Bank in 1889. His desire to go against the grain, to self-educate and to read, can be seen as one of the leading factors in his sons having such strongheld self-belief in their principles and ideals. Much has been written regarding the influence James had on the formative years of Patrick. This is very much 'an exercise in speculation'.[112] Brian Crowley perhaps sums him up best 'as a traditionalist and modernist, a religious believer who could interrogate his faith', and through that lens 'we may find in Pearse the father of a nation much more suited to the complexities of twenty-first century Ireland than we have hitherto imagined'. By telling his story, I hope more people become aware of the Pearse family gravesides and of the forgotten legacy of the master stonemason James Pearse.

An Unassuming Gentleman: Sir Thomas Farrell

Another prolific but forgotten sculptor buried in Glasnevin is Sir Thomas Farrell, who lies in his mother's family vault, No. 26 in the Dublin section. He gave Dublin some of its finest stone memorials and statues of the nineteenth century. Born in 1827, he trained as a sculptor in the workshop of his father Terence on Lower Mecklenburg Street (today Railway Street).[113] In 1842 he entered the modelling school of the Royal Dublin Society and managed to establish himself in the early 1850s with a commission for a monument commemorating the late Catholic Archbishop Daniel Murray.[114] It can be seen today in St Mary's Pro-Cathedral, Marlborough Street. His sculptural output was extensive and features a Neoclassical style unlike much from the same period, which reflects the popular Gothic style. Many of these works can still be enjoyed today.

Another early monument completed by Farrell was to Captain John McNeill Boyd (1864), commemorating the sailor who had drowned in a storm in 1861 while leading a rescue mission for a sinking vessel off Kingstown (now Dún Laoghaire) pier. It can be seen today in St Patrick's Cathedral, Dublin. He became heavily influenced by similar Neoclassical designs around Dublin by contemporaries like Francis Chantrey and John Henry Foley.[115] It was his monument to Archbishop Murray, however, that put him on the map after 1854. It allowed him to establish himself as an independent sculptor free from his father's workshop. Elected as a full member of the RHA in 1860, he became the Academy's professor of sculpture until 1862. Subsequently he became a council member for three years, an auditor for one and treasurer for twenty-two. In 1893 he was elected as president.[116]

In the 1850s Farrell was awarded the commission to model one of the base panels for the Wellington Memorial in the Phoenix Park. The job was originally meant for his father, Terence, under the family business of 'The Messrs Farrell', but Thomas completed it. He chose to illustrate the Battle of Waterloo in its closing moments. It was finished in March 1860 and cast in South Molton Street in London, where it was completed in 1861. Some of his other works include his bronze statue to William Dargan outside the National Gallery of Ireland (1863), his funerary monument to Richard Whately, the Protestant Archbishop of Dublin, at St Patrick's Cathedral (1865), his bronze statue to Lord Ardilaun (Arthur Edward Guinness) at St Stephen's Green (1893) and his bust to Sir Patrick Keenan, the only Catholic Resident Commissioner of Education in Ireland (1899), now at the Department of Education on Marlborough Street. Keenan is buried in Glasnevin in the South section (PD 41).

Other works completed by Farrell include a number of pieces that had particularly strong links to Irish nationalism. His statue of William Smith O'Brien on O'Connell Street in Dublin, unveiled in 1870, caused much controversy because of its associations with the attempted insurrection in Tipperary from 1848. The monument beside O'Brien's to Sir John Gray is also the work of Farrell and was completed in 1879. Controversy relating to his monument to the Irish Republican Brotherhood and Young Irelanders intended for the grave of Terence Bellew McManus in Glasnevin (completed in 1866) meant it wasn't erected until 1933 due to its perceived political significance.[117]

Farrell's main competition during his lifetime came from John Henry Foley. Amidst fierce competition and delays, the commission to design the Daniel O'Connell monument on Sackville (O'Connell) Street was awarded to Foley. Appeals to give the commission to an Irish artist living and working on the island were rejected and Farrell and his brother's separate applications were never seriously considered.[118]

Farrell continued to produce fine sculptural pieces following this disappointment. In 1882 he completed his statue to Cardinal Paul Cullen at the Pro-Cathedral in Dublin. Later, in 1887, he added the prone figure of Archbishop Edward McCabe to Ashlin's earlier elaborate exterior mausoleum in Glasnevin.[119] In the cemetery you can see a number of his monuments including a statue of the actor Barry Sullivan in his favourite role as Hamlet (South New Chapel: RE 33). There is a white marble bust of Sir John Gray carved on a pedestal above his vault, and another monument (on Row D, Number 93 of the Old O'Connell Circle) is an interpretation of the flight of the soul for the wife of the Lord Chief Baron's wife, Ellen Palles (1839–85).[120]

Sir Thomas died on 2 July 1900; he had asked before he died for his death not to be made public for three days. He was a shy and reserved man and hated big occasions celebrating the unveiling of his works. He wished to maintain that in death. His obituary in *The Irish Times* said he was a 'great genius, the successor of Foley and Hogan whose death left a gap which it would be hard to fill'.[121] The RHA held a meeting weeks after his burial in Glasnevin and expressed its sadness and frustration that his final wishes had prevented them from displaying publicly 'the honour and esteem in which they held him'.[122] He was described in 1864 as 'a most amiable and unassuming gentle man'.[123] The only place you will see his name in Glasnevin is on the side of his statue to Barry Sullivan.

Writers and Poets

Glasnevin houses its fair share of uncelebrated literary talent. Beneath an ornately decorated Celtic cross beside the Tolka River at the back of the cemetery, you will find the grave of Irish-language activist William Rooney. Some of his best remembered poems include 'The Men of the West', ''Ninety Eight', 'An tSean Bhean Bocht' and 'Wrap the Green Flag Round Me'. He worked closely with Arthur Griffith for most of his life and together on 25 November 1900 they founded Cumann na nGaedheal to act as an umbrella organisation to help better coordinate the activities of different nationalist bodies.[1] Central to his politics was language revivalism.[2] He died of typhoid fever at the young age of 27 on 6 May 1901. Today his headstone remembers his Celtic connections and devotion to the Irish language. In his brief life he became a formative influence on the revolutionary generation of 1916. He was held in such high regard that when Sinn Féin opened its headquarters at 6 Harcourt Street, it was a portrait of William Rooney that greeted people as they entered the main door.[3] Rooney's story is one of many that has not received the recognition it deserves.

Glasnevin Cemetery *c*. 1865–1914. (Reproduced courtesy of the National Library of Ireland)

The Mistress of the Macabre

Beneath another ornate Celtic cross in the Old Chapel Circle section (WA 51.5) close to the adjoining gates to the National Botanical Gardens lies another forgotten literary legacy. It is the final resting place of Lady Gilbert and her husband John T. Gilbert. She is better remembered as Rosa Mulholland and is one of the cemetery's most forgotten literary figures. In one of the many ghost stories written by her she said, 'The lonely graveyard is far away, an' the dead man is hard to raise.'[4] This is from her short story 'Not to Be Taken at Bed-Time' (1865). It is a good introduction to the woman who was known as the 'Mistress of the Macabre'.

Rosa was born in Belfast on 19 March 1841 to Dr Joseph Mulholland and Maria Coleman from Newry. She was privately educated and spent some time travelling in the west of Ireland, where she developed a love for the countryside, its superstitions, folklore and an understanding of the extreme poverty existing at the time.[5] She studied art in South Kensington, London, but ideas of becoming a painter were short-lived.

Charles Dickens greatly encouraged Rosa and published some of her work in his monthly magazine called *All the Year Around*. She became one of a select group of authors employed by Dickens to write stories for his popular magazine.[6] It was Dickens who published her first novel, *Dunmara* (1864), under the pseudonym 'Ruth Murray'.[7] He continued to encourage her up until his death in 1870. Other notable works by Rosa within his magazine included her 'Not to be Taken at Bed-Time' for the 1865 Christmas edition called *Doctor Marigold's Prescriptions*.[8] Her second and third novels – *Hester's History* (1869) and the *Wicked Woods of Tobereevil* (1872) – were also serialised in this same magazine. She wrote probably her best ghost stories for these magazines: 'The Ghost at the Rath' (14 April 1866) and her 'Haunted Organist of Hurly Burly' (19 November 1866).[9] Her novella *The Late Miss Hollingford* was later published by Dickens from 4 April to 2 May 1868. It was such a hit that it was immediately reprinted in a Tauchnitz (European publishers) edition.[10] The novella was published without her real name and for many years *The Late Miss Hollingford* was speculatively attributed to Charles Dickens and Wilkie Collins. This remained the case until 1886 when it was republished with her full name on the cover.[11] After Dickens' death she gradually began to drift away from London and back to Ireland.

The 1870s were productive for her. Her children's publications, highly sought-after today, were richly illustrated and are pieces of art in their own right. Her story 'The Little Flower Seekers: Being adventurers of Trot & Daisy in a Wonderful Garden by Moonlight' (1871) was illustrated by W.H. Frith, W. French and F.E. Hulme. The latter parts of the nineteenth century saw Rosa achieve great popularity and her works received high praise. She published over forty novels in a fifty-year writing career.[12]

Back in Ireland she became close friends with Fr Matthew Russell, SJ. He was the editor of the *Irish Monthly* magazine and as a result she became a regular contributor. His brother Francis, later Lord Russell of Killowen, was married to her elder sister Ellen Clare Mulholland, who was also a children's author.[13] In the *Irish Monthly* some of her most notable works included: 'The Strange Schooner' (June 1876), 'A Scrap of Irish Folklore' (December 1894) and 'The Girl Under the Lake' (August–December 1881). The plot of her story 'A Scrap of Irish Folklore' centred on a man who had returned from his grave with the ghosts of two children and who tried to kiss his widow. He left her with lips permanently blue and ice-cold. Her themes varied from those of the macabre to those of fantasy. At the same time she continued to write for *All the Year Around* with 'The Mystery of Ora' (1 July 1879), 'A Strange Love Story' (3 July 1882) and 'The Hungry Death' (1 July 1880).[14]

Both *Marcella Grace*, which had originally featured as a series in the *Irish Monthly*, and *A Fair Emigrant* dealt with the themes of emigration from Ireland to America. Shortly after they were published, Rosa married John T. Gilbert on 29 May 1891 at the Pro-Cathedral on Dublin's Marlborough Street. He was a famous historian who was knighted in 1897, and so she became better known as Lady Gilbert. They lived in Blackrock, County Dublin at his impressive house called 'Villa Nova'. It was filled with his unique collection of Irish historical and archaeological works.[15] During his own life he published some noted historical works. His *History of the City of Dublin* (1861) and a seven-volume *History of the Irish Confederation* (1882–91) are the most famous. The marriage sadly lasted only seven years. John died on 23 May 1898 aged 69 and was buried in the Old Chapel Circle section (WA 51.5). They had one son together, Henry, who died in infancy.

With her parents, husband and young child all dead, Rosa was left with just her siblings Ellen Cecilia and Clara as family after 1898. She went on to publish a two-volume biography of her husband in 1905 entitled *The Life of Sir John T. Gilbert: Irish Historian and Archivist* (1905). She also donated his massive collection of manuscripts to the City of Dublin Corporation.[16] She remained incredibly busy in the 1890s with over a dozen novels published by Blackie Novels, often featuring richly decorated covers. Some of these included her *Banshee Castle* (1895), *The O'Shaughnessy Girls* (1911), *Twin Sisters* (1911), *Fair Noreen* (1912), *The Daughter in Possession* (1915) and *Narcissa's Ring* (1916).[17] A sign of her status at the end of the nineteenth century is given by W.B. Yeats, who anthologised her works in 1891 with his *Representative Irish Tales.*[18] In some of her later novels, such as *The Return of Mary O'Morrough* (1908), she tried to acknowledge the new reality for small farmers in Ireland with the failure of conciliation with Britain after Parnell died and the Land Wars had come to a conclusion.[19] She also published three volumes of poetry in her lifetime.[20]

Her final years were spent at 'Villa Nova', where she died on 21 April 1921 aged 80. James H. Murphy summed her up as: 'the leading exponent of an upper-middle-class Catholic fiction which sought to modify the adverse image of Irish nationalism during the years of the land war and home rule crisis, and to promote the claims of its own class to national leadership'.[21] News of her death was covered widely. The *Irish Independent* reported on the 'passing of a gifted authoress'.[22] *The Freeman's Journal* led with the headline 'Distinguished Irish writer Passes Away'.[23] Her obituary in *The Irish Times* said:

> Always an indefatigable worker, she contributed largely to the lighter periodicals of the days, and her shorter tales, dealing for the most part with varied aspects of Irish social life, were favourably read with pleasure. All of these bore the stamp of clever workmanship, exhibiting moreover, a cultivated mind, a deep and sensitive nature, and a characteristic of purity of fancy ...[24]

She was buried alongside her husband in the Old Chapel Circle. In 2021, to remember her life, a publication was released with some of her works. It is called *Rosa Mulholland: Feminist, Victorian, Catholic and Patriot* (2021), published by Edward Everett Root and edited by James H. Murphy. On the anniversary of her death in April 2021, the publication was placed on the grave inside a plastic folder and was weighted down with some small stones. It was nice to know that someone had remembered Glasnevin's 'Mistress of the Macabre'.

'Dark Rosaleen'

A short walk away from Rosa Mulholland's grave in the Garden section (JB 34) lies Ireland's forgotten national poet, James Clarence Mangan. His grave is marked by a modest rectangular headstone inscribed with the final words of his poem 'Dark Rosaleen'. It was many years after his death that his uncle, Michael Smith of Copper-Alley, had the modest rectangular headstone placed over his grave. Sadly for the Mangan family, James' brother William, a cabinet-maker, only survived his elder brother by a couple of weeks and was buried in the adjoining grave.[25] William was the last of the Mangan family and all today lie in the Garden section of the cemetery.

James Clarence Mangan was born on Fishamble Street, Dublin, likely on 1 May 1803. A plaque can be found outside what is today F.X. Buckley's steakhouse to mark where his birthplace once stood beside Christ Church. A short walk to St Stephen's Green also reveals a bust of the poet by sculptor Oliver Sheppard. It was unveiled to remember Mangan in 1909. His father, a former schoolteacher also called James, ran a grocery business, which eventually went bankrupt. His mother was Catherine Smith. Her family owned farmland in County Meath as well as some commercial property in Dublin.[26] He was educated at the Jesuit school Saul's Court for a time before spells at other schools in Derby Square, Arran Quay and Chancery Lane, where he was taught Latin and several European languages. By the time he was 15 years old, he had attended three different schools before being forced to leave full-time education to help support his family. He worked in a scrivener's office called Kenrick's on York Street.[27]

A scrivener was traditionally a person who could read and write and usually provided secretarial and administrative duties, including dictation and keeping records. It was during this time that Mangan began to write and publish his own poems for two of the most popular almanacs of the day, *Grant's* and the *New Ladies*.[28] After ten years he left, and managed to live by just writing occasional pieces for magazines. His family left Fishamble Street and moved to Charlemont Street.[29] It was noted that they kept one servant and were on the move frequently. In his teenage years the family lived at a residence on Chancery Lane. This laneway, running from Bride Street to Golden Lane, would have been in the immediate locality of Mangan's birthplace.[30] He left a detailed description of what living there was like:

> It consisted of two wretched rooms, or rather holes, at the rear of a tottering old fragment of a house, or, if the reader please, hovel, in Chancery Lane. These dens, one of which was above the other, were mutually connected by means of a steep and almost perpendicular ladder, down which it was my fortune to receive many a tumble from time to time upon the sloppy earthen floor beneath ...[31]

By 1826 Mangan had become a legal copyist at Matthew Frank's offices in Merrion Square. He later described these years as the worst of his life and partly blamed them for his later abuse of alcohol.[32] It has often been speculated that Mangan was addicted to more than just alcohol. James Price, a long-time friend of the poet, was of the opinion that anyone who claimed to really know him would be aware that 'it was in his attempt to escape from the terrible drug which had obtained an almost complete mastery over his senses that he fell into the other habit, not less potent for evil, not less personally degrading. He conquered the opium fiend after a fierce ordeal of self-torture, but it is certain that his second state was worse than his first.'[33] A favourite pub of the poet's was the Bleeding Horse tavern on Camden Street. He enjoyed it there because it had a 'free and easy' feeling every evening.[34] Friends managed to find him employment for short periods in both Trinity College Library and the Ordnance Survey department and at the same time he submitted poems and prose to various Dublin publications. His contributions appeared in the *Dublin University Magazine*, and he wrote several pieces for the newly created *The Nation* newspaper. Sometimes he used the nom-de-plume 'the man in the cloak', and became one of Dublin's most mysterious characters.[35] The years 1826–31 were barren ones for Mangan.[36] He contributed no completed works for *The Nation* until 1846.[37] Nearly all of his contributions to that newspaper came in 1846 and included 'Dark Rosaleen', 'The Dream of John McDonnell', 'Siberia', 'A Cry for Ireland', 'A Vision of Connaught in the Thirteenth Century' and 'A Lament for Sir Maurice Fitzgerald'.[38]

The only collection of Mangan's poems to appear during his life was the *Anthologia Germanica*, a selection of some translations from German published in Dublin in 1845.[39] The greater part of his verse all appeared in different Dublin periodicals and magazines up until his death. According to D.J. O'Donoghue, the total number of his poems and translations amounts to 800–900 but only about half of these have ever been collected in book form.[40]

He produced translations of many German works by Schiller and Goethe. He could not speak Irish but used translations by Eugene O'Curry and John O'Donovan to write more nationalistic-themed works in his later literary career. O'Curry is buried in the South section of Glasnevin (KD 49), while John O'Donovan lies in a vault on the Old O'Connell Circle on Row D, Vault 21.5. Both men died within a year of each other and played a considerable part in influencing Mangan's work. O'Curry and O'Donovan's translations were used by Mangan to help produce versions of old Irish poems. The most notable example is his 'My Dark Rosaleen'. He wrote many of his poems to the memory of a mysterious 'Frances'. This was likely a reminiscence of a love that had gone wrong for him in his younger years.

Mangan's first translations from Irish appeared in the *Irish Penny Journal* between August 1840 and January 1841. These were 'The Woman of Three Cows', 'Lament for the Princes of Tyrone and Tyrconnell (Buried in Rome)', 'Kincora' and 'Kathleen Ní Houlihan.' He relied heavily on prose translations given to him by O'Curry. It had been suggested at the time that Mangan simply copied these translations for his own benefit. In letters to Thomas Davis, one of the founders of *The Nation* newspaper, however, O'Curry and O'Donovan both protested any such idea that Mangan had used their original translations for this purpose.[41] Between 1829 and 1838 Mangan was employed at Leland's solicitor's office on Fitzwilliam Square. During this time, he contributed to periodicals including George Petrie's *Dublin Penny Journal*, the infamous *Dublin Satirist*, the unionist *Irish Monthly Magazine* and also the nationalist *Vindicator*.[42] Between 1847 and 1849 he began to apply himself seriously to the study of the Irish language.[43]

Opium addiction came to take its toll on the poet. John Mitchel, a member of the newly created *Nation* newspaper and leading figure in the *Young Irelander* movement, chronicled his final years. He reflected on the man he observed: 'those who knew him … could do nothing for him; he would not dwell with man, or endure decent society; they could but look on with pity and wonder'.[44] Mitchel linked Mangan's poetry with his own later personal suffering to describe him as 'a type and shadow of the land he loved so well'.[45]

Having spent days in the Kilmainham fever sheds suffering from cholera, Mangan was eventually discovered in a state of severe malnutrition by Dr Wilde (the father of Oscar) during one of his antiquarian studies among Dublin's poorest districts.[46] He was admitted to the Meath Hospital where he died on 20 June 1849.[47] He was only 46 years old. Charles Gavan Duffy, founder of *The Nation*, described him as 'truly born to sing deathless songs as Keats or Shelley ... He was so purely a poet that he shrank from all other exercises of his intellect.'[48] Gavan Duffy had described the poet in his twenties and early thirties: 'He looked like the spectre of some German romance rather than a living creature.'[49] In contrast James Price, his close friend, ten years later, said:

> ... thin even to emaciation, and slightly stooped in the shoulders, like many men of studious habits and close application. In his dress, the eccentric city of his mind was outwardly displayed. His coat, a very little coat, tightly buttoned, was neither a frock coat, dress coat, morning coat, nor shooting coat, and yet seemed to partake of the fashioning of all four ... You could not laugh at that deathly pale and visibly dream-haunted man, whose thin, worn features spoke of unhealthy seclusion, close study and heart-weariness. You could not even laugh at the grisly moustache which, with a strange notion of he himself knew not what he clothed his upper lip. You could not; for in his eye, on his cheek, you must have read the struggle of genius with adverse circumstances; you must have felt that he was no ordinary man, singularly attired though he was, on whose wan face and attenuated form the band of death was visibly strengthening its grasp.[50]

In this you get a good sense of how quickly the poet deteriorated. Mangan was buried with his father, mother and brother John. According to C.P. Meehan, only three mourners attended the funeral.[51] There are few newspaper reports of it, except in *The Nenagh Guardian*. It made use of already published material from the *Dublin Evening Packet* and was written nearly four months later. It describes in great detail the final hours of the poet's life: 'The humblest coffin, the humblest hearse, then bear those poor remains to the pauper's grave. No cenotaph, no slab, no mound, marks the spot where "after life's fitful fever" sleeps one, the greatest fancy the most fertile in intellectual resources, the most original in genius that this age has produced ...'[52]

It is Mangan's semi-autobiographical *Nameless One* (likely published in 1842) that gives us his own poetic narrative of his life. He wrote:

Tell thou the world, when my bones lie whitening
Amid the last homes of youth and eld,
That there was once one whose blood ran lightning
No eye beheld.

In the decades following he assumed the status of Ireland's *poète maudit*. He was remembered as a person who had lived on the fringes of society while producing pieces of bleak and despairing work. Both Joyce and W.B. Yeats were admirers and saw in him the ideal of the tragic artist. International writers like Edgar Allen Poe and Herman Melville were also influenced by his works.[53] Some of his poems featured regularly in Irish school texts for much of the twentieth century.

As in life, his grave today remains on the fringes. D.J. O'Donoghue, one of his earliest biographers, reflected that 'Of no man of equal gifts and fame belonging to this nineteenth century is there so little recorded, and there is hardly another poet known in literature about whom so much mystery has been made …'[54]

Dora Sigerson Shorter: The Sacred Fire

Back at the main gates of the cemetery on the Finglas Road, you will come to Glasnevin's *Pieta* monument beside the cemetery office. It acts as a homage to the executed leaders of 1916. The *Pieta* in this monument, unlike Michelangelo's, depicts Mother Ireland embracing the dying figure of Patrick Pearse, his face veering off at an angle in his famed side pose in part of a volunteer uniform. The back of the monument features the poem 'The Sacred Fire' inscribed onto a bronze plaque:

They lit a fire within their Land
that long was ashes cold
With splendid dreams they made it glow,
threw in their hearts of gold.
They saw thy slowly paling cheek
And knew thy failing breath,
They bade thee live once more, Kathleen,
who wert so nigh to death.

> And who dare quench the sacred fire,
> and who dare give them blame,
> Since he who draws too near the glow
> shall break into a flame?
> They lit a beacon in their land,
> built of the souls of men,
> To make thee warm once more, Kathleen,
> To bid thee live again.

The poem was written by Dora Sigerson Shorter and the monument was designed and commissioned by the same woman. Today it is commonly referred to as the Sigerson Memorial. She raised funds for its erection through her poetry. Just weeks before her own death, she compiled a volume of poetry published posthumously in America in 1919 under the title *Sixteen Dead Men: And Other Poems of Easter Week*. The work was reissued in 1922 entitled *The Tricolour: Poems of the Irish Revolution*. The 1922 reissue can be viewed online. The editor's note at the beginning of the 1922 version tells the reader that:

> The publication of this book is a sacred obligation to one who broke her heart for Ireland. Dora Sigerson in her last few weeks of life, knowing full well that she was dying, designed every detail of this little volume, the dedication of the tricolour, and the order in which the poems were to be printed. Any profit that may arise from the sale of the book will be devoted, as are all the copyrights of the author, to a monument which she herself sculptured with a view to its erection over the graves of the 'Sixteen dead men' when circumstances place their ashes in Glasnevin.[55]

Sadly, she did not live to see her *Pieta* finished. The sculpted piece was originally unveiled in 1927 behind the Mortuary Chapel, nine years after her death.[56] It was only moved to its current position beside the front gates in 2007.[57] It now acts as a focal point for all remembrance services to those who died in 1916 and is an enduring legacy for the poet in the cemetery.

Dora was born on 16 August 1866 at 17 Richmond Hill, Rathmines. Her father was the noted physician and Gaelic scholar George Sigerson and her mother, Hester Varian, was a novelist. The family later lived at No. 3

Image of Sigerson monument to Patrick Pearse and his comrades from *The Tricolour* (Dublin: Maunsel and Roberts Ltd, 1922).

Clare Street. A plaque can be seen outside the building today, remembering her father's achievements. The Sigerson Cup, the main Gaelic football championship for higher educational institutions in Ireland, still uses the trophy given to the GAA by her father. Her parents' interests in both literature and the Celtic Revival instilled in Dora a strong passion for Irish nationalism. Hester and George were titans of the Celtic Revival. They regularly held salons at their home on Clare Street that were attended by the famed names of Yeats, Casement, MacDonagh and Pearse.[58]

She was the second of four children. Her siblings included Anna Hester (1870), George Patrick (1864), an infant brother William, who died before she was born, and her elder brother George Patrick, who died at the young age of just 36. As a child Dora developed a deep interest in art and sculpture. Poetry was not an immediate passion. It was from the many influences at her family home that she accumulated so much knowledge of art and literature. She showcased a literary talent from a young age and regularly contributed verses to newspapers and magazines such as *The Irish Monthly*, *United*

Ireland, The Pilot (Boston), Detroit Free Press, Young Ireland, Catholic Times, Derry Journal and *The Nation.*[59] She was to become a leading figure in the late Victorian literary revival, and Douglas Hyde was to become an admirer of her work.[60]

Both of her parents were highly active in the Irish Literary Revival movement of the late nineteenth century. As a result she became involved with contemporary political organisations such as the Pan-Celtic Society.[61] She supported Charles Stewart Parnell from an early age and was an advocate for Home Rule. Both W.B. Yeats and the important critic John O'Leary became her friends and advisors, and served as inspiration to the young poet.[62] Her first collection of poetry, called *Verses*, was published in 1893 when she was 27. This was followed by numerous volumes of poetry, four books of tales and sketches and two novels: *The Country-house Party* (1905) and *Do-well and Do-little* (1913).[63] Her *Collected Poems*, made up of 148 works, appeared in the year 1907. More patriotic poetry would follow later in her life.

In 1895 Dora married the critic and editor of *The Illustrated London News*, Clement King Shorter, and moved to London. She spent the rest of her life there. Her husband was the editor of the *Sphere* magazine from 1900 up until his death in 1926.[64] They had no recorded children. Through her marriage and relocation to London, she began to make friends with other noted literary figures of the time, including Thomas Hardy, George Meredith, Algernon Swinburne and Katharine Tynan.[65] George Meredith spoke about how 'she has the gift of metrical narrative', while Thomas Hardy wrote 'How She Went to Ireland' in remembrance of her death.[66] Her work today is often characterised within the nationalist arena. In her early years of writing, however, there is also a sense of the eerie, the Gothic and the macabre, with titles such as 'The Rape of the Baron's Wine', 'The Dead Wife' and 'The End of the World'.

Dora's mother Hester died in Dublin aged 69 in 1898. The family had her buried in the family vault in the Old O'Connell Circle Row E, Vault 28. Dora's brother, George Patrick, joined his mother three years later, on 1 July 1901. The years 1899 to 1902 saw Dora publish *My Lady's Slipper and Other Verse, The Father Confessor, Stories of Danger and Death* and *The Woman Who Went To Hell: And Other Ballads and Lyrics.* Other works include her short Irish mythological and macabre tales: 'The Ballad of the Little Black Hound', 'The Fairy Thorn Tree' and 'The Old Violin'. 'The Fairy Thorn Tree' tells the reader the story of a woman who tries to deal with the

Devil to claim back the body and soul of her long-lost love. These early works are polar opposites to her later nationalist publications. Dora knew some future leaders of the 1916 Rising from her childhood and nationalist themes became the dominant force in her work in the early twentieth century. Most notable were *Love of Ireland: Poems and Ballads* (1916) published for both general and private circulation, and *Sixteen Dead Men* (1919) published posthumously in America. Examples of poems in her *Love of Ireland* included 'The hill-side men', 'Conscription', 'The Choice', 'Sixteen Dead Men' and 'The Sacred Fire'.[67]

The events of 1916 were a massive shock to Dora; her poetry expresses her agony and heartbreak. Within *The Tricolour: Poems of the Irish Revolution* (1922) is the poem 'Sick I Am and Sorrowful', which depicts her mood after 1916 quite well and starts:

> Sick I am and sorrowful, how can I be well again
> Here, where fog and darkness is, and big guns boom all day,
> Practising for evil sport? If you speak humanity,
> Hatred comes into each face, and so you cease to pray.[68]

Along with her husband, Dora campaigned unsuccessfully to overturn Roger Casement's death sentence.[69] In her poem 'Sixteen Dead Men' she reflected on the executions of all the leaders from the rebellion, while 'The Choice' specifically honours Casement.[70] It was later stated by her husband and her friends that the heartbreak she suffered because of the failure of 1916 contributed to her death.[71] Although likely not the cause of her death, this has added to a sense that she had a 'romantic and supernatural bond' with her country.[72]

Dora died at her home at Marlborough Place, St John's Wood, London, on 6 January 1918. She was 46 years old. News of her death was widely reported and a death notice can even be found in the *Brooklyn Daily Eagle* newspaper in New York.[73] She wished to be buried in Ireland, so her remains were brought back to Dublin. *The Freeman's Journal* reported on the funeral on 9 January and said that the mourners included Mr and Mrs George Gavan Duffy, Mr and Mrs Darrell Figgis, Count Plunkett MP (father of executed Joseph Plunkett), Countess Plunkett, Mrs and Miss Pearse, Madame O'Rahilly, Madame MacBride (Maud Gonne) and Seán MacBride.[74] Éamon de Valera also attended the burial service in Glasnevin.[75] She was buried not

Portrait of Dora Sigerson (Mrs Shorter) (*c.* 1870–1918) by John Lavery, oil on canvas, 75 x 63cm. (Courtesy of the National Gallery of Ireland, presented by Mr C. Shorter, 1921, NGI.831)

in the family vault but close by, in the Old O'Connell Circle on Row F, Vault 34. Today her grave is unmarked and not many people know she is buried in the cemetery.

The Sigerson family story came to an end with the death of Dora's father, George, on 17 February 1925. He was 89 years old and was acting as a senator in the newly formed Irish Free State. He was buried in the family vault with his wife and two sons. Meanwhile Dora lies a few metres away. The reason she was buried in a separate vault perhaps has something to do with remaining space in the main vault and a wish for her parents to be laid to rest together when they died. The words of one of her critics, William Archer, in remembering her work, said:

> There is race in her work; it smacks of the soil; it is no mere imitative culture-product but an expression of innate emotion and impulse. Mrs Shorter has all the fanciful melancholy, the ardent spirituality, and the eerie pathetic invention of the western Celts. The unseen world of semi-malignant elemental beings is quite as real to her as the tangible world of her five senses. Her imagination is nourished on folklore, and even Christian conceptions of life and death she instinctively translates into terms of that ancient and exquisite paganism which seems like a natural emanation from the green hills and rushing waters of Ireland. All the characteristics of the Celtic Spirit are exemplified in Mrs Shorter's poetry.[76]

A portrait of Dora by the artist John Lavery, commissioned in 1919 after her death, was presented to her husband Clement Shorter in 1921. It is held by the National Gallery of Ireland. Trinity College Dublin holds much of her published material in their Early Printed Books and Special Collections, while their Manuscripts and Archives Research Library holds several manuscript notebooks, sketches and typescripts of her work.[77]

The Mammy of Irish Cookery

On the Yew Tree pathway in the Dublin New Chapel section (EF 24), close to where Arthur Griffith is buried, a small, weathered headstone reads simply 'Maura Laverty 15th May 1907 to 21st July 1966'. Her son James was later buried in the same grave in 1974 and his name also features on the base of the memorial. There is no trace of her literary talents.

Mary Kelly (her birth name) was born in Rathangan in County Kildare on 15 May 1907. She was the third of nine surviving children of Michael Kelly and his wife, Mary Anne Treacy. Her father married late in life, at 57, and had thirteen children in total. Once a farmer with a sizeable 200-acre site, he later set up a drapery shop but was an unsuccessful businessman. He ran into financial troubles and eventually lost the farm. This loss, coupled with bad gambling habits, resulted in hard times for the family. It was Mary Anne who managed to maintain the family by dressmaking.[78]

Michael died from cancer while in hospital in Dublin on 2 March 1921.[79] Maura was just 14 years old at the time. In her semi-autobiographical work *Never No More* (1942), in which the character Delia Scully acts as her alter ego, she made reference to these early years. She specifically referred to 'five bewildering miserable years' before her father's death. He was buried in her home parish of Rathangan and today Maura's family are all buried in that grave.[80]

Maura went to the local national school in Rathangan before attending the Brigidine convent in Tullow County Carlow.[81] As a child she was extremely close to her maternal grandmother. It was with her that she spent much of her childhood and developed her interest in cookery.[82] The death of her grandmother ended her early ambitions of becoming a teacher and instead she decided to leave Ireland for Spain in 1924.

In Spain she worked briefly as a governess before becoming a secretary and a journalist on the Madrid Catholic paper *El Debate*.[83] She got engaged to a Hungarian engineer she had met while working for the newspaper. Before her wedding, she came home to Ireland. It was on this trip home that she was to meet James (Seamus) Laverty. He was an athletics coach to the Defence Forces and later became a journalist. In a storyline like something from a television soap drama, she married him almost immediately, on 3 November 1928, at the Church of St Patrick's in Rathangan. She returned to Spain briefly, where she continued to pursue her journalistic career. During that time, she kept busy sending articles, poems and stories to Irish magazines. She even worked as a freelance correspondent for Irish newspapers, translating Spanish headlines into English.[84] Notably, in Ireland she wrote for the women's magazine *Woman's Life*, often writing under the name of Mrs Wyse, an agony aunt who tried to answer women's problems in 1930s' Ireland.[85]

She had three children with Seamus: two daughters, Maeve (1931) and Margaret Finbarr, nicknamed Barrie (1935), and a son James born in 1948, who became the famous artist 'Barry Castle'.[86] When Maura began to write fiction in the early 1940s, it was her childhood that provided inspiration. Her experiences of growing up in rural County Kildare allowed her to showcase accurate depictions of country characters. She knew what it was like to go from a comfortably well-off lifestyle to a very poor one. Her grandmother was later immortalised as Delia Sally in her first novel *Never No More* in 1942. Her second followed, *Touched by a Thorn* (1943), which was also published under the titles *Alone We Embark* and *No More Than Human* (1944). This second novel was originally banned by the Irish censor, but it went on to win the Irish Women's Writer's Award.[87]

By 1928 Maura had decided to settle fully in Ireland. She took up her new job as a journalist and broadcaster with the newly established 2RN (later becoming Radio Éireann in 1937). It was an exciting time in her life. Writing as a career only truly began to take off for Maura after her husband experienced a failed business venture with the Irish Sweepstakes.[88] Her marriage eventually failed – a combination of financial difficulties and Maura's dedication to her work were the two main factors. In his later life, Seamus moved back to his native County Antrim, where he worked for various newspapers in Belfast. He died in June 1967 and his death was reported in the *Irish Independent*: 'Mr Seamus Laverty, the well-known journalist has died in Belfast.'[89]

Maura's work continued with 2RN, where she was put in charge of women's and children's programmes.[90] She broadcast on female issues of the time, such as cooking, domestic economy and household tips. She also played the role of the station's agony aunt. Through this work, she forged an impressive career as a well-known cookery writer. In 1941 during the 'Emergency', she was commissioned by the government to write *Flour Economy* (1941) for housewives dealing with wartime shortages. Other cookery books she published included *Kind Cooking* (1946). This had illustrations by the famed artist Louis le Brocquy. It was chosen as the Irish non-fiction 'book of the month' in America.[91] Her most famous cookery book, however, was *Full and Plenty* (1960). It was enormously popular with the Irish public. The book was made up of over 100 Irish recipes and ran to 500 pages. It included everything from wholemeal brown bread, fruit scones, lamb stew to beef pot-roast and roast chicken. It became a definitive reference book for every Irish kitchen.

Her final novel, *Lift Up Your Gates* (1946), took inspiration from her time living in Fitzwilliam Lane to highlight the high levels of extreme poverty in these environments.[92] It was ultimately banned by Ireland's Censorship of Publications Board.[93] Two years later she began working with the Irish political party Clann na Poblachta in their campaign for the 1948 general election.[94] Although her work was never overtly political, she produced a film on a similar theme for the party that highlighted what urban life was like for those stuck in the tenements of Dublin. Other subject matter in the video was the ongoing issue of tuberculosis for many in Ireland, long dole queues and the State's inability to deal with the high levels of extreme poverty.

Her mother, Mary Ann Treacy, died on 12 February 1944. She was buried in the old graveyard in Rathangan.[95] It was a sad time for Maura, despite the fact that her career as a radio personality and literary figure was taking shape. In an undated piece she wrote that 'my mother, who was dependent on us, got a stroke from which she died'.[96] Shortly after her mother's death, Maura was appointed as president of the Women's Writers Club.[97] *Lift Up Your Gates* was later adapted for the stage and renamed *Liffey Lane* (1951). Both Micheál MacLíammóir and Hilton Edwards, who had previously written to Maura in the 1940s, were the instigators behind this shift from novels to plays for Maura. As a play on the Gate Theatre stage, *Liffey Lane* was less likely to be banned than her novels. Two more plays followed: *Tolka Row* (1951) and *A Tree in the Crescent* (1952). It was *Tolka Row* that was to become her biggest success. It was adapted to become RTÉ's first ever soap drama. The soap began broadcasting in 1964 with a half-hour programme once a week.

Her plays at the Gate gave the theatre some much-needed box-office success at a time when its future was uncertain. The *Irish Independent* in 1951, under the heading 'Another intimate study of Dublin life', praised Maura and said, 'In her new play, *Tolka Row* ... Maura Laverty has added another corner to her glowingly original tapestry of Dublin Life ...'[98] Maura's plays for the Gate drew comparisons from many critics with the playwright Seán O'Casey.[99] *The Irish Press* stated on 5 November 1951 that the play 'is the voice of Dublin at the moment and it may be said that Mrs Laverty is the only authentic Dublin voice since O'Casey'.[100] Its themes took the form of a social commentary of Ireland in the 1950s.

Her plays acted as a vehicle for Laverty to discuss taboo subjects including birth control, a subject rarely spoken about in Ireland at the time. *Liffey Lane* featured passages unafraid to discuss these topics.[101] At a time when censorship would have banned such discourse in literature, it was through the medium of live theatre that Maura was able to exercise her voice. Among those who came to see *Liffey Lane* was the famed film actor Orson Welles. He attended on the night of 18 December 1951. He was no stranger to that theatre, having trodden its boards in his early theatrical career in 1931.[102] Between 1947 and 1953 the BBC began to serialise some of Maura's works for radio. On 2 November 1957 her *Tolka Row* was broadcast on the BBC's Radio 4 *Saturday Night Theatre* show.[103]

Maura wrote all the episodes of her adapted *Tolka Row* for the television screen single-handedly up until her death in 1966. As the first Irish television soap opera, its portrayal of the urban working class became very important.

The State in this period had a preoccupation with depicting a largely rural culture. It became a way for ordinary people around the country to begin introducing themselves to how the other half lived. Her hard work in writing all the scripts for *Tolka Row* meant she had a steady income for the rest of her life. She purchased a house in Rathfarnham on Butterfield Drive and it was there that she spent the final years of her life alone.

Maura died in July 1966, just two months after the 100th episode of *Tolka Row* aired. She was 63 years old. Her recorded cause of death is as a result of a heart attack. There is uncertainty about the precise date she died, as her body was not discovered for several days. Her hard-working writing lifestyle was the reason her body lay undiscovered.[104] She had in fact been falling behind on deadlines for scripts and trying to catch up with them. On her desk were found radio scripts completed two months in advance up to August 1966.[105] *The Irish Times*, in her obituary on 28 July 1966, wrote that 'she got to know the life of Dublin's poor and she wrote about the slums in her fourth novel ...'[106]

Her death was widely reported in the *Irish Independent*, *The Irish Press* and the *Irish Farmers Journal*. It was also reported in *The Times* of London on 28 July. Her funeral to Glasnevin took place on 29 July. A trip to Rathangan reveals a flowerbed that memorialises its famous writers; Maura Laverty is one of them. No other memorial to this talented writer exists. In 2017 Seamus Kelly published his *The Maura Laverty Story from Rathangan to Tolka Row*. Without his work I would not have become as aware of her forgotten legacy as I am today. He states that she has had 'a good press, indeed a "Full and Plenty" press in more recent years, mostly in relation to her cookery books ...'[107] Her papers are held in the National Library of Ireland and can be viewed upon special request and even contain her passport.[108]

Maura Laverty's many achievements as writer, broadcaster, radio producer, script writer and culinary personality are deserving of our respect. She was a household name. Her novels were published at a time when censorship and the discussion of taboo subjects were highly controversial. Her work from 1942–52 was nothing short of prolific, and the way in which she was found dead speaks volumes to her work ethic and commitment to screenwriting. Next time you find yourself strolling along the yew tree pathway in Glasnevin and you come to the grave of Arthur Griffith, stop and take a look along the row of graves behind his unfinished colonnade and you will see the final resting place of the 'Mammy of Irish Cookery'.[109]

Religious Figures

Ready. Present. Fire: Fr Eugene MacCarthy

James Connolly was the last leader of the Rising executed in Kilmainham Gaol in the early hours of 12 May 1916. He entered the stonebreaker's yard blindfolded on a stretcher. Connolly's execution was arranged to take place at the opposite end of the yard to where the others had taken place because of his injuries. His leg was badly wounded during the week of fighting close to the GPO. Lorcan Collins tells us that: 'Connolly … unable to stand unaided, was placed in a chair wearing only his pyjamas. His head lolling backwards; the injection of morphine, which had been administered by the military doctor, affected his senses.'[1] Ready. Present. Fire.

Fr Eugene MacCarthy was present for the execution of Connolly. He 'went over and anointed Connolly' according to the Capuchin Fr Aloysius, who was also present at the execution.[2] The sacristan of St James' at the time, Hubert O'Keeffe, penned a small memoir that recalled these events and his words were quoted during the 150th anniversary of the parish: 'Fr Eugene McCarthy officially attended at each execution being taken from bed each morning at 4am. The prisoners having been placed against the wall and the

---

An aerial shot of the cemetery taken in 2019. (© Warren Farrell)

firing party having fired, his duty was to anoint the body where it fell.'[3] For Fr MacCarthy the executions of 1916 left a strong imprint on his mind:

> In giving a description of James Connolly's execution Fr McCarthy told me that the prisoner, who was in a bad condition, elected to stand like the rest but failed. He was then tied to a chair but slumped so much that he overbalanced. Finally he was strapped to a stretcher [*sic*] and placed in a reclining position against the wall. The sight left an indelible impression on Fr McCarthy. Describing the scene to me afterwards he said: 'The blood spurted in the form of a fountain from the body, several streams shooting high into the air.'[4]

Robert Barton, a member of the Provost Marshals staff, on talking to Major Harold Heathcote of the 6/7 Sherwood Foresters said:

> [Connolly] was lifted into a chair where he sat in an extended position with his head falling backwards ... Heathcote previously arranged with two of the firing party to aim at Connolly's head. Both shots took effect penetrating at each side of his nose, the remainder entered his chest with the exception of one which entered his abdomen. He died without a movement but, unlike any of the other prisoners, he bled quite a deal. The back of the chair on which he sat was shattered by the volley, a piece being blown out of the top of it.[5]

Fr MacCarthy was born in Scotland in the parish of Paisley outside Glasgow on 20 December 1863 to Rundal (Randal) MacCarthy and his wife, Bessie (Elizabeth) Ginnane. He was baptised on 29 December 1863 in the church of St Mirin's. By 1901 he had made his way to Dublin and lived in a house at 7 Lower Exchange Street, a parochial house in the parish of St John. On the night the 1911 census was recorded, he was visiting the address of 10 Echlin Street at Usher Quay. Head of that house was Patrick Fee. He was in the company of two others: Christopher Flood and Edward Morrissey. Morrissey was another chaplain who would later be present in Kilmainham during the executions.

As fighting broke out across Dublin on Easter Monday 1916, Fr MacCarthy would have heard the shots from nearby South Dublin Union (today St James's Hospital) as the rebels under the command of Éamonn

Ceannt fought to keep control of the workhouse and prevent British Army reinforcements making their way into the city. He later became part of a wider network of priests from the parish of St James and friars from the Capuchin community of the Church Street area who would stay with the leaders in Kilmainham until the very end. [6] Fr Aloysius Travers, Fr Patrick Browne and Fr Augustine Hayden all stayed close to the men's prison cells and gave them absolution and council. Others delivered letters and final messages to the prisoners' loved ones. Fr MacCarthy, as one of the prison chaplains, gave holy communion and last confessions to some of the leaders in their cells, visited others in their final moments and stood in the yard to watch as they made their last journey to face the firing squad.

His last important act was to anoint their dead bodies. Patrick Pearse, Thomas MacDonagh and Thomas Joseph Clarke were the first three that he watched. He was not the only prison chaplain present. He was with another priest from the area, Fr Edward Morrisey. These executions took place on the morning of 3 May 1916 before 4.15 a.m.[7] The prisoners did not receive the last rites of the Catholic Church because of the express orders of the gaol commandant, W.S. Lennon. Protests were led by Fr Aloysius Travers and consequently the rest of the leaders executed were given the last rites.[8] The bodies of Pearse, MacDonagh and Clarke were taken to Arbour Hill and buried together in a mass grave. The chaplain at Arbour Hill, Fr Francis Harrington, was given the task of overseeing the burial services. He accounted that they arrived 'in pools of blood, still warm and limp, eyes bandaged and mouths open'.

On 4 May, Edward (Ned) Daly, William Pearse, the brother of Patrick, Michael O'Hanrahan and Joseph Mary Plunkett were executed. Significantly, the night before their deaths, Plunkett was permitted to marry his fiancée, Grace Gifford, in the Catholic chapel of the prison. Grace had seen in the newspaper that the first three executions had been carried out. One of them, Thomas MacDonagh, was her brother-in-law. The arrangements for the wedding were hastily put together. A British non-commissioned officer, Sergeant Desborough, recorded that he was given the order to deliver a message to the commandant of the prison from Richmond Barracks. The contents of the message: 'Yes tonight. The lady in question may take her own priest and he must be recognised by the prison chaplain who must assist.'[9]

The priest who presided over the ceremony was Fr Eugene MacCarthy. Grace had agreed that he should carry out the ceremony. She was led into the chapel in the gaol. There, Joseph's handcuffs were removed and MacCarthy carried out the brief ceremony with two soldiers present acting as witnesses by candlelight. The gas supply had failed due to the damage caused to the city. There was no kissing permitted and no conversation. Grace later in life reflected that she was 'never left alone with him … not for a minute'.[10] In an account of the marriage given by Grace's sister Sidney Czira, née Gifford (her pseudonym as a journalist was John Brennan), she recalled:

> At 6 o'clock that evening she was summoned to the Gaol. For two hours she walked up and down, alone, in a prison yard, while Joe, she was told, waited in a cell. At 8 o'clock she was taken to the prison chapel, and, as she entered, her fiancé was led in by a party of soldiers with fixed bayonets. The soldiers remained in the chapel, while, at the altar, Father Eugene MacCarthy, the prison chaplain, read the marriage service by the light of a candle (the gas supply having failed). Two soldier witnesses shifted their rifles from hand to hand as they assisted at the ceremony. Immediately afterwards the newly married couple were separated. Grace was taken to lodgings found for her by Father MacCarthy in Thomas Street and Joe was escorted back to his cell.[11]

Fr MacCarthy had arranged the temporary lodgings for Grace to be as close to the prison as possible on nearby Thomas Street. Four hours later a letter arrived for Grace from the commandant of the gaol giving her permission to visit her husband in his prison cell. She was taken to cell number 88 on the top landing of the prison compound and was permitted ten final minutes with Joseph. An armed guard stood outside with a watch to count down the seconds.[12]

Fr Augustine and other Capuchin friars spent time with Joseph in his final hours. Fr Sebastian, another friar from Church Street, recorded: 'His face reminded me of St Francis … no fine talk, no heroics … a distinguished tranquillity that came from his nobility of soul and his faith.'[13] He was executed after Michael O'Hanrahan between 4 and 4.30 a.m. on the morning of 4 May 1916. Fr MacCarthy walked to his lifeless body and anointed him. John MacBride was executed on 5 May. He was attended to by Fr Augustine Hayden in his final hours. *The Irish Times* poignantly listed the marriage in its births, marriages and death column on 6 May 1916, two days after Plunkett's execution.[14]

The priest who anointed John MacBride was Fr MacCarthy. Con Colbert, Seán Heuston, Éamonn Ceannt and Michael Mallin were next to be executed. Ceannt was anointed by Fr Augustine following execution, not by Fr MacCarthy. An account left by Fr Augustine recalls him saying to Ceannt, 'When you fall, I will run out and anoint you.' Ceannt replied, 'Oh, that will be a grand consolation.'[15] Fr MacCarthy spent a good deal of time with Mallin in his cell and gave him his last confession. Before his execution, Mallin was visited by his wife, Agnes, his sons, James, John and Joseph, his daughter, Una, his brothers, Thomas and Bartholomew, his sister, Katie, and his mother, Sarah. Mallin, in his final letter, named Fr MacCarthy as someone his wife should seek out: 'Father MacCarthy has just been in with me and heard my Confession and made me so happy and contented. He will see to the Education and general welfare of our dear ones; you must go and see him my darling, Fr McCarthy James St, God Bless him …'[16]

Seán Mac Diarmada and James Connolly were the last to be executed, on 12 May. Mac Diarmada was attended to by Fr MacCarthy at about 3 a.m. on the morning of 12 May and the priest listened to his last confession.[17] Mac Diarmada was led to the stonebreaker's yard a few minutes before 3.45 a.m. and executed by firing squad. Fr MacCarthy anointed his body. He later gave Seán's final words to Min Ryan (his fiancée):

> I go to my death for Ireland's cause as fearlessly as I have worked for that sacred cause during all my short life. I have asked the Reverend Eugene MacCarthy, who has prepared me to meet my God, and who has given me courage to undergo this ordeal, to convey this message to my fellow countrymen. God Save Ireland. Seán MacDiarmada, Kilmainham Prison, 12 May 1916.[18]

Throughout the War of Independence and the Civil War that followed, Fr MacCarthy continued his work in the parish of St James in Dublin. His last known address is the Presbytery in Arran Quay in 1930. He had been witness to one of the most defining episodes in Irish history and had played a role in creating stories that are told and sung to this day. He died on 27 October 1930, aged 64. His cause of death is given as 'apoplexy' or stroke. His funeral mass took place in St Paul's church on Arran Quay at 11 a.m. and the archbishop presided over the service.[19] He was buried on the afternoon of 31 October at 1.25 p.m. in the South section of the cemetery (BA 68). The grave had originally been purchased for the burial of his father, Randal, in 1908, who had worked as a civil servant in Dublin. His mother is also buried in this grave. She died in 1918 aged 75.

The presence of people like Eugene MacCarthy in Kilmainham Gaol during the executions of 1916 was very significant. As Brian Barton puts it, 'ultimately they helped influence popular perceptions of the Rising itself, by later providing some of the most graphic accounts of the final hours of the condemned men'.[20]

Priest, Republican and Inventor

There are countless other significant but forgotten religious figures buried in Glasnevin including Fr Michael O'Flanagan (1876–1942), the parish priest and prominent republican activist. He first came to national attention on 1 August 1915 when he led the funeral prayers at the graveside of Jeremiah O'Donovan Rossa at Glasnevin alongside his friend Patrick Pearse. The previous evening, he had given an oration in Dublin's City Hall on Rossa's life, but this was overshadowed by Pearse's subsequent fiery graveside oration at the cemetery.[21] Many of those present at the funeral would go on to become household names in the years following revolution and Civil War, but Fr O'Flanagan has been largely forgotten by historians since his death in 1942.

Born on 13 August 1876, at Kilkeevan, near Castlerea, County Roscommon, his parents were Edward Flanagan, a small farmer, and his wife, Mary Crawley. Both parents were bilingual, speaking English and Irish, and both of his parents' families were active in the Fenian movement and the Land League.[22] After an education at Cloonboniffe national school, Summerhill College in Sligo (1890–94), and St Patrick's College, Maynooth (1894–1900) he worked as professor of Irish at Summerhill between 1900 and 1904. He was selected to travel to America on a fundraising mission and there he established himself as a talented orator and preacher. Returning in 1910, he joined Sinn Féin and was elected to the Executive Committee of the Gaelic League, who sent him back to the USA on another fundraising mission. In both 1912 and 1914 he was invited to preach at a selection of churches in Rome.[23]

In August 1914 O'Flanagan was transferred to the parish of Cliffoney in Sligo where he engaged in the local economic and social issues there. Cliffoney was his first rural posting after many years of travelling and fundraising.[24] He repeatedly called on the government to engage in land redistribution there and to increase food production, while denouncing the exportation of food from Ireland owing to the risk of a new famine. He also led a local protest which secured his parishioners' rights to cut turf on the local bogs.[25] Despite local protests, which included locking the village church for ten weeks, he was transferred to Crossna, County Roscommon in October 1915 by the conservative Bishop Coyne. The bishop was upset by O'Flanagan's many public speeches and appearances, and his separatist-inclined attitudes.

Fr Michael O'Flanagan standing in the back pictured with (seated left to right) Mrs Mary O'Donovan Rossa, Eileen O'Donovan Rossa and Thomas Clarke in 1915. (Reproduced courtesy of the National Library of Ireland)

O'Flanagan became a driving force for Sinn Féin as a political entity during the by-elections of 1917.[26] He organised the campaign for Count George Noble Plunkett in January 1917, which was the first electoral victory for Sinn Féin. This made him a very well-known figure in the republican movement and he was elected joint vice-president of the newly consolidated party at the end of the Ard-Fheis that October.[27] Because of his republican and political activities, he was suspended by Bishop Coyne in the summer of 1917 and again in May 1918.[28] These censures did not stop him taking an active part in the general election of 1918, when he was the main platform speaker during a series of nationwide rallies in support of Sinn Féin. When the first Dáil met in the Mansion House on 21 January 1919, O'Flanagan was invited to recite the opening prayers for the assembly and was appointed as chaplain.[29]

When de Valera set off for America, O'Flanagan became the unofficial acting president of Sinn Féin. He caused outrage within the party when he sent a telegram to British Prime Minister David Lloyd George in response to his offer of exploratory peace talks. In it he asked the prime minister to lay out his proposals and to meet with him and the unionist leader Edward Carson. For many in the republican movement this was beyond his brief.[30]

He rejected the Anglo-Irish Treaty, which was signed while he was on a fundraising tour in America and Australia. He remained out of Ireland until 1925, when he was recalled to participate in a series of by-elections for Sinn Féin, which resulted in another clerical suspension.[31] He actively opposed de Valera's move in 1926 to leave Sinn Féin and establish Fianna Fáil. In 1933 he was elected president of Sinn Féin and held that position for two years until forced to resign due to a controversy surrounding his acceptance of an appointment for a Place Names Commission with Fianna Fáil.[32] He was later fully expelled from the party for an appearance in a re-enactment of the opening of the first Dáil on the State-run radio service.[33] Later in life he reconnected with the Sinn Féin party.

O'Flanagan was a critic of the Irish fascist movement, the 'Blueshirts', under Eoin O'Duffy in Ireland. He supported and raised funds for the republican forces in the Spanish Civil War fighting against General Franco, despite much backlash from the Catholic Church for his views. He went to Barcelona to show his support for republicans there and believed in the rights of workers and small farmers from Spain.[34] His views in support of the Republic in Spain, against O'Duffy in Ireland, and his support for

Advertisement for Fr O'Flanagan's swimming googles in the *Catholic Bulletin*, July 1928.

the separation of powers between Church and State did nothing for his reputation with his clerical superiors. By 1939, however, he was reinstated as a parish priest after negotiations with the Bishop of Elphin. He retired to Dublin where he acted as a chaplain at two convents and a hospital.

Aside from his political activism throughout his life, O'Flanagan was also an inventor. Most famously, he is known as the inventor of the swimming goggles, which he patented in July 1926 in the USA.[35] He managed to make some extra income from selling them from his home in Bray, County Wicklow, at 7 Sydenham Villas, for seven shillings and sixpence per set.[36] In the *Catholic Bulletin* of July 1928, an advertisement for his patented goggles can be seen proudly proclaiming 'surround your eyes with airtight chambers'.[37] He got the idea while experimenting in a glass-bottomed boat while in Sligo in 1914 and many years later, amidst his busy political career, he developed the idea further while travelling in America. An article in *The Irish Press* from 1932 reported on his invention: 'Seeing under water, the story of an Irish Priest's Invention, Hidden Beauties.'[38]

O'Flanagan died on 7 August 1942 in a Dublin nursing home, a week before his 66th birthday, due to stomach cancer. He was given a State funeral with a requiem mass at the Franciscan church on Merchant's Quay and was buried metres away from where he had said prayers by the grave of O'Donovan Rossa twenty-seven years earlier in the South New Chapel section (TD 22). Taoiseach Éamon de Valera, Tánaiste Seán T. O'Kelly, Seán MacEntee, Frank Aiken, Gerry Boland and Oscar Traynor were all in attendance.[39] Jim MacEoin reflected on the life of Fr O'Flanagan and said:

> He was I think the best open-air orator of his time. He possessed a deep, resonant voice, with a pleasant rolling Western quality, and he had, in addition, a fund of native humour that never failed him … In conversation he was the soul of wit and good humour. He had fought and suffered but he had not grown embittered. To the end he preserved the ideals of his youth and he recognised that no matter what differences had arisen or what setbacks had been encountered, much that he had striven for had been obtained.[40]

Since his death he has been all but forgotten. In recent years great work has been undertaken by the Fr Michael O'Flanagan Memorial Group in Cliffoney

OKLAHOMA CITY, OKLA., FRIDAY, MAY 7, 1937.

SPEAKS FOR SPANISH AID

Father Michael O'Flanagan, one-time Sinn Fein vice-president, who is touring the U. S. to plead for medical aid for Basque Catholics and other Spanish loyalists under the auspices of the Medical Bureau to Aid Spanish Democracy, 381 Fourth Ave., New York City. "There will be more of the spirit of religion in Spain if democratic government is established over the entire country," the priest says. He is shown wearing special glasses he invented to protect divers' eyes.

Image of Fr O'Flanagan during a fundraising tour of the USA in 1937 to support those fighting against Franco in the Spanish Civil War. He is pictured wearing his famed swimming goggles. (Picture from the *Oklahoma City, Okla.*, 7.5.1937)

to reclaim this extraordinary man's life. A new headstone was unveiled on his grave in 2019 by the National Graves Association and Martin Byrne, who has created the Fr Michael O'Flanagan historical website, played the uilleann pipes at his graveside during the ceremony.

Spratt and St Valentine

Beside the steps leading down to the vault of Daniel O'Connell is the final resting place of Dubliner and Carmelite priest John Francis Spratt (1796–1871). His biographer, Fergus D'Arcy, contends that he has been completely overlooked in modern histories of nineteenth-century Dublin and Ireland.[41] He was baptised on 5 January at St Catherine's church in Dublin. His parents were James Spratt and Elizabeth Bollard. Following a period in Spain, he was received into the Carmelite order in December 1816, before completing his noviciate as a member of the Carmelite province of Castille and being ordained on 26 February 1820.[42]

Spratt later joined the community of Calced Carmelites on Cuffe Lane beside French Street in Dublin and established a school in Longford Street.[43] He also acquired a site on Whitefriar Street and it is largely through his work that today you can visit Our Lady of Mount Carmel's Carmelite church (commonly known as Whitefriar Street church).[44] Designed by John Papworth, it was completed in 1826 and consecrated a year later. As the church's first prior, he travelled to Rome in 1835 and Pope Gregory XVI was so affected by his words that he decided to send the Carmelite priest a gift to the church at Whitefriar Street – the remains of St Valentine, who had been buried in the cemetery of St Hippolytus in Rome. The remains arrived in Dublin on 10 November 1836 and were placed under the altar of Whitefriars.[45] As they arrived they were met at the front gates of the church by forty robed priests and Archbishop Murray.[46] According to legend, St Valentine was a Christian martyr who lived during the third century AD in Rome. He was known for his compassion, performing secret marriages for young couples during a time when marriage was forbidden by the Roman Emperor Claudius II. St Valentine's actions were discovered and he was imprisoned and eventually executed on 14 February, which later became St Valentine's Day.

While the story of St Valentine's remains coming to Dublin and their connection with Fr John Spratt is widely accepted and rightly celebrated, it is important to note that the historical authenticity of the relics themselves has been a subject of debate. Nonetheless, the story and its significance hold a special place in the hearts of many who visit the Whitefriar Street Carmelite church seeking inspiration and blessings in matters of the heart. Today the church continues to be a popular destination for visitors seeking to pay homage to St Valentine, and some even propose next to the relics. Spratt also purchased a wooden statue of the Virgin. This was later proven to be of late medieval origin and with both these relics inside the church it became a popular pilgrimage site in Ireland.

It is, however, for his many philanthropic works that Spratt is best remembered today. He founded St Peter's orphanage and the free schools at Whitefriar Street in 1860. He also established the Catholic Asylum for the Female Blind and founded St Joseph's Night Refuge for women and children.[47] Spratt was heavily involved in the temperance movement, founded the French Street Temperance Society and was closely aligned to Fr Mathew.[48] During the Famine he organised an interdenominational relief committee, was heavily involved politically with O'Connell's Emancipation and Repeal campaigns and was vocal in support of tenant farmers.[49]

In 1871 he began to suffer from ill health and his doctors advised that he take alcohol to ease the pain, but he refused. On 27 May 1871, while he was administering the total abstinence pledge, he died aged 75 of a sudden heart attack at Whitefriar Street Carmelite church. Many things he achieved lived on, including his St Peter's school and shrine to St Valentine, but according to his biographer he is 'hardly remembered today beyond the confines of the Carmelites'.[50] Originally, he was buried in the Garden section in the Carmelite plot but was later moved on 15 October 1873 to the O'Connell Tower Circle (A 1). His brother, Fr James Spratt, was later buried in the same plot, on 9 June 1879. John Francis Spratt was buried next to his hero Daniel O'Connell and an impressive four-sided bas-relief Celtic cross marks his final resting place. The headstone includes a detailed description of his achievements in life and the side panels depict his many legacies left behind for his beloved Dublin. Certainly one of the most politically active priests of the nineteenth century in Ireland, his legacy is overlooked today. John Spratt, according to D'Arcy, 'deserved better of his city and his country'.[51]

Conflict, Revolution and War

A Long Train of Suffering: The Napoleonic Wars

The cemetery has links to many major conflicts, dating back to the Battle of Waterloo in 1815. It is a place that can remember conflict through multiple narratives and at times conflicting perspectives. It is not possible to recall all those buried in the cemetery who died due to conflict in a single chapter. In the Curran Square section (J 35) close to the old entrance gates, metres away from the first-ever burial from 1832, a modest but impressive headstone tells the fascinating story of a soldier from the Napoleonic Wars. His epitaph reads:

> He served with his corps to the close of the Peninsular War. At the siege of Burgos his leg was shattered and his left eye carried away by a ball. He received two gunshot wounds in the chest at Waterloo. One of the balls fractured the collar-bone and penetrated the lung, in which it became embedded. The long train of suffering ensuing, and the haemorrhage it induced, ultimately proved fatal.

The period between 1798 and 1816 on the European continent was one of war, alliance, coalitions and eventual defeat for Napoleon at the Battle of Waterloo.

Glasnevin Cemetery *c.* 1865–1914. (Reproduced courtesy of the National Library of Ireland)

France was trying to expand its territory on the continent into Switzerland. Great Britain demanded that France withdraw but France refused, leading to Great Britain declaring war in 1803. Fighting would, in time, break out all over Europe. For over fifteen years there was almost uninterrupted war. Important battles from this period include Trafalgar, Leipzig and Waterloo. Throughout the period Great Britain joined a number of alliances and was part of five coalitions against the French. While involved in these various power struggles in Europe, Great Britain was also fighting against the USA in the War of 1812. The war in Europe came to an end in 1815 when Napoleon suffered defeat at Waterloo.

The Peninsular Campaign (1807–14) was a conflict between Spain and Portugal (with the help of Great Britain) and the invading forces of the French for control over the Iberian Peninsula. The French, having crossed the Franco-Spanish border in early October 1807, came to occupy both Lisbon in Portugal and Madrid in Spain, but the invading forces were not readily accepted and insurrections broke out across both regions. Great Britain decided to back the Spaniards and the Portuguese. Sir Arthur Wellesley (the Duke of Wellington) landed with the British Army at the mouth of the Mondego River in Portugal in October 1808. The French eventually capitulated.

Henry Quill, the soldier buried in Curran Square, was baptised in Tralee, County Kerry on 27 September 1784, five days after his twin brother. Henry had four brothers and six sisters. His father, Thomas, was born sometime around the year 1738, while his mother (a little younger) was born around 1755. Henry's name appears in the attestation papers for the British military in March 1809.[1] For a young, single, 25-year-old man, a career with the British Army was an attractive choice in the context of late eighteenth- and early nineteenth-century Ireland. He joined at the rank of ensign. This was the lowest commissioned rank in the British Army until 1871.

Henry was attached to the 32nd Regiment of Foot.[2] This was a regiment dating back to the turn of the eighteenth century and was one that landed in Portugal in 1808 under the command of Arthur Wellesley. It took part in many of the battles and sieges of the Peninsular campaign and suffered heavy casualties. Kevin Linch and Matthew McCormack have looked at soldiering in this period:

> From around 1740 to 1815 Britain's armed forces underwent a massive and sustained expansion in response to a series of ever more demanding

> wars. In this '70 Years War,' as it has been termed, Britain was more often than not at war with France ... By far the largest proportion of this growth (in the military) was outside the British Army, such that of the 630,000 rank and file soldiers that Britain could claim to have in 1805, only some 160,000 (23%) were in the regulars ...[3]

Henry Quill joined the army at a time when they needed all the recruits they could get. As an Irishman he was not alone. It has been estimated that, during the Peninsular campaigns and Napoleonic Wars, the Catholic Irish contingent in some regiments ranged from about 8 to 50 per cent.[4] Nicholas Dunne-Lynch accounts for the six Irish infantry battalions stationed in the peninsula during this period:

> The size of the Irish contingent is out of proportion to Ireland's share of the total UK population, especially as most Irish troops were drawn from Ireland's Catholic population of about 4 million, or about 28% of the UK population. The proportion of Irish officers, which may have been as great as one third of the officer corps, came mainly from Ireland's Anglican community of less than 5% of the total UK population ... Overall, Ireland contributed much more than its share in terms of population.[5]

Rather than being attached to any of the six Irish infantry battalions during his time in Spain, Portugal or later (present day) Belgium, Henry was one of thousands of Irishmen who served in English and Scots regiments. James Deery tells us that the majority of Irish soldiers from the Peninsular campaign served not within Irish regiments but as a part of those like the 32nd Regiment of Foot.[6] In fact the 1/32nd(Cornwall) Regiment of Foot had within its ranks just under 27 per cent Irish-born men during the Iberian Peninsula campaign.[7] This regiment had been stationed in Ireland for a period prior to the Peninsular War.[8] About 40 per cent of those in the regiment that went to fight at Waterloo were from Ireland, with twenty-seven different countries also represented.[9] Henry Quill's socio-economic standing mirrored the rank and file of the regiment. Whatever differences existed between the Kerryman and his English and Scottish colleagues mattered little. They formed a distinct familial bond replicated across all of Wellington's army.[10]

Henry's military records show us that he saw action at Salamanca.[11] In the column entitled 'number of actions admitted in each case' there is a tick with the number 1 beside it. Most soldiers on this record show similar ticks and a number '1' beside them. This is reflective of the life of a soldier at this time. Although away for long periods of time on active service, it did not mean constant fighting and battles. Much of Quill's time was spent waiting around. Linch and McCormack say:

> Taking the campaigns of the Peninsular War as an example, and counting all the battle, skirmishes, and sieges … at most a British soldier could have undergone 355 days in combat out of a total of 2,085, equivalent to 17%. Needless to say, it is highly unlikely any soldier, even an officer or general, was at every battle of the Peninsular War.[12]

Quill's action at the Battle of Salamanca would have lasted somewhere in the region of 24 to 36 hours. It was fought between the Anglo-Portuguese forces led by the Duke of Wellington and the French forces of Auguste-Marmont. It took place on 22 July 1812 and resulted in defeat for the French. The next action that he encountered was in the trenches outside the castle of Burgos, about 200km north of Madrid in Spain. The Duke of Wellington laid siege to the castle between 19 September and 21 October 1812 but failed to seize the fortress and was forced to retreat to Portugal. It was a siege reminiscent of the Middle Ages. Ladders, axes and mining beneath the walls were all used to try to breach the fortress. It was during preparations for this attack that Henry received his first nasty injury. In his military records it states, 'in the trenches before Burgos in Spain, loss of one eye'.[13] He lost his entire left eye due to a musket ball, and his leg was also shattered.[14] It was not until the Crimean War (1853–56) that battlefield hygiene began to take hold and it was not until the American Civil War (1861–65) that morphine became available on the battlefields. In this context his injuries become more gruesome; it is a miracle he survived. However, he made a full recovery and returned to full service with the 32nd Regiment of Foot in May 1815 on mainland Europe, where he saw action once more at Quatre Bras, two days before the Battle of Waterloo on 18 June 1815.

The engagement at Quatre Bras was the preliminary battle to Waterloo and took place on 16 June. Quatre Bras (the four arms) was an important crossroads that set the scene for what was to follow two days later. Napoleon sent his 'North Army' (Armée du Nord) under the command of General Michel Ney to Quatre Bras. Patrick Geoghegan contextualises the events of these pivotal few days, saying:

> On June 16th 1815 Napoleon won his final military victory. At Ligny, a town in present day Belgium, he defeated the Prussian Army under General Gebhard von Blücher but was unable to achieve the knockout blow he desired. The same day Wellington took on a French Army under Ney at Quatre Bras, having been outfoxed by Napoleon's troop movements … Wellington won the field, narrowly, but was forced to retreat North towards Brussels upon hearing of the Prussian defeat. The small town of Waterloo, a key strategic location on the road to Brussels, now assumed a massive significance.[15]

Fatalities and injuries at this battle have been estimated at somewhere between 8,000 and 10,000 men killed or wounded on both sides. Unfortunately for Henry, he suffered another horrific injury on this battlefield. Two musket balls hit him directly in the chest. One fractured his collarbone and the other penetrated his lung.[16] His military record states: 'at Quatre Bras in Flanders June 1815 a severe wound of the lungs'.[17] By this time he had been promoted to the rank of lieutenant on the recommendation of General Ogilvie Colonel of the 32nd Regiment of Foot.[18] In a fascinating entry in his military record in Henry's own handwriting he wrote how:

> The wound which has deprived me of one of my eyes has impacted the sight of the other especially for the last two years … the wound of the lungs from which the ball has now been extracted has so afflicted me with agonies of ill health as to make me unfit or incapable of returning to the service … you will see by a reference to the medical certificate in the late … at the War Office I have received another wound in the leg which so shattered it was narrowly to escape amputation and for which I have never made any injury claims of any kind.[19]

Through his own testimony we know that he had one of the musket balls successfully removed. The second musket ball however became embedded within his lungs. The surgeons deemed it too risky to extract it and it was left inside. Now he could say that there was a piece of the Waterloo campaign inside his own chest. He was moved to half-pay as a result of his injuries.[20] Napoleon meanwhile was defeated. Wellington went on to become prime minister in the years ahead, while Henry Quill spent a number of years recovering in Jersey before making his way to London sometime around 1821.[21]

Determined not let these injuries get in the way of his life, he met a woman called Margaret Prendergast. They married at St Margaret's Church in Westminster, London and went on to have four children: Ellen, their firstborn (11 October 1822), Henrietta Maria (24 December 1824) and Henry Francis and Thomas (between 1831 and 1833).[22] By the time Henrietta was born, the family were back in Ireland. This was due to the fact that the 32nd Regiment of Foot had returned to Bandon, where it had been based prior to its initial deployment to the Iberian Peninsula. Henry later took up a residence at 26 Talbot Street in Dublin with his family. *The Cork Examiner* features a story that tells us his son Henry was arrested for: 'being about to have a hostile meeting at Howth … whereby a breach of the public peace may be committed'.[23] A sergeant went to Talbot Street, where Henry Quill Jr was placed under arrest. His father was described as a 'military gentleman, who stated that he knew the duel would happen if his son and those involved were not arrested'. Bail was met and Henry was released days later. It is an interesting snapshot into Henry senior's life after military service.

For his military service and injuries, he was given a pension of £70 per year in 1813 and a further £70 per year from 1816 onwards.[24] He left the military after nineteen and a half years' service. In 1847 Henry was awarded the Military General Service Medal (MGSM) for his actions in the period 1793–1814. The medal was designed to hold a number of clasps to represent each action the combatant had taken part in. A maximum of twenty-nine could be attached. He received a clasp for his service at Salamanca in 1812 when he was nearly 65 years old, just weeks before he died. His death was covered in the *Kerry Evening Post* and *The Kerry Examiner*.[25]

Henry was buried in Glasnevin, where today his epitaph makes people stop and consider the 'long train of suffering' he went through. He was buried with the remnants of the musket ball still inside him. It had shifted internally causing bleeding, which led to death. He had lived for over thirty-four years with the scars of the Iberian Peninsula and Waterloo visible on his body. His wife, Margaret, was later buried in the same grave on 26 January 1873, aged

80. She died in her home on Anne Street, Dundalk, close to her daughter Ellen and her family. She was brought back to Dublin and buried with her late husband on 31 January 1873.

Today the most noticeable monument to Wellington is in the Phoenix Park. Nobody, however, remembers the ordinary Irishmen who sacrificed so much in this period. The Irish soldier in the British Army from 1793 to 1815 remains an understudied figure and deserves more attention. Quill is not the only Irishman with links to this period buried in Glasnevin. There are also the graves of Lieutenant Theobold Butler in the Garden section (BE 32), who served during the Peninsular Wars at Rolica, Vimiera, Corunna, Salamanca, Pyrenees, Nivelle, Nive and Orthes with the 32nd Foot, as well as at Waterloo.[26] There is Captain Benjamin Walker Nicholson, also in the Garden section (AB 62), who was a lieutenant during Waterloo in the 2nd Battalion of the 30th Regiment of Foot. His battalion suffered heavily with a 50 per cent casualty rate.[27] His wife is also buried in the same grave. The inscription on the headstone gives an intriguing insight into her role: 'In memory of Maria the affectionate wife of Capt. B.W. Nicholson Late 30th Regt. who died May 5 1853. Aged 74 years. She accompanied him in his campaigns to the East Indies, Cape of Good Hope, St. Helena and was in Antwerp during the days of Waterloo where her husband was engaged.'

Other graves include Lieutenant William Talbot in the Garden section (RA 70). From Wexford, he served with the 27th Foot Inniskilling's during the Peninsular War at Toulouse and Vittoria. He was also present at Waterloo but escaped with no injuries.[28] These stories have become virtually forgotten. James Deery states that 'very few Irish families can or indeed have the inclination to trace a relative serving in the ranks of Wellington's army. However, the success of the Peninsular army and the Irish contribution to that success should be taken as the starting point for Irish involvement in the British army throughout the Victorian era culminating in the First World War …'[29]

Henry Quill's is a singular story amongst thousands around Ireland. At the end of the battle at Waterloo only 131 of his regiment were left standing and he lived the rest of his life with the physical scars of these experiences. For others with links to conflict in the cemetery, the Fenian and rebel path was chosen. Over six decades there existed many splinter Fenian groups. They can all be characterised as secretive, oath-bound organisations with their main aim to liberate Ireland from the British Empire by whatever means necessary.

The Fenians

The origins of the Fenians can be seen in the early 1840s with the emergence of the Young Ireland Society and the Irish Confederation in America (later the Young Irelanders), who viewed the changes brought by Daniel O'Connell's political successes, with Catholic Emancipation (1829) and his later campaign for the Repeal of the Act of Union between Great Britain and Ireland, as too slow. The death of O'Connell in May 1847 and the onset of the Great Famine pushed more people towards radical, physical-force Fenian organisations. The late historian Shane Kenna summed up their importance by stating:

> The Irish Republican Brotherhood (IRB), better known as the Fenians, was one of the most important revolutionary organisations within Irish history and that had a profound influence on the emergence of Ireland as we understand it today. Through sixty years of secretive conspiracy it bestrode Irish history like a colossus. It was a key factor in the emergence of cultural and political organisations in the late nineteenth and early twentieth centuries, played an active role in the Irish revolution 1916–1921 and was a crucial group in terms of the negotiations of the Anglo-Irish Treaty of 1921 and the emergence of the Irish Free State.[30]

As revolution swept Europe in Austria and France, the Young Irelanders staged their attempted rebellion on 29 July 1848 at Ballingarry. This was to become known as 'The Battle of Widow McCormack's Cabbage Patch'. It took place on a small piece of farmland in County Tipperary. The leaders of the Young Ireland movement, however, had misjudged the mood of the population, who were far more concerned about the third year of Famine. Its failure led to men like James Stephens, John O'Mahony, Michael Doheny, Terence Bellew McManus, John O'Leary and others going on the run and ultimately hastened the disintegration of the Young Irelanders. In its place came the new Irish Republican Brotherhood (IRB) founded on St Patrick's Day 1858 by James Stephens. The IRB and its American branch (the Irish Fenian Brotherhood) later played a significant role in leading its own rebellion in 1867. Many of its members also took leading roles in the 1916 Rising.

The cemetery today is the final resting place for many of these notable names. A short walk to the Republican Plot and you will see two large Celtic crosses above the graves of James Stephens (the founder of the IRB) and John O'Leary, who is next to him. O'Leary himself took part in the failed 1848 insurgency and was later immortalised by the words of W.B Yeats in his poem 'September 1913'. There is also the grave of veteran Fenian Jeremiah O'Donovan Rossa. Rossa was buried next to Stephens and O'Leary on 1 August 1915 resulting in Pearse's famous graveside oration. The Fenian John Devoy is five graves away. He spent much of his life in America in exile and was buried in 1928. Beneath an impressive structure sculpted by Sir Thomas Farrell you can also visit the grave of Young Irelanders: John O'Mahony, Terence Bellew McManus and other members of that same organisation.

D. George Boyce said that the two decades after the Famine were 'an era of fragmentation in political terms ... it seemed impossible to establish any kind of clear direction; and it was not until the end of the 1860s that the emergence of Fenianism as a threat to both Britain and British Rule in Ireland concentrated political minds ...'[31] The Fenian leadership and their ideas have been well documented by other historians but less talked about have been the stories of the rank and file members of the organisations. Glasnevin is the final resting place for not only the well-known Fenians but also many forgotten ones and they too deserve to have their lives remembered.

The Silk Weaver and the Irish Tricolour

Not far from the grave of Henry Quill is the grave of Edward Hollywood in the Garden section (G 88.5). The headstone originally suggested to mark this grave sadly never materialised after his death and up until 2012 it lay unmarked.

Hollywood was born on 11 January 1814 in Dublin. Not much is known about his formative years, but we know that he was baptised on 23 January at St Catherine's on Meath Street. His parents were Francis Hollywood and Mary Harbourne. He was the first-born child of seven. He lived in the Liberties of Dublin and became a leader of an early trade union for artisans. He worked as a weaver of silks for the well-respected Irish poplin manufacturers Messrs O'Reilly, Dunne and Co.[32] According to *The Nation* newspaper Hollywood was 'regarded as being one of the most skilled men in his craft'.[33]

Between 1840 and 1848 he was increasingly involved with the newly emerging Young Irelander movement and became treasurer of the Davis Confederate Club.[34] As popularity for O'Connell began to fade along with his energy and youth, along came figures like Charles Gavan Duffy, John Blake Dillon, John Mitchel and Thomas Davis. Through their newspaper *The Nation* they had begun a new conversation about the promotion of Irish nationalism. The premature death of Thomas Davis in 1845 meant the Young Irelanders by 1846 were led by the Protestant Limerick landowner William Smith O'Brien. Under his leadership they broke away from O'Connell's Repeal movement and formed the nationalist Irish Confederation. Edward was a member of the movement by 1848 and was very active in gathering opposition to O'Connell's Repeal movement in favour of the newly emerging Confederation. Michael Doheny wrote of the work undertaken by Hollywood in 1849:

> Late in the autumn of 1846, some men, few in number and humble in condition, undertook the desperate task of remonstrating with the Repeal Association. Among them, Mr. Keeley and Mr. Hollywood, Mr. Crean and Mr. Halpin, were prominent. Their undertaking was gigantic, considering the formidable obstacles they proposed to encounter. They proceeded silently and sedulously; and, in a few weeks, a remonstrance against the course pursued by the Association was signed by fifteen hundred citizens of Dublin ...[35]

The Irish Confederation as a movement had many internal divisions and different schools of thought. To many, the use of violence and insurrection was still a contested issue. Only a minority truly supported such an approach. Boyce states that: 'the great majority of Young Irelanders were not fiery revolutionaries, bent on leading a starving peasantry in the manner of the great French Revolution of 1789; and in the autumn of 1847 and the spring of 1848 they followed the propensity of many Irish political movements ... they split.'[36]

Leaders like John Mitchel began to voice their views for peasants to begin arming themselves against evictions. The Confederation saw the resignations of people like Mitchel, Martin and Thomas Devin Reilly. They all disagreed with the organisation's focus on agrarian agitation and arms. Rival newspapers were set up and opinions became hotly contested. Regardless of these internal divisions, events in France forced many moderates into action. Three weeks after the Irish Confederation had debated the use of violence to achieve their aims, a revolution in Paris had overthrown the monarchy of King Louis Philippe. A popular provisional government was set up, led by reformists like Alphonse de Lamartine and the radical Louis Blanc. They proclaimed the dawn of the Second French Republic. News of this reached the Young Irelanders and all differences within were put to one side.

Philosophical debates, deliberations and delays followed. While arguments continued on how to act on this inspirational news, *The Nation* of 18 March 1848 has a lengthy article outlining what was said at a meeting on the previous day in Dublin. It was noted that a Eugene O'Reilly came forward to second the adoption of a proposed congratulatory address to loud cheers and applause, before a Mr McGee came forward to say: 'I have to move Mr. Chairman, the following resolution: that Wm Smith O'Brien, Thomas F. Meagher and Edward Hollywood, be requested to convey this address to Paris, and present it to the provisional government of France; and that any members of our Council who are now in Paris are requested to accompany the deputation.'[37]

Hollywood was one of the four men who travelled to Paris as part of the small delegation. They presented the provisional government and the French principal leader de Lamartine with a congratulatory address.[38] While in Paris they were inspired by de Lamartine and his work. They were particularly impressed by his passion in ensuring the future of the *Tricolore* as being the national flag of France. Its unifying message was noticed by the Irishmen. Hollywood, O'Brien and Meagher remarked on how such a symbol could have similar potential back in Ireland and it was decided that they should return to Ireland with a flag based on the French emblem with the amended colours of green, white and orange. The expertise of Hollywood as a silk weaver was called upon to make this flag a reality; as Conor Dodd has said, 'as a silk weaver (he) was undoubtedly important in their efforts.'[39]

On the delegation's return to Ireland, the silken Irish tricolour was flown from number 33 The Mall in Waterford City and in Enniscorthy, Wexford throughout March 1848. The meaning of the flag was explained by Meagher on 15 April 1848: 'The white in the centre signifies a lasting truce between the "orange" and the "green" and I trust beneath its folds, the hands of the Irish Protestant and the Irish Catholic may be clasped in generous and heroic brotherhood.'[40]

Edward Hollywood himself is noted in Meagher's memoirs, published by Michael Cavanagh in 1892, as wearing a silken neckerchief fashioned by his own hands while in Waterford after returning from France: 'Mr Edward Hollywood … produced a neckerchief of green silk with an orange border. As an emblem of the union of "Orange and Green!" the article soon became popular with the Confederates in Dublin, and throughout the country, and its originator was a man who consistently stood by his colours …'[41]

Later in 1848, on 29 July, Edward took part in the events staged at Ballingarry in Tipperary. Many leaders had been arrested and deported in the weeks and months before this. Membership of the Confederation was now seen as sufficient grounds for arrest by the authorities.[42] Those who remained (including William Smith O'Brien) felt the only option left to them was to make some form of stand. The idea of any form of violent insurrection was not a popular one, even within the minority that had previously argued for one. In spite of this, Edward Hollywood was one of about forty Irish Confederates, alongside James Stephens, William Smith O'Brien and Terence Bellew MacManus, who took a chance and attempted to stand against the Irish Constabulary.

Afterwards, O'Brien was arrested and transported. Meagher, Doheny and MacManus were later sent to Van Diemen's Land. Edward, for his part, managed to evade arrest and was listed as an outlaw. Some months later *The Cork Examiner* said that he was 'proclaimed as an outlaw in the last number of the *Hue and Cry*'.[43] The *Belfast News-Letter* later reported on 17 October 1848 that: 'In a letter received in Dublin on Thursday, it is stated by the writer, that Edward Hollywood, silk weaver, and who had been one of the deputation to France, had effected his escape to Boulogne.'[44]

Hollywood would not return to Dublin for many years and lived happily in France until the beginning of the 1860s. It is footnoted in the memoirs of Thomas Francis Meagher that following the failed insurrection of 1848 Edward lived in France for a number of years with his wife and family. His wife, the footnote says, died while he was in France and afterwards he made the decision to return to Dublin. On his return he attended the funeral of another well-known Young Irelander, Terence Bellew MacManus, in 1861 at Glasnevin. A sign of Hollywood's long-standing reputation within the movement can be seen at this occasion. *The Nation* noted, 'Mr Hollywood was present at the [funeral] arrangements, and was one of the pall-bearers of his colleague's coffin.'[45]

Edward attended Glasnevin again on 9 October 1872 for the burial of his young nephew Francis Hollywood. Francis, the child of his brother Richard, who had also made his living on Dublin's Cork Street as a silk weaver, was recorded as just 4 years, 4 months and 6 days old and today lies in an unmarked grave in the Garden section (NE 202).

The latter part of Edward's life was spent in Dublin. Although he was alive to see another attempted Fenian rebellion in 1867, he did not play an active role. He died on 16 September 1873 aged 59 and was buried two days later. His recorded cause of death is as a result of 'Bronchitis'. He died at his home at 18 Cork Street, Dublin. *The Nation* covered the sad occasion on 20 September: 'We regret to announce the death of one of the staunchest of the men of '48, Mr Edward Hollywood … It was suggested that his old colleagues should themselves erect his tomb and open a short subscription for that purpose, May god have mercy on his soul.'[46] The small white headstone today is inscribed with his name and tells the passer-by that he was part of the deputation to France in 1848. In 2016, to mark the centenary

Edward Hollywood, bottom right.
(Courtesy of the New York Public Library Digital Collections, 1866)

of the Easter Rising, a flagpole was placed beside his grave. Each time the Easter Rising is commemorated at the cemetery, the tricolour is now flown over his grave.

The Battle of Tallaght

For young Stephen Donohoe, the events of 1867 took him from his house at 6 Werburgh Street in Dublin, where he was living with his father, brothers and sisters, to Tallaght on the outskirts of Dublin. The rebellion began on 11 February 1867 with a planned attack in Chester, England to seize arms and return them to Ireland. A nationwide rebellion was to follow. These plans were foiled by spies and informers. Before the rising had even begun, the authorities were informed not only of its date but also the basic strategy of the Fenians.[47]

Despite countless setbacks, lack of ammunition or any real prospect of success, the Fenian rising went ahead on the morning of 6 March. Men began to gather towards the lower reaches of Mount Seskin, a mountain above Jobstown. Stephen Donohoe, just 30 years old, journeyed out from the centre of Dublin to join them. There were two principal routes which the Fenians took from the city: one was Crumlin–Walkinstown–Greenhills and the other Rathmines–Rathgar–Roundtown (Terenure). Within Dublin city, the police had observed large numbers of outside cars leaving the Coombe and Kevin Street areas. The sergeant from Crumlin police station stated that 'the Dublin road is crowded with young men all taking the direction of Tallaght'.[48]

Stephen was in charge of one of three groups that arrived in Tallaght. One had thrown stones at the police before diverting and the other was read the Riot Act. Donohoe's group (the third) had approached Tallaght from the direction of Roundtown. They chose to open fire on the police with what little ammunition they had. According to later police testimony: 'One of the insurgents, who appeared to be their leader [likely Donohoe] ordered them to fire by calling out, "Now, boys! now fire!" A volley of not less than fifty shots was then discharged at us by the insurgents. Burke (the inspector) immediately commanded us to kneel and fire, which command was obeyed.'[49]

An account of the whole incident has survived in a document written by an unidentified Fenian who took part. He pointed out three reasons why

Donohoe's group had caused the 'disaster'. Firstly, they were poorly armed: the 150 men had only twenty rifles. Secondly, Donohoe had failed to drill his members properly. The twenty rifles they had were given to 'a few who knew and some who boasted they knew how to use them'. Thirdly, the group not only disobeyed orders that the Fenians should not attack the police but some seem to have pressed for an attack, with some 'very young fellows' – a number of youths of about sixteen or seventeen years of age featuring among the ranks.[50]

In the disorder and chaos, the police responded with rifle fire. Both Stephen Donohoe and another Fenian, Thomas Farrell, were mortally wounded. *The Cork Examiner* on 8 March reported at length on the events under the headline 'The Fenian Insurrection in Dublin':

> … large bodies of men were observed by the police last night at the Rathmines, Crumlin and Harold's Cross stations to be making their way in groups along the roads shortly after dusk until a late hour at night …. The man who was mortally wounded is supposed to be an Attorney's Clerk named Stephen Donohoe who resided with his father, and brothers, and sisters at Werburgh Street. The ball entered his right lung and went out the back. He was attended this morning by the surgeon of the 52nd who was out with his regiment and afterwards by Dr Seward, but the wound was of that character that surgical aid was unavailing and the man died this morning at ten. His body is at present at Tallaght station. The other wounded man also lies there. He is quite a young man. He is supposed to have been a working man named Byrne who had been employed at Mr Ireland's establishment on Ellis-Quay. It is believed that several others of the party were wounded but no other wounded were found by the police. Possibly they were brought off by their own party.[51]

The events of 6 March became known as the Battle of Tallaght. There were other small successes in County Cork, a small stirring in Ballyhurst, Tipperary and an attack on Kilmallock police barracks in Limerick, but no nationwide uprising materialised. For their role in suppressing the rising the Irish Constabulary were given the prefix 'Royal' and became better known as the RIC. Stephen Donohoe was buried in the Garden section (CE 197.5) of Glasnevin on the morning of 8 March. Four years later Terence Byrne, who had fought alongside him at the Battle of Tallaght, was buried in the plot beside Donohoe (CE 197). Byrne had been arrested after the events of that day, and after four years in prison immediately signed up for war service on the French side in the Franco-Prussian War.[52]

Today if you walk to these graves, you will see a detailed headstone complete with symbols of the Rising Moon, Irish Wolfhound, the Irish Harp and Ancient Monastic sites carved on it. The stone was erected in 1885 by the Young Ireland Society and features not just the name of Stephen Donohoe but also that of Byrne. Thomas Farrell, who was mortally wounded in the events of 1867, is also recorded, but he is not buried in either of the graves. The headstone features an inscription in Irish that translates as: 'In evil days they devoted their lives to advance the cause of Irish freedom transmitting towards the hope which animated them of seeing Ireland a nation once again.'

The Nation reported on the unveiling of the monument over the graves of Donohoe and Byrne on 28 November 1885, an event at which Michael Davitt spoke.[53] Despite the abortive nature of the rising of 1867, it 'kept the Irish and British public in a state of alarm'.[54]

The *Catalpa* Rescue

A small headstone erected by the National Graves Association of Ireland in the Garden section (XG 47) provides another forgotten story from this period. It is the grave of Denis Duggan. He was born in Dublin in 1842. He was a coach maker by trade, from 21 Upper Dominick Street, and attended school with John Devoy. By 1861 he was a member of the IRB.[55] Similarly to his schoolmate Devoy, he was arrested on 14 February 1866, but due to lack of evidence was released on the condition he leave Ireland. He journeyed to London where he joined the London Irish Volunteers. Having risen through the ranks, he was put in charge of one of the largest circles in Dublin city before the 1867 uprising. He returned to Ireland secretly in preparation. He was second-in-command of one of the small groups that captured the police barracks at Stepaside and Glencullen about the same time that Stephen Donohoe was engaging the police in Tallaght. Unlike Donohoe, Duggan survived the events of 1867.

Previously, in 1865, Duggan was part of a daring plan to free James Stephens from jail. On 24 November 1865 Superintendent Daniel Ryan of the DMP wrote to his superiors: 'I beg to state that at 5.20am this morning a constable of E. Division stated that the G. Division office that Marquess, Governor of the Richmond Bridewell, directed him to call and say that James Stephens, who was confined there on a charge of high treason, had made his escape.'[56]

Peter Fitzsimons gives a great account of the escape on a very stormy night in Dublin: 'nearing midnight 10 Fenians approach the prison walls … John Devoy himself gets into position near the section of wall whence the Captain (Stephens) is supposed to come …'[57] Stephens had befriended two sympathetic prison guards inside and was able to open his cell door and make use of two tables stacked on top of each other to climb out over the boundary wall. Seven doors had to be unlocked before he was able to get to the wall.[58] Once at the exterior wall he waited. Those outside threw a rope over. They held tightly and began to hoist Stephens up. Amongst the men on the outside were John Devoy with his personal bodyguards. One of those was Denis Duggan.[59] Fitzsimons says that Devoy selected him for this role because of his 'courage and calm when under pressure'.[60] In later years, during the Irish War of Independence, one of Michael Collins' famous spies, Eamon (Ned) Broy, came across secret police reports from 1865 detailing these events. In one of his Bureau of Military History statements he includes what he had copied:

> The escape was affected mainly by Warders Byrne and Breslin … Breslin's brother Michael, a member of the Dublin Metropolitan Police carried all the correspondence between Stephens in prison and the Fenians outside and brought in all the keys made to fit the 7 doors mentioned in the police report … Colonel Kelly and John Devoy had a party outside [including Duggan] the prison wall to receive Stephens after he had been conducted there from his cell by warders Breslin and Byrne … The rescue was affected between 1 and 2 a.m … Stephens had to climb to the top of the 17 ft prison wall by means of a knotted rope thrown over by his friends outside then he slid down outside with his back to the wall …[61]

The escape was a success and Stephens made his way to America. Denis was subsequently arrested in February 1866 and was incarcerated at Mountjoy Prison before being transferred to Belfast.[62] He was later released on bail on condition that he leave the country. He travelled to London, where he spent

Denis Duggan, top left. (Courtesy of the New York Public Library Digital Collections, 1866)

some time helping the London Irish Volunteers before returning to Ireland in time to take part in the events of 1867 at Tallaght. Following the rising, Duggan managed to flee to America as the suppression of the movement gathered pace in Ireland. Other Fenians who were convicted of treason-felony as a result of the rising were transported to Australia. Many ended up in the infamous Fremantle Prison in Western Australia. Sixty-two Fenian prisoners were transported to this prison after 1867 aboard the *Hougoumont*. They began to arrive in January of 1868. By 1869 pardons had been issued to a number of the men but some faced more time and uncertainty there.

In America John Devoy had been planning, as far back as 1872, for what was to become one of the most dramatic prison breaks in Irish, British and Australian history. *The Connaught Telegraph* featured a detailed article on the planning behind the proposed escape:

> The sum of $20,000 was needed … When the requisite sum had been procured steps were instantly taken to put the plan into execution … The whaling bark *Catalpa* was enlisted in the service and the plan of action was drawn up under the eyes of men who were acquainted with the coast of Western Australia … At length the *Catalpa* was got ready for sea and on April 29th, 1875 she sailed from New Bedford. There was only one agent of the Nationalists on board of her; Mr Dennis Duggan who went as ship Carpenter … In September 1875, Mr Breslin the chief rescue agent started for Western Australia by way of San Francisco accompanied by Captain Desmond of that city and they were to be joined on the arrival at that destination by Mr John King of New South Wales who had with him £700 collected in Australia for the rescue project.[63]

In 1872 John Devoy had received a letter from the former Fenian James Wilson, who was one of the few Fenians left in Fremantle at that stage, asking for help to escape. Once funds had been raised, the whaling vessel *Catalpa* was obtained. The official representative on board for the IRB was Denis Duggan. He faced opposition in the form of Thomas Brennan, a long-standing member of Clan na Gael, but Devoy opted to stick with his trusted schoolmate.[64]

The *Catalpa* left New Bedford on 29 April 1875 and would not complete its mission until 19 August 1876. The crew consisted of the captain, George Anthony (who was not Irish but an experienced seaman), First Mate Samuel Smith and a number of Malays, Sandwich and Cape Verde Islanders. The Islanders presumed they were embarking on a two-year whaling expedition. Other Fenians, Breslin and Desmond, sailed from Los Angeles directly to Fremantle and embedded themselves into the community, acting as the eyes and ears of the operation.

Controlling the crew of the *Catalpa* became a serious challenge. As the real reason for the voyage became clearer, they grew restless. By October 1875 the vessel had reached the Azores. The crew realised they were unlikely to make any money from this expedition and asked to be left behind. As tensions on board continued to rise, Duggan did little to de-escalate the situation and it was reported that, in the port of Fayal, he took a number of the crew ashore on a drunken rampage. He apparently got so drunk that he fell out of the rowing boat no fewer than three times on the way back to the

Catalpa.[65] Replacements were recruited to fill the places of the crew who left. By 20 November 1875 the ship had reached Tenerife. Bad weather forced it to head in the direction of the Seychelles, before finally reaching Bunbury (about 70 miles south of Fremantle) on 28 March 1876. Breslin, who had been in Fremantle for months scouting out the location, made his way to the captain to inform him of the plans. The *Catalpa* was to stand 10–12 miles offshore, well out in international waters. It was to send a whaleboat to Rockingham Beach. The prisoners would be expected to break away from their working parties and, in rented horse carriages driven by Breslin and Desmond, make a 20-mile journey from Fremantle to Rockingham and from there to freedom.

The six prisoners – Wilson, Hogan, Harrington, Cranston, Darragh and Hassett – made it to the beach and met the captain, who waited for them to row out to the vessel. It took over 28 hours of rowing in the open whaling boat on the Indian Ocean before they reached the *Catalpa.* The vessel was spotted by the British vessel, the *Georgette*, which fired across the bows of the *Catalpa.* Cleverly the *Catalpa*'s captain hoisted the American flag and declared to the British that if they fired at the ship they were firing on the American flag. The vessel was shadowed for some distance, but ultimately the *Georgette* gave up its pursuit and the mission made land in New York on 19 August 1876.

In America the freed prisoners were greeted with applause, cheers and crowds of over 20,000 in some places.[66] It was a massive success for John Devoy and Clan na nGael.[67] Denis Duggan later earned the name 'The Carpenter of the *Catalpa*'.

Duggan returned to Ireland and his native Dublin in May 1884 after sustaining a bad injury to his head caused by a brick while labouring in New York City. He spent time at St Vincent's Hospital in New York before funds were raised to bring him home to Dublin.[68] He died on 9 September 1884 aged just 42. The register of Glasnevin records him as 'single' at the time of death and living with his family. His recorded cause of death is as a result of phthisis (a form of TB). *The Buffalo Times* in New York reported on 16 September:

> An impressive demonstration occurred yesterday in Dublin on the occasion of the funeral of Dennis Duggan. The cortege comprised fully 20,000 people, and included Mr Michael Davitt and Mr William

> O'Brien. The coffin bore a plate on which was inscribed 'A solider in the Army of Ireland.' It was draped with the stars and stripes and the green flag of Ireland, intertwined and surmounted with a trophy of pikes. Masses for the repose of Duggan's soul were said in the principal churches.[69]

In Ireland both *The Nation* and *The Irish Times* featured detailed accounts of Duggan's death and funeral in the Garden section. *The Nation* said on 13 September 1884: 'On Tuesday morning there passed away in Dublin an Irish man who took a prominent part in the numerous events of the stormy Politics of 1861 to 1867 …'[70] A week later the paper reported:

> At many points along the line of the route strong contingents joined in the procession, so that before it had travelled any great distance it had assumed most imposing proportions. At the end of the marching body came the mourning coach, containing the mother and two sisters of the deceased, who appeared to be in a very great grief, and a long stream of carriages and cabs … Great crowds of spectators assembled along the line of march … The Spectators appeared all to be deeply impressed by the scene, and reverently doffed their hats as the hearse containing the remains of the deceased man passed … As it went, like a snowball rolling, the cortege added to itself and increased its dimensions or, like a rapid river … gained in strength as it flowed from its source in Cuffe Street, and poured itself into the great human sea at Glasnevin … The funeral had only reached its full dimensions when the horsemen, who rode some distance in front of the hearse, had pulled up at the gate of the chief entrance to the cemetery. The coffin was then borne upon the shoulders of friends of the deceased inside the Mortuary Chapel …[71]

A Forgotten Leixlip Fenian

One other forgotten Fenian story in Glasnevin is that of William Francis Roantree, who lived through the rebellions of 1848, 1867 and the Easter Rising. His involvement with the Fenians covers six decades, but his story, like the others, has slipped from public memory and he has become known as the forgotten Fenian from Leixlip.

Born in 1828, Roantree was baptised on 17 August 1828 in the parish of Maynooth in County Kildare. His parents are listed as 'James Roundthree' and 'Anne O'Brian'. His father was an auctioneer and a butcher. William was part of a large family, and records from the Leixlip area show that he had several brothers and at least one sister.[72] The family lived at number 33 Main Street in Leixlip. There is a plaque outside the address today but little else is known about his early years. His family survived the Famine years of 1845–52 and, like many later Fenians, this experience, coupled with emigration, played a significant part in shaping his political outlook on Ireland.

Roantree played no part in 1848. Instead, he emigrated. Records show that he arrived in Philadelphia, Pennsylvania in September 1854.[73] Between 1855 and 1860 he gained valuable military experience both as a soldier of fortune and in the American Navy. William travelled to Nicaragua with the American mercenary adventurer General William Walker. Nicaragua was in a state of civil war at the time and it appears General Walker had been hired by one of the factions involved.

There are numerous contradictions and inaccuracies about Roantree's life during this time. What we do know of this period is that he departed San Francisco in 1855 and, according to John Devoy (who later in life became a very close friend of William's), took part in all the fighting in Nicaragua alongside a fellow Irishman called Hugh Byrne from Wicklow.[74] On his return he joined the US Navy with his brother James. He joined at the rank of private and his enlistment date is given as 15 January 1858, with his station recorded on board the USS *Wabash*.[75] John Devoy said at this time, '[he] saw most of the great ports of the world. On his return to New York he joined the Fenian Brotherhood and became acquainted with John O'Mahony and most of the Fenian leaders.'[76] It is noted that he returned to Ireland for the Fenian Trials of 1859, and is recorded in some proceedings as one of a number of prisoners facing charges for 'conspiring and combining with the members of a secretive society called the "Fenian Brotherhood".'[77] The presence of a brother-in-law at Greenstreet Courthouse during the trials tell us he had married a woman called Isabel Casey by this time.[78] They had two daughters together: Catherina Anna Maria (or Kathleen; born 1862) and Isabella (1864).

When the American Civil War began, Roantree joined the Fenian Brotherhood back in New York. He worked as a sutler (a person who followed the army and sold provisions to them), but by 1861 he had returned to Ireland permanently, where he joined the IRB and was one of the group, with Edward Hollywood, who organised the funeral to Glasnevin of veteran Fenian Terence Bellew McManus in November 1861.[79] He became a trusted member of the IRB and was put in control of the 'Leixlip Circle'. Under his leadership in Kildare, it became one of the largest in the country and took in large parts of Maynooth, Celbridge, Lucan and some areas of counties Meath and Dublin.[80] By late 1862 Roantree had gained a place amongst the Fenian Executive. His name can be found in the Fenian newspaper *The Irish People* alongside O'Donovan Rossa, John O'Connor, Denis Dowling Mulcahy, James Stephens, John O'Leary and Charles J. Kickham.[81] By 1862 he was one of the most senior figures in the organisation. He was constantly on the move, travelling between Dublin and Leixlip, and returned to America in 1863 on Fenian business and to provide for his family.

By the end of 1863 he had committed himself fully to the Fenian cause. In particular he led the recruitment of Irishmen serving in the British Army into the IRB and was highly successful at it.[82] As plans began to gather momentum for an insurrection, the authorities arrested the main leaders of the Fenian movement. The rank and file were later rounded up and in total nearly 3,000 suspected Fenians were arrested, leaving plans for a rebellion in ruins. William was arrested on Dublin's Dame Street. The regiments of the British Army, from which Roantree had recruited so many members, were moved outside of Ireland and William was sent to Richmond Bridewell.

He was in his cell on the night of 24 November 1865 when Devoy, with Denis Duggan and other Fenians, managed to help Stephens escape. This was not to follow for Roantree. Instead, along with thirty-five other Fenians, he was transferred to the more secure Kilmainham Gaol on the night of 2 December. They were some of the first Fenians to be sent to the new gaol.[83] While in Kilmainham he wrote a number of letters to his wife, Isabel. Today these letters are in the National Archives and provide some insights into his personality and what he was going through while in prison. The letters cover everything from his strong beliefs and convictions to jokes about the clergy. The letters also contain some of his worries and reactions to the news that his mother died while he was in Kilmainham on 3 January 1866. On receiving this news, he wrote a postscript at the bottom of one letter to his wife dated 3 January 1866: 'Mother is dead. 'Tis very hard that I am deprived of that poor consolation of attending her funeral. 'Tis always darkest the hour before day.'[84]

Roantree played no part in the 1867 uprising. He had been charged with treason-felony at Greenstreet Courthouse on 24 January 1866 and given ten years' penal servitude. He spent time at Mountjoy before being transported to Pentonville in London. Later, with other Fenians, he was transferred to Portland Prison, which was a hard labour prison. He also spent time at Woking Prison, where he stayed until his release. He was pardoned in January 1871 under the condition that the Fenians go into exile in America as part of a wider amnesty for prisoners. He arrived in New York once again with many other released Fenians and their families. The president at the time (President Grant) received them at the White House on 22 February 1871, no doubt conscious of the importance of the Irish-American vote.[85]

Life for William, his wife and children was tough. The time he had spent in prison had taken its toll and it was noted that Roantree, though still relatively young, looked old and had grey hair.[86]

In New York, away from Fenian activities, he set about trying to find employment and settled in Atlantic City, New Jersey with his family. He set up a pub called the New York House.[87] A report in *The Irishman* paper, however, tells us he was suffering with lung problems by 1871.[88] As Devoy began to

William Francis Roantree. (Courtesy of the National Library of Ireland)

organise the Irish American exiles into his new Clan na Gael, Roantree played an important role, mainly in fundraising. Clan na Gael became the dominant Fenian organisation in America and it absorbed many of the Fenians living in exile following a series of earlier splits and division into its ranks. Roantree was particularly important in helping to raise funds in Philadelphia for the *Catalpa* and the escape from Fremantle prison.[89]

In 1877 Roantree visited Glasnevin once again, for the burial of John O'Mahony. The funeral was another massive occasion. There was a requiem mass in New York before the Fenian's body was returned to Dublin via Cobh. The procession through Dublin on 4 March 1871 was marshalled by Roantree on horseback. *The Irishman* paper commented on him: 'He was well mounted … (he) rode in front and rendered invaluable service in getting the procession into line.'[90] In 1884 he became a member of the Ancient Order of Hibernians back in Philadelphia.[91] This society was one close to his heart. It was a symbolic moment for the now aging Fenian. Not much within the movement developed in the 1890s, apart from a continuation of fundraising for Clan na Gael. In 1900 Roantree made the decision to return to Dublin. Isabel chose to stay in America and went to live with one of their daughters, who had married and was reluctant to make the trip back to Ireland.[92]

Roantree meanwhile secured a job in Dublin Corporation and was assigned to its electricity and lighting department before it appears, due to his old age (he was now over 70), he was given the job as a 'canvasser'.[93] This job required him to put up canvas coverings for those involved in outdoor works and appears to have been given to Roantree as a way of acknowledging his services to the Fenian organisations. The corporation employed many prominent nationalists from the IRB.

In 1901, James Stephens, the founding father of the IRB, had been buried in Glasnevin. His memorial stone, in the shape of a large Celtic cross, was unveiled in 1909 and it was William Roantree who was chosen to give the graveside oration. The *Drogheda Argus and Leinster Journal* described the scenes:

> Major Roantree said that in revering the memory of Stephens it was not so much to the man they rendered homage as to the movement he originated … he hoped that ere long suitable memorials would be erected over the remains of Terence Bellew McManus, O'Mahony

> and others of the faithful few who died for Ireland, and who lay there sleeping in that cemetery in neglected graves.[94]

He was never officially given the title or rank of 'Major', but many sources in his later life cite him as such, perhaps out of respect for the aging famous Fenian. In 1911 he was living as a boarder at 16 Blessington Street. His occupation is listed as a 'Municipal Official'.

In his final years, Roantree maintained a keen interest in the reemerging IRB and its new plans for another insurrection. According to *The Freeman's Journal*, his post from America was being interfered with by officials in Dublin Castle and he was kept under watch despite his old age.[95] He lived to witness the events of 1916 but not in the way he would have hoped. His health was failing and, although living on Gardiner Street, close to the city centre, at the start of the Rising he was removed to the Mater Hospital.[96]

Following the events of 1916 he was released from his job in the corporation due to ill health and awarded a regulation pension of £23.8.0 per year.[97] On 20 February 1918, William Francis Roantree died at his residence at 33 Upper Gardiner Street. He was 90 years old. His obituaries in the newspapers contained some fanciful tales about his life; many should be taken with a pinch of salt. Some point to his time in Dartmoor Prison, despite the fact that he never set foot there. Others tell stories relating to his time in Cuba as a soldier of fortune. Another of the many tales told about Roantree is the story that he made his way to the GPO on Easter Monday 1916 from Gardiner Street and shouted, 'The best of luck to all involved inside.' Michael Kenney argues that despite these many tall tales '[he] certainly led an eventful and interesting life' surviving 'military action, imprisonment and exile'.[98]

His funeral took place two days later, on the morning of 22 February. His remains were laid out at the Pro-Cathedral on Marlborough Street. After requiem mass, he was removed and taken for burial.[99] *The Freeman's Journal* in its account of the proceedings said, 'the attendance in the church and at the graveside testified to the esteem and respect in which the deceased gentleman was held'.[100] The *Irish Independent* obituary, although littered with inaccuracies surrounding his life, ended with the lines: 'His fine old figure and noble presence, which were familiar to Dublin citizens, will be sadly missed.'[101] His grave is in the Dublin section (MA 4). His nephew, Vincent James Roantree, was in charge of making the appropriate arrangements, but William was buried in a grave with his wife's family, the Caseys, and it lay forgotten and unmarked until 2009, when a limestone slab was finally placed on top. This was thanks to the work of locals from Leixlip, his relations and the National Graves Association.

Countless other Fenians buried within the cemetery have similar stories, but these four men were chosen to tell a story of sacrifice, hardship and an unrepentant belief in a cause that they were willing to take to their graves. None lived to see their dream become a reality, but Roantree, at least, lived to see 1916.

Strange Bedfellows

Over the course of the 1916 rebellion, 488 people died. Many were civilians simply caught up in the chaos. As bodies began to literally pile up in places, funerals gathered pace, many arriving at the gates of Glasnevin. The business of burying the dead was not an easy one for staff in the weeks after the rebellion. They struggled to cope with the demand over such a short period. The first week in May 1916 saw an average of fifty bodies at a time reaching the cemetery gates for burial. It was decided that in order to make burials more manageable, a communal plot was to be opened in the St Paul's section of the grounds. This is where an unexpected burial took place on 5 May 1916 for Richard Simpson (KA 37.5).

Richard was born on 13 October 1865 in County Antrim.[102] He was born into a family who were Presbyterian in faith and was brought up and educated in the unionist tradition. He lived on Richmond Street just off the Shankill Road in Belfast and was one of the first to sign the Ulster Solemn League and Covenant of 1912. Amongst republicans, nationalists and civilians it is unusual to find an Ulster unionist at rest in this plot.

With the outbreak of the First World War many Ulster Volunteer Force (UVF) men joined the British Army (in particular the 36th Ulster Division). They would have been eager to show the empire that they were willing to do their duty for their nation. Richard Simpson was one of these men. He was described in his military file as being of 'fair' build with a fair head of 'grey' hair, brown eyes, weighing 143lbs, 5ft and 2½ inches in height with a distinctive tattoo in the shape of an R on his forearm and a scar on his left scapula.[103] He was provisionally passed fit for active service on 5 September 1914 in Belfast. When it came to actually being posted to serve overseas, however, difficulties would arise in the shape of his lungs. He would eventually find himself in Dublin City instead. He was posted to Wellington Barracks (today Griffith College) on the South Circular Road.

When he arrived in Dublin at the end of March 1916 he was listed as a private on duty in the barracks.[104] On the evening of 22 April 1916 two of his friends went into his room in Wellington Barracks wondering where he was. They found find him lying dead on the floor. At the time they noted a strong smell of gas in the room. His body was taken to the morgue and a coroner's inquest was ordered. The death certificate for Richard Simpson states that he died as a result of 'gas poisoning'. Before burial could be arranged, however, the rebellion had broken out and everything was put on hold. His body lay in the morgue almost forgotten about. A military cordon was placed around the city and no funerals could take place. He remained there until May 1916. The *Irish Independent* on 8 May had a grim section on page four listing the dead of Easter Week buried 'without inquests'. In it we can see the name of: 'Pte R. Simpson, asphyxiated by gas in Wellington Barracks.'[105] Due to the delay, his remains were buried in the new communal plot at Glasnevin. Today he lies in his British military uniform and is buried alongside people from the Irish Volunteers, the Irish Citizen Army and many civilians.

The Eye Opener and Thomas Dickson

Another example of the many unexpected and unexplored narratives from the 1916 Rising at rest in the cemetery is the grave of Thomas Dickson in the Garden section (VG 78). He was born in Glasgow in 1884, to Samuel Dickson, a plumber and gas fitter with Glasgow Corporation, and his wife, Annie. Both were Irish and Roman Catholic. In 1901 the family were living at 28 Glebe Street in Glasgow in tenement conditions and Thomas was working as an advertising agent. By 1910 he had moved to Dublin, probably for work, where he could be found living at 31 Bolton Street, employed as a grocer and provisions dealer.[106]

The Mountjoy Prison General Register states that on 13 May 1910 he was committed for trial having 'embezzled and converted to his own use money, to wit £24/18/10 and £36/3/1' but was discharged just a few days later, on 19 May.[107] On 20 March 1912 he was sentenced to nine months' hard labour in Mountjoy for obtaining the sum of 13 shillings by false pretences. By that time he was a commission agent living at 85 Lower Camden Street,

Dublin. In the prison register he is described as '4 foot 7¼ inches in height, 103 pounds, both legs deformed, brown eyes, dark brown hair, with a fresh complexion'.[108] *The Weekly Irish Times* in 1917 stated that 'during his business career some of his undertakings had involved himself and other persons in very unfortunate consequences'.[109] In essence he was a convicted fraudster.[110]

Later, in February 1916, he launched a controversial periodical called the *Eye Opener* and, according to Conor Morrissey, it has a 'claim to be one of the most vitriolic Irish Periodicals of the 20th century in Ireland'. Its circulation was tiny but featured anti-Semitic content and a good deal of sexually salacious material. It featured attacks on Jewish businessmen, allegations of municipal corruption, xenophobia and 'innuendo laden cryptic accounts' of alleged non-marital affairs to blackmail people he disliked.[111]

As the Rising began on Easter Monday 1916, Captain John Bowen-Colthurst, who appears to have been suffering the effects of a mental breakdown, engaged in an extraordinary series of killings. On 25 April, Francis Sheehy Skeffington, who had been seeking to prevent looting in the city, was arrested and brought to Portobello Barracks. Later, he was taken on a patrol of the city led by Bowen-Colthurst to capture more rebels. If they were fired at, Bowen-Colthurst said, Sheehy Skeffington would be shot. The party advanced into the city and came to the corner of Camden and Harrington streets, where Bowen-Colthurst shot dead an innocent 19-year-old cycle mechanic called James Coade.[112] Coade was buried in the St Bridget's section (CH 214) on 3 May 1916. His cause of death is recorded as a 'result of gunfire'.

Next, the patrol approached Kelly's tobacco shop, where Thomas Dickson, along with another journalist, Patrick McIntyre, was arrested and taken back to Portobello. Shortly after 10 a.m. on 26 April, Bowen-Colthurst asked to speak with Sheehy Skeffington, Dickson and McIntyre in the barracks yard. When all three were together, he had them shot without warning, trial or cause by seven members of the guards on duty.[113] Bombardier McCaughey, a member of the firing squad, described to the Royal Commission of Inquiry how Dickson was 'very knock-kneed and small and he wore his hat in a curious way on the back of his head'.[114] Bowen-Colthurst was eventually placed under arrest after a fellow officer, Sir Francis Vane, pressured the authorities. At a court martial he was found guilty but insane, and was detained at Broadmoor lunatic asylum for two years before emigrating to Canada, where he died in 1965.[115]

The Royal Commission looked into the circumstances around the men's deaths and found that 'the shooting of unarmed and unresisting civilians without trial constitutes the offence of murder, whether martial law had been proclaimed or not'.[116] Thomas Dickson, despite his controversial periodical and fraudulent career, was just 31 years old and engaged to a Dublin lady at the time of his death. His parents only learned of their son's death through a statement made in Parliament by the prime minister. His two brothers came over from Glasgow to claim his body and he was buried in Glasnevin on 19 May 1916 (VG 78). His effects were collected from the 3rd Royal Irish Rifles, Victoria Barracks, Belfast, on 22 May 1916 by his mother and brother Samuel, who both lived in Glasgow.[117]

The events in Portobello Barracks on 26 April 1916 are among the most infamous of the Easter Rising. Today Francis Sheehy Skeffington, the more famous victim of the three, is still remembered, but Dickson and McIntyre are often just footnotes in his story. Sheehy Skeffington and Dickson are both buried in Glasnevin, while McIntyre is buried in Deansgrange Cemetery.

Gearóid O'Sullivan: Hoist the Tricolour above the GPO

At twelve noon on 24 April, the GPO on Sackville Street was seized by members of the Irish Volunteers, Irish Citizen Army, Na Fianna Éireann and Cumann na mBan. The Proclamation of the Irish Republic was read outside the GPO to a bemused small crowd sometime before 1 p.m. In the chaos and confusion of the day the youngest officer of the Irish Volunteers, at 25 years of age (three months younger than Michael Collins), was handed a folded up Irish tricolour flag and instructed to go to the roof and raise it. This was to be one of two flags flown above the GPO during the Rising. The second was the flag of the Irish Republic, which is held today at the National Museum of Ireland in Collins Barracks.

This was an extraordinary honour for a young man from County Cork called Gearóid O'Sullivan. He was born on 28 January 1891 in the small townland of Coolnagarrane, a short distance from Skibbereen, County Cork. Born to parents Michael Sullivan and Margaret McCarthy, he was the fifth of nine children.[118] A newspaper account of his father says he 'was a quiet, hard-working, industrious farmer, a fluent speaker of Irish, honest and straightforward in his dealings'.[119]

Gearóid grew up in a rural setting with his five brothers and three sisters.[120] His story has many parallels with that of Michael Collins: they were born in the same area, were of similar age and were born into farming families, but Collins' legacy is the one that has assumed legendary status. Up until 2020, no biography on the life and legacy of O'Sullivan existed. It was in that year that Joni Scanlon published *A Sacrifice of the Heart: The Biography of Irish Patriot Gearóid O'Sullivan*. A former journalist and newspaper editor, she became impassioned about telling his forgotten story:

> He was forgotten by history … as a former journalist the sense of justice is so strongly engrained in me that the idea that he contributed so much and was forgotten bothered me. I had always known about him, he was my grandfather's first cousin … my grandparents in fact named their first son after him … but as a child I didn't really know a lot about him. Growing up in the United States of America it wasn't something I was really focused on. It was really in 2006 that I visited the Skibbereen Heritage Centre … and when I walked in there the archivist when I mentioned my grandfather said you have someone really famous in your family …[121]

He is today buried a short walk away from Michael Collins in the South section (UA 23). During his life he fought at the GPO during the Rising, played a major role in the Irish War of Independence, becoming adjutant general of the IRA from 1920–21, and he later became adjutant general of the Irish Free State Army (1922–24) before resigning. He held a seat in the Dáil for much of the period 1920–30 and became judge advocate general for the State between 1927 and 1937.[122]

Gearóid went to school in the town of Skibbereen, where he attended St Fachtna's.[123] He was strongly influenced by the interest in Irish heritage, culture and language in his family. He would have heard stories about the Famine years (1845–52), in which his local area was very badly affected. His father, Michael, defiantly completed the 1911 census fully in Irish, while his grandparents' home on his mother's side was turned upside down by members of the RIC in the days after the Rising. These raids, as Joni Scanlon tells us, happened on more than one occasion, culminating in the entire residence being burned to the ground in March 1921 during the War of Independence.[124] The legacy of local IRB members like Jeremiah O'Donovan Rossa would also have played their part in Gearóid's beliefs.[125]

Two of Gearóid's friends, James Duggan and Peadar O'Hourihane, also influenced him greatly. Duggan was a friend of the family and later a Sinn Féin organiser in the area. O'Hourihane was heavily involved with the Gaelic League and was editor of *The Southern Star* newspaper. These men encouraged him to sign up to the Gaelic League in 1901.[126] The records of his local branch show that in his formative years he took part in various feiseanna and debates, winning prizes for reciting Irish poetry.[127] His involvement in the League allowed him to meet many of the leaders within the republican movement, including Seán Mac Diarmada, Patrick Pearse, Tom Clarke, Maud Gonne and Éamon de Valera. He met Mac Diarmada in Skibbereen, shortly after turning 17; they would forge a close relationship, with Gearóid holding Mac Diarmada in great regard.

Gearóid moved to Dublin to pursue his studies and took lodgings at 44 Mountjoy Street. He began his studies at St Patrick's College, Drumcondra, to pursue his interest in teaching. He graduated as a national school teacher and later returned to study at UCD where he graduated with an honours degree in Celtic Studies in 1913.[128] His flair for education saw him receive his Higher Diploma in Education (1914) and later his full Master's in Education (1915).[129] He taught at Kildorrery in his native County Cork before returning to Dublin to teach at St Peter's school in Phibsborough.[130] He also taught Irish at 44 Mountjoy Street and later at 44 Parnell Square, the headquarters of the Gaelic League's Keating branch. Members of this branch included Collins, Mac Diarmada, Cathal Brugha, Richard Mulcahy and Piaras Béaslaí.[131] Regarded as a very talented teacher, an old student from St Peter's in Phibsborough in later years said, 'Irish was one thing he could teach in a way a boy could learn it from him.'[132]

The files of the Military Archives of Ireland show that Gearóid joined the Irish Volunteers at their inaugural foundation meeting in November 1913 at the Rotunda. He became a member of F Company, 1st Battalion, Dublin Brigade.[133] His officer commanding was Captain Fionán Lynch, who was lodging with Gearóid at 44 Mountjoy Street. This address was later to become known as the most raided house in Dublin. Through his connections with Mac Diarmada, he met Tom Clarke[134] – these two men became the masterminds behind the Rising. O'Sullivan was in the room and was part of many of their inner conversations. Mac Diarmada and Gearóid were known to share meals and have long, deep conversations about politics. Such was the impact of this new friendship that O'Sullivan would later, in an unpublished memoir of his life, say, 'Seán was one of the most serious of all the conspirators and yet the one who had the greatest sense of humour ... [he] appears to be the least mentioned of the 1916 leaders, tho' without doubt he and Tom Clarke were the two persons most responsible for the insurrection in 1916 and the events which led up to it.'[135]

At 44 Mountjoy Street, two days before the planned Rising, Gearóid was woken in the early hours of the morning by knocking on the door. In the house that night were Mac Diarmada, Mort O'Connell and Fionán O'Doherty (both Volunteers) and his roommate, Fionán Lynch.[136] It was a messenger. The news was bad. Roger Casement had been arrested. After receiving this news, Gearóid and Lynch set off by taxi to St Enda's in Rathfarnham to collect Pearse and bring him to Liberty Hall for crisis talks.[137]

The arrest fundamentally changed the nature of the Rising. Eoin MacNeill issued countermanding orders to be published in the *Sunday Independent*, cancelling all Volunteer manoeuvres for Easter Sunday, the planned day of the Rising. That afternoon, 23 April, the RIC raided 44 Mountjoy Street. Most of the Volunteers staying in the residence at the time were out, but one man, Con Collins, was arrested and charged with 'possession of a gun and ammunition'. A sizeable cache of ammunition stored by Gearóid above the ceiling in his room went undetected by the police.[138]

The Supreme Council of the IRB met on Parnell Square. They voted to go ahead with the insurrection a day later than planned. Gearóid was briefly in charge of guarding Bulmer Hobson, who had been busy travelling around the country on MacNeill's direction, reinforcing the cancellation orders. He had been placed under arrest to prevent any more such orders being distributed.

Gearóid spent the night before the Rising in Flemings Hotel at 32 Gardiner Place with Mac Diarmada. His official role during Easter Week was to be his friend's aide-de-camp.[139] On Easter Monday, he left the hotel before 8 a.m. to carry mobilisation orders and messages around the city. His next duty was to travel to the Citizen Army headquarters at Liberty Hall, where he was given the task of transporting the GPO's main store of ammunition.[140] He commandeered a horse-drawn taxi for the job and set off for the GPO with everything on board. As the taxi turned the corner past Abbey Street onto Sackville Street, he saw Volunteers beginning to run towards the GPO. At that same moment the floor of the horse-drawn cab split apart with the weight. Hundreds of rounds of ammunition spilled onto the street.[141]

A vehicle caught his eye coming down Sackville Street. It was a chauffeur-driven motor car carrying a wealthy and affluent judge and a lady. When he stopped the car to try and transfer the ammunition to it, the judge asked, 'Do you know who I am?' The lady interjected, 'If you do not, go away immediately, I will positively call a policeman.' O'Sullivan replied, 'If you do not obey my order it will be my painful duty to shoot you both!'[142] They both gave way and let him take the car. Once inside the GPO he was handed the Irish tricolour. He was instructed to hoist it above the building on the Henry Street-facing corner. Éamonn Bulfin hoisted the Irish Republic flag at the Prince's Street side.

A week of fighting intensified around the city of Dublin until the shells finally found their mark on the roof of the GPO. The decision was made to evacuate and head towards the warren of streets around Moore Street. Michael Joseph O'Rahilly (or The O'Rahilly) had gathered a number of men and made plans for a charge towards the barricade on Moore Street. He hoped that this would clear a path for the remaining Volunteers to get out of the GPO and retreat. Gearóid volunteered to join this group and standing next to him was Seán MacEntee. In future years, MacEntee and Gearóid would take up opposing sides in Dáil Éireann and share many heated debates.

Gearóid survived the charge and found himself on Henry Place, while The O'Rahilly bled to death in a nearby laneway called Sackville Lane (today The O'Rahilly Parade). Those left alive huddled in doorways and lanes. Eventually they managed to work their way safely to Moore Lane. Gearóid ended the week fighting a losing battle at 16 Moore Street alongside Clarke, Mac Diarmada, Pearse and a badly injured James Connolly.[143] After the Volunteers surrendered, an overnight sojourn outside the Rotunda was followed by a stay at Richmond Barracks, where he waited with the others to learn his fate.[144] With spirits low, Gearóid gave those interned a small morale boost when he stood up to a British military officer called Major Orr. Batt O'Connor recalled the incident:

> It was one of our duties to clean out the latrines used by us and this was done by the fatigue party appointed for the day. On the fifth morning it was the turn of a party led by Gearóid O'Sullivan. When they had done their job they received an order to clean the latrines used by the English soldiers. Gearóid at once refused. He said he was prepared to take his turn in attending to the requirements of his comrades, but

> that nothing would induce him to do so for the English soldiers … The Major arrived immediately in a towering rage. O'Sullivan repeated his refusal. Saying he would give him two minutes to obey, the Major walked back five paces and, drawing his revolver, he took his watch in the other hand. This scene took place in the barrack yard, and from the window of the room in which we were imprisoned we watched all that was passing below … We could see the Major's lips moving and the resolute expression and unflinching attitude of Gearóid. I have thought the world of him since that day.[145]

After some time in solitary confinement, Gearóid and the men in his party faced a court hearing on the matter. It found that it was not the prisoners' duty to clean British soldiers' latrines.[146] Because of this incident, however, he missed his chance to say goodbye to his friend Mac Diarmada, who was court-martialled and executed.

Gearóid was in one of the last groups to leave the barracks in the summer of 1916 and ended up in Wandsworth Prison in England and later Frongoch internment camp in Wales. While in Wandsworth he kept company with some fellow Corkmen, most notably Michael Collins and Pádraig Ó Caoimh.[147]

In Frongoch, a close friendship began to grow between O'Sullivan and Collins. Bernard O'Driscoll commented that 'Gearóid had no mind of his own, he copied Mick Collins.'[148] Not everyone there at the time agreed with that view, but it shows how close the West Cork men had become. Gearóid, in this period, emerged as a natural leader amongst the prisoners. Tensions rose considerably with the threat of possible conscription into the British military as the First World War continued. A camp-wide hunger strike was arranged to protest and Gearóid became extremely ill. O'Driscoll described him at the time as being 'thin and weak … we put him between us in bed to keep him warm.'[149] The strike was called off a week later.

Gearóid stayed at the camp until his release in December 1916. During his time there his name was on the list of fifty-four prisoners who made up the 'General Council of Frongoch.'[150] After his release he became an integral part of Collins' inner circle, and their friendship was talked about so much that people have since falsely claimed that they were cousins.[151]

Between 1917 and 1919 his teaching career restarted in Carlow.[152] At the same time he became brigade commandant for the Volunteers in Carlow.[153]

His work with them involved a great deal of effort in recruiting, training and drumming up support in the local area. By 1917 he had been elected to the Supreme Council of the IRB.[154] The years 1917 and 1918 also saw him speak at many rallies to help set up Sinn Féin branches on the ground. British Intelligence was keen to arrest Gearóid and in March 1918 they got what they wanted. He had travelled home to County Cork to take part in a series of speeches being given by Collins and was arrested for 'unlawful assembly meeting persons to commit crime' according to the prison register from Cork County Gaol.[155]

As the War of Independence began, Gearóid left teaching behind and was constantly on the move. He had a seat at the table of the army's GHQ staff by the beginning of 1920. Due to the nature of his work the threat of arrest was ever present. He was arrested in January 1919 for 'seditious speeches' in County Clare, but the charges were later dropped.[156]Arrested again in August 1919 for 'unlawful assembly and drilling in possession of arms and ammunition', he was handed a six-month sentence. [157] After three months in Mountjoy Prison he was released under a new act called the 'Prisoner's Temporary ill-health Discharge Act', introduced by the British government to tackle the issue of republican hunger strikes.[158] Under the act he was temporarily released for his health but was to return to the prison once recovered. He did not return. Instead, he joined Collins on the list of wanted men on the run.[159]

The nature of Gearóid's work in the early days of the War of Independence was done on what can be termed an ad-hoc basis.[160] This was due to a lack of funds to pay many in the Volunteer Executive. Collins was effectively working multiple roles as the only paid member of staff for a time. It had been the intention of the Volunteer Executive as early as 1917 to have a paid professional GHQ staff, but this did not become a reality for some time. During the period 1917–20 both men carried out dual roles on an equal footing before Gearóid became adjutant general of the IRA in January 1920. The job entailed being head administrator for the IRA and one major responsibility was communications in the field.[161]

Joseph E.A. Connell Jnr notes how many addresses Gearóid would have been working and staying in. His head office was on Eustace Street (today where the Irish Film Institute is located) in early 1920.[162] He shared this premises with Richard Mulcahy, but due to frequent raids moved to 21 Henry Street, the premises of Jennie Wyse-Power. Vaughan's Hotel was another regular meeting spot. Safe houses were numerous. Of particular note was 16 Airfield Road, Rathgar, the home of Julia and Fionnula Donovan, the aunt and grandmother of Gearóid. It was one of two houses favoured by Collins. The other was 31 Fitzwilliam Street Upper.

Gearóid's offices were later located at 30 Ormond Quay over a tailor's shop where he carried out many of his duties.[163] A sign of his prominence in this period is a Dublin Castle file titled 'Gerald Sullivan'. There is one line that shows the seriousness of his work: 'Attempt made to assassinate him in 1920 and 1921.'[164] Gearóid was with Collins on the morning of 22 November 1920, the day after Bloody Sunday, when they attended the wedding of Elizabeth Clancy and Michael J. O'Brien at 16 Airfield Road. There is a famous photograph of the wedding with Collins hiding his face next to Gearóid.[165] The previous night both had dined at the house following the bloodiest day of the War of Independence. They attended the wedding on the morning after out of necessity. The bride's brother (Joe Clancy) was the owner of the Elgin Hotel in Skibbereen and Collins relied on this as a safe place to meet in West

Michael Collins and Gearóid O'Sullivan (second and third left back row) pictured at the wedding of Elizabeth Clancy and Michael J. O'Brien, 22 November 1920. (Courtesy of Joni Scanlon)

Cork.[166] O'Sullivan was present for the meetings before Bloody Sunday at Donovan's pub in Rathgar.[167]

The final major offensive by the IRA in the War of Independence was the attack on the Customs House on 25 May 1921. Gearóid travelled to the home of the late Michael O'Rahilly at 40 Herbert Park where Collins, Mulcahy and others approved the plan for the assault, which resulted in heavy casualties and many arrests. The situation left the IRA in Dublin close to breaking point. It was around this time that Gearóid was elected as Sinn Féin TD to Dáil Éireann for Carlow–Kilkenny. He was later re-elected in the third Dáil for this constituency in 1922 before retiring in 1923.

A truce was called in July 1921 and during the long period of negotiations that followed Gearóid gave many passionate speeches around the country. His presence at Glasnevin was noted on 21 November 1921, at an event marking the first anniversary of the killing of Dick McKee and Peadar Clancy in Dublin Castle.[168] In an advisory role to Collins, Gearóid was with the negotiators of the Anglo-Irish Treaty in London in the tense early hours of 6 December when the decision was made to sign. The Treaty was brought back to Dublin on the night of 7 December and Gearóid made a large contribution to the debates that followed.

On 6 January after listening to the Treaty debates in the Dáil and considering his view on what was the right decision, he delivered a speech to the public session:

> I rise to support the motion for the ratification of this Treaty … I don't believe that the acceptance of this Treaty by the people of Ireland is dishonourable … The Treaty gives the Irish people a chance of living their own lives in their own way. Our President said a few days ago that he was anxious, not only for the good of Ireland but for the good of humanity that this strife should cease. I am also anxious not only for the good of Ireland, but for the good of the whole human race that this strife should cease … those who advocate its rejection have not, in my opinion, given me any reason why I should conscientiously vote for its rejection. The Minister for Labour, I think, objected to our association with England because England oppresses Egypt and India. I have already said that there are many Irishmen at present oppressing India; and if Ireland accepts this Treaty the opinion of the Irish people on British rule in India and in Egypt will be expressed … I would ask

> the assembly to remember that England is not the only Empire that oppresses small nations, though I believe she is the worst.[169]

The Treaty was passed by 64 votes to 57. The evident divisions over it set the scene for the Civil War. Gearóid's own brother Tadg took up an anti-Treaty position and their relationship remained unreconciled until the 1930s. Gearóid, in his role as adjutant general of the IRA, now swapped his office premises at 30 Ormond Quay for Beggars Bush Barracks and later Portobello Barracks. He later assumed the role of adjutant general of the new Irish Free State Army. His new office was made up of seven separate sections, including a records branch, prisoners' section, discipline section, legal department, medical services, chaplain and a central registry office.[170] It was a time of rapid change, when people like Gearóid and Mulcahy had to try to establish a regular army with no guidelines or precedent. They had to do this at the same time that British troops were withdrawing from barracks in twenty-six counties and the RIC was being gradually disbanded.

During the Civil War, Gearóid's job became increasingly difficult. News reached Portobello Barracks on the morning of 23 August 1922 from Major General Emmet Dalton that Collins had been killed at Béal na Bláth. Charlie Dalton recalled the moment the news filtered through: 'He [Gearóid] did not greet me as customarily … but stood rather bewildered-looking for a second or two and then broke down weeping and spoke in a rather uncertain voice, saying, "Charlie, The Big Fella [Collins] is dead."'[171]

Collins was buried in Glasnevin on 28 August. Gearóid's relationship with him was described by Con Collins as embodying the phrase *Fidus Achates* (faithful friend).[172] An indication of their closeness was the fact that they had arranged to get married in a double wedding to the Kiernan sisters from Granard, County Longford. Collins was to marry Kitty, while Gearóid was to marry Maud. A date had been set for 18 October 1922. Tragically the day went ahead without Collins. There is Pathé news reel footage of the wedding featuring Kitty smiling sadly into the camera dressed in black. *The Freeman's Journal* wrote of the wedding: 'A very pretty wedding took place yesterday at University Church, Stephen's Green … As Miss Kiernan entered the Church the bridal march from Lohengrin (Wagner) was played … Attired in pale old gold satin and cream veil, and carrying a fragile spray of flowers, the bride, attended by bridesmaid and page, also in old gold satin, looked exceedingly pretty …'[173]

The Freeman's Journal image of Gearóid and Maud's wedding. (Courtesy of Joni Scanlon)

There was no time for a honeymoon. The couple lived initially at Temple Villas in Rathmines, close to where Gearóid was working, but later moved to Grosvenor Road, Rathmines. They had four children. Away from family life, Gearóid, with Mulcahy as commander in chief, Seán McMahon (chief of staff), Joseph McGrath (director of intelligence) and Diarmuid O'Hegarty (director of organisation) entered a new phase of the Civil War – the executions of old friends. A month after his marriage to Maud, Gearóid began to preside over and sign off on the executions of anti-Treaty prisoners under the newly introduced Public Safety Act.

In total there would be eighty-one official executions by the Irish Free State in this period. Gearóid also dealt with anti-Treaty prisoners. One of the most notable was Éamon de Valera in Kilmainham Gaol. As adjutant general, he kept de Valera under strict watch. De Valera was to be seen by no other prisoners while exercising. All reading material was pre-approved by Gearóid and all of de Valera's correspondence was sent to his office for preview. There was even a special note attached to instructions for on-duty guards close to his cell that 'under no circumstances will any person be permitted to enter the Special Wing unless in possession of a permit signed by the ADJUTANT GENERAL; and being duly recognised by the officer in charge.'[174]

Many terrible acts happened during the Civil War. It often fell to Gearóid to investigate. A case in Kenmare, County Kerry, involving two sisters (the McCarthys), made for some difficult reading. The sisters had declined invitations by two Free State soldiers to attend a Kerry Command Dance, saying they would not 'have anything to do with murderers'. Consequently their home was raided on 2 June 1923 by three disguised men who violently assaulted them and rubbed heavy axle grease into their hair. It was found that one of the men involved was Paddy O'Daly, General Commander for the Kerry Command of the Irish Free State.[175] Gearóid, as adjutant general, received the garda report and, with the involvement of Commander in Chief Richard Mulcahy, the attorney general, Hugh Kennedy, and legal advice from Cahir Davitt, the judge advocate general, a court of inquiry was established. No charges were ever brought against O'Daly.[176] War of Independence loyalties seem to have saved him. Legal advice had sought to have O'Daly court-martialled, but this never happened. The atrocities of the Civil War left a lasting impact on many local communities and many have still not been adequately explored 100 years later. The desire to move forward, heal and forget what happened afterwards means that events like those from Kenmare are not widely remembered today.

The Civil War officially came to an end in May 1923. Gearóid's time as adjutant general ended in controversy due to the Army Mutiny of 1924. Mutineers were angry and disillusioned with mass demobilisation within the army and frustrated by perceived instances of favouritism among the elite in the Army Council. They branded themselves the 'Old IRA'. Gearóid gave orders to arrest the mutineers and after raids on their locations, they were taken to Arbour Hill Barracks. The mutiny ended with the resignations of O'Sullivan and most of the Army Council, including Mulcahy from his role as Minister for Defence. An inquiry ultimately found that the mutineers were solely to blame and Gearóid's reputation remained untarnished.

After his exit from the military, Gearóid held a number of civil service jobs and focused on family life. He took up study of law and was called to the Irish Bar in 1927; later he was appointed judge advocate general for the State. He held this post until 1932. The assassination of Kevin O'Higgins in 1927 pushed him back into politics. He won O'Higgins' empty seat and was duly elected as a member of the fifth Dáil for Cumann na nGaedheal (1927–32). He was now in the Dáil opposite many people whom he had fought against a decade earlier and was noted for speaking his mind, particularly in exchanges with Seán MacEntee, with whom he had charged out of the GPO in 1916. Scanlon says 'their mutual banter could be amusing and their respect for one another despite their political views is hard to miss'.[177]

After 1932, Cumann na nGaedheal fell out of power and was replaced by de Valera's Fianna Fáil administration. Gearóid swapped seats for the opposition benches where he remained until 1937. He briefly became a senator and was a member of the Cultural and Education Panel (1938). After 1938 he took up a role as the Commissioner for Ireland's Special Tax Acts and focused on his private legal career.

On 28 October 1940 his wife, Maud, died of kidney failure and was buried in a grave with her first child in Glasnevin (UA 23 South). Those close to Gearóid noted a marked shift in his personality afterwards. He sent his children to boarding school in Tipperary and drank heavily.[178] He was married a second time, to a woman called Mary (Mae) Brennan in November 1942, and they moved to Dartry, County Dublin. Mae came from Belfast and worked as a civil servant. As Gearóid's health began to decline, she became his carer. Although only 56 years old at the time of his death, his daughter Ann remembered him as having the body of an old man.[179] He died on Good Friday, 26 March 1948 at St Gerard's in Dartry. His recorded cause of death is as a result of 'cancer'. *The Cork Examiner* featured a notice of his death in both the Irish and English language, while *The Irish Times* and *The Irish Press* published substantial obituaries on his life.[180] A feature from *The Southern Star* gave an account of his funeral as told by Peadar O'Hourihane (an old friend of Gearóid's) who noted:

> I saw a few ex-Ministers of the Fianna Fáil Government present, and the new Taoiseach (John A. Costello) with General Mulcahy and their friends were to the fore. His relatives who were present … must have found comfort with witnessing the high honour paid to their dead hero, for a military funeral can be very impressive indeed. In many parts along the route today the side paths were thronged and traffic was held up wherever necessary. Such honour and respect have not been shown to a Skibbereen man in our time nor possibly ever before. It was a most impressive procession from one side of the city to the other.[181]

Gearóid was buried in the South section at 12.22 p.m., 29 March 1948, with his late wife, Maud, and infant child. The funeral took place on Easter

Monday 1948, the same day that he had raised the Irish tricolour above the GPO thirty-two years previously. As a mark of respect, the funeral passed the GPO where the tricolour hung at half-mast. The hearse then continued its journey northwards. Thousands are pictured in newspaper images on O'Connell Street. His coffin was draped in the same tricolour that had covered Michael Collins' coffin before he was buried.

Gearóid's second wife, Mae, remained at their home in Dartry.[182] She had considered moving back to Belfast but, for the sake of his children from his first marriage, decided to stay in Dublin. She was eventually awarded a meagre pension of £66 pounds per annum, which increased modestly as the years passed but never exceeded £260 per year.[183] Gearóid's estate was not released until October 1949 and so she had no choice but to take on lodgers. She later moved back to Belfast to live with her family until her death in 1984. Gearóid's last surviving child, Sibéal, died in 2011.

Emmet Dalton: 'Drive like Hell'

In the same area of the cemetery where both Alfie Byrne and William Dargan are buried, you will find the grave of Emmet Dalton, whose story is multifaceted. During his life he was a decorated British soldier in the First World War, a high-ranking IRA man in the War of Independence and a major general in the Irish Free State Army, before becoming a film pioneer. He is also the man who sat beside Michael Collins when he was killed at Béal na Bláth. Sean Boyne, in *Emmet Dalton: Somme Soldier, Irish General, Film Pioneer*, notes:

> [He] packed much into his eighty years. His soldiering took him on a hazardous journey, from the Somme to Bealnablath, from Palestine and Salonika to the Battle of the Four Courts. He had an amazing record – a founding father of the Irish Defence Forces; first Senate Clerk; pioneering film-maker and founding father of Ireland's first film studio. It is noteworthy that a former Civil War enemy described him as 'a fearless soldier' and 'among the noblest of men'. Not a bad epitaph for Major General Emmet Dalton.[184]

Dalton was born in the USA on 4 March 1898 to Irish-American parents, James Francis Dalton and Katherine Lee Riley. The family later moved to

Ireland around 1900 and by 1911 had settled in Drumcondra, at 8 Columba's Road Upper. Dalton was educated at O'Connell's School.[185] He later enlisted with the British Army to fight in the First World War and, during the Easter Rising, was in Kilworth Camp, Cork, when he heard about the unfolding events. He fought at the Somme, Palestine and Salonika between 1914 and 1918, and later said that it was an 'existence that is hard to conjecture today. I don't think that today's generation could survive it. It's amazing to me that we did, in at least those of us did [*sic*].'[186] He was stationed at Trones Woods with Tom Kettle on the evening before the assault on Guillemont and Ginchy on 8 September 1916. Dalton was second in command of A Company and Kettle was in command of B Company. At 5 p.m. on 9 September, they led their men in an assault on what was left of the town. Dalton recalled the moment when Kettle was hit:

> I was just behind Tom when we went over the top. He was in a bent position, and a bullet got over a steel waistcoat that he wore and entered his heart. Well, he only lasted about one minute, and he had my crucifix in his hands. Then Boyd took all the papers and things out of Tom's pockets in order to keep them for Mrs. Kettle, but poor Boyd was blown to atoms in a few minutes. The Welsh Guards buried Mr. Kettle's remains. Tom's death has been a big blow to the regiment, and I am afraid that I could not put in words my feelings on the subject.[187]

Emmet Dalton in his First World War British military uniform.

Dalton was given a Military Cross for his bravery. Between 1917 and 1918 he was sent to the 7th Battalion of the Royal Dublin Fusiliers, 30th Brigade, 10th Irish Division in Salonika, Egypt and Palestine. He spent the final few months of action at the Western Front with the 6th Leinsters.

After his demobilisation he returned to a greatly changed Ireland. His brother Charlie was already an active Volunteer and later became a member of Collins' 'Squad'. Emmet became quite close to Collins and was a trusted ally. He served as his liaison officer and assistant director of training, and was at the heart of IRA GHQ operations during the War of Independence.[188] In May 1921 he was given the task of coming up with an audacious escape plan to rescue Seán MacEoin from Mountjoy Prison.[189] The attempt was ultimately unsuccessful. Following the Truce of July 1921, he became the assistant chief liaison officer and Dublin Brigade assistant liaison officer.[190] Dalton was with the Irish delegates as they made their way to London for negotiations and was asked by Collins to make provisions for a special squad to be arranged to protect him and to purchase an aeroplane in case of an emergency.[191]

In 1922 he became director of military operations in the National Army. On 28 June 1922 he ordered the bombardment of the Four Courts where anti-Treaty leaders had been gathered for months – this was the beginning of the Civil War. As the Battle of Dublin ended and the National Army gained control of the capital, attention turned to other counties. Dalton, from the outset, was a big advocate of seaborne landings for troops.[192] He successfully landed 500 Free State Army soldiers at Passage West in Cork and quickly took control of the city. On 18 August Dalton communicated to Collins that he had it on good authority that talk of peace negotiations was not possible with anti-Treaty leaders. On 22 August Collins was shot dead during an inspection tour of the south-western command on which Dalton had accompanied him. Much of the blame for his death was subsequently unfairly placed in Dalton's lap and ever since there have been allegations and baseless conspiracy theories that he had a role to play in the killing of Collins.

Emmet married Alice Shannon in Cork on 9 October 1922, less than two months after the loss of his friend Michael Collins. Accusations of conspiracy with the British Intelligence network, along with the mental trauma he had endured in the First World War, took their toll and Dalton began to drink heavily. After he resigned from his military post in the National Army, the Free State government, in recognition of his services, offered him the £1,000 a year clerkship of the Seanad. He accepted and became the first clerk of Seanad Éireann. His time in this position ended on 11 December 1925. The strain of handling his father's estate, which had placed great financial burdens on his son, meant he was too often absent from the chamber.[193]

Following the end of the Second World War he emerged surprisingly as a pioneer film-maker. A lucky meeting with David Rose, the head of the British branch of Paramount Studios on the golf course at the Hermitage in Dublin resulted in a job as a salesman for the Hollywood movie studio.[194] Dalton moved to London and, in 1948, became Samuel Goldwyn's representative in Britain and Ireland.[195] He believed that there was a big market for Irish-produced films on American television and managed to secure the support of the Abbey Theatre to adapt a series of Abbey plays for television. Due to their modest success, he was able to convince Taoiseach Seán Lemass that there could be great potential for an Irish Film Industry. Ardmore Studios in Bray, County Wicklow, was the end result.

Dalton was the joint managing director of the operation and it was financed by a sizeable loan from the Industrial Credit Corporation. Notable successes of the studio included *Shake Hands with the Devil* (1959) starring James Cagney, and *This Other Eden* (1959) starring Leslie Phillips, Milo O'Shea and Dalton's daughter Audrey. His daughter also appeared in *Titanic* (1953). Dalton's final film with Ardmore was the unsuccessful *The Devil's Agent* (1962) starring Christopher Lee.[196] Ardmore survived receivership and under new management his long-term vision came to fruition. The studio is now over sixty years old and many major TV series, shows and films have used the facility to produce their creations, including *Penny Dreadful.*

In the final chapter of his varied life, Dalton gave a number of significant TV interviews discussing events at Béal na Bláth, his experiences in the First World War and his opinions on the revolutionary period. Many of these can be viewed through the RTÉ archives or YouTube. He died 'with military precision' on his 80th birthday, 4 March 1978, on the 200th anniversary of the birth of Robert Emmet after whom he was named.[197] He was at his daughter Nuala's house in Ballsbridge. The night before his death, the documentary *Emmet Dalton Remembers* was broadcast by RTÉ. It received much acclaim, but Dalton did not live to see the reaction.

At his funeral he received full military honours. His coffin, draped in the tricolour, was brought to the cemetery on a gun carriage. The Last Post was sounded and he was lowered into his plot (JD 56) metres away from Michael Collins.[198] Vinny Byrne (a former member of Collins' Squad) led the final salute.[199] *The Irish Times* in its editorial noted the failure of Fianna Fáil representatives to attend. His headstone is a small, modest, white rectangular stone with no words or epitaph.

In the immediate aftermath of Dalton's death, his name was once again linked to the death of Collins, which deeply hurt the Dalton family. Baseless conspiracy theories, TV programmes and the use of testimony from anti-Treaty IRA men have all led to tenuous links between him and the death of Collins. An anti-Treaty Civil War veteran, Sean Dowling, later stated: 'Emmet Dalton was not only the most fearless of soldiers, he was also among the noblest of men, and he idolised Collins.'[200] Undoubtedly rumours and conspiracies have done much to damage the attention given to his grave. Hopefully, with the inclusion of his name in this book, people will remember him as soldier, general, film-maker, husband and father.

Fatalities from the First World War

The cemetery can tell stories from both the revolutionary period and the First World War. In the Garden section, two graves lie side by side: Sergeant Patrick Dunne (AG 23.5) and Volunteer Edward Ennis (AG 24.5). Patrick enlisted with the Royal Dublin Fusiliers in the First World War and died from meningitis on 30 June 1916. He was 20 years old. Beside him lies Edward, who worked as a chimney cleaner in Dublin. He joined the Irish Volunteers and died during the 1916 Rising on 29 April along the railway line at Grand Canal Street. He was 31 years old. Their headstones tell two very different stories. Sergeant Dunne's grave is marked by a Portland stone Commonwealth War Graves memorial. Volunteer Ennis' grave is marked by a National Graves Association of Ireland memorial. The two died in 1916 for different causes but show how multiple narratives lie side by side in Glasnevin.

On a walk around the cemetery, you will come across more of these small Portland headstones. In 2012 a project between the Commonwealth War Graves Commission and Glasnevin was launched to remember all those buried in the cemetery who had fought and died as members of the British military in both world wars. Irishmen fought not just with the British military in the First World War but also with the Americans, Canadians, Australians and New Zealand Armed Forces. Glasnevin is the final resting place for over 200 of the resulting casualties.

George Cronin was born in Dublin's Rotunda Hospital on 14 October 1895 to Christopher Cronin, a bookmaker's clerk originally from Scotland, and his wife, Anne, née Philpot. By 1901 the family were living at Wood Quay in number 20 Carman's Hall. After leaving school George worked as a bootmaker and lived with his grandmother, Mary Mulhall, on Gardiner Street. In May 1915 he enlisted for service with the Royal Navy. He served on board HMS *Victory II*, which was an administrative vessel. On his navy enlistment card we see that he first served on board on 21 May 1915. His character is described as being 'Good'.[201] He is also described as being 5ft 7¼ inches tall, having brown hair and blue eyes and having a 'fresh' complexion.[202] His last service date as a member of the Royal Navy was 22 April 1916, after which he was discharged from the administrative vessel and was no longer required. He emigrated to the USA where he made his way to Pittsburgh, Pennsylvania. He intended to work as a labourer but spent much of his time unemployed. In June 1917 he registered in the US draft for the First World War and enlisted as a private.[203]

The USA entered the war officially on 6 April 1917. Private Cronin was sent to France with the American Expeditionary Force. He was shot and killed in a confusing incident during a battle near Chateau-Thierry (just east of Paris) on 5 June 1918. The incident is recorded as 'accidentally shot'.[204] The American Expeditionary Force had a policy of allowing bodies to be repatriated to families for burial, unlike the British War Office, which buried its dead where they fell. Most of the graves today marked by the Commonwealth War Graves Commission in Glasnevin are for men and women who had been badly wounded and brought home to recover from their injuries, but who sadly later died. George Cronin was buried in an unmarked plot in the St Paul's section on 9 November 1921 (VC 98). The funeral took place at 11.50 a.m. He was buried two days before the Armistice on 11 November 1918. His remains had made the difficult journey home from France to America before finally being brought to Dublin. After a request from his mother, Anne, to the Cemetery Committee, his body was moved to the St Bridget's section (BH 89).[205] The grave was purchased by his mother. He is the only person killed on 'active service' at the Front to be buried in the cemetery, but his grave is unmarked and covered by a small patch of stones today. As a member of the American Expeditionary Force, his grave did not come under the remit of the Commonwealth Graves Commission project.

With many mothers and wives waving goodbye to their loved ones as they departed Ireland for the battlefields of the First World War, it is hard to imagine the feelings of worry they must have felt. Mary Martin was one of those. Her son, Charles Andrew Martin, joined the Royal Dublin Fusiliers. He was destined for the Balkans and Salonika in Greece. The Allies had delayed coming to the aid of the Serbs, who had been overrun by the invading forces of Austria, Germany and Bulgaria. The Serbs had evacuated as many of their remaining armed forces as possible to Corfu to regroup before the Allied nations of France and the UK (mainly the 10th Irish Division) agreed to land forces at Salonika (now Thessaloniki) in October of 1915. Many of the men involved had already been through a gruelling experience at Gallipoli.

The 10th Division eventually ended up in a mountainous region called Kosturino. They were ill-equipped to deal with a harsh mountainous winter. News reached Mary Martin in mid-December 1915 that her son had been reported missing in action. In an attempt to stay positive, she began a diary. In it she included notes of events, news and daily life so that Charlie could read everything on his return home. This diary provides an invaluable insight into Dublin life between January and May 1916, a very important time in Irish history.[206] She began on Saturday 1 January 1916, shortly after finding out her son was missing in action: 'Dear Charlie, since I heard you were missing as well as wounded, it has occurred to me to write the diary in the form of a letter. We hope to hear from you soon. Till then we cannot communicate with you and later on when you read this it will let you know what has been happening …'[207]

Mary was a widow living with her family in the affluent Dublin suburb of Monkstown. The census of 1911 tells us that the Martin family were living at a house called 'Green Bank', with over thirteen rooms and eleven outhouses. The family had made its name through a shipping line and timber business and was well known as an Irish Catholic merchant family from the nineteenth century.[208] Mary Aloysius Moore had been born on 21 June 1868 in Castleknock, Dublin at her family home 'Ashton House' next to the Phoenix Park to Andrew Moore and Anne Levins. On 16 April 1890 she married Thomas Patrick Martin at Westland Row Church. The couple had twelve children together between 1891 and 1907.

The family suffered tragedy on 17 March 1907 when, on the sixteenth birthday of their eldest son, Tommy, his father 'accidentally shot himself', apparently with a hunting gun. The coroner's inquest said that 'he did not intend to shoot himself, that the discharge of the revolver was accidental'. The Glasnevin registers list his death as a result of a 'Haemorrhage from brain from an accidental revolver shot.' He was buried on 20 March in the South New Chapel section (BF 7). He was just 42 years old.

Mary later said goodbye to two of her sons – Charlie and Tommy – as they went to fight in the British military in the First World War. Two of her daughters – Marie and Ethel – served with the Voluntary Aid Detachment (VAD).[209]

Her diary depicts a Dublin quite different to the well-known narrative of rebellion in 1916. It is a story of the everyday and written from the perspective of a woman who viewed the Easter Rising at arm's length – her worries elsewhere. While others faced one reality in the city centre, Mary gives a rather different account of events.

Up until St Patrick's Day 1916, the diary depicts a comfortable life except for the concern for Charlie. From Monday 24 April it gives an interesting account of the rebellion:

> Monday 24th of April 1916. Ethel and Violet started off to go with Aunt Rita to Fairyhouse and had a very pleasant day until they got back to town. Here they discovered to their cost there was a Sinn Fein Rising and Dublin was in a state of siege … No trains or trams running, the streets and bridges were barricaded. The GPO, Westland Row station, Four Courts in occupation of the rebels. The furniture of these places being thrown out on the street …[210]
>
> Wednesday 26th of April 1916 … Still no authentic news but it appears the Sinn Feiner's still hold the city… In the afternoon I went to the tea rooms, we had a good many soldiers and sailors most of the Staffordshire regiment. This has been a glorious day. It is too terrible to think how it is being desecrated with murder and pillage …[211]
>
> Thursday 27th of April 1916. Things still as bad as ever. There were big fires in town during the night. Got a *Daily Mail* but there is very little news …[212]
>
> Friday 28th April 1916. A perfectly glorious day. Ethel and I were off to mass where we met Jack and Leo on the Avenue … Reports today are that the Boland's bakery has been taken from the Sinn Feiners … It is reported that Connolly & Countess Markievicz & Sheehy Skeffington have been shot. The boys marked out the Tennis Court so I presume play will now begin for the Season.[213]
>
> Saturday 29th of April 1916. Fighting still continuing as fierce as ever in Dublin and fires were seen during the night and one could hear the big guns firing. We hear great rumours of the damage that is being done to the City by the cannonade …[214]
>
> Thursday 4th of May 1916. Made up our minds to go to Dublin

> today some trains and trams are running. I got out at Grafton Street to do some shopping. Switzers and a few other shops are open ... there's some evidence of the attacks on the Sinn Fein stronghold in the College of Surgeons, in the shops of bullet holes in the windows and mirror. Front of the college is much marked with bullets but the structure is not damaged. After lunch we walked down to Sackville Street and although prepared for great havoc it is much worse than I anticipated ... From O'Connell Bridge to Cathedral Lane past Earl Street is destroyed only a heap of smouldering rubbish with a few facades standing ... The GPO is only a skeleton front ... the interior completely gone ...[215]

The entries, although inaccurate in places, tell a story of uncertainty and fascination. The diary also shows a disconnect between those of wealth and those within the city centre caught up in the fighting. The last entry is dated 25 May 1916. Charles would never read it. Official word reached Mary days later that he had died of his wounds soon after his capture in December in 1915. His name today is recorded on the Doiran Memorial in Greece. He was awarded the Order of the White Eagle 5th Class for his service in Serbia.[216]

Mary Martin later moved away from Monkstown and sold the house in 1949 to the Sacred Heart Sisters who set it up as a school.[217] The family moved to St Margaret's on Cross Avenue, Booterstown, County Dublin. She lived there until her death on 9 August 1955 aged 87 years. She was buried in the same plot as her husband in the South New Chapel section (BF 8). Her voice can still be heard today through her diary written for Charlie.

Christmas 1915 was also a tragic time for Pioneer William Coleman of the Royal Engineers. He was making the journey home to Dublin from the Western Front in France to bury his 4-year-old son, Christopher. William's wife, Bridget Hyland, had died on 17 November 1913. She was buried on 20 November, at just 34 years old, and left behind three sons: Edward (1901), William (1905) and their youngest Christopher, born on the 19 December 1911. She died as a result of 'syncope' (her death was likely the result of a brain haemorrhage).

William Coleman was born in Dublin on 10 December 1868 to Edward Coleman and Bridget McCourt at 23 Marlborough Street. Following his marriage to Bridget Hyland, they moved to 133 Thomas Street, where Edward was born, before they made the move to 5 Earl Street. William worked as a 'Labourer' and went from job to job trying to make ends meet. After the death of his wife, he secured a good job at the Guinness Brewery and began work there on 31 August 1914. He worked in the highly skilled cooperage department. His record in the brewery reveals that he left this position on the 14 August 1915 before he 'reassigned' himself 'to join Army'.[218] Three days later he was in Southampton. He enlisted for active service with the 2nd Labour Battalion of the Royal Engineers 13th Company as a Pioneer.[219] The terms of service were for the duration of the war, and he landed in France on 23 August. While he was away he left his children with his brother-in-law William Lawlor and his sister Mary at their house on School Street.[220]

William was attached to the 7th Entrenching Battalion. Such battalions were effectively small groups of men appointed at Corps level from where replacements could be called up to the front lines at short notice on the request of the infantry. News reached William while in France that his youngest son, Christopher, had died on 28 December 1915. He was granted leave to return to Dublin to make arrangements for the funeral. Tragedy was to strike, however. In a letter from G.M. Court, Captain for Colonel Commanding, 2nd Battalion Royal Engineers: 'The officer Commanding his company has received a letter from the man's sister-in-law which states that he was killed as a result of falling from the Irish night Express between Euston and Holyhead … 20.1.1916.'[221]

William fell from an open compartment door on one of the train's carriages as he made his way home. The train was about 2 miles outside Rugby train station and was on its way to Holyhead to deliver the mail back to Dublin. *The Belfast Evening Telegraph* on Monday, 3 January 1916 reported on a 'Soldier's Fall From Train':

> The door of a compartment having been noticed open, the train was stopped, and a search made, when the body of the deceased was found on the line. It was supposed that, when going down the corridor of the train, he opened the door by mistake. The medical evidence showed the deceased's neck was broken, he had a compound fracture of the skull, and the right foot was severed, any of these injuries being in itself sufficient to cause death. The jury found that death resulted from misadventure.[222]

His brother-in-law replied in a letter to Brompton Barracks dated 6 January 1916 and said that:

> He had £17.10.0 and an old (and paid £4.10.0 for coffin to bring him home) metal watch and it was handed over to me by request of the Coroner as when he left Guinness Brewery … With regards his kit the Captain of his Batt. wrote and told me that he took all his belongs when he was going on leave and when I got it the only things that was in it was a signet his sister sent him, one drawers, old grey shirt, one old blue jersey and canteen can, one tin of cooked corned beef, if you like I will send them back the way I received them.[223]

William did not die while 'performing military duty' so did not qualify for any supports. On the official letter sent by the War Office regarding army funds it said, 'Pioneer William Coleman, Royal Engineers, was not engaged in the performance of military duty when he met with the accident which caused his death, his widow is not eligible for pension from Army Funds. Mrs. Coleman and the Regimental Paymaster should be informed accordingly …'[224]

William's 4-year-old son was buried in the St Paul's section (AA 35) on 30 December 1915 and joined his late mother. He had died as a result of 'inflammation of the bowels'. William was later buried in the South section (LB 10) on the morning of 5 January 1916. Today a large tree covers his grave. Jutting up out of the earth beside the trunk you can see a small rectangular Portland headstone with the name William Coleman. For many years his grave lay unmarked. His headstone was unveiled in 2012 as part of the project with the Commonwealth War Graves Commission. His name is not featured on the Guinness Brewery Roll of honour for the First World War. His story is not one from the battlefield. It is one of the ordinary, everyday and tragic.

Riddled by Bullets: Detective Sergeant Patrick Smyth

The cemetery can also tell the stories of many people who died in the Irish War of Independence and the subsequent Civil War. Conor Dodd, through his book *Casualties of Conflict* (2023), explores the lives and deaths of over 300 people buried in Glasnevin who died between 1919 and 1923. Visitors regularly visit the Republican plot to pay their respects at many of these graves. There are other perspectives, however, telling a different story of that period, of those who served with the RIC and the DMP. A campaign to boycott the police forces of the RIC and DMP in Ireland was promoted by the IRA during the War of Independence and this grew in intensity throughout 1920–21.

On the night of 30 July 1919, Detective Sergeant Patrick Smyth of the political crime section (G Division) of the DMP was on his way home to 51 Millmount Avenue, Drumcondra. It was about 11 p.m. He disembarked a tram and began his routine walk. Following him were five members of the newly created Special Duties Units set up by Michael Collins. This later formed the basis of 'The Squad'. They had waited several nights for the opportune moment. They open fired on the unarmed DS Patrick Smyth. Although Smyth was hit in the back, thigh and hip by bullets, he still managed to stagger towards his house. He got to Drumcondra bridge (today Frank Flood bridge) where he collapsed. He managed to get up again and continued towards his house. On hearing the gunfire some of his children had made their way outside. They saw their father lying against the wall of a nearby house. His hands were clamped onto one of his hips in pain. His eldest sons and daughter grappled with him to get him inside. As they carried him, he said, 'I am shot; call an ambulance.'[225]

A newspaper article from *The Freeman's Journal* published on the day following the shooting begins with the headline: 'City Detective Shot in the Streets, Riddled by Bullets at own door.'[226] It tells us:

> [T]he wounded policeman was taken at once to the Mater Hospital. Sergeant Smyth was conscious when he reached the hospital, and was treated by Dr. Butterly, the house surgeon … His condition is considered to be grave … It is concluded that there are in all four bullets in the body, as one of the injuries appears to be an exit wound. A bullet fell out of his clothes while he was being examined at the hospital …[227]

DS Smyth remained in the Mater Hospital and died of his wounds on 8 September 1919. On his deathbed he gave a full statement to Sergeant Lynch of the DMP. *The Irish Times* on 23 September reported that he said:

> When I got off the tram at the end of my own avenue I saw four or five men against the dead wall and a bicycle resting against the curb stone. Just as I turned the corner into Millmount Avenue I was shot in the back. I turned and said to them 'You Cowards,' and three of them fired again with revolvers at me and one bullet entered my leg. I then ran away and they pursued me to within about fifteen yards of my own door and kept firing at me all the time. In all about ten or twelve shots were fired at me. I shouted for assistance but no one came to me except my own son. I had no revolver myself and I am glad now that I had not one as I might have shot some of them when I turned around after the first shot, as I would not like to have done that.[228]

Patrick Smyth was born on 28 December 1867 in the town of Lizaherty, Granard, County Longford to Francis Smyth, a local schoolmaster, and Mary Murtagh. He began his career with the DMP on 18 August 1893 at the age of 25. The DMP Register Books state that he was a farmer, 5ft 10¾ inches tall and a Roman Catholic. He was assigned to E Division. This Division meant he worked as a police officer around an area to the south of the Grand Canal, south of the Liffey at Chapelizod up to the Merrion railway crossing on the coast.[229] On 22 February 1895 he was moved to A Division, where he operated south of the River Liffey before making his last move to G Division on 9 April 1897. He became a sergeant on 4 December 1908 and by 1 September 1918 he was earning £3 and 5 shillings a year.[230] His wages were not high for the standards of the time. He married a Kildare woman, Annie Bourke, who was living at 19 Vernon Street in Dublin. They had seven children before his death in 1919: Francis Joseph, Patrick Matthew, Thomas Bernard, Eugene, Peter Paul, Mary Elizabeth and Anna Teresa.

The men who had been selected for the Drumcondra assassination were chosen by Michael Collins. They included Mick McDonnell, Jim Slattery, Tom Kehoe, Tom Ennis and Mick Kennedy. The actual order to carry out this attack was delivered to the men either by Liam Tobin or Tom Cullen, who were both heavily involved in intelligence gathering for the IRA with Frank Thornton. They branded the detective as 'The Dog' Smyth from G Division. Detectives like Smyth had 'amassed a considerable amount of information about their movements and activities'.[231] Collins and members of the republican movement put together a plan to target 'G men'. The aim was to try and get them to drop charges against members of Sinn Féin and the Volunteers. Smyth likely earned his nickname due to his work in G Division keeping leading figures under constant surveillance. Formally, The Squad was not set up until September 1919 at 46 Parnell Square in Dublin. DS Patrick Smyth, however, is recognised as the first member of G Division (special branch) and the wider British Intelligence network to be killed by The Squad. For what was to become The Squad, these events also acted as a lesson. Their choice of .38 revolvers used in the Drumcondra attack proved too weak and resulted in too many bullets having to be fired.[232] Afterwards it was agreed to use .45 revolvers for assassination attacks.

Dominic Price provides great insight into the initial makeup of what were the Special Duties Units. There were two: Unit 1 and Unit 2. They were mostly made up of men in the Dublin Brigade of the IRA. Both joined to form The Squad. Unit 1 was responsible for the operation to kill DS Smyth. Mick Kennedy was chosen to take part as he knew what Smyth looked like. Jim Slattery, according to Dominic Price, recounted that 'they waited for Smyth for five nights and when Smyth eventually passed Mick Kennedy he was not sure if it was him and the opportunity passed'.[233] After some tense nights of observation it was the night of 30 July that they opened fire on Smyth. McDonnell was not best pleased with the operation and in one account stated they had made a 'right mess of it'.[234]

DS Smyth's funeral procession made its way to Glasnevin and he was buried in the St Bridget's section (DH 225.5).[235] His grave is close to the wall that separates the cemetery from the National Botanical Gardens. He had been in line for promotion to inspector. He was buried at 11.50 a.m. on the morning of 11 September 1919. He was 51 years old. Hours later, on the night of 12 September, Daniel Hoey, another member of G Division, was killed by The Squad on Townsend Street. This time there was no mistake and there was no riddling of bullets.[236] Between 1919 and 1922 Richard Abbot has accounted for 502 police fatalities. DS Smyth was one of fifteen who died in 1919. His story is a reminder that while Glasnevin Cemetery is the final resting place for many men and women who fought in the War of Independence, it is also the final resting place for those of different political perspectives. By telling Smyth's story I have tried, as historian Peter Hart puts it, to blur the 'effect of uniforms and titles, which lend themselves to stereotypes, statistical aggregation and erasure'.[237]

The Funeral of Tobias O'Sullivan

Patrick Smyth is not the only member of the DMP or RIC buried in the cemetery. There are designated sections for both forces. Another member of the RIC who is noteworthy from the period is Tobias O'Sullivan from Galway. His funeral at Glasnevin was one of the largest unionist funerals ever to come through its gates during the Irish War of Independence. A married Catholic man with three children, O'Sullivan was born on 14 May 1877. He had joined the RIC on 16 November 1899 and had served in both Donegal and Galway.[238] On his promotion to the role of sergeant, he was transferred to Maryborough in Laois. Later he was stationed at Athea in Limerick, before being re-stationed to Kilmallock. He was the sergeant in charge when the barracks in Kilmallock was successfully defended on 28 May 1920 from an IRA raid. In the raid Sergeant Thomas Kane and Constable Joseph Morton both died. Kane today is buried beside the RIC plot in the Garden section of Glasnevin (JF 233.5). O'Sullivan for his part received some injuries but later recovered. This would have been a worrying time for his wife, Mary Maguire, whom he had married in Abbeyleix on 8 February 1915.

For his role in the defence of Kilmallock Barracks, O'Sullivan was decorated with the Constabulary Medal by General Tudor, the police advisor to the authorities in Ireland, and was promoted to head constable.[239] On 26 September 1920 he was promoted to district inspector and sent to Listowel in Kerry with a handpicked number of men from Limerick. His task was to try and restore discipline following the Listowel Mutiny – an event when fourteen policemen resisted transfer orders, appealed for IRA support, and in some cases abandoned their posts, with some IRA defections. There had been previous attempts by the IRA to shoot and kill O'Sullivan, and he had a double bodyguard for most of his time in County Kerry.

Tobias O'Sullivan.

On 20 January 1921, an IRA party lay in wait in Stacks pub on the main street of Listowel. It was located 100 yards from the RIC barracks. The plan was to shoot him as he went home for lunch. At 13.20 p.m., having just dismissed his bodyguards, O'Sullivan was shot by Daniel O'Grady and Cornelius Brosnan on Church Street. The shooting took place in plain sight of his wife and child. His family maintain he was holding his son by the hand when killed.[240] At the funeral his widow, Mary, his two sons, John and Bernard, his brothers John and Bernard, his sisters and two cousins, Sergeant T. O'Sullivan and Sergeant Charles O'Sullivan, RIC, were in attendance.[241] It was recorded by Pathé News Reel and a simple search of his name on YouTube shows the size of the event. *The Cork Examiner* described the 'impressive' scenes:

> Since his arrival in the city on Saturday the remains of the police officer had rested in James Street Catholic Church and thence the funeral procession made its way through two miles of streets lined by crowds of people who bore a reverent attitude as it passed by. The cortege was headed by troops of cadets of the Auxiliary Division of the Royal Irish Constabulary, followed by the bands of the military, the Dublin Metropolitan Police and the RIC, who in turn played appropriate marches. Then came the coffin on a gun carriage and covered with the Union Jack, surmounted by flowers. Immediately behind the coffin walked General Tudor, Police Advisor to the government, accompanied by Lieutenant Col. Edgeworth Johnstone, Chief Commissioner of the Dublin Metropolitan Police and other officers of the military and RIC. A large force of RIC with arms reversed, and a body of DMP followed by carriages conveying the bereaved relatives and closed carriages sent by high officials in Dublin.[242]

Due to a gravediggers' strike, the grave was dug and filled by RIC men and Auxiliaries.[243] O'Sullivan was buried in the St Patrick's section (CK 329). The funeral can be viewed as a show of strength by the authorities. Its aim was to show that they too could honour their dead with all the relevant pomp and ceremony required.

The RMS *Leinster*

A large anchor stands close to the pier at Dún Laoghaire today. It is a reminder of the greatest loss of life ever recorded on the Irish Sea – the sinking of the RMS *Leinster* on 10 October 1918. To many the 'Leinster disaster' is not well-remembered. Stephen Ferguson, assistant secretary and museum curator in An Post, wrote that 'the loss of the RMS *Leinster* was the greatest disaster ever to occur on the Irish Sea, but for whatever reasons, memory of the tragedy has been obscured over the years and many Irish people will never have heard of it at all'.[1]

The ship was built in 1897 at Laird Brothers in Birkenhead for the City of Dublin Steam Packet Company. At the time she was one of the fastest ships at sea with a speed of 24 knots.[2] This was essential to ensure people received mail in a fast and efficient way. Between 1850 and 1920 the City of Dublin Steam Packet Company operated a mail and passenger service between Dún Laoghaire (then Kingstown) and Holyhead in Wales. Four ships carried mail across the Irish Sea. Each ship had an on-board mail sorting room. It was staffed by members of Dublin Post Office. The ships were nicknamed the 'Provinces': RMS *Connaught*, RMS *Leinster*, RMS *Munster* and RMS *Ulster*

Rainbow over Glasnevin Cemetery, 2021. (© Warren Farrell)

(RMS stood for Royal Mail Steamer).[3] In addition to the crew and sorting staff, there were civilian passengers. People used the ships as a convenient and fast way to travel. As the First World War continued, many soldiers who came home on leave began to use the service. The RMS *Leinster* was said to be the public's favourite, especially with Irish MPs, who were given free passage as a thank you for their parliamentary support for the ship's owners.[4] Only days before tragedy struck, it was recorded that the King of Portugal, Manuel II, had been on board.[5]

As the First World War progressed, military authorities asked the Dublin Steam Packet Company to help with crossings of soldiers. While normal passengers could turn up and queue for a ticket, space was often set aside for soldiers to make use of the *Leinster* and her sister ships.[6] As the war unfolded and Germany enforced an exclusion zone around the waters of Great Britain, the military authorities and government of the United Kingdom were aware that any ships within this area were legitimate targets for sinking by German submarines. Ships carrying military personnel or weapons and supplies were especially vulnerable. The torpedoing of the *Lusitania* off Kinsale (1915) is a famous example of this policy. The RMS *Leinster* was viewed as 'a legitimate target'[7] and all the 'Provinces' were painted in camouflage and equipped with a gun placed in the stern.[8] The crew and postal workers would have been in no doubt about the dangers that they potentially faced on board.

The events of 10 October 1918 resulted in at least 501 souls being lost. The latest research shows that the figure could be as high as 569 or more.[9] More Irish people died on the RMS *Leinster* off the coast of Dublin than on the *Titanic* or *Lusitania*. Philip Lecane, in his *Women and Children of the R.M.S Leinster* (2018), with the help of the National Maritime Museum and An Post, has helped in putting together this small selection of stories for those who were on board that morning and who are today buried in Glasnevin.

John Joseph Higgins was one of the twenty-two postal workers to report for work that morning. John was born on 12 October 1880 at Lisburn Street, off Church Street in Dublin. His parents, Peter Higgins, a labourer, and Mary Rourke, lived at a series of addresses around the Smithfield and Grangegorman areas. By 1901 John had moved out of the family home and had settled on Arran Quay with his wife, Mary Kenny, whom he married in the church of St Paul's on 19 August 1900. John and Mary Higgins had eight children, with five surviving. They spent periods of time living on Viking

Road in Smithfield and Manor Place before making the move out to Prospect Square in Glasnevin. John worked as a 'Sorter at the G.P.O.'

That day, the mailbags were loaded on board by porters, and then John Joseph Higgins and his colleagues in the mailroom began to sort their contents. This all happened below decks. At the same time, along two gangways above the mail workers on the port side of the ship, passengers began to board.[10] Amongst these were Florence Margaret Scroope, Sheelah Isabel Plunkett, her sister-in-law Lucy Harrington Plunkett and Elizabeth Susan Woodhouse. There were people of all walks of life on board – crew members, civilian nurses, soldiers, children and even three couples on their honeymoon.

We don't know why Florence was travelling on the ship. What we do know is that she was born in Cork on 12 July 1871. She was the eldest of the eleven children of Henry Scroope, who had been working with the National Bank when he married Catherine (Kate) Hackett in 1870. Florence's father was an accountant from Tipperary. His own father had settled in Ireland having left Yorkshire, and he became a member of the Anglo-Irish community. Her mother was a native of County Cork and her mother's father (Bartholomew Hackett) had been mayor and deputy lieutenant of Cork.[11] Florence moved around Ireland a good bit with her family. By 1877 the family had moved to Castlerea, Roscommon. Henry had become bank manager there. They later moved to Ballina in Mayo and finally to Dublin. Her mother, Kate, sadly died in Ballina in 1908. In the period afterwards Florence witnessed her siblings all move out, get married or move into various posts in the British military, the Indian civil service and to work as doctors.[12] Florence was left alone with her father. By the time they moved to 7 Ashbrook Terrace, Leeson Park, Dublin, she was eager to embark on some form of adventure.

Also boarding that morning were Sheelah Isabel Plunkett and her sister-in-law Lucy Harrington Plunkett. Sheelah was born in Dublin at 83 Merrion Square on 21 June 1897. She was the daughter of the Maltster John Randall Plunkett and Cecilia Read. Her father had made his money supplying malt to the Guinness Brewery. The Plunketts owned a summer residence out at the Baily in Howth called 'Earlscliffe'. By 1911 they had moved from Merrion Square to 1 Herbert Street, Dublin. Sheelah was the youngest of six siblings and as the First World War broke out she volunteered with the Red Cross–St John's Ambulance Joint War Committee's Irish War Hospital at 40 Merrion Square. Her father, John Randall, died in April 1915 and was buried in the Garden, Curran Square section (J 38.5). In early 1907 her brother Leo emigrated to Canada and while in Winnipeg met his wife, Lucy Harrington. The couple married on 6 July 1910.[13] The following October they returned to Ireland. As the First World War continued, Leo Plunkett joined the Royal Dublin Fusiliers. By 1918 he had become second lieutenant. Lucy's brother (John Elliot Harrington) was serving with the Canadian Expeditionary Force and was seriously injured in August 1918. He was taken to a hospital in Northampton.[14] Both women were on a trip to visit him.

Elizabeth Susan Woodhouse, aged 30, was the twin sister of Emily Mary, born to parents John Henry Woodhouse and Emily Bradley. Their father's occupation is listed as a bookseller from 61 Lombard Street in Dublin. Elizabeth and Emily's father was Church of Ireland but his wife and children, according to the records available, were all Roman Catholic. The census in 1911 shows that Emily had followed in her father's footsteps as a 'bookkeeper'. Their address is given at an upstairs apartment at 49 Grafton Street. Elizabeth was living with her twin sister and was employed to purchase hay in County Wicklow on behalf of the British government before boarding the RMS *Leinster*.[15] Their mother died in 1919 aged just 48. Her address on the death certificate gives the Lock Hospital Asylum. Her cause of death is recorded as being a result of 'Pneumonia 6 days, general paralysis insane'.

The RMS *Leinster*, under the command of Captain William Birch with 771 souls on board, left Kingstown (or Dún Laoghaire today) just before 9 a.m. from the Carlisle Pier. On board were an estimated seventy-seven crew, twenty-two postal workers, 250 sacks of mail, 180 civilians and about 500 soldiers. Between 9.30 and 9.40 a.m. the ship passed the Kish Light.[16] She passed the RMS *Ulster* inbound to Kingstown.[17] All, seemingly, was well. The weather was mixed, with a rough Irish Sea. The crew on board had just finished serving breakfast and many of those on board were either in or heading to their cabins for what should have been a quick journey. Those without a cabin went on deck to brave the choppy conditions. At 9.50 a.m. Captain Birch gave the order to begin a zig-zag course; standard anti-submarine procedure.

Unknown to those on board, however, the German U-boat UB-123 was patrolling the waters close to the Kish Light. UB-123's commander, Robert Ramm, spotted the *Leinster* and gave orders to prepare for an attack. The torpedoes were loaded. The tubes on board the submarine were flooded and it positioned itself on the port side of the *Leinster*. As people on board went about their tasks and passengers sat back or gazed out along the horizon, Ramm gave the command to fire the first torpedo. It whizzed its way towards the ship beneath the surface, missing narrowly and passing across her bows. Some on board saw it and presumed it was a whale. Shortly afterwards a second torpedo was fired. On the bridge Seaman Hugh Owen pointed to it approaching from the port side.[18] Captain Birch gave the order for evasive action, but it was too late. It hit on the port side where the mailroom was.

John Joseph Higgins gave an account of what happened to the Controller of the Dublin Postal District, Henry Tipping:

> At the moment of impact all lights went out and except for a very faint glimmer from the port lights which were mostly under water the place was in darkness. Mr Attwooll was standing nearest the door of the enclosure and I was next to him. I told him he had better get out but he made no answer. I passed by him and stepped out into the Sorting Office and was immediately over my waist in water. I looked all around and saw none of my colleagues, I saw nothing but falling beams and twisted iron of the sorting divisions. I heard no sound but the roaring of water. I clambered over some bags in the centre of the office with the water rising higher as I advanced and reached the stairway with wood floating round my face. The stairway had entirely disappeared but there was light from the opening overhead. I struggled for the opening and caught some electric wires hanging from the roof and hauled myself up floating to thc Mail Shed.[19]

As he struggled to escape, a final torpedo was fired. By this time Captain Birch had managed to turn the ship 180 degrees and it now faced back towards Kingstown. As the third torpedo sped towards the right-hand side of the ship a lifeboat was being lowered with people inside and it was blown to pieces. The *Leinster* began to sink head first.[20] Sheelah Isabel Plunkett and her sister-in-law Lucy Harrington Plunkett were on deck at the port side wearing life jackets. Shortly after the impact of the second torpedo, the ship quickly keeled over and the two young women were thrown into the rough sea. They became separated in the chaos. Lucy's life jacket came loose and fell off, but luckily she was pulled onto a raft by a fellow struggler. Sheelah Isabel, her young sister-in-law, was sadly lost.

By this time John Joseph Higgins had swung himself down a long rope towards a lifeboat where he spotted a colleague from the postal staff. It was a man called Alfred McDonnell, 'Then the second torpedo [this is the third torpedo fired as only two hit the ship] struck the ship and I did not see him again. The ship turned sideways and went down headfirst.'[21]

For Florence Margaret Scroope and Elizabeth Susan Woodhouse, we do not know what their final moments were like. It is assumed both were on deck. Florence's body was later recovered and brought to the morgue in Dublin. Elizabeth's body was also later recovered and returned to shore. Higgins sat shivering on a lifeboat as the *Leinster* sank beneath the Irish Sea after just twenty minutes. Of the postal workers on board, he was the only survivor. The submarine left the scene with hundreds of passengers, soldiers and crew flailing about in the rough sea. The submarine was later blown up, resulting in the deaths of the entire crew as it passed through a minefield in the North Sea.

Florence's body lay unidentified for some time. Her family eventually recognised a picture of her in the *Evening Telegraph*. In the *Belfast News-Letter* we are told that 'as of yesterday [16 October] there were 8 bodies in the morgue, two of these a woman and a child of about five, were unidentified ...'[22] The woman was most likely Florence. Later in the same article it gives us a list of those 'definitely' lost in the disaster and not recovered. In this list we see 'Miss Florence Scroope, daughter of Mr. Henry Scroope, 7 Ashbrook Terrace, Leeson Park.'[23] The Scroope family had presumed her body was lost at sea. Her remains were taken from the morgue and brought to Glasnevin for burial in the South section (VA 53.5). The plot had been purchased by the Lord Mayor of Dublin to allow for the dignified burial of those not identified as a result of the sinking.

The burial register states that Florence was buried on the morning of 21 October 1918 at about 10.45 a.m. Later, the Scroopes purchased the plot beside it and made it a family one. Lynn Brady, in researching this grave with John O'Grady, uncovered the burial of a young unidentified child in the same plot. The young child was buried there in accordance with the Lord Mayor of Dublin's wishes. The burial register states that an 'unknown child' was buried at 10.45 a.m. on 21 October 1918 with Florence. It also states that the cause of death for the child was 'drowning' and its last known address was listed as 'S.S *Leinster*, Irish Sea.'

This research suggests that the name of the child, a young girl, is Angela

Gould. Philip Lecane explains that she had been on board with her family. The Goulds suffered by far the greatest number of deaths in the sinking. Angela had boarded the RMS *Leinster* with her mother, Catherine, and her five other siblings: May, Essie, Alice, Michael and Olive, their ages ranging from 12 months to 21 years old.[24] It is believed they were travelling to England where their father, John, was working. Only one member of the family survived: Essie (Ellen). Their mother was thought to have been the only Gould recovered from the sea. She was later buried at Mount St Laurence Cemetery in Limerick.[25] The Scroope family over the subsequent years buried more family in the same plot, unaware that Catherine's 5-year-old daughter Angela was also at rest there.

Elizabeth Susan Woodhouse's funeral was covered in *The Freeman's Journal*. It tells us that 'the bodies of the following victims were interred yesterday in Glasnevin Cemetery, Miss Woodhouse, Grafton Street, Dublin, Mrs O'Mahony, Oxford Road … and Mrs Georgina O'Brien, London.'[26] In *The Irish Times* a small memorial reads: 'To the loving memory of Elizabeth (Betty) killed on the R.M.S. *Leinster* on the 10th October 1918.'[27] She was buried on the morning of 15 October, five days after the sinking, at 11.20 a.m. She was 30 years old. Her occupation is listed as a 'book-keeper' and it appears her twin sister purchased the grave to bury her in. Today she lies in an unmarked grave in the St Paul's section (PD 23).

Sheelah Isabel Mary Plunkett's body, also presumed lost at sea, is in fact in Glasnevin. The *Belfast News-Letter* stated that 'the body of Miss Sheila Plunkett … was removed on Tuesday night'.[28] Her father, John Randal Plunkett, and other descendants are buried in (J 38). Sheelah is buried in the plot beside them (J 38.5). The burial is listed as having taken place at 9 a.m. on the morning of 16 October 1918. Her age is listed as being just 21 years old.[29]

Lastly there is John Joseph Higgins. Following his miraculous escape, he recounted: 'After being some hours adrift we were rescued by a destroyer. I was taken to the Red Cross station at Dún Laoghaire where I received every attention and afterwards rode in a military lorry to the G.P.O. where I got down as I did not wish to go to hospital.'[30] Once he got off the military lorry he grabbed his bicycle from the GPO, at the time located at the Rotunda. He cycled home to Prospect Square where his wife opened the door to see him in an awful state. Newspapers both in Ireland and abroad picked up on this survivor's story. *The Freeman's Journal* reported: 'the surviving member of staff J.J Higgins who lives with his wife and family at 17 Prospect Square ... Mr Higgins who described his escape as a most providential one, said he had but a hazy idea of what had really occurred, and beyond this he could go no further.'[31] *The Cork Examiner* stated, 'the postal staff on the *Leinster* ... are believed to have all been lost save one, J.J. Higgins who was saved.'[32] The *New York Tribune* even recounted: 'Of the mail clerks on board the *Leinster* ... killed outright by the explosion and the twenty-first [twenty-second] was blown through the side of the ship, being picked up at sea later.'[33] Later in life Higgins recounted that his lasting memory of that day was of 'swimming through a sea of white letters' with water up to his chin as he tried to make his escape from the sinking ship.[34]

Higgins had a long career in the post office. He died on 4 October 1955, six days before the thirty-seventh anniversary of the sinking. He was buried in the St Patrick's section (RK 268) at 10.50 a.m. on 6 October 1955 aged 74. When remembering those hours waiting to be rescued, he said, 'I am not likely to forget the happenings of that day, but one particular occurrence which is burned in my memory is when the *Leinster* plunged to her last resting place to see hundreds of people who could not get off in time being brought down with the ship.'[35]

There are at least thirteen known victims of the RMS *Leinster* buried in Glasnevin today and approximately 150 recovered military dead buried in Grangegorman military cemetery.[36] People of many countries are represented amongst the dead, including Ireland, Wales, Scotland, England, Guernsey, Australia, New Zealand, Canada and the USA. War weariness, a changing political landscape in Ireland or the absence of a full investigation in the immediate aftermath of the sinking can all help to explain why this event became so lost to history.

Death of Two Labourers in Dublin's GPO

We never know when tragedy or disaster is going to strike or affect us, as is the case with the tragic deaths of John Ledden and Henry McMahon. The GPO on O'Connell Street in the lead up to the 1916 Rising had undergone a programme of restoration.[37] It is noted that the railings outside the building had been removed, the main entrance doorway was brought to the front and old critics of what was described as a dingy and dark public office space were happy to see it opened out as a spacious, light-filled area to do business. New

Burmese teak counters and mosaic floors, coupled with a public telephone box over which hung a new clock, impressed many who visited the building in early 1916.[38]

The public didn't get the opportunity to enjoy the restoration works for long. After a week of intense fighting in and around the building during Easter 1916, all that remained was a shell. The building was left smouldering. Eventually workmen were permitted to try and salvage what they could. The sight of men sifting through charred documents and furniture must have been sad for the Board of Works. It took thirteen years to fully restore and reopen the building for its primary function as a post office. Works went on between 1916 and 1929 and were halted on many occasions, but on 24 October 1919 disaster struck.

Thirty-six-year-old John Ledden was a married man with four children living at 113 Lower Gardiner Street, and he had begun work that morning in the GPO. Alongside him was Henry McMahon. He was single, aged 44 and living on Dublin's Hanover Street. They had been employed to help in the demolition of the remaining floors inside. The aim was to gut the building and to leave just the original Francis Johnston facade. Ledden was standing with one foot on the wall, or so he thought, and another on the floor when he heard a shout that the floor was giving way. With no time to get off the disappearing floor, he fell towards the ground. The slabs of flooring falling from above crushed and killed him. Henry McMahon was also on the first floor as it collapsed and he shared the same unlucky fate.

In the National Archives there is a file entitled 'GPO, Collapse of floor during demolition, death of two labourers', which gives many of the nasty details of both men's deaths. The file is made up of newspaper clippings from the inquiry and inquests into what happened. It also features a series of letters by Mr Fairweather, the Commissioner's Surveyor for the Board of Works. In one of these letters, it is stated: 'A portion of the slab seemed to have fallen and taken them with it and the main slab about 6ft x 5ft x 6ft thick fell afterwards and crushed them before they could get clear … the event took place between 12–1:35pm that afternoon.'[39]

At the inquest held at Jervis Street Hospital it was stated by Mr Kane, another labourer who had been close to both men on the day, that:

> The section of the floor they were working on was about ten feet eight inches, supported by iron girders, while the other end had been

> broken through by workmen. On top of the floor from the wall to the iron girders were two planks about 18 inches wide; on which the men were supposed to stand and break with sledge hammers the floor from these planks, but for some reason unknown the men stepped on to the floor and engaged in breaking it.[40]

Dr John M. Ryan, the house surgeon at Jervis Street Hospital, reported that both John Ledden and Henry McMahon were dead on arrival at the hospital: 'In the case of Ledden it was due to haemorrhage. In the case of McMahon death was due to fracture of the skull and lacerations of the brain, caused by a heavy mass falling on his head.'[41]

The jury at the inquest found that while it was a very unfortunate event, there was no safer way at the time of carrying out the works and that the cause of death was accidental.[42] In the official file it also states that 'It is regrettable that this should have occurred just as the demolition had got so near the ground level, the higher reaches having been removed without mishap.'[43] Health and Safety was not a top priority in 1919. The men's causes of death in Glasnevin are recorded as 'a result of injuries suffered from falling through a floor' and 'floor fell on him'. John Ledden was buried on 27 October in the St Patrick's section (OL 290.5) close to the Tolka River. Henry McMahon was buried on the same date in the St Paul's section (CC 68). Both graves are unmarked. The funerals arrived at 12.20 p.m. and their hearses separated at the gates in different directions to their graves. The GPO officially reopened to the public on Thursday, 11 July 1929. President W.T. Cosgrave gave a speech on the occasion where he complimented the workmen who had brought the building back to life.[44] He did not mention the deaths of the two men.

The Portobello Bridge Omnibus Disaster

Another forgotten tragedy with links to Glasnevin is the Portobello Bridge Omnibus disaster. On the night of 6 April 1861, the horse-drawn No. 7 tram was approaching Portobello Bridge along the Grand Canal at 9.25 p.m. It was the sixth time that the driver, Patrick Hardy, and the conductor, Patrick Costello, had made the journey that day.[45] Two horses pulled the carriage back and forth across the Grand Canal: 'Badger', an experienced grey and a younger but steady bay mare.[46] On board that night were eight passengers.

John Keeley and his young son from 4 Camden Villas had got onto the carriage at what would today be the Terenure Crossroads. Also on board were Christopher Cunningham, a watchman from the North Docks, and a Mr Gunn, from the firm Gunn and Sons of 13 Westland Row; the firm was noteworthy in the city for its expertise in organ and piano building. Mary Anne Byrne was also seated on the carriage. She lived at 29 South King Street with William Byrne, who worked as an assistant at Dycer's Horse Repository beside St Stephen's Green. Mary Anne, a milliner, was with her 2-year-old daughter. Both were sitting close to Susan O'Connell, the wife of Charles O'Connell, a solicitor from Liscannor, County Clare. Susan was accompanied by her 18-year-old daughter, Matilda. They were coming home after visiting a family friend, Dr Cahill.[47]

Approaching the bridge, Keeley signalled to the conductor that both he and his son wished to get off. The conductor brought the bus to a halt at the crest of the hill over the bridge. The driver pulled in and Keeley and his son disembarked. Six passengers remained on the ground level of the omnibus.[48] Its final stop was to be Nelson's Pillar, at 9.30 p.m. Hardy tried to get the horses to move forward, but they refused. Instead, they began to walk backwards, pushing the carriage with them. Both horses began to turn their heads in an eastward direction and, despite the efforts of Hardy to jolt them forwards and over the crown of the bridge, they continued to push backwards. The four wheels then partially locked in one direction, moving the carriage to the western side of the bridge near the old turnpike.

The carriage was pushed up against the wooden barrier that separated the bridge from the lock below. As the fragile and worn beams broke, the carriage was momentarily left hanging off the side of the stone-built base of the bridge before falling into the lock. Water began to pour and foam inside the interior while the six passengers tried desperately to escape. As the carriage filled with water a policeman, Michael Gaffney, and a soldier named Smith from the 4th Light Dragoons arrived on the scene. Shocked onlookers began to gather. The constable managed to lie over the edge of the bridge and grab the driver from the front. Hardy was unharmed and taken to the nearby Meath Hospital.[49] Costello, the conductor, was also saved in the chaos.

The passengers were not so lucky. Desperate attempts were made to rescue them, but they could not be reached. The lock continued to pour foaming dirty water into the carriage. *The Freeman's Journal* gave a gruesome depiction of what the onlookers saw:

> In the distance was to be heard nothing but the continuous and mournful fall of the water over the canal flood-gates, and the exclamations of those who were trying to render assistance to those who had just passed beyond the reach of human aid … Near one of the great throughfares from the southern side of the city, and in a chamber of one of the locks of the Grand Canal, six human beings, six fellow citizens were struggling for their lives within the narrow area of the omnibus sunk beneath the water … Men called on me in loud and vehement language, and each vied with the other to render assistance; but no help no matter how vigorous, could avail. Midst the darkness rendered melancholy visible by the sickly flickerings of the lamps on the bridge, crowds pressed excitedly forward to get a view of the Omnibus in which were engulfed the lifeless bodies of six persons … The din and confusion which prevailed was great. Its effect was much aggravated by the desperate struggling of the horses as they rose and fell, snorting, neighing and plunging in their death agonies. Impetuously, desperately they fought and vainly strived to sink their Iron-shod hoofs in the slimy walls of the lock, but the sullen water still kept rolling over those who but a few minutes before were full of hope and life, and who no doubt were expected at their firesides at that particular moment. It was one of those sights that lives in the mind as a great horror.[50]

All six passengers on board and both horses died. The deceased passengers were removed to Mercer's Hospital, except for the O'Connells, who were taken to the Meath Hospital.[51]

The inquest, led by Dr James Kirwan, began on Tuesday 9 April. Dr Kirwan at the time was also employed as cemetery doctor for Glasnevin. Mr Sidney appeared for the company who owned the omnibus company, Messrs Wilson proprietors.[52] The evidence went to prove that the occurrence was wholly accidental so far as the bus driver and conductor were concerned, and that the utmost exertions were made to rescue the unfortunate passengers. The verdict found that several persons lost their lives by simple drowning owing to the omnibus having suddenly fallen into the Grand Canal. They were satisfied that all involved 'exerted themselves at the best of their judgement on the occasion'. The jury did, however, make a request that the omnibus owners put brakes on each bus.[53]

The funerals of Susan O'Connell and her daughter, Matilda, made its way to Glasnevin on 11 April 1861. It was attended by a large number of people, the crowds made up of relatives, friends and Dublin citizens. *The Waterford News and Star* reported: 'The lamented deceased Mrs O'Connell was a lady of rare moral excellence and her daughter an accomplished girl whose acknowledged beauty was enhanced by a kind and amiable disposition.'[54] They were both buried in the Garden section of the cemetery (ZD 44); the grave is unmarked today. Despite the fact that causes of death were not officially recorded by the cemetery in 1861, their record features the pencilled-in appendage: 'drowned in an Omnibus in the Grand Canal'. *The Freeman's Journal* summed up the public reaction:

> Accidents at sea involving loss of life, railway disasters or shipwrecks, or death resulting from causes in which peril is incurred are things for which people are more or less prepared, but six human beings to be drowned in an omnibus before the eyes of thousands is a terrible novelty, a fearful warning, a desperate illustration of the insecurity of life, even where it was regarded to be most secure and protected![55]

Spanish Flu Pandemic 1918–19

For much of the time I spent writing this book, the Covid-19 pandemic was ever present. The situation, although different, provided some perspective on the Spanish flu pandemic from 1918 to 1919. The same sense of mourning, loss and powerlessness felt by thousands of families in Ireland today was felt by thousands of families over a century ago. Glasnevin saw more than 3,000 burials in the period between July 1918 and April 1919. Per month, burials saw daily spikes in October to November 1918 and March to April 1919. The biggest peak for burials came with the second wave of the virus in late March to early April 1919.[56] Many records show the causes of death as a result of 'influenza' or 'pneumonia'. Both can be regarded as a consequence of the pandemic.

Due to the many different official causes of death recorded during 1918–19, an exact number of burials for those who died as a result of the virus is difficult to ascertain. It is estimated, however, that 3–4,000 are buried in Glasnevin. Ida Milne provides some data on burials. She states that 'between the first and twenty-first of October 1918, 490 people were buried in Glasnevin compared with 243 in the corresponding period in 1917'.[57] By the end of that period there were on average twenty-three burials a day in the cemetery, culminating with 343 in the last week of October 1918.[58] *The Irish Times* said:

> Yesterday, from early morning till well after midday, cortege after cortege reached Glasnevin Cemetery, sometimes as many as three corpse-laden hearses being seen proceeding up Sackville Street at the same time. Close on forty orders for interment were issued at the Cemeteries office yesterday, and, inclusive of the remains brought for burial on the previous day, which had been temporarily placed in vaults overnight, there were close on one-hundred bodies for sepulchre.[59]

The acting superintendent for Glasnevin reported in the first week of November 1918:

> Since Saturday last up to the present time, we have buried at full depth 176, in vaults there are 35. We have orders on hand for 64 burials. I need hardly say that the week has been a very great strain on workmen and officers, all of whom are working very well. The office work of course is greatly in arrears as all our time is taken up with actual burials.[60]

The cemetery had not seen such high demand for burials since it first opened its gates in 1832 and had to deal with a cholera epidemic. By the end of February 1919 it was clear that a second wave was on the way. Staff at Glasnevin were paid double-time for Sundays due to the constant procession of bodies requiring burial. Ida Milne states that in March 1919, the second wave of burials eclipsed the first wave, with 1,192 burials compared with 593 in the same period from 1918.[61] The burial orders for the cemetery continued to grow day by day. Staff struggled to cope. The official tallies for the dead from the pandemic interestingly do not mirror the corresponding burials in the cemetery from these periods. This suggests that many deaths were not initially attributed to the second wave of the pandemic. Behind these statistics are individual tales of loss. Life-altering events for many unfolded across Dublin and the island of Ireland. I selected the grave of a young woman whose family was greatly altered by the perfect storm of conflict on the Western Front and influenza in Dublin to reflect on this period.

Catherine Moran was born on 8 January 1894 at 2 Walls Square, Dublin, to Christopher Moran and Catherine Reilly. Her father was a blacksmith and general labourer. She would go on to marry Charles Heatley, a 'trunk maker', son of Charles, a lithographer, and Mary Jane Heatley from 52 High Street in Dublin. They married on 18 October 1910 in St Audeon's Church. Catherine made the decision to keep her maiden name and add her husband's to become Catherine Moran Heatley. Both 20 years old in 1911, they lived at 1 Fish Street with their son, Charles (or Charlie), who had been born shortly after their marriage at the Rotunda. Two more sons followed: Frederick (1912) and Christopher (1913). By the time they had their third son they had moved to 1 High Street. This address would have been very close to both Catherine's family home on Nicholas Street and only a couple of doors away from her in-laws' house at 52 High Street.

From High Street they moved into more spacious accommodation in the Iveagh Trust buildings on Bride Street. In 1914 Catherine's husband was one of the first to sign up with the British Army. He enlisted in the 1st Battalion of the Royal Dublin Fusiliers.[62] He survived Gallipoli before being sent to France. Charles was reported missing in action on the first day of the Battle of the Somme. An official telegram reached Catherine in mid-1917 telling her that her 25-year-old husband was presumed dead. His body was never recovered from the battlefield. His name is one of over 72,000 carved at the Thiepval Memorial in France – men who have no known grave.

Financially, Catherine qualified for the army's Widows' Pension Fund. Her parents and in-laws nearby tried to help her through an incredibly difficult time. Then, the first wave of the Spanish flu hit Ireland, with Leinster and Ulster feeling the worst affects. Catherine contracted the virus in the last week of October 1918. With nobody to look after her children, she had little choice but to try to carry on as normal. Her parents made the decision to move their daughter back into the family home on Nicholas Street in the Liberties, but Catherine died as a result of 'influenzal pneumonia' on 4 November in her parents' house, surrounded by her three sons.[63] She was 25 years old.

Her funeral took place three days later, on 7 November. She was buried in the Garden section (WE 194) at 11.50 a.m., just four days before the end of the First World War. This particular section of the cemetery today contains many similar tales of loss and tragedy. For nearly a century her grave lay unmarked. Charles' sister Christina, or 'Cissy', raised her brother's three sons like her own. She died on 20 December 1949 and was buried in the Heatley (spelled Heatly on the Glasnevin register) family plot in Glasnevin. The plot also contains the remains of both Charles and Mary Jane Heatley, Catherine's in-laws. Her father-in-law was buried on 24 November 1922, while her mother in-law followed on 12 December 1930. The plot is in the same Garden section as Catherine (ZE 115.5). If you stand at their grave you can see Catherine's a few metres away.

On the morning of 23 December 1949, as Christina, the sister of Charles was being buried, her three nephews, Charles, Fred and Chris, all in their thirties stood around the graveside. Unknown to them, their mother's grave was just behind them. They had no idea she was there. It remained that way until 1998, when Fred Heatley, the grandson of Catherine, began his search for her grave. He found her death certificate and made his way to Glasnevin. He inquired about finding a family grave. A member of staff walked him to the plot. When he got there a bare patch of overgrown grass met his eyes.

In 2018 RTÉ's *Nationwide* put together a small documentary on the Spanish flu pandemic. In it, Fred recalled:

> No one in the family knew about it; they didn't know where she was buried … I vowed then that I would have the grave marked and that I would visit it and I would bring other members of the family to visit it so that in time she would always be remembered and people could come and put their flowers on it and say their prayer. She was now no longer just a photograph on the wall, she was more than just a death certificate, she was now like everybody else, like every other mother: she had a grave.[64]

Often such stories are lost to statistics and figures in global pandemics. Catherine Moran Heatley's grave was lost even to her family for nearly 100 years. Today it is marked by a modest wooden cross. The cross is painted black and dark grey, and features a photograph of Catherine alongside her husband in his military uniform. The laminated photograph is attached using thumbtacks. Around the grave a low metal railing and some stones map out the plot. Thanks to her grandson's investigative work, her story can be remembered properly.

As the memory of the pandemic drifted out of people's heads, so too did the stories of those who died. Peter Ross, in his book *A Tomb with a View,* contends, 'you die twice, once when your heart stops beating, and again on the last occasion someone mentions your name'.[65]

Politics and Law

Politicians, barristers, lawyers and judges are not hard to find in Glasnevin Cemetery. Most are well remembered and have fine funerary monuments. In the South New Chapel section (GD 57) you will find the grave of the shaking hand of Dublin, Alfie Byrne. He had the distinction of being a councillor, alderman, lord mayor of Dublin, an MP in Westminster, a TD in Dáil Éireann and a senator in the Seanad. He was the lord mayor of Dublin for a record ten times, including nine terms of office in a row (1930–39). Trevor White, in his 2017 publication *Alfie: The Life and Times of Alfie Byrne*, has thankfully brought this Dublin legend's story back to life.[1] Traffic was held up along O'Connell Street for nearly a half hour during his funeral and according to the *Evening Herald*: 'at all junctions along the route to Glasnevin people silently gathered to pay tribute to one of Dublin's most famous sons'.[2] Yet his achievements in the world of politics sadly don't attract large amounts of visitors to his graveside today. This is true too of many who devoted themselves to the legal profession.

One example is Timothy Healy (1855–1931), buried in the South New Chapel section (CE 4). He was the first governor general of the Irish Free State. Before being appointed to this role, he had a long-standing career in

---

Glasnevin Cemetery Mortuary Chapel and O'Connell Tower. (© Alan Cleary)

the Houses of Commons as an MP with the IPP. Another is Hugh Kennedy, whose grave is in the South section (Z 21). He became the first attorney general of the Irish Free State in 1923.[3] Later he was the legal adviser to the Department of Local Government under the First Dáil and played an important role in helping to draft the 1922 constitution of the new State.[4] As attorney general, his first task in 1923 was to help establish a new court system, and afterwards he was elevated to the position of chief justice. He was also a member of the first delegation from the Irish Free State to travel to the League of Nations in 1923.[5] Today he is regarded as one of the best judges ever to have graced the Irish bench since independence.[6] Byrne, Healy and Kennedy's graves, although not visited by many, have fitting headstones above their graves. There are others, however, who are less well memorialised.

Earnán de Blaghd

Ernest Blythe (or, as he preferred, Earnán de Blaghd) is buried in the Garden section (GG 138.5) beneath a small, weathered, leaning headstone. During his life he was many things: journalist, republican, Irish-language enthusiast, Minister for Finance and later Posts and Telegraphs, senator, hunger-striker and managing director of the Abbey Theatre. A search through newspaper articles from 1910 to 1975 reveals over 4,000 articles featuring his name. Blythe was a member of the first seven Dáils from 1919 to 1933 and a member of both the 1931 Seanad (1931–34) and the 1934 Seanad (1934–36). Daithí Ó Corráin states 'that while no recent work treating the opening decade of the Irish State has failed to draw on Blythe's papers … Blythe's role in the reorientation of thinking on the national question has not received the historical attention it deserves'.[7] David Fitzpatrick's biography, *A Double Life: Ernest Blythe's Revolutionary Education* (2019), is a welcome step in helping to bring his story back to life.

He was born on 13 April 1889 into a Presbyterian and unionist family in a place called Magheragall, close to Lisburn in County Antrim. At the young age of 15 he made his way to Dublin. His first guiding presence on his journey from 'the Orangeman' to 'the Fenian' was Seán O'Casey, who introduced him to the IRB.[8] Ernest recounted in his Bureau of Military History statement:

> Seán began to talk to me about the Fenians … One Saturday evening coming home on the tram from the Phoenix Park … when we came

> to the end of Blessington Street he asked me to leave the tram as he wanted to talk to me. We walked up Hardwicke Street, and he proceeded to inform me that the Fenian organisation was still alive today … He asked me if I would join. Having read something about the Invincibles, I told him that I did not favour assassination and would have nothing to do with an organisation which countenanced it. Seán said that the Fenians were completely against assassination, and that their policy was to prepare to make open war on England … When I told Seán I was willing, he said that, as I was a stranger to Dublin and unknown to the people with authority in the organisation, I should be kept under observation for some months …[9]

Ernest worked as a boy clerk in the Department of Agriculture. Despite his family background, he joined not only the IRB but also the Irish Volunteers. He also joined the Gaelic League and was taught Irish by Sinead Flanagan, the future wife of Éamon de Valera. He also spent some time in the West Kerry Gaeltacht to improve his fluency of the language. Prior to becoming a member of the IRB, he was placed under observation. Ernest stood out as someone from Ulster and a Protestant.[10] He recounted how he was 'very embarrassed when a school pal who was in the RIC called one day to see me and I got rid of him as quickly as I could but I had to go for a drink with him in a pub and I was afraid that my chances of ever getting into the organisation would be ruined if I was seen drinking with this man in uniform in the pub!'[11]

In his twenties he became a junior reporter with the *North Down Herald.* Around that same time he became a member of the Orange Order. David Fitzpatrick contends that 'if that fact had become widely known, Blythe's revolutionary and political ambitions would have been immediately and permanently dashed'.[12] On 26 September 1910 the Newtownards District Orange Lodge confirmed the admission of a 21-year-old recruit into Volunteers' Lodge 1501. He was returned as Ernest Blythe of East Street, exactly where he was living as a correspondent with the *North Down Herald.*[13] He remained a member of the Order until his resignation in February 1912. It is hard to tell what his true intentions were. Those from where he was born remained loyal and friendly to Ernest, despite his nationalist outlook.

Between 1912 and 1916 he gained a reputation within republican circles in Ulster as 'an inveterate inmate of prisons'.[14] He also built a reputation as a talented propagandist and organiser within the Irish Volunteers and IRB. He became close friends with Bulmer Hobson and Denis McCullough. The Defence of the Realm Act (DORA), a piece of emergency legislation speedily introduced in the UK during the First World War, gave the British government the power to design regulations to control its populations and prevent people from providing information to the enemy in a time of war. DORA came to police everything from public outdoor gatherings, sporting events, the use of the Irish language and cultural demonstrations, publications and speeches. In July 1915 Ernest was jailed for failing to leave Ireland and reside in Britain. He had been ordered to leave the country because of his recruitment and organisational role within the Irish Volunteers.[15] He spent three months in Crumlin Road Gaol in Belfast. Later he was sent to a small town in Berkshire called Abingdon, where he was required to report to the local police station each day. His failure to report on a few occasions resulted in a short spell in Oxford Prison. He later spent time in Arbour Hill, Brixton and Reading jails. Due to these sentences, he played no part in the Rising of 1916.

In 1914 Ernest Blythe was taking part in rallies and speeches on the topic of proposed Home Rule and unionist objections. In a strong letter to the editor of the *Irish Independent* dated 21 May 1914, Blythe is already at pains to point out feelings within the nationalist community in Ulster. He titled this letter the 'Evils of Exclusion, Danger of Unionist Triumph' and said:

> The hope that Ulster can be wooed and won is a hope that can only be entertained by people utterly ignorant of the conditions prevailing in the North. If exclusion takes place it will be looked upon as a Unionist triumph, and the triumph will almost certainly be celebrated by the rowdiest Orange element with an anti-Catholic outburst in the factories and workshops. This may quite conceivably be followed by certain forms of retaliation. At any rate, it will involve a disastrous increase of ill-feeling and sectarian hatred, which may not be confined to Ulster ... If the Orangemen were given actual personal experience of the rule of an Irish Government, I (who am of his race and creed) am well assured that he would soon become the proudest and most patriotic Irish citizen. Exclusion, however, will not permit him to have that experience ... Exclusion will in fact, stereotype his opposition to Irish National aspirations. If we cannot have Home Rule for an

> undivided Ireland, it will be a hundred-fold better for us to turn from the Liberal doorstep and see what efficacy may be found in the arms of the Irish Volunteers.[16]

In the 1918 general election he was duly elected as MP for North Monaghan. He joined his fellow TDs in assembling at the Mansion House, Dublin, for the first sitting of Dáil Éireann. He was given the ministerial position of Trade and Commerce, which he held until 1922.

For Ernest the period between 1919 and 1922 was a time when the threat of arrest loomed large. He had been arrested in February 1918 before being appointed Director of Trade and Commerce. He was rearrested in September 1919 but released in November.[17] It is during these spells in prison in both Cork and Mountjoy that he went on hunger and thirst strikes. In February 1918, while in Cork Gaol, he began a hunger and thirst strike lasting five days before being moved to Dundalk. His description of his first experience gives a sense of what it was like:

> The effects of the thirst-strike began to be felt very soon. I found the skin coming off my lips, and on one occasion towards the end I woke up and had to put my finger into my mouth to take my tongue off my palate. During the last day or so I slept a great deal, and, although I had never even tasted stout in my life, I dreamed, every time I dozed off, of a huge tankard of stout with an enormous head on it ...[18]

Following this he was court-martialled for failing to comply with the order to leave Munster, and served twelve months' imprisonment in Dundalk, Belfast and Mountjoy. On 1 November 1919 he began another hunger strike while in Mountjoy and was released on 6 November.

Despite only being appointed as a minister to the Dáil cabinet in early 1922, he held a seat at the cabinet table long before this. In the Dáil files there is a record of proceedings dated 17 June 1919 with a letter from Éamon de Valera in which it says:

> I do not know that there is any provision for it in the Constitution, but I think it important, so that the number in the Cabinet may not be too small. And that it may include a sufficiency of different types of opinion, to make good the deficiency in number during my absence

> (his time in America) by the temporary admission of one of the present extra Cabinet Ministers, and if this be ratified by Dáil Éireann Earnán de Blaghd, Minister for Trade and Commerce be thus admitted.[19]

Ernest, after his release from prison in November 1919, said:

> I had been intending at this point to go back to Skibbereen, but Michael Collins had said to me that I ought to stay in Dublin, and had in fact told me the day before that he and others would look out to see if they could get me a job in Dublin. Consequently I accepted de Valera's offer, and my appointment as Director of Trade and Commerce was confirmed by the Dail a day or two afterwards.[20]

In this role he worked on policies ranging from the introduction of an Irish Industrial Scheme (1921) to the more mundane tasks of sourcing a new manager for the Dead Meat Factory in Waterford at their request (on 28 May 1920).[21] It was a ministerial portfolio ranging from the most local of matters to those of a more international nature, including efforts to obtain recognition for the Republic from the 'Russian Socialist Federated Soviet Republic'.[22]

The Anglo-Irish Treaty signed on 6 December 1921 established the new Irish Free State as a self-governing, semi-autonomous dominion within the British Commonwealth. It also more controversially included an oath of allegiance to the reigning monarch of the United Kingdom. It further agreed to the partition of the six counties in the north-east of the island. Debates, division and disillusionment followed. Ernest was a supporter of the Treaty. He was appointed Minister for Finance in 1923 by President of the Executive Council W.T. Cosgrave in the newly established Irish Free State following the end of the Irish Civil War. In the Treaty debates on 22 December 1921 he spoke two words to members of the house who were condemning Michael Collins for what had been agreed. He interrupted Deputy MacEntee to say, 'Trust Him.'[23] A lengthier contribution followed on Tuesday, 3 January 1922:

> I believe that in making my choice I am not fettered by the oath I took as a member of this Dáil. I believe that if I hold myself back from doing what I believe would be best for the Irish nation because it conflicted with the terms of that oath, it would be doing wrong, because I took

> that oath as President de Valera took it – as an oath to do my best for the freedom of the Irish nation … Republicanism is with me not a national principle but a political preference. I am against monarchy, because I believe monarchies in the world as it is today are effete and out of date. I believe the Irish people, when they voted for a Republican majority in this Dáil, and when they declared themselves for an Irish Republic were not thinking of constitutional privileges very much, but were thinking of the complete freedom of Ireland. I think that is the ideal for which the Irish people have declared … but I believe the main thing that was in their minds was the securing of the complete independence of Ireland. As far as I am concerned, I wanted the Irish Republic, as I believe the people of Ireland did, in order that Ireland might be free. With me the Republic was a means to an end and not an end in itself.[24]

Michael Collins responded with a resounding 'Hear, Hear'. Ernest continued:

> In fact, people who are willing to agree to external association and refuse to accept the Treaty seem to me to be the people who have swallowed the camel and are straining at the gnat. We have before us the alternatives of ratification and rejection. What would follow rejection is, I think, to a considerable extent, a matter of speculation. We would have chaotic conditions, certainly …[25]

Ernest, in his lengthy contribution, also discussed the legal exponents of the Treaty document, the role of the plenipotentiaries in the negotiations and their decision to sign the document under the threat of immediate and terrible war. His other contributions included a rebuttal of the suggestion by Deputy Robinson on 6 January 1922 that Collins only came to Ireland to avoid conscription. There is one last contribution from 9 January, on the issue of the resignation of de Valera from his role as president of the Irish Republic. Blythe stated:

> What is in my mind is to assure you that anything that will be done here to-day will be something that will rather tend to prevent people who have worked together so long, and who are still out for the same ultimate end, to prevent them from arriving at a situation where they

> may begin shooting one another ... I think we are heading straight for a situation in which chaos of the worst kind will result.[26]

The Civil War that followed put an enormous strain on the country financially. Ernest became the new Minister for Finance. To some he is remembered unfairly as the minister who decreased the old age pension by a shilling. He also managed to fund the Shannon Hydroelectric Scheme, arguably the biggest achievement of the Cumann na nGaedheal administration (1923–32). As Minister for Posts and Telegraphs between 1923 and 1932 he was also vice president of the Executive Council and second in command to W.T. Cosgrave during a decade of nation building. David Fitzpatrick describes him as being 'a controversial minister in W.T. Cosgrave's executive council ... he was an effective if conservative minister for finance'.[27]

The 1933 general election saw de Valera and his new party, Fianna Fáil, rise to power. Ernest lost his seat and began his period in Seanad Éireann. He continued working as a senator for Cumann na nGaedheal and later with the newly formed Fine Gael in 1933.

To many historians, Ernest's political career after 1933 is a source of confusion to this day. In the build-up to the 1933 election he was selected as a candidate, and his sentiments in the campaign of 1932–33, only a decade after the end of the Civil War are remarkable. Ernest, himself a proponent of the republican cause, began to label those against Cumann na nGaedheal as being 'Republicans' who will cause 'chaos and bankruptcy'. David Fitzpatrick contends: 'His seminal role in the Blueshirts movement and Irish fascism continues to bemuse historians.'[28]

According to an article in *The Irish Press*, at a gathering in Cashel of about 200 members of the Army Comrades Association (ACA) Blythe said:

> The A.C.A is a vigorous national organisation, which will serve the people in a much wider way than simply securing the preservation of free speech or maintaining order at public meetings. The A.C.A is the successor of the great national organisations which in the past encouraged and raised up the people and brought about the establishment of national freedom, the Gaelic League, the Volunteers and the pre-Truce and pre-Treaty Sinn Fein. Through the A.C.A the nation will go ahead until this generation will see the country under one flag from sea to sea, free, prosperous, strong and proud.[29]

It is also noted in the article that General Felix Cronin, who went on to marry Kitty Kiernan, also spoke. Cronin and Kiernan are buried two graves away from General Eoin O'Duffy, who in 1933 became chief of staff to the ACA and later the National Guard. Adopting the symbols of fascism and featuring a distinctive blue uniform, they became better known as the 'Blueshirts'.

In September 1933 the political parties Cumann na nGaedheal and the Centre Party merged with the Blueshirts movement to form Fine Gael. Eoin O'Duffy was elected its first leader. A year later he resigned.[30]

By 1936 Blythe had retired from politics and shifted his focus to matters of the Irish language and to resolving the partition question. He encouraged theatrical impresarios and promoters like Micheál Mac Liammóir and Hilton Edwards to set up an Irish-language theatre in Galway called *An Taibhdhearc*. He also set up a publishing company, *An Gúm*, dedicated to Irish-language literature printing for the Irish government. On the topic of partition, he became a prominent voice, often at odds with those in power. His opinions regularly received backlash in the press. In the *Donegal News* there is an article from 4 November 1950 sarcastically entitled 'The Wisdom of Ernest Blythe'. The author gives a damning opinion on his contentions about the border. It goes on to suggest that:

> We have not the space to follow Mr Blythe through the maze of half-statements, qualifications and conditions with which he bolsters up his amazing case that partition is really the fault of those who are in the Anti-Partition movement, he writes of a smear campaign against Stormont, as though the vindicative bigots in Belfast and the small towns of this area were really injured by innocents to whose good name justice demands that full reparation be done, presumably by Mr Blythe, but we consider he has a cool cheek to describe the blackguardly gerrymandering devices by which Orangeism sets the will of the majority at defiance as amounting merely to a 'slight temporary lack of balance' ...[31]

Blythe's writings promoted the ideals of persuasion over coercion for the unionist population. In 1959 he published a pamphlet entitled 'A New Departure in Northern Policy'. Daithí Ó Corráin believes that Blythe's writings on partition looked mainly at the 'internal inconsistencies of the nationalist position', which insisted 'that Ireland was really one nation, yet

[was] unable to find any convincing way of reconciling that claim with the refusal of unionists to accept that they belonged to the nation'.[32] His attitude and opinion on reunification remained the same throughout his life.[33] In his old age he remained a prominent voice in the newspapers, although there is only a footnote in his writings on the beginnings of the Troubles. He left some remarks in an internal document entitled 'Politicians and the Ulster Question':

> Changes forced upon Protestants by outside pressure will tend to make them more determined to hold on by various stratagems to all that remains of their power. In a word, the campaign now going on in the North may secure Catholic Civil Rights as fully as they might have been secured say fifteen years ago by a Catholic policy of non-coercion and non-segregation in politics which would have brought about Catholic-Protestant co-operation, but the securing of reform by the enlistment of British help, will probably operate to preserve politico-sectarian segregation and so buttress Partition for a further period.[34]

He could not have foreseen the horrors that lay in wait for his province during the Troubles. He welcomed the historic meeting of Seán Lemass and Terence O'Neill in January 1965. It symbolised what he called in the *Irish Independent* 'a breakthrough to common sense'.[35]

After his retirement from the political arena, Ernest's most notable appointment was as managing director of the Abbey Theatre, a position that he held for twenty-six years (1941–67). He continued to work as a member on the board of directors at the Abbey until 1972. His tenure in the role was a controversial one. His past links to unionist communities in Ulster raised some eyebrows, while assertions that he engaged many actors on the basis of their knowledge of the Irish language rather than their acting skills caused upset to others. There were also allegations that he favoured 'popular' material over new productions to help increase box office receipts. Leslie Faughnan suggested in 1966 that the Abbey's tendency towards traditionalism was inclined to make it dull and that Ernest Blythe had 'served it well as an able and dedicated administrator … but an administrator he has been, and not in any full sense a man of the theatre'. The period of the Board of Directors of which Blythe was the head up until 1967 was described by Tomás MacAnna (Irish theatre director and playwright who later became artistic adviser to the Abbey Board in 1966 and was artistic director from 1972–79 and 1984–85) as a time when the directors 'did a disservice both to the Abbey and to O'Casey'.[36]

The Cork Examiner covered the story of Blythe's full retirement from the Abbey on 9 September 1972. In the article it quoted the chairman of the Board of Directors, Michael Ó hAodha:

> We are deeply conscious of Mr Blythe's exceptional and distinguished service to the National Theatre both as Director and manager. He first became interested in the work of the theatre as long ago as 1905, and he had seen and can recall practically every play staged at the Abbey since its foundation … Mr Blythe has been singled out as a target for criticism. His determination to preserve the Abbey as a distinctively Irish Theatre has frequently been either misrepresented or misunderstood, but when the definitive history of the Abbey is written, it will become clear that he more than anyone else since Yeats, has remained steadfast in upholding the aims of the founders of the National Theatre.[37]

Cyril Cusack, Joan Plunkett and Ernest Blythe at the Olympia Theatre 21st anniversary party, 17 March 1962. (Used with kind permission of Mediahuis Ireland/NLI Collection)

Ernest Blythe died in Dublin's Mount Carmel Hospital on 23 February 1975 at the age of 85 from heart failure. His funeral took place at St Patrick's Cathedral in accordance with his religion and he was later buried in Glasnevin. A special programme was broadcast on RTÉ radio that same evening on the life of Blythe.[38] His funeral was covered by all the major newspapers of the time. *The Cork Examiner* ended its coverage with: 'In subsequent comments on the Civil War, Blythe made his deep feelings on the division within the country known. His own actions and those of his colleagues at the time were regrettable but necessary. He said controversial as well as brilliant things and took a firm stand on the partition question …'[39] The *Evening Herald* remembered him as the 'unflappable Mr Blythe'.[40] *The Cork Examiner*, on Tuesday 25 February, described how a group of about 150 people with the Taoiseach, Liam Cosgrave, were in attendance at his removal.[41] His wife, Annie, formerly Miss Annie McHugh, who was born in Dunlavin, County Wicklow, had died years earlier, in 1957.

Blythe's legacy has become lost to more popularised tales of the revolutionary period 1916–23. Liam Cosgrave said of him:

> his deep and abiding interest in the Irish language and his work to promote it will be remembered as indeed will his contribution to the development of the theatre in Ireland by his long service to the Abbey Theatre. Earnán de Blaghd was one of a remarkable generation of Irishmen who contributed to the founding of this State and who nursed it through those first difficult years.[42]

Sir John Gray and Vartry

A walk up Dublin's O'Connell Street reveals six monuments, to Daniel O'Connell, William Smith O'Brien, James Larkin, Fr Mathew and Charles Stewart Parnell. The sixth can be seen at its finest after leaving Eason's bookshop or standing outside Supermac's. Most people walk past it without realising the significance behind the person it remembers. If you stop to read the inscription however it reveals a multi-faceted man from 19th-century Ireland. It states: 'Erected by public subscription to Sir John Gray Knt. MD JP, Proprietor of *The Freeman's Journal*; MP for Kilkenny City, Chairman of the Dublin Corporation Water Works Committee 1863 to 1875 during which period pre-eminently through his exertions the Vartry water supply was introduced to city and suburbs. Born July 13 1815, Died April 9 1875.'

There is another monument to Gray on the O'Connell Tower Circle in Glasnevin. Made from fine Sicilian marble, it is inscribed with the words: 'He is not dead but sleepeth.' Both monuments were sculpted by the prolific nineteenth-century Irish sculptor Sir Thomas Farrell. Gray's memorial in the cemetery is made up of a sculpted shaft with a massive bust of his head on top. It also includes a series of faces on its shaft where four carved figures can be seen. Each figure reflects on an important part of his life. They represent the spirit of the Vartry, of enfranchised religion, an Irish maiden with the fruits of a land blessed with security and peace, and the image of Education spreading her teaching out of an open book, while her finger points towards heaven symbolising the greater lessons to be learned from above. W.J. Fitzpatrick said in 1900 that: 'The likeness not alone preserves the lineaments but conveys somewhat of the thought, purpose and character of the man.'[43]

Born on 16 July 1816 in Claremorris, County Mayo, to John Gray, a farmer and excise officer, and Elizabeth (Eliza) Wilson,[44] he was the third of six sons and four daughters. His family were raised in the Presbyterian

Sir Thomas Farrell's monument to Sir John Gray, Glasnevin Cemetery, O'Connell Tower Circle. (© Warren Farrell)

faith. He went to study medicine at Glasgow University before returning to Dublin to practise in 1839. His practice was located on Dublin's North Cumberland Street.[45] Before too long his career took a twist and a life in politics beckoned. He threw his full support behind Daniel O'Connell in his fight for Repeal of the Union with Great Britain. He wished to see a parliament in Dublin and also supported O'Connell's earlier successful campaign for Catholic Emancipation. He would later throw his full support behind another of Ireland's 'uncrowned Kings', Charles Stewart Parnell.[46] In 1841 he purchased the Dublin Catholic daily paper *The Freeman's Journal* and became the newspaper's political editor as well as owner. He used its pages to support O'Connell during his campaign and to attend many of the Liberator's meetings.[47]

These activities did not go unnoticed and he was arrested on charges of treasonable conspiracy in October 1843, and later charged, along with five other men, in 1844 and sentenced to nine months at Richmond Bridewell (today Griffith College). As a political prisoner and respected newspaper proprietor, he was kept in great comfort while in prison. The Bridewell was also used to imprison Daniel O'Connell for a short period in 1844. Gray was released on 4 September that same year following appeals on his behalf in the House of Lords.[48]

After O'Connell's death in 1847, Gray became involved in tenant-rights agitation and played a big role in the establishment of a fire brigade and cattle market on Dublin's North Circular Road. Described as an 'improver', he did much to improve living standards throughout Dublin. Most significantly as chairman of Dublin Corporation's Waterworks Committee (1853–75) he oversaw the construction of the Vartry water scheme (1862–69). He was knighted by the viceroy in 1863 in recognition but declined to accept election as lord mayor of Dublin in 1868.[49] David Dickson contends that 'his political acumen was vital in securing the enabling legislation and the finance for the mountain reservoir, the twenty-four-mile pipeline and a suburban distribution reservoir at Stillorgan'.[50] It cost £541,000 to build and the first water arrived via its pipes in July 1867.[51] This new high-pressure supply of water went through 110 miles of pipes to all locations in the city and was a major construction feat of its day.[52] This is why his headstone features links to Vartry.

In July 1865 Gray was elected as MP for Kilkenny, a position he held unopposed up until his death. During his time in Westminster he argued for

Church disestablishment and land reforms. He held his own conservative views on Home Rule, but in 1874 he was counted among the fifty-nine supposed Home Rulers returned and he later moved towards the more militant Home Rulers led by Joseph Biggar.[53] Ironically, for a man so devoted to clean water for the city of Dublin during his life, it is fitting that he died in the town of Bath on 10 April 1875.

The funeral made its way to Glasnevin on 15 April and was reported in many newspapers as being 'nearly a mile in length'.[54] The procession made its way past his home in Rathmines, Charleville House (later the St Louis Convent) to the O'Connell Tower Circle where he was buried in Vault 8. He died at the age of 59 due to cancer of the liver. The route to the cemetery was 'densely thronged, and the progress of the funeral was marred occasionally by expressions of emotion from the people who assisted'.[55] There were several MPs, leading figures from Dublin Corporation and deputations from many local authorities.[56] *The Irish Times* reflected:

> [There] was a strong muster of police stationed along the route … regulating the traffic … easily performed, indeed there seemed to be a great dignified position to aid in the proper carrying out of the last act of duty to an eminent public man … The body was enclosed in an oak coffin … on it were placed a number of garlands and wreaths of everlasting flowers …[57]

His statue today on O'Connell Street is forgotten and overshadowed by the Spire, but next time you turn the tap on for a glass of water, stop and think of Sir John Gray, without whom countless Dubliners would not be alive today.

A Multi-faceted Man: J.J. O'Kelly

Another neglected parliamentarian buried in a vault in the Dublin section (D 18) is James Joseph O'Kelly. He was one of Parnell's parliamentarians; not a noted orator, but a complex and multi-faceted character. He was born in Dublin to John O'Kelly, a blacksmith, dray maker and petty landlord, and Bridget Lawlor. He was sworn into the Fenians in 1861 at the age of just 16.[58] After the death of his father that same year he moved to London to live with his uncle, the distinguished sculptor John Lawlor, and helped to establish the London IRB.[59]

In 1863 he was elected captain of the London Irish Volunteers but instead enlisted in the French Foreign Legion, which saw him travel to Algeria and later Mexico. There he was made a prisoner by the Mexican General Canales but escaped and returned to Ireland having learned of plans for an uprising through John Devoy, his boyhood friend.[60] On his return, however, he saw that the Fenians were ill-equipped to stage a successful rebellion and opposed the idea. He moved back to London in 1868 where he entered the next phase of his life as a journalist and news correspondent for *The Irishman*.[61] He also become secretary of the IRB's Supreme Council and for two years was the leading arms agent for the IRB in London.[62]

James O'Kelly MP. (Reproduced with permission from the Library of the Houses of the Oireachtas)

On 25 February 1868 he arrived in America. He got a job as art editor and drama critic for the *New York Herald*, and later became its war correspondent. He travelled to Cuba for interviews with guerrilla fighters during the campaign for independence in 1873, to Brazil in 1874 to accompany the emperor through his tour of the USA, and in 1875 he was attached to the American Army in its war against the Sioux, during which time he was with General Custer.[63] He wrote a book about his experiences in Cuba called *The Mambi Land* (1874). It remains in print in Cuba to this day.

He met Parnell in a series of interviews in Paris in 1877 and became convinced of his politics. At the same time he was a leading figure in the Fenian fundraising organisation of Clann na Gael with Devoy and persuaded him to support his call for an Irish nationalist parliamentary party to be established at Westminster. Unsuccessfully in 1879 he also tried to persuade the IRB to give military aid to the Zulus in their war against Britain.[64] Disillusioned with the Irish revolutionary movement in the 1880 general election, he decided to stand for parliament for the Land League and was elected for County Roscommon.[65] During 1882 he was imprisoned at Kilmainham Gaol along with Parnell for their support of the Irish Land

League and Michael Davitt. He was held until 2 May 1882.[66] By the mid-1880s the radical Fenian O'Kelly had become Parnell's chief spokesman in parliament on British foreign policy. He maintained his war correspondent position and travelled to Sudan to cover the conflict from behind enemy lines from 1883 to 1885.[67]

After the scandal relating to Parnell and Catherine O'Shea became public knowledge, he backed his ally in parliament. This is no surprise as O'Kelly was no stranger to scandalous headlines. He had been forced to marry a young American woman whom he had made pregnant in 1875. He sent her to live with his brother Aloysius in Paris. Later that same year he married the singer, Harriet Clark. When news broke about his bigamous lifestyle, Harriet divorced him in 1876 and newspapers featured the story prominently.

Following the splits and divisions within the IPP after Parnell's death, O'Kelly lost his seat in parliament. He regained it in 1895 and held it unopposed up until his death in 1916. In the latter parts of his life, he held strong pro-Boer sentiments during the South African War (1899–1902) and worked as London correspondent for the *Irish Independent* but was dogged by ill health and financial difficulties.[68] It was a surprise to his Fenian friend John Devoy when he voiced his support for Irishmen enlisting to fight as the First World War commenced. That was to be the first and last time they disagreed, as J.J. O'Kelly died of pneumonia in London on 22 December 1916. He never spoke about what had happened during the Easter Rising but his death caused the famous by-election in Roscommon in 1917 won by Count George Noble Plunkett for Sinn Féin.

His death was widely reported in *The Irish Times*, *The New York Times*, the *Irish Independent* and *The Freeman's Journal*. The *Ulster Herald* reported that his life was 'crammed with exciting adventures'.[69] The *Irish Independent* led with 'veteran nationalist buried' on 29 December 1916 and it wrote about his funeral to Glasnevin the day before. His body was taken from the Pro-Cathedral, his coffin was carried by a number of local Roscommon men and a wreath was laid by John Redmond and the IPP in recognition of his life as a nationalist and MP.[70] Carla King noted that symbolically his death was the first signal that the old IPP was about to be overwhelmed by a political revolution and the emergence of a whole new generation of Irish nationalists.[71]

The Sullivans

Alexander Martin (A.M.) Sullivan (1830–84) was born on 15 May 1830 in Bantry, County Cork to a house painter, Daniel Sullivan, and Catherine Baylor. His brother was the famous T.D. Sullivan, who later became lord mayor of Dublin (1886–88). After an education in the locality, A.M. Sullivan displayed exceptional intellect and inspired by Fr Mathew, the Irish Catholic priest and teetotalist reformer, he held a lifelong commitment to temperance.[72] He worked as a clerk of Famine relief works in the Skibbereen district (1845–57) and what he saw led him to become actively involved with the emerging Young Ireland movement.[73]

In 1853 he moved to Dublin to work as an illustrator for the *Dublin Expositer.*[74] At the same time he began contributing to *The Nation* and became close to many leaders in the Fenian movement, including Charles Gavan Duffy and William Smith O'Brien.[75] Two years later he became the paper's assistant editor and part owner, and in 1858 bought out his partners to become the sole proprietor of *The Nation*. He held the position for over twenty years and 'throughout … his pen was constantly active in defence of the Nationalist side in politics'.[76] His brother T.D. would take over the newspaper in 1876.

Although a nationalist, he distanced himself from the Fenians and their Proto-Phoenix Society in October 1858, which afterwards saw many of his public speeches disrupted by Fenian agitators accusing him of 'felon-setting' (betraying nationalist activists to the authorities).[77] Many also blamed him for the numerous arrests and trials of Phoenix activists, although he actively campaigned for a Fair Trial Fund in their defences. From 1859 to 1860 he started both the *Morning News* and *The Weekly News* to try and compete with Sir John Gray's *Freeman's Journal*, but both closed by 1864. Elected to Dublin Corporation in December 1862, he objected to Gray's proposal to erect a statue to Prince Albert instead of Henry Grattan on College

A.M. Sullivan Senior. (Reproduced with permission from the Library of the Houses of the Oireachtas)

Green.[78] Grattan's statue still stands today on College Green, while Albert's stands behind a large bush on Leinster Lawn.

He married Frances Genevieve Donovan of New Orleans on 27 April 1861. They had three sons and five daughters together. He publicly condemned the executions of the Manchester Martyrs in 1867 and helped stage a mock funeral for Larkin, Allen and O'Brien in Dublin.[79] In February 1868 he was jailed for six months for seditious libel and served three months.[80] He became one of the leading constitutional nationalists of the nineteenth century in Ireland and approved of physical force but also appreciated there was no point in violence without a prospect of success.[81] He enrolled at the King's Inns in 1873 and later moved to London to study for the English Bar. He was admitted to the Irish Bar in 1876 and the English Bar in 1877. In his legal career he defended Patrick Egan from December 1880–January 1881 when leaders of the Land League were tried for conspiracy charges. He also defended the Ladies' Land League against charges of 'unwomanly conduct' from Cardinal Edward McCabe (buried opposite Sullivan's grave).

He excelled in the world of politics and was present at the founding meeting of the Home Rule Party at Bilton's Hotel, Dublin, on 19 May 1870 with Isaac Butt; he was also elected Home Rule MP for Louth in February 1874.[82] Five years later Philip Callan campaigned against him in Louth. He was backed by the drinks trade and Sullivan; although he retained his seat was outpolled by Callan and so he resigned in protest staying true to his Temperance morals.[83] In May 1880, however, he took up a seat as MP for Meath to replace Parnell, who had also been elected in Cork leaving the Meath seat unfilled.

With his brothers T.D. and D.B. Sullivan, he produced *Guilty or Not Guilty? Speeches from the Dock* (1867), an account of the trials of rebels from 1798 to 1867. The book became the central text for popular nationalism and was reprinted as late as the 1960s. In his final years he developed a serious heart condition that nearly killed him in August 1881. He resigned from parliament shortly afterwards but continued to work for the parliamentary Bar and within the Home Rule movement. In September 1884 he suffered another heart attack and spent his final few days with his close companion William Martin Murphy (also buried metres away from him in Glasnevin) at his residence in Dartry. A.M. Sullivan senior died aged 54 on 17 October 1884 and was buried in Glasnevin three days later in the South section (SE 49), beside the steps leading down to O'Connell's vault.

The Nation reported, 'Not Ireland alone, but the civilised world as well, has lost a fearless champion of popular rights ...'[84] Continuing the family's tradition of excellence, Alexander Martin Sullivan Jr (1871–1959) followed in his father's footsteps and also made his mark on the legal profession. Born on 14 January 1871 in Bantry, he was called to the Irish Bar in 1892 and the English Bar in 1899, took silk in Ireland in 1908 and in England in 1919. To take silk was to become Queen's or King's Counsel. He was first cousin to Timothy Healy, and his uncle T.D. Sullivan had written with A.M. Sullivan (his father) 'God Save Ireland'.[85]

His legal career mirrored that of his father. He rose to prominence as a barrister, known for his meticulous preparation, sharp legal analysis and persuasive advocacy. Later he was given the ceremonial title of King's serjeant in law, a title dating back seven centuries. He became third serjeant in 1912, second in 1913 and first in 1920. Today he is remembered as the last person to hold the title of serjeant in law in Ireland.

Sullivan, aged just 14, had participated in the campaign for the election of William Redmond at Fermanagh North in 1885.[86] He became part of the anti-Parnellite contingent during the splits in the IPP of the 1890s.[87] His politics differed from those of his father. As Angus Mitchell contends, 'sons do not inevitably share the political sympathies of their fathers'.[88] His career began like his father's in the world of journalism in New York.[89] He married Helen Keiley in August 1900 in Brooklyn at a private ceremony, and afterwards they set sail for Dublin.[90] They had twelve children.

Sullivan later accepted the brief for the defence of Roger Casement on the charge of high treason at the Royal Courts of Justice on the edge of London City. The case ran from 26 to 29 June 1916. Sullivan is featured standing in the portrait of 'High Treason' by John Lavery, which hangs in the King's Inns, Dublin.[91] He had not been the first choice and in England was only a junior counsel. His relations with Casement have been well documented in Angus Mitchell's account of Roger Casement's life as part of the *16 Lives* series: 'Casement and Sullivan disliked each other from the outset ...'[92] Mitchell argues that Sullivan's main motivation for taking the case was reputational and financial gain. Rather than fighting the case on the grounds of an Irishman having the right to act against England, as Casement had wanted, he instead wanted to use legal technicalities against the charge of treason.[93] George Gavan Duffy, as Casement's solicitor, also made things difficult as he was married to Sullivan's sister.

In his closing speech at the trial, Sullivan had a form of mental breakdown and had to be relieved by Artemus Jones, though he returned the next morning to finish the address.[94] On doctor's orders, he did not attend the final day of proceedings. It took the jury less than an hour to reach a verdict of 'Guilty'. Casement was hanged on 3 August 1916. Sullivan declined to look at Casement's Black Diaries, detailing his homosexuality and produced by the prosecution with the aim of turning public opinion against him and dividing his many well-placed allies.[95]

In the years following the trial he wrote *The Last Serjeant* (1952) and included details about what had happened and what was said. In 1956 René MacColl published a biography of Casement quoting Sullivan stating that Casement 'gloried in it' when discussing the diaries.[96] A controversy followed in which Sullivan denied the comments and said that in fact Casement had told him nothing to help his case. The controversy culminated with two members of the Irish Bar demanding that Sullivan clarify if he had or had not received the express consent of his client Casement to reveal what confidential instructions had been discussed in 1916. Sullivan protested against what he described was 'a public controversy about what is now a matter of ancient history'.[97] Thirty-four members of the Irish Bar then presented a memorial to the benchers for Sullivan's removal on the grounds of 'gross and dishonourable professional conduct'. Sullivan later requested that his name be completely removed from the roll of benchers.

Following 1922 and establishment of the Irish Free State, he found his politics incompatible with the new regime and took up practice in England. After 1949 and the Republic of Ireland Act, he disqualified himself from practice in Ireland as he rendered himself an alien in England.[98] Despite his father's links to the Young Irelanders and his own role in the defence of Roger Casement, he was opposed to Sinn Féin and was a fierce critic of the War of Independence. The IRA even tried to assassinate him in Tralee in January 1920, and again on his travels from Cork to Tralee on his way to give evidence against the group of men who had tried to kill him the first time.[99]

Sullivan spent his final years back in Ireland, in Terenure at Greenmount Road, before leaving for England, where he died on 9 January 1959 in Kent. He was buried in the South section (YA 22) at Glasnevin, a ten-minute walk from his parents' plot and beside the grave of Francis and Hannah Sheehy

Skeffington. John A. Costello said that 'Serjeant Sullivan was regarded as a very great advocate in his practice at the Irish Bar, but his outlook on Irish affairs did not always coincide with the view of the majority of the people. He was a very controversial figure in the Ireland of his time and he continued to be a very controversial figure.'[100] The Sullivan family's influence in the legal profession and their active involvement in Irish politics is mostly forgotten today.

Epilogue

While famous names such as Michael Collins, Charles Stewart Parnell, Countess Markievicz, Grace Gifford and many more rightfully capture our attention, this book I hope has helped to shed light on some of the neglected legacies that lie beneath the cemetery's surface. These lesser-told stories of people who rest in eternal slumber alongside renowned figures of Irish history also deserve our remembrance and recognition. In exploring the lives behind these neglected burials, I have tried to highlight the diverse tapestry of Irish society that has found its final refuge in Glasnevin. From poets and artists, activists and workers, revolutionaries to soldiers, each headstone and grave marked or unmarked holds a story waiting to be told. These untold and forgotten narratives reveal many struggles and triumphs of everyday people who helped shape Ireland's cultural, political and social fabric.

By illuminating these overlooked legacies within Glasnevin, this book serves as a reminder of the inherent value of every life regardless of fame or fortune. It calls on you to look beyond the surface, to recognise that beneath the shadows of the celebrated lie other hidden gems of Irish history. These forgotten burials, once neglected by time, now have their stories written and remembered. In writing this book, my aim is to remind you that the strength

Memento Mori in Old Chapel Circle Glasnevin. (© Warren Farrell)

of a nation lies not solely in the achievements of its most famous figures, but in the collective stories of all its people. By seeking out these legacies, we can reshape our understanding of history and ensure that no voice remains unheard. We can also better appreciate the complexities of our shared past without simplifying narratives.

As you close this book, remember that among the grandeur of Glasnevin's famed monuments there is an intricate mosaic of lives waiting to be discovered. They are some of the important threads that help to weave Irish history together. By honouring these figures, we also honour the resilience, spirit and shared humanity that unites us all. I hope their stories serve as a timeless reminder of the power of remembrance and of the enduring relevance of Glasnevin Cemetery today.

The Research: Some Essential Points

There has been much written about the cemetery and many of the people buried on its grounds over the last 200 years. It is not my intention in this book to repeat common knowledge and I do not intend to write a full historiography of each person named. My aim is to make people more aware of some of the forgotten individuals buried in Glasnevin and to highlight some of their often-overlooked contributions to society, both in Ireland and abroad. In putting together my research I have tried to follow these steps for each story:

- All chosen names for this book were located using the records of Glasnevin Cemetery. This was a task undertaken with the great help of Glasnevin's then resident genealogist, Lynn Brady. Dublin Cemeteries Trust has immaculate records that date back to the first interment in Goldenbridge Cemetery in 1828. This means that the records pre-date the establishment of Prospect Cemetery (today Glasnevin). Initially, only basic records were kept with a first and last name along with the person's last known address, age, grave location and date of burial. However, post-1872, the cemetery began to record a lot more valuable information. From 1872 first name, surname, age, gender, last known address, address where they died, plot number, date of death, date of burial (sometimes the time of burial), religion, occupation, marital status, cause of death, who informed the cemetery of the person's death and the date that the issuing order for burial was made were all recorded. In the cases of young children, the names of the parents are always recorded. It was common when burying young children to only register the child's surname. For women buried in the cemetery it is extremely common for their occupation to be listed as 'spinster' if unmarried, or as 'the wife of' whatever their husband's profession was if they were married (i.e. shopkeeper's wife). This sadly remained the case up until 1981. Many of these women contributed much to the world during their lives and deserve recognition. All records have been digitised and can be accessed via the Dublin Cemeteries Trust website using genealogy credits.

- Once all individuals were located and a burial register obtained, the next step was to locate birth, marriage and death certificates. This task could be lengthy and challenging, depending on the date each person was born and died. Most were accessible through www.irishgenealogy.ie. Others did not have digitised copies and the General Registers Office located at Werburgh Street, Dublin, was used. The accessibility of these records is bound by certain date parameters online. Currently all births in Ireland from 1864–1923 are accessible through Irish Genealogy. All civil marriages from 1845–1948 and all death records from 1871–1973 are available through this site and provide vital links in piecing these stories together. For some, it was only possible to obtain baptismal records. No birth records are accessible in Ireland pre-1845. For help in obtaining some of these baptismal records, Lynn Brady must be thanked again. The General Registers Office is open to the public and if you prefer to do your research through their reading room you can. In a minority of cases where people were born outside of Ireland, records were obtained through a combination of online genealogical sites like Ancestry.com and newspaper clippings. A special thank you to Fionnuala White of the Glasnevin Genealogy Group for birth certificates for those born in Scotland.
- For individuals where a birth, marriage or death certificate could not be found, academic sources, military records or books were used. For marriage dates that could not be located the same approach was taken. In the absence of a death certificate, the Glasnevin records were used.
- Census records from 1901 and 1911 were also used. Unfortunately owing to the destruction for the Public Records Office at the beginning of the Irish Civil War in June 1922, only the 1901 and 1911 censuses are currently available to the public. There are other census records that will be released in the coming years but due to laws

governing the releasing of such documents there is a 100-year rule in place restricting access. The next census records that will be made public will be the 1926 census in April 2026. The returns for 1926 to 1946 and part of those for 1951 are held in the National Archives today but they remain under the control of the Central Statistics Office (CSO), to the extent that the staff of the National Archives are not permitted to examine them for any purpose.

- I am indebted to the many historical organisations, institutions, historians, archivists, relatives, friends, colleagues and places of interest in helping to gather more information about the people in this book. In my endnotes and references I have made every effort to attribute people's pre-existing work as much as possible. If I have missed a reference to anyone's research I apologise.
- I have used as many books and articles as I could for each person. For some there was a voluminous amount, while for others not so many. Emails and visits to the National Archives of Ireland and the National Library of Ireland have helped greatly in shaping the stories of those less written about in this collection, while the Irish Newspapers Archives also played a central role in shaping many of the stories written about in this book.

Endnotes

INTRODUCTION

1 MacThomáis, Shane (2010), *Glasnevin: Ireland's Necropolis*, Dublin: Glasnevin Cemeteries Trust, p. 10.
2 MacThomáis, Shane (2012), *Dead Interesting*, Cork: Mercier Press, p. 10.
3 Kelleher, Aoife (2014), *One Million Dubliners*, Dublin: Underground Films.
4 Griffith, Lisa Marie and Wallace, Ciarán (2016), *Grave Matters: Death and Dying in Dublin, 1500 to the Present*, Dublin: Four Courts Press, p. 35.
5 Quoted in *The Freeman's Journal*, 24.9.1823, p. 3.
6 Dodd, Conor (2023), *The Funeral that Led to a Cemetery Exhibition*, Dublin: Dublin Cemeteries Trust.
7 Ibid.
8 Griffith and Wallace (2016), *Grave Matters*, p. 40.
9 Connell, Carmel (2004), *Glasnevin Cemetery, Dublin, 1832–1900*, Maynooth: Maynooth Studies in Local History, p. 34.
10 Loudon, J.C. (1843), *On the Laying Out, Planting, and Managing of Cemeteries; and on the Improvement of Churchyards*, London: Longman Brown, Green and Longmans, p. 13, available at https://wellcomecollection.org/works/asb5kt7g/items?canvas=5 (accessed April 2020).
11 Ibid., p. 14.
12 Byrne, Patricia M. (2009), 'O'Kelly, Matthias Joseph', available at www.dib.ie/biography/okelly-matthias-joseph-a6835 (accessed 9 December 2022).
13 Dublin Cemeteries Committee (1879), *A Guide Through Glasnevin Cemetery*, Dublin: M.H. Gill & Son, pp. 95–6.

STRANGE THINGS

1 De Courcy, Catherine (2019), *Dublin Zoo: An Illustrated History*, Italy: Mabel Way Press, p. 1.
2 *The Freeman's Journal*, 8.11.1867, p. 3, www.irishnewsarchive.com.
3 De Courcy, *Dublin Zoo*, p. 17.
4 RZSI Visitor Notebook Feb. 1859–June 1866, entries on 30, 31 August 1864 and later April 1865, accessed courtesy Trinity College Dublin, TCDMS 10608/1/8.
5 De Courcy, *Dublin Zoo*, p. 23.
6 Ibid.

7 Ibid.
8 Ibid.
9 *The Irish Times*, 10.06.1903, p. 10 and 12.06.1903, p. 3.
10 RZSI Minute Book Dec. 1900–Dec. 1904, accessed courtesy Trinity College Dublin, TCDMS 10608/1/7, pp. 228–231.
11 *The Irish Times*, 10.06.1903, p. 10 and 12.06.1903, p. 3.
12 RZSI Minute Book Dec. 1900–Dec. 1904, accessed courtesy of Trinity College Dublin, TCDMS 10608/1/6, pp. 231–233, and 10608/1/7, pp. 228–231.
13 *The Irish Times*, 12.06.1903, p. 3.
14 *The Irish Times*, 18.05.1861, p. 3.
15 Ibid.
16 Ibid.
17 *Munster Express*, 19.12.1863, p. 6, www.irishnewsarchive.com.
18 *The Freeman's Journal*, 27.05.1861, p. 5, www.irishnewsarchive.com.
19 *The Belfast News-Letter*, 15 May 1861, p. 4, www.irishnewsarchive.com.
20 Ibid.
21 Ibid.
22 Ibid.
23 *The Irish Times*, 18.05.1861, p. 3.
24 Ibid.
25 Ibid.
26 *The Cork Examiner*, 29.05.1861, p. 4, www.irishnewsarchive.com.
27 *Leinster Express*, 22.06.1861, p. 8, www.irishnewsarchive.com.
28 *Irish Independent*, 24.03.1932, p. 6, www.irishnewsarchive.com.
29 Moore, Andrew (2006), 'De Groot, Francis Edward (Frank) (1888–1969)', *Australian Dictionary of Biography*, available at https://adb.anu.edu.au/biography/de-groot-francis-edward-frank-12881 (accessed 12 October 2022).
30 *Irish Independent*, 24.03.1932, p. 6, www.irishnewsarchive.com.
31 Moore, Andrew (2005), *Francis De Groot, Irish Fascist, Australian Legend*, Sydney: The Federation Press, p. 13.
32 Ibid.
33 Ibid., p. 14.
34 Ibid., p. 21.
35 Ibid.
36 Ibid.
37 Ibid.
38 Ibid., pp. 26–7.
39 Ibid., pp. 30–1.
40 Ibid.
41 Moore, 'De Groot, Francis Edward (Frank) (1888–1969)'.
42 Moore, *Francis De Groot*, pp. 36–7.
43 Moore, 'De Groot, Francis Edward (Frank) (1888–1969)'.
44 Moore, *Francis De Groot*, p. 42.

45 Moore, 'De Groot, Francis Edward (Frank) (1888–1969)'.
46 Ibid.
47 Moore, *Francis De Groot*, p. 64.
48 Moore, Andrew (2005), 'The New Guard and the Labour Movement 1931–35', *Labour History*, 89(1): 55–72, p. 57.
49 Ibid., p. 69.
50 Ibid., p. 62.
51 Ibid.
52 Moore, *Francis De Groot*, p. 134.
53 Ibid., p. 144.
54 Ibid.
55 *The Irish Press*, 02.04.1932, p. 1, www.irishnewsarchive.com.
56 *Offaly Independent*, 26.03.1932, p. 3, www.irishnewsarchive.com.
57 *Irish Independent*, 18.11.1932, p. 9, www.irishnewsarchive.com.
58 Moore, 'The New Guard and the Labour Movement 1931–35', p. 69.
59 Ibid.
60 Ibid., p. 169.
61 Ibid.
62 Moore, 'De Groot, Francis Edward (Frank) (1888–1969)'.
63 Ibid.
64 Moore, *Francis De Groot*, p. 178.
65 Ibid., p. 179.
66 Ibid.
67 Ibid., p. 178.
68 Ibid., p. 181.
69 Moore, 'De Groot, Francis Edward (Frank) (1888–1969)'.
70 Moore, *Francis De Groot*, p. 193.
71 *The Irish Press*, 02.04.1969, p. 6, www.irishnewsarchive.com.
72 Moore, *Francis De Groot*, p. 193.
73 Ibid., p. 204.
74 *The Irish Times*, 12.11.1951, p. 1.
75 McPherson, Douglas (2015), 'When a Lion Roamed Loose in Dublin', *Ireland's Own*, available at www.irelandsown.ie/when-a-lion-roamed-loose-in-dublin/ (accessed 17 August 2022).
76 Ibid.
77 Lee, Joe and Whelan, Bill (2015), *Fortune's Wheel: The Life and Legacy of the Fairview Lion Tamer*, available at https://repository.dri.ie/catalog/c534vb51f (accessed 17 August 2022).
78 Ibid.
79 Ibid.
80 Ibid.
81 Ibid.
82 Ibid.

83 Ibid.
84 *The Irish Times*, 14.11.1951, p. 3.
85 *The Irish Press*, 13.11.1951, p. 1, www.irishnewsarchive.com.
86 Ibid.
87 McPherson, 'When a Lion Roamed Loose in Dublin'.
88 Ibid.
89 Lee and Whelan, *Fortune's Wheel.*
90 Ibid.
91 McPherson, Douglas (2015), 'Death of a Lion Tamer's Wife: Mai Stephens 1924–2015', available at http://circusmania.blogspot.com/2016/01/death-of-lion-tamers-wife-mai-stephens.html (accessed 28 September 2022).
92 *Irish Independent*, 08.01.1952, p. 6, www.irishnewsarchive.com.
93 McPherson, 'Death of a Lion Tamer's Wife'.
94 Lee and Whelan, *Fortune's Wheel.*
95 *Limerick Leader*, 06.09.1952, p. 7.
96 Lee and Whelan, *Fortune's Wheel.*
97 Ibid.
98 Ibid.
99 *Irish Independent*, 30.01.1953, p. 7, www.irishnewsarchive.com.
100 Lee and Whelan, *Fortune's Wheel.*
101 Ibid.
102 McPherson, 'Death of a Lion Tamer's Wife'.
103 *The Irish Press*, 05.02.1953, p. 1, www.irishnewsarchive.com.
104 Murphy, David (2009), 'O'Kelly, Countess Mary de Galway', available at www.dib.ie/biography/okelly-countess-mary-de-galway-a6853 (accessed 10 April 2023).
105 RTÉ Radio (1993), *In the Shadow of Death*, available at www.rte.ie/radio/doconone/646590-radio-documentary-shadow-of-death-countess-mary-de-galway-mary-cummins-belgian-resistance (accessed 21 April 2023).
106 Ibid.
107 Murphy, 'O'Kelly, Countess Mary de Galway'.
108 Ibid.
109 Ibid.
110 *The Irish Times*, 3.07.1999, p. 20.
111 *The Irish Times*, 22.06.1999, p. 31.
112 RTÉ Radio, *In the Shadow of Death.*

SPORT

1 *Saturday Herald*, 13.02.1913, p. 2, www.irishnewsarchive.com.
2 *Irish Independent*, 11.11.1963, p. 11, www.irishnewsarchive.com.
3 *Saturday Herald*, 15.02.1913, p. 2, www.irishnewsarchive.com.
4 Ibid.
5 Ibid.

6 Ibid.
7 Ibid.
8 Moore, Cormac (2015), 'Why this small Island had two international soccer teams', *History Ireland*, 23(6), available at www.historyireland.com/the-irish-soccer-split/ (accessed 20 February 2021).
9 *Irish Independent*, 11.11.1963, p. 11, www.irishnewsarchive.com.
10 *Sunday Independent*, 14.10.1956, p. 16, www.irishnewsarchive.com.
11 Ibid.
12 *Irish Independent*, 25.09.1905, p. 3, www.irishnewsarchive.com.
13 The Everton Collection, 'Object of the Month – Valentine Harris – cigarette card', available at www.evertoncollection.org.uk/article?id=ART74616 (accessed 4 January 2021).
14 Griffiths, Darren (Everton FC Broadcast and Liaison Manager), 'Val Harris Everton Career' (unpublished research kindly shared with me).
15 *Irish Independent*, 21.04.1939, p. 14, www.irishnewsarchive.com.
16 *Sunday Independent*, 14.10.1956, p. 16, www.irishnewsarchive.com.
17 *The Freeman's Journal*, 05.05.1914, p. 11, www.irishnewsarchive.com.
18 *Irish Independent*, 21.04.1939, p. 14, www.irishnewsarchive.com.
19 Ibid.
20 *The Cork Examiner*, 04.07.1946, p. 6, www.irishnewsarchive.com.
21 *Irish Independent*, 21.04.1939, p. 14, www.irishnewsarchive.com.
22 *Irish Independent*, 04.05.1939, p. 12, www.irishnewsarchive.com.
23 *Sunday Independent*, 14.10.1956, p. 16, www.irishnewsarchive.com.
24 Ibid., p. 12.
25 *The Irish Press*, 11.11.1963, p. 3, www.irishnewsarchive.com.
26 *Irish Independent*, 11.11.1963, p. 11, www.irishnewsarchive.com.
27 *Pastime*, 1895 (courtesy of Robert McNicol Librarian at the All-England Lawn Tennis Club).
28 Little, Alan (1984), 'Vere St Leger Goold: A Tale of Two Courts', Kenneth Ritchie Wimbledon Library.
29 Eaves, Simon J., and Lake, Robert J. (2019), 'The Forgotten Powerhouse: Analyzing the Brief Rise to Prominence of Lawn Tennis in Ireland in the Late-Nineteenth Century', *The International Journal of the History of Sport*, 36:11: 959–981, p. 964.
30 Bunbury, Turtle, 'The Golden Age of Irish Tennis', available at www.turtlebunbury.com/history/history_irish/history_irish_tennis.htm (accessed 20 September 2020).
31 Eaves and Lake, 'The Forgotten Powerhouse', p. 964.
32 Ibid., p. 965.
33 *Pastime*, 26 May 1886, p. 347.
34 ESPN, 'Frank Stoker, Ireland, Players and Officials', available at http://en.espn.co.uk/ireland/rugby/player/764.html (accessed 3 October 2020).
35 Murphy, Meadhbh, 'A Pim Wins Wimbledon' from *Heritage Collections of the Royal College of Surgeons*, available at https://rcsiheritage.blogspot.com/2015/06/ (accessed 4 October 2020).

36 Eaves and Lake, 'The Forgotten Powerhouse', p. 970.
37 Ibid., pp. 970–1.
38 *The Irish Times*, 10.01.1939, p. 13.
39 *The Freeman's Journal*, 27.05.1899, p. 5, www.irishnewsarchive.com.
40 *The Yorkshire Post and Leeds Intelligencer*, 8.07.1922, p. 8.
41 Ibid.
42 Pinfold, John, *Lady Margaret Nelson and Ally Sloper* (private research of John Pinfold kindly shared with me 2 June 2020).
43 Ibid.
44 *The Cork Examiner*, 21.08.1922, p. 1, www.irishnewsarchive.com.
45 *The Irish Times*, 10.07.1922, p. 2.
46 *The Yorkshire Post and Leeds Intelligencer*, 8.07.1922, p. 8.
47 Ibid.
48 *The Scotsman*, 'Sporting News', 08.04.1932, p. 15.
49 *Belfast News-Letter*, 27.03.1915, p. 3, www.irishnewsarchive.com.
50 Pinfold, *Lady Margaret Nelson and Ally Sloper.*
51 O'Connor, Michelle (2019), 'Celebrating Lady Nelson, Glasnevin's link to the Grand National', *Teaching Matters*, p. 57.
52 *Belfast News-Letter*, 27.03.1915, p. 3, www.irishnewsarchive.com.
53 Ibid.
54 O'Connor, 'Celebrating Lady Nelson', p. 57.
55 *The Cork Examiner*, 29.03.1915, p. 10, www.irishnewsarchive.com.
56 *Belfast News-Letter*, 27.03.1915, p. 3, www.irishnewsarchive.com.
57 Pinfold, *Lady Margaret Nelson and Ally Sloper.*
58 *The Irish Times*, 08.04.1932, p. 7.
59 *The Courier and the Adventurer*, 08.04.1932, p. 5.
60 *Drogheda Independent*, 25.06.1932, p. 12, www.irishnewsarchive.com.
61 Vamplew, Wray and Kay, Joyce (2004), *Encyclopaedia of British Horse Racing: 'The Grand National'*, London: Routledge, p. 147.

MURDER AND MYSTERY

1 Kenna, Shane (2019), *The Invincibles: The Phoenix Park Assassinations and the Conspiracy that Shook an Empire*, Dublin: O'Brien Press.
2 *The Irish Times*, 23.05.1896, p. 5.
3 *The Nenagh Guardian*, 20.05.1896, p. 4; *The Ballinrobe Chronicle*, 23.05.1896, p. 3, www.irishnewsarchive.com.
4 *The Irish Times*, 23.05.1896, p. 5.
5 *The Freeman's Journal*, 19.05.1896, p. 6, www.irishnewsarchive.com.
6 Registry of Old Offenders, Grangegorman, 9.06.1896.
7 General Register of Prisoners, Grangegorman Prison, No. 143.
8 Ruxton, Dean (2022), *Death on Ireland's Eye: The Victorian Murder Trial that Scandalised a Nation*, Dublin: Gill Books, p. 235.

9 *The Anglo-Celt*, 03.01.2013, p. 32, www.irishnewsarchive.com.
10 Ibid.
11 *The Kerry Sentinel*, 11.07.1884, p. 4, www.irishnewsarchive.com.
12 *The Belfast News-Letter*, 09.07.1884, p. 5, www.irishnewsarchive.com.
13 *The Kerry Sentinel*, 11.07.1884, p. 4, www.irishnewsarchive.com.
14 *The Cork Examiner*, 09.07.1884, p. 2, www.irishnewsarchive.com.
15 Ibid.
16 Ibid.
17 Ibid.
18 Ibid., p. 5.
19 Ibid.
20 *The Irish Times*, 12.07.1884, p. 5.
21 Ibid.
22 Ibid.
23 Ibid.

TV, MOVIES AND STAGE

1 Long, Patrick, 'O'Dea, James Augustine ('Jimmy')', *Dictionary of Irish Biography*, available at www.dib.ie (accessed 28 March 2023).
2 Ryan, Philip B., (1990), *Jimmy O'Dea, The Pride of the Coombe*, Dublin: Poolbeg Press, p. 232.
3 *Evening Echo*, 30.01.1907, p. 2, www.irishnewsarchive.com.
4 Mikhail, E.H. (1988), 'Looking back on the Abbey, May Craig' in *The Abbey Theatre: Interviews and Recollections*, Basingstoke: Macmillan, pp. 79–80.
5 Clarke, Frances (2010), 'Craig, Mary ('May')', *Dictionary of Irish Biography*, available at www.dib.ie, (accessed 8 September 2021).
6 Ibid.
7 Clarke, 'Craig, Mary ("May")'.
8 Abbey Theatre, Online Catalogue, 'May Craig', available at www.abbeytheatre.ie/archives/person_detail/14299/ (accessed 20 November 2021).
9 Abbey Theatre, 'May Craig'.
10 Ibid.
11 Mikhail, 'Looking back on the Abbey, May Craig', pp. 79–80.
12 Clarke, 'Craig, Mary ("May")'.
13 *The Irish Times*, 09.02.1972, p. 6.
14 Clarke, 'Craig, Mary ("May")'.
15 *The Irish Press*, 18.12.1963, p. 9, www.irishnewsarchive.com.
16 *The Irish Press*, 09.02.1972, p. 3, www.irishnewsarchive.com; *The New York Times*, 10.02.1972, p. 46.
17 *The Irish Press*, 12.02.1972, p. 4, www.irishnewsarchive.com.
18 *The Irish Times*, 09.02.1972, p. 6.
19 Ibid.

20 *Limerick Leader*, 29.11.1975, p. 10, www.irishnewsarchive.com.
21 Ibid.
22 Long, Patrick (2009), 'Margaret Tisdall (Dell, Peggy)', *Dictionary of Irish Biography*, available at www.dib.ie (accessed 14 December 2021).
23 Long, 'Margaret Tisdall (Dell, Peggy)'.
24 *Limerick Leader*, 29.11.1975, p. 10, www.irishnewsarchive.com.
25 Ibid.
26 Long, 'Margaret Tisdall (Dell, Peggy)'.
27 *Limerick Leader*, 29.11.1975, p. 10, www.irishnewsarchive.com.
28 *Irish Independent*, 18.07.1935, p. 3, www.irishnewsarchive.com.
29 *Sunday Independent*, 23.02.1975, p. 15, www.irishnewsarchive.com.
30 Long, 'Margaret Tisdall (Dell, Peggy)'.
31 *Limerick Leader*, 29.11.1975, p. 10, www.irishnewsarchive.com.
32 Myler, Thomas (2016), *Showtime at the Royal: The Story of Dublin's Legendary Theatre*, Dublin: Liffey Press, pp. 257–8.
33 Ibid.
34 *Limerick Leader*, 29.11.1975, p. 10, www.irishnewsarchive.com.
35 Ibid.
36 Long, 'Margaret Tisdall (Dell, Peggy)'.
37 *The Evening Herald*, 08.07.1971, p. 2, www.irishnewsarchive.com.
38 Long, 'Margaret Tisdall (Dell, Peggy)'.
39 *The Irish Press*, 01.05.1979, p. 4, www.irishnewsarchive.com.
40 *Irish Independent*, 01.05.1979, p. 1, www.irishnewsarchive.com.
41 *The Irish Times*, 05.05.1979, p. 9.
42 *Evening Press*, 01.05.1979, p. 5, www.irishnewsarchive.com.
43 Ibid.
44 *Evening Herald*, 04.05.1979, p. 3, www.irishnewsarchive.com.
45 *Limerick Leader*, 29.11.1975, p. 10, www.irishnewsarchive.com.
46 Ibid.
47 Chambers, Anne (1989), *La Sheridan Adorable Diva: Margaret Burke Sheridan, Irish Prima-Donna 1889–1958*, Dublin: Wolfhound Press, p. 8.
48 Ibid.
49 Ibid.
50 Ibid.
51 Walsh, Derek (2009), 'Sheridan, Margaret (Burke) ("Margherita")', *Dictionary of Irish Biography*, available at www.dib.ie (accessed 10 February 2022).
52 Chambers, *La Sheridan Adorable Diva*, p. 26.
53 Ibid., p. 27.
54 Ibid.
55 Ibid., p. 32.
56 Walsh, 'Sheridan, Margaret (Burke) ("Margherita")'.
57 Chambers, *La Sheridan Adorable Diva*, p. 35.
58 Ibid., p. 9.

59 Ibid., p. 45.
60 Ibid., p. 42.
61 RTÉ, *The Silenced Voice* (1958).
62 Walsh, 'Sheridan, Margaret (Burke) ("Margherita")'.
63 MacThomáis, Shane (2010), *Glasnevin: Ireland's Necropolis*, Dublin: Glasnevin Trust, p. 89.
64 Walsh, 'Sheridan, Margaret (Burke) ("Margherita")'.
65 Chambers, *La Sheridan Adorable Diva*, pp. 117–51.
66 Ibid.
67 Walsh, 'Sheridan, Margaret (Burke) ("Margherita")'.
68 Myler, *Showtime at the Royal*, pp. 69–71.
69 Chambers, *La Sheridan Adorable Diva*, p. 103.
70 *Evening Echo*, 14.10.1989, p. 5, www.irishnewsarchive.com.
71 Chambers, *La Sheridan Adorable Diva*, p. 103.
72 Ibid., p. 110.
73 Myler, *Showtime at the Royal*, p. 95.
74 *The Irish Press*, 18.04.1958, p. 6, www.irishnewsarchive.com.
75 Walsh, 'Sheridan, Margaret (Burke) ("Margherita")'.
76 *Evening Echo*, 14.10.1989, p. 5, www.irishnewsarchive.com.
77 Walsh, 'Sheridan, Margaret (Burke) ("Margherita")'.
78 Chambers, *La Sheridan Adorable Diva*, p. 142.
79 Ibid., p. 147.
80 Walsh, 'Sheridan, Margaret (Burke) ("Margherita")'.
81 Chambers, *La Sheridan Adorable Diva*, p. 158.
82 Ibid., p. 179.
83 Walsh, 'Sheridan, Margaret (Burke) ("Margherita")'.
84 Chambers, *La Sheridan Adorable Diva*, p. 191.
85 Ibid., p. 192.
86 Ibid.
87 *The Nenagh Guardian*, 26.04.1958, p. 3, www.irishnewsarchive.com.
88 *Irish Independent*, 19.04.1958, p. 7, www.irishnewsarchive.com.
89 Chambers, *La Sheridan Adorable Diva*, p. 155.
90 Clavin, Terry (2013), 'Ryan, Agnes', *Dictionary of Irish Biography*, available at www.dib.ie (accessed 10 June 2022).
91 Ibid.
92 Ibid.
93 *The Irish Times*, 18.12.1985, p. 12.
94 Clavin, 'Ryan, Kathleen'.
95 *The Irish Press*, 19.07.1944, p. 3, www.irishnewsarchive.com; *The Irish Times*, 19.07.1944, p. 3.
96 *The Irish Press*, 03.07.1933, p. 3, www.irishnewsarchive.com.
97 Clavin, 'Ryan, Agnes'.

98 Ibid.
99 *The Irish Times*, 18.12.1985, p. 12.
100 Clavin, 'Ryan, Kathleen'.
101 *The Irish Times*, 18.12.1985, p. 12.
102 Clavin, 'Ryan, Kathleen'.
103 *Evening Herald*, 22.03.1960, p. 3, www.irishnewsarchive.com.
104 Clavin, 'Ryan, Kathleen'.
105 Collins, Liam (2019), 'Kathleen Ryan – the Irish actress who became forgotten star of Hollywood', available at www.independent.ie/entertainment/movies/kathleen-ryan-the-irish-actress-who-became-forgotten-star-of-hollywood-38819032.html (accessed 10 June 2022).
106 Ibid.
107 *The Irish Times*, 18.12.1985, p. 12.
108 Ibid.
109 Maume, Patrick (2011), 'McAvin, Josie (Josephine)', *Dictionary of Irish Biography*, available at www.dib.ie (accessed 20 June 2022).
110 *The Irish Times* (2004), 'Setting the Standard', available at www.irishtimes.com/culture/setting-the-standard-1.1148214 (accessed 21 June 2022).
111 Ibid.
112 *The Irish Times* (2005), 'Set designer who received Oscar approval', available at www.irishtimes.com/news/oscar-winner-josie-mcavin-85-dies-1.410374 (accessed 10 June 2022).

PIONEERS AND INNOVATORS

1 Fallon, Donal (2022), *Three Castles Burning: A History of Dublin in Twelve Streets*, Dublin: New Island Books, p. 171.
2 Ibid., p. 172.
3 Mulligan, Fergus (2014), *William Dargan: An Honourable Life 1799–1867*, Dublin: Lilliput Press, p. 3.
4 Ibid.
5 Ibid., p. 6.
6 Ibid.
7 Mulligan, *William Dargan*, p. 202.
8 *Dundalk Democrat*, 16.02.1867, p. 6.
9 *The Irish Times*, 12.02.1867.
10 Mulligan, *William Dargan*, pp. 202–4.
11 Aldridge, Albert H., MD (1961), 'Thomas Addis Emmet Presidential Address', *American Journal of Obstetrics and Gynecology*, 82(5): 961–9, p. 962.
12 Wall, L. Lewis (2002), 'Thomas Addis Emmet, the Vesicovaginal Fistula, and the Origins of Reconstructive Gynecologic Surgery', *International Urogynecology Journal*, 13(1): 145–55, p. 146.
13 Francavilla, Lisa A. (2021), 'John Patten Emmet (1796–1842)', *Dictionary of Virginia*

Biography, available at https://encyclopediavirginia.org/entries/emmet-john-patten-1796-1842/ (accessed 10 December 2022).

14 Wall, 'Thomas Addis Emmet', p. 146.
15 Francavilla, 'John Patten Emmet (1796–1842)'.
16 Ibid.
17 Wall, 'Thomas Addis Emmet', p. 146.
18 Ibid.
19 Ibid., p. 147.
20 Ibid.
21 Aldridge, 'Thomas Addis Emmet', p. 963.
22 Emmet, T.A. (1911), *Incidents of My Life: Professional–Literary–Social, with Services in the Cause of Ireland*, New York: G.P. Putnam's Sons, p. 166.
23 Wall, 'Thomas Addis Emmet', p. 148.
24 Aldridge, 'Thomas Addis Emmet', p. 964.
25 Ibid., p. 963.
26 Wall, 'Thomas Addis Emmet', p. 149.
27 Ibid., p. 150.
28 Kelly, Howard (1928), 'Thomas Addis Emmet', in Kelly, H.A., and Burrage, W.L. (eds), *Dictionary of American Medical Biography: Lives of Eminent Physicians of the United States and Canada, from the Earliest Times*, New York: D. Appleton and Co., pp. 381–4.
29 Wall, 'Thomas Addis Emmet', p. 151.
30 Ibid., p. 152.
31 Ibid., p. 149.
32 Aldridge, 'Thomas Addis Emmet', p. 965.
33 Ibid., p. 966.
34 Ibid.
35 Ibid., p. 967.
36 Wall, 'Thomas Addis Emmet', p. 154.
37 *The Tribune*, 25.11.1905, p. 7.
38 *Medical News*, 2.8.1919, p. 156.
39 *The Daily Progress*, 08.03.1919, p. 1.
40 Goffe J.R. (1919), 'In Memoriam, Thomas Addis Emmet, M.D., LL.D., 1828–1919', *Surgery, Gynecology and Obstetrics*, 29(1): 521–4.
41 *The Freeman's Journal*, 14.09.1922, p. 5, www.irishnewsarchive.com.
42 *Irish Independent*, 15.09.1922, p. 2, www.irishnewsarchive.com.
43 Goffe, 'In Memoriam, Thomas Addis Emmet'.
44 Kerr, Steven, College Librarian, RCSED, Royal College of Surgeons of Edinburgh, information obtained in May 2020.
45 Lunney, Linde (2009), 'Murray, Sir James', *Dictionary of Irish Biography*, available at www.dib.ie (accessed 4 January 2023).
46 Ibid.
47 *The Freeman's Journal*, 19.12.1871, p. 8, www.irishnewsarchive.com.
48 Lunney, 'Murray, Sir James'.

49 Fitzpatrick, W.J. (1900), *History of the Dublin Catholic Cemeteries*, Dublin: Dublin Cemeteries Committee, p. 132.

50 Ibid.

51 Lunney, 'Murray, Sir James'.

52 Ibid.

53 Clarke, Frances (2009), 'Murray, John Fisher', *Dictionary of Irish Biography*, available at www.dib.ie (accessed 4 January 2023).

54 *The Freeman's Journal*, 19.12.1871, p. 8, www.irishnewsarchive.com.

55 Fitzpatrick, *History of the Dublin Catholic Cemeteries*, p. 132.

56 *The Dundalk Democrat*, 16.12.1871, p. 2.

57 *Kerry News*, 16.04.1928, p. 7, www.irishnewsarchive.com.

58 Ibid.

59 Fennelly, Teddy (2019), 'James Fitzmaurice – Ireland's greatest aviator', *History Ireland*, 27(2): 40–2, p. 41.

60 Ibid.

61 *Kerry News*, 16.04.1928, p. 7, www.irishnewsarchive.com.

62 Fennelly, 'James Fitzmaurice', p. 42.

63 The United States Navy Memorial, 'Floyd Bennett', available at https://navylog.navymemorial.org/bennett-floyd-1 (accessed 28 December 2023).

64 Long, Patrick (2009), 'Fitzmaurice, James Christopher', *Dictionary of Irish Biography*, available at www.dib.ie (accessed 28 December 2022).

65 Ibid.

66 MacThomáis, Shane (2010), *Glasnevin: Ireland's Necropolis*, p. 40.

67 Long, 'Fitzmaurice, James Christopher'.

68 Ibid.

69 MacThomáis, *Glasnevin: Ireland's Necropolis*, p. 40.

70 Ibid.

71 Ibid.

72 Long, 'Fitzmaurice, James Christopher'.

73 Ibid.

74 MacThomáis, *Glasnevin: Ireland's Necropolis*, p. 40.

75 Long, 'Fitzmaurice, James Christopher'.

76 *The Irish Press*, 27.09.1965, p. 1, www.irishnewsarchive.com.

77 Ibid., p. 4.

78 *The Evening Herald*, 28.09.1965, p. 1, www.irishnewsarchive.com.

79 Fennelly, 'James Fitzmaurice', p. 42.

80 Ibid.

81 Long, 'Fitzmaurice, James Christopher'.

CHISEL AND HAMMER

1 Bhreathnach-Lynch, Síghle, (2019), *Expressions of Nationhood in Bronze and Stone*, Dublin: Irish Academic Press (ebook), pp. 161–3.

2 Ibid., p. 76.

3 Bhreathnach-Lynch, Síghle, (2009), 'Power, Albert George', *Dictionary of Irish Biography*, available at www.dib.ie (accessed 26 May 2022).

4 Bhreathnach-Lynch, *Expressions of Nationhood in Bronze and Stone*, p. 151.

5 Ibid., p. 105 and pp. 79–80.

6 Ibid.

7 Ibid., pp. 72–4.

8 Ibid., pp. 71–2.

9 Ibid., pp. 120–2.

10 Ibid., pp. 118–20.

11 Bhreathnach-Lynch, 'Power, Albert, George'.

12 Ibid.

13 Bhreathnach-Lynch, *Expressions of Nationhood in Bronze and Stone*, p. 151.

14 *The Irish Times*, 11.07.1945, p. 3.

15 Ibid., p. 2.

16 Casey, Christine (2005), *The Buildings of Ireland: Dublin*, Yale: Yale University Press, p. 422.

17 *The Irish Times*, 06.12.1905, p. 9.

18 *Dictionary of Irish Architects*, 'Ashlin, George Coppinger', available at www.dia.ie (accessed 4 October 2020).

19 *The Irish Times*, 14.12.1921, p. 3.

20 *Irish Independent*, 23.8.1923, p. 6, www.irishnewsarchive.com.

21 O'Brien, Emmet, 'Bank Building in Nineteenth-Century Ireland', *Irish Arts Review Yearbook*, Vol. 11 (1995), pp. 157–62, p. 161.

22 *Dictionary of Irish Architects*, 'Ashlin, George Coppinger'.

23 Grimes, Brendan (2015), 'Patrons and architects and the creation of Roman Catholic church architecture in nineteenth-century Dublin', *Dublin Historical Record*, 68:1: 6–20, p. 9.

24 Ibid.

25 *The Irish Times*, 14.12.1921, p. 3.

26 *Dictionary of Irish Architects*, 'Ashlin, George Coppinger'.

27 Long, Patrick (2009), 'McCarthy, James Joseph', *Dictionary of Irish Biography*, available at www.dib.ie (accessed 4 April 2023).

28 Ibid.

29 *Dictionary of Irish Architects*, 'Ashlin, George Coppinger'.

30 McGee, Caroline Martha, '"A Reverence Peculiarly Its Own": The Boys' Chapel at Clongowes Wood College', *An Irish Quarterly Review Studies*, Vol. 103, No. 412, The Jesuits in Ireland: Before and After the Suppression (Winter 2014/15), pp. 499–515, p. 501.

31 Grimes, Brendan (2007), 'Patrick Byrne and St Paul's, Arran Quay, Dublin', *History Ireland*, 15:1: 24–9, p. 24.

32 From Alistair Rowan, 'Irish Victorian Churches: Denominational Distinctions', *Ireland: Art into History*, p. 208, quoted in Brian Crowley (2004), '"His Father's Son": James and Patrick Pearse', *Folk Life*, 43:1, 71–88, p. 75.

33 Grimes, 'Patrick Byrne and St Paul's, Arran Quay, Dublin', p. 24.

34 Ibid., p. 25.

35 Curran, C.P. (1944), 'Patrick Byrne: Architect', *Studies: An Irish Quarterly Review*, 33:130: 193–203, p. 193.

36 Grimes, Brendan (2005), 'The Architecture of Dublin's Neo-Classical Roman Catholic Temples 1803–62', doctoral thesis, Dublin: National College of Art and Design, p. 76.

37 Ibid.

38 Grimes, 'Patrick Byrne and St Paul's, Arran Quay, Dublin', p. 26.

39 Grimes, 'The Architecture of Dublin's Neo-Classical Roman Catholic Temples 1803–62', p. 77.

40 Connell, Carmel (2004), *Glasnevin Cemetery, Dublin, 1832–1900*, Kildare: Maynooth Studies in Local History, p. 17.

41 Ibid.

42 Connell, *Glasnevin Cemetery, Dublin, 1832–1900*, p. 43.

43 Ibid.

44 Ibid., pp. 40–1.

45 Ibid.

46 Ibid., p. 42.

47 Grimes, 'The Architecture of Dublin's Neo-Classical Roman Catholic Temples 1803-62', p. 77.

48 Curran, 'Patrick Byrne: Architect', p. 198.

49 Grimes, 'The Architecture of Dublin's Neo-Classical Roman Catholic Temples 1803–62', p. 85.

50 Connell, *Glasnevin Cemetery, Dublin, 1832–1900*, p. 44.

51 Ibid.

52 Ibid., p. 45.

53 Ibid.

54 Ibid., p. 48.

55 Ibid.

56 Grimes, 'Patrick Byrne and St Paul's, Arran Quay, Dublin', pp. 24–5.

57 Curran, 'Patrick Byrne: Architect', p. 200.

58 Ibid., p. 199.

59 Connell, *Glasnevin Cemetery, Dublin, 1832–1900*, p. 44.

60 Ibid.

61 Grimes, 'Patrick Byrne and St Paul's, Arran Quay, Dublin', p. 25.

62 Andrews, Helen (2009), 'Patrick Byrne', *Dictionary of Irish Biography*, available at www.dib.ie (accessed 20 August 2021).

63 Curran, 'Patrick Byrne: Architect', p. 203.

64 Connell, *Glasnevin Cemetery, Dublin, 1832–1900*, pp. 50–1.

65 Pearse, Patrick, 'Autobiography unpublished fragment', from the Pearse Museum, available at http://pearsemuseum.ie/patrick-pearse/ (accessed 20 February 2021).

66 Ibid.

67 Crowley, Brian (2004), '"His Father's Son": James and Patrick Pearse', *Folk Life*, 43:1, 71–88, p. 71.

68 Thornley, David (1971), 'Patrick Pearse and the Pearse Family', *An Irish Quarterly Review*, 60(239), pp. 332–46, p. 336.
69 Dudley Edwards, Ruth (2006), *Patrick Pearse*, Dublin: Irish Academic Press, p. 7.
70 Ibid.
71 Ibid., pp. 7–8.
72 Crowley, '"His Father's Son"', p. 73.
73 Ibid., pp. 72–3.
74 Pearse, 'Autobiography unpublished fragment'.
75 Dudley Edwards, *Patrick Pearse*, p. 7.
76 O'Donnell, Ruán (2016), *Patrick Pearse: 16 Lives*, Dublin: O'Brien Press, p. 15.
77 Dudley Edwards, *Patrick Pearse*, pp. 7–8.
78 Crowley, '"His Father's Son"', p. 75.
79 Maume, Patrick (2017), 'Pearse, James', *Dictionary of Irish Biography*, available at www.dib.ie (accessed 15 March 2021).
80 Dudley Edwards, *Patrick Pearse*, p. 8.
81 Ibid.
82 Maume, 'Pearse, James'.
83 Ibid.
84 Crowley, '"His Father's Son"', p. 75.
85 Dudley Edwards, *Patrick Pearse*, p. 8.
86 Crowley, '"His Father's Son"', p. 75.
87 Dudley Edwards, *Patrick Pearse*, p. 9.
88 Ibid.
89 Pearse, Patrick, unpublished autobiographical fragment, Pearse Museum, quoted in Crowley, '"His Father's Son"', p. 76.
90 O'Donnell, *Patrick Pearse: 16 Lives*, p. 18.
91 Exhibition of Irish Arts and Manufacturers 1883, Rotunda, Dublin, Complete Official Catalogue (1882), Dublin: Irish Exhibition Company, p. 60.
92 Crowley, '"His Father's Son"', p. 78.
93 Ibid.
94 Ibid., pp. 78–9.
95 Maume, 'Pearse, James'.
96 Ibid.
97 Harbison, Peter (2016), *Glasnevin Celtic Crosses: A Selection*, Dublin: Glasnevin Trust, p. 31.
98 Ibid.
99 O'Shea, Shane (2000), *Death and Design in Victorian Glasnevin*, Dublin: Dublin Cemeteries Committee, p. 212.
100 Connell, *Glasnevin Cemetery, Dublin, 1832–1900*, p. 49.
101 Ibid.
102 Maume, 'Pearse, James'.
103 Thornley, 'Patrick Pearse and the Pearse Family', p. 338.
104 Crowley, '"His Father's Son"', p. 79.

105 Pearse, Patrick, unpublished autobiographical fragment, Pearse Museum, quoted in Crowley, '"His Father's Son"', p. 76.

106 Thornley, 'Patrick Pearse and the Pearse Family', p. 338.

107 *The Freeman's Journal*, 07.05.1900, www.irishnewsarchive.com.

108 Crowley, '"His Father's Son"', p. 83.

109 *Irish Independent*, 8.05.1900, p. 6, www.irishnewsarchive.com.

110 *The Irish Times*, 10.09.1900.

111 *The Freeman's Journal, 10.09.1900*, p. 6, www.irishnewsarchive.com.

112 Crowley, '"His Father's Son"', p. 84.

113 Minch, Rebecca (2009), 'Farrell, Sir Thomas', *Dictionary of Irish Biography*, available at www.dib.ie (accessed 2 April 2023).

114 Ibid.

115 Murphy, Paula (1993), 'Thomas Farrell, Sculptor', *Irish Arts Review Yearbook*, 9(1): 196–207, p. 197.

116 Ibid., p. 198.

117 Minch, 'Farrell, Sir Thomas', available at www.dib.ie (accessed 2 April 2023).

118 Murphy, 'Thomas Farrell, Sculptor', p. 201.

119 Ibid., p. 202.

120 Murphy, Paula (2000), 'Farrell, Thomas (1827–1900)', available at www.sculpturedublin.ie (accessed 2 April 2023).

121 *The Irish Times*, 5.07.1900.

122 *The Irish Builder*, 1.08.1900.

123 Murphy, 'Thomas Farrell, Sculptor', p. 197.

WRITERS AND POETS

1 Murphy, William (2009), 'Rooney, William (Ó Maolruanaidh, Liam)', *Dictionary of Irish Biography*, available at dib.ie (accessed 10 May 2022).

2 Kelly, Matthew (2007), '"… and William Rooney spoke in Irish"', *History Ireland*, 15(1), available at www.historyireland.com/and-william-rooney-spoke-in-irish/ (accessed 22 May 2022).

3 Fallon, Donal (2022), *Three Castles Burning: A History of Dublin in Twelve Streets*, Dublin: New Island Books, p. 146.

4 Mulholland, Rosa (2019), *The Ghost at Wildwood Chase and Other Stories*, Black Heath Editions (ebook).

5 Murphy, James H. (2009), 'Mulholland, Rosa (Lady Gilbert)', *Dictionary of Irish Biography*, available at www.dib.ie (accessed 30 June 2022).

6 Ibid., p. 19.

7 Ibid.

8 Dalby, Richard (2017), 'Rosa Mulholland, Mistress of the Macabre', *The Green Book: Writings on Irish Gothic, Supernatural and Fantastic Literature*, 9(1):19–23, p. 19.

9 Ibid., pp. 19–20.

10 Ibid.

11 Dalby, 'Rosa Mulholland', p. 19.
12 Murphy, 'Mulholland, Rosa (Lady Gilbert)'.
13 Ibid.
14 Dalby, 'Rosa Mulholland', p. 20.
15 Ibid., p. 21.
16 Ibid.
17 Ibid., pp. 21–2.
18 Murphy, 'Mulholland, Rosa (Lady Gilbert)'.
19 Ibid.
20 Dalby, 'Rosa Mulholland', pp. 21–2.
21 Murphy, 'Mulholland, Rosa (Lady Gilbert)'.
22 *Irish Independent*, 23.04.1921, p. 7, www.irishnewsarchive.com.
23 *The Freeman's Journal*, 23.04.1921, p. 4, www.irishnewsarchive.com.
24 *The Irish Times*, 23.04.1921, p. 5.
25 McCall, John (1975), *The Life of James Clarence Mangan*, Dublin: Carraig Books, p. 30.
26 Ryder, Sean (2009), 'Mangan, James Clarence', *Dictionary of Irish Biography*, available at www.dib.ie (accessed 23 June 2022).
27 Ibid.
28 Ibid.
29 O'Donoghue, D.J. (1897), *The Life and Writings of James Clarence Mangan*, Dublin: M.H. Gill & Son, p. 12.
30 Ibid.
31 Ibid., p. 16.
32 Diskin, Patrick (1960), 'The Poetry of James Clarence Mangan', *University Review*, 2(1): 21–30, p. 21.
33 O'Donoghue, *The Life and Writings of James Clarence Mangan*, p. 109.
34 Ibid., p. 148.
35 Ryder, 'Mangan, James Clarence'.
36 O'Donoghue, *The Life and Writings of James Clarence Mangan*, p. 22.
37 Ibid., p. 131.
38 Ibid., p. 161.
39 Diskin, 'The Poetry of James Clarence Mangan', p. 21.
40 Ibid.
41 Ibid.
42 McCall, *The Life of James Clarence Mangan*, pp. 18–21.
43 Diskin, 'The Poetry of James Clarence Mangan', p. 27.
44 O'Donoghue, *The Life and Writings of James Clarence Mangan*, p. 150.
45 Ryder, 'Mangan, James Clarence'.
46 *The Nenagh Guardian*, 26.09.1849, p. 1.
47 Ryder, 'Mangan, James Clarence'.
48 McCall, *The Life of James Clarence Mangan*, pp. 27–8.
49 O'Donoghue, *The Life and Writings of James Clarence Mangan*, p. 23.

50 Ibid., pp. 102–3.
51 Ryder, 'Mangan, James Clarence'.
52 *The Nenagh Guardian*, 26.09.1849, p. 1, www.irishnewsarchive.com.
53 Ryder, 'Mangan, James Clarence'.
54 O'Donoghue, *The Life and Writings of James Clarence Mangan*, p. xv.
55 Shorter Sigerson, Dora (1922), *The Tricolour: Poems of the Irish Revolution*, Dublin: Maunsel and Roberts Ltd, available at https://archive.org/details/tricolour poemsof00sho/page/n7/mode/2up?ref=ol&view=theater (accessed 5 July 2022).
56 Dodd, Conor (2016), 'Wreath Laying Ceremony at Glasnevin Cemetery', pamphlet, Dublin: Dublin Cemeteries Trust, p. 3.
57 Ibid.
58 March, Jessica (2009), 'Shorter, Dora Sigerson', *Dictionary of Irish Biography*, available at www.dib.ie (accessed 1 July 2022).
59 Ibid.
60 Dodd, 'Wreath Laying Ceremony at Glasnevin Cemetery', p. 3.
61 Bleiler, Richard (2019), 'Dora Sigerson Shorter (1866–1918)', *The Green Book: Writings on Irish Gothic, Supernatural and Fantastic Literature*, 13(1): 30–7, p. 31.
62 Ibid., p. 31.
63 March, 'Shorter, Dora Sigerson'.
64 Ibid.
65 Bleiler, 'Dora Sigerson Shorter (1866–1918)', p. 31.
66 Ibid., p. 30.
67 Mawe, Shane (2015), 'Sixteen Dead Men', *Early Printed Books and Special Collections*, available at www.tcd.ie/library/1916/sixteen-dead-men/ (accessed 4 July 2022).
68 Shorter Sigerson, *The Tricolour: Poems of the Irish Revolution*.
69 Mawe, 'Sixteen Dead Men'.
70 Shorter Sigerson, *The Tricolour: Poems of the Irish Revolution*.
71 March, 'Shorter, Dora Sigerson'.
72 Bleiler, 'Dora Sigerson Shorter (1866–1918)', p. 36.
73 *Brooklyn Daily Eagle*, 07.01.1918, p. 2.
74 *The Freeman's Journal*, 10.01.1918, p. 4, www.irishnewsarchive.com.
75 Bleiler, 'Dora Sigerson Shorter (1866–1918)', p. 30.
76 *The Freeman's Journal*, 07.01.1918, p. 2, www.irishnewsarchive.com.
77 Mawe, 'Sixteen Dead Men'.
78 Clarke, Frances (2009), 'Laverty (Kelly), (Mary) Maura', *Dictionary of Irish Biography*, available at www.dib.ie (accessed 5 July 2022).
79 Kelly, Seamus (2017), *The Maura Laverty Story from Rathangan to Tolka Row*, Kildare: Naas Printing Ltd, p. 22.
80 Ibid.
81 Clear, Catriona (2003), '"The red ink of emotion": Maura Laverty, women's work and Irish society in the 1940s', *Saothar*, 28(1): 90–7, p. 90.
82 Clarke, 'Laverty (Kelly), (Mary) Maura'.
83 Ibid.

84 Clear, '"The red ink of emotion"', p. 91.
85 Ibid.
86 Clarke, 'Laverty (Kelly), (Mary) Maura'.
87 Ibid.
88 Craven, Paul, (2016), 'Maura Laverty – The Creator of Irish TV's First Soap Died 50 Years Ago', available at www.irelandsown.ie/maura-laverty-the-creator-of-irish-tvs-first-soap-died-50-years-ago/ (accessed 6 July 2022).
89 Kelly, *The Maura Laverty Story*, p. 306.
90 Craven, 'Maura Laverty'
91 Clarke, 'Laverty (Kelly), (Mary) Maura'.
92 Ibid.
93 McFeely, Deirdre (2021), 'Maura Laverty at the Gate: Theatre as Social Commentary in 1950s Ireland', in Marguérite Corporaal and Ruud van den Beuken (eds), (2021), *A Stage of Emancipation: Change and Progress at the Dublin Gate Theatre*, pp. 39–54, p. 39.
94 Ibid.
95 Kelly, *The Maura Laverty Story*, p. 42.
96 Ibid., p. 43.
97 Ibid., p. 31.
98 *Irish Independent*, 09.10.1951, p. 8, www.irishnewsarchive.com.
99 McFeely, 'Maura Laverty at the Gate', p. 40.
100 *The Irish Press*, 05.11.1951, p. 4, www.irishnewsarchive.com.
101 McFeely, 'Maura Laverty at the Gate', p. 41.
102 Kelly, Seamus (2018), 'Tolka Row and Orson Welles', available at www.irelandsown.ie/tolka-row-and-orson-welles/ (accessed 9 July 2022).
103 Kelly, *The Maura Laverty Story*, p. 31.
104 Craven, 'Maura Laverty'.
105 Kelly, *The Maura Laverty Story*, p. 285.
106 *The Irish Times*, 28.07.1966, p. 7.
107 Kelly, *The Maura Laverty Story*, p. 29.
108 Ibid.
109 Ibid., p. 27.

RELIGIOUS FIGURES

1 Collins, Lorcan (2016), *The 1916 Rising Handbook*, Dublin: O'Brien Press, p. 307.
2 Rev. Fr Aloysius Capuchin Friary, Chaplain to Irish Volunteer Leaders, 1916, Bureau of Military History Witness Statement (BMH WS) 200, p. 36.
3 Hubert O'Keeffe quoted in Fitzpatrick, Martin (1994), *Celebrating 150 Years 1844–1994: The Place, The Parish, and the People A Brief and Random History*, Dublin: St James's Parish Committee p. 16.
4 Ibid.
5 Barton, Brian (2010), *The Secret Court Martial Records of the Easter Rising*, Stroud: The History Press, p. 343.

6 Fitzpatrick, *Celebrating 150 Years 1844–1994*, p. 16.
7 Barton, *The Secret Court Martial Records of the Easter Rising*, p. 157.
8 Connell, Joe, 'Ministering to Republicans 1916–1924', available at https://kilmainhamtales.ie/priests-and-friars---ministering-to-republicans.php (accessed 15 November 2020).
9 Barton, *The Secret Court Martial Records of the Easter Rising*, p. 204.
10 Ibid.
11 Mac Lochlainn, Piaras (1996), *Last Words: Letters and Statements of the Leaders executed after the Rising at Easter 1916*, Dublin: Stationary Office Books, p. 95.
12 Barton, *The Secret Court Martial Records of the Easter Rising*, p. 204.
13 Ibid., p. 205.
14 *The Irish Times*, 06.05.1916, p. 1.
15 Barton, *The Secret Court Martial Records of the Easter Rising*, p. 236.
16 Mac Lochlainn, *Last Words*, pp. 121–2.
17 Barton, *The Secret Court Martial Records of the Easter Rising*, p. 322.
18 Collins, *The 1916 Rising Handbook*, p. 182.
19 *The Irish Times*, 30.10.1930, p. 1.
20 Barton, *The Secret Court Martial Records of the Easter Rising*, p. 142.
21 Duggan, Eamonn (2017), 'Fr Michael O'Flanagan, The Maverick Priest', *Ireland's Own 1917 Centenary Souvenir Edition*, pp. 54–6.
22 Maume, Patrick (2009), 'O'Flanagan, Michael', *Dictionary of Irish Biography*, available at www.dib.ie (accessed 4 June 2023).
23 Ibid.
24 Byrne, Martin and the Fr. Michael O'Flanagan Memorial Society in Cliffoney, available at http://carrowkeel.com/frof/1915cliffoney.html (accessed 20 April 2020).
25 Ibid.
26 Maume, 'O'Flanagan, Michael'.
27 Carroll, Denis (1993), *They Have Fooled You Again: Michael O'Flanagan (1876–1942) Priest, Republican, Social Critic*, Dublin: The Columba Press, pp. 54–9.
28 Duggan, 'Fr Michael O'Flanagan, The Maverick Priest'.
29 Ibid.
30 Ibid.
31 Carroll, *They Have Fooled You Again*, pp. 149–50.
32 Maume, 'O'Flanagan, Michael'.
33 Ibid.
34 Duggan, 'Fr Michael O'Flanagan, The Maverick Priest'.
35 Byrne, Martin and the Fr. Michael O'Flanagan Memorial Society in Cliffoney, available at http://carrowkeel.com/frof/1915cliffoney.html (accessed 20 April 2020).
36 *Irish Independent*, 26.07.1927.
37 *The Catholic Bulletin*, 1928, p. 6.
38 *The Irish Press*, 27.05.1932, p. 4, www.irishnewsarchive.com.
39 *The Irish Press*, 11.08.1942, p. 4, www.irishnewsarchive.com.
40 *The Irish Press*, 07.08.1942, p. 2, www.irishnewsarchive.com.

41 D'Arcy, Fergus (2018), *Raising Dublin, Raising Ireland: A Friar's Campaigns*, Dublin: Carmelite Publications, p. 13.

42 Murphy, David (2009), 'Spratt, John Francis', *Dictionary of Irish Biography*, available at www.dib.ie (accessed 23 January 2023).

43 Ibid.

44 Ibid.

45 D'Arcy, *Raising Dublin, Raising Ireland*, p. 118.

46 Ibid.

47 Ibid., pp. 225–7.

48 Murphy, 'Spratt, John Francis'.

49 Ibid.

50 D'Arcy, *Raising Dublin, Raising Ireland*, pp. 225–7.

51 Ibid.

CONFLICT, REVOLUTION AND WAR

1 The National Archives UK, reference WO 25/771, pp. 97–8.

2 Ibid.

3 Linch, Kevin, and McCormack, Matthew (2013), 'Defining Soldiers: Britain's Military, c. 1740–1815', *War in History*, vol. 20, no. 2: 144–59, p. 145.

4 Dunne-Lynch, Nicholas (2007), 'Humour and Defiance: Irish Troops and their humour in the Peninsular War', *Journal of the Society for Army Historical Research*, 85(341): 62–78, pp. 63–4.

5 Ibid., p. 64.

6 Deery, James (2020), 'The contribution of the Irish Soldier to the British Army during the Peninsula campaign 1808–1814', *The Journal of Military History and Defence Studies*, 1(1):1–65, p. 4.

7 Molloy, Peter (2011), 'Ireland and the Waterloo campaign of 1815', MA thesis, NUI, Maynooth, p. 26, cited in Deery, 'The contribution of the Irish Soldier to the British Army during the Peninsula campaign 1808–1814'.

8 Dodd, Conor (2015), *Waterloo 1815-2015 Glasnevin Cemetery*, Dublin: Glasnevin Trust, p. 1.

9 Ibid.

10 Pockett, C.I. (1998), 'Soldiers of the King: British soldiers and identity in the Peninsular War, 1808–1814', MA thesis, Queen's University, Ontario, p. ii.

11 The National Archives UK, reference WO 100/2.

12 Linch and McCormack, 'Defining Soldiers', p. 145.

13 National Archives UK, reference WO 25/771, pp. 97–8.

14 Dodd, *Waterloo 1815–2015 Glasnevin Cemetery*.

15 Geoghegan, Patrick (2015), 'A Battle of Giants: Waterloo, Wellington and Ireland', *History Ireland*, 23(3): 22–26, p. 22.

16 Dodd, *Waterloo 1815–2015 Glasnevin Cemetery*, p. 1.

17 Ibid., p. 98.

18 The National Archives UK, WO 25/771, pp. 97–8.
19 Ibid. p. 97.
20 Ibid., p. 98.
21 Ibid.
22 *The Freeman's Journal*, 31.12.1824, p. 3, www.irishnewsarchive.com.
23 *The Cork Examiner*, 26.06.1848, p. 4, www.irishnewsarchive.com.
24 The National Archives UK, WO 25/771, pp. 97–8.
25 *The Kerry Examiner*, 06.04.1849, p. 3, www.irishnewsarchive.com.
26 Dodd, *Waterloo 1815–2015 Glasnevin Cemetery*, p. 1.
27 Ibid., p. 2.
28 Ibid., p. 3.
29 Deery, 'The contribution of the Irish Soldier to the British Army during the Peninsula campaign 1808–1814', p. 36.
30 Kenna, Shane (2015), *Conspirators: A Photographic History of Ireland's Revolutionary Underground*, Cork: Mercier Press, p. 7.
31 Boyce, D. George (2005), *Nineteenth Century Ireland: The Search for Stability*, Dublin: Gill & Macmillan, p. 136.
32 *The Nation*, 20.09.1873, p. 13, www.irishnewsarchive.com.
33 Ibid.
34 Doheny, Michael (1920), *The Felon's Track or the History of the Attempted Outbreak in Ireland: Embracing the Leading Events in the Irish Struggle from the Year 1843 to the Close of 1848*, Dublin: M.H. Gill and Sons Ltd, p. 305.
35 Ibid., p. 112.
36 Boyce, *Nineteenth Century Ireland*, p. 127.
37 *The Nation*, 18.03.1848, p. 3, www.irishnewsarchive.com.
38 Dodd, Conor (2016), 'Wreath Laying Ceremony at Glasnevin Cemetery' for Sigerson, Kearney and Hollywood booklet 27.03.2016, Dublin: Glasnevin Trust, p. 2.
39 Dodd, 'Wreath Laying Ceremony at Glasnevin Cemetery', p. 2.
40 '1848 Tricolour Celebration', *History Ireland*, 19(2) (2011), pp. 6–7.
41 Cavanagh, Michael (1892), *The Memoirs of General Thomas Francis Meagher*, Dublin: Messenger Press, p. 280.
42 Boyce, *Nineteenth Century Ireland*, p. 129.
43 *The Cork Examiner*, 22.09.1848, p. 3, www.irishnewsarchive.com.
44 *Belfast News-Letter*, 17.10.1848, p. 2, www.irishnewsarchive.com.
45 *The Nation*, 18.03.1848, p. 3, www.irishnewsarchive.com.
46 *The Nation*, 20.09.1873, p. 13, www.irishnewsarchive.com.
47 Takagami, Shin-Ichi (1995), 'The Fenian Rising in Dublin, March 1867', *Irish Historical Studies*, 29(115): 340–62, p. 347.
48 Takagami, 'The Fenian Rising in Dublin, March 1867', p. 347.
49 NAI, Fenian briefs, 6(a), quoted in Takagami, 'The Fenian Rising in Dublin, March 1867', p. 356.
50 Takagami, 'The Fenian Rising in Dublin, March 1867', p. 357.
51 *The Cork Examiner*, 08.03.1867, p. 3, www.irishnewsarchive.com.

52 The National Graves Association (1915), *The Last Post: Glasnevin Cemetery Places of Historic Interest*, Dublin: National Graves Association of Ireland, p. 53.
53 *The Nation*, 28.11.1885, p. 6, www.irishnewsarchive.com.
54 Boyce, *Nineteenth Century Ireland*, p. 158.
55 Fitzsimons, Peter (2019), *The Catalpa Rescue: The Gripping Story of the Most Dramatic and Successful Prison Break in Australian and Irish History*, London: Constable, p. xviii.
56 Dorney, John (2013), *Griffith College Dublin: A History of the Campus 1813–2013*, Dublin: Griffith College, pp. 20–1.
57 Fitzsimons, *The Catalpa Rescue*, p. 21.
58 Dorney, *Griffith College Dublin*, pp. 20–1.
59 Fitzsimons, *The Catalpa Rescue*, p. 25.
60 Ibid.
61 Colonel Eamon Broy, BMH WS 1284, pp. 1–8.
62 *The Nation*, 13.9.1884, p. 5, www.irishnewsarchive.com.
63 *The Connaught Telegraph*, 16.09.1876, p. 2.
64 Fitzsimons, *The Catalpa Rescue*, p. 179.
65 Ibid., p. 195.
66 Ibid., pp. 330–3.
67 *The Anglo-Celt*, 06.08.1904, p. 1, www.irishnewsarchive.com.
68 *The New York Herald*, 03.05.1884.
69 *The Buffalo Times*, 16.09.1884, p. 1.
70 *The Nation*, 13.09.1884, p. 5, www.irishnewsarchive.com.
71 *The Nation*, 20.09.1884, p. 2, www.irishnewsarchive.com.
72 Kenny, Michael (2018), *Brothers in Arms: The Remarkable Story of William and James Roantree from Leixlip, Co. Kildare*, Kildare: Naas Printing Ltd, p. 11.
73 Passenger and Immigration Lists Index, 1500s–1900s, Source Publication Code: 9307 from the United States Works Projects Administration (accessed via Ancestry.com on 4 July 2021).
74 *The Gaelic American*, 16.03.1918.
75 US Marine Corps Muster Rolls 1798–1958, William F. Roantree, accessed via Ancestry.com on 06.07.2021.
76 *The Gaelic American*, 16.03.1918.
77 *The Anglo-Celt*, 02.12.1859, p. 3, www.irishnewsarchive.com.
78 Kenny, *Brothers in Arms*, p. 12.
79 Ibid.
80 Ibid., p. 13.
81 Kenna, *Conspirators*, p. 23.
82 Kenny, *Brothers in Arms*, p. 16.
83 O'Sullivan, Niamh (2007), *Every Dark Hour: A History of Kilmainham Gaol*, Dublin: Liberties Press (e-book), loc.1170.
84 Ibid., William Francis Roantree to his wife, 2–3 January 1866.
85 *The New York Times*, 23.02.1871.
86 NAI, Fenian Papers (1871), R. Series, Carton 12, 'Report of the Commissioners

appointed to enquire into the treatment of treason felony convicts in English prisons', London, p. 5.

87 Kenny, *Brothers in Arms*, p. 35.

88 *The Irishman*, 10.06.1871, www.irishnewsarchive.com.

89 Kenny, *Brothers in Arms*, p. 36.

90 *The Irishman*, 10.03.1877, www.irishnewsarchive.com.

91 Kenny, *Brothers in Arms*, p. 40.

92 Ibid., p. 41.

93 *The Gaelic American*, 18.03.1918.

94 *Drogheda Argus and Leinster Journal*, 07.08.1909, p. 6, www.irishnewsarchive.com.

95 *The Freeman's Journal*, 18.03.1918, www.irishnewsarchive.com.

96 Kenny, *Brothers in Arms*, p. 42.

97 Ibid., p. 43.

98 Ibid.

99 *The Freeman's Journal*, 22.02.1918, p. 1, www.irishnewsarchive.com.

100 *The Freeman's Journal*, 23.02.1918, p. 6, www.irishnewsarchive.com.

101 *Irish Independent*, 21.02.1918, p. 2, www.irishnewsarchive.com.

102 The National Archives UK, Richard Simpson Reg No. G/1030, Case No. 425, Medical Card, accessed 18.02.2021 via Ancestry.co.uk.

103 The National Archives UK, Description of Richard Simpson on enlistment, accessed 18.02.2021 via Ancestry.co.uk.

104 The National Archives UK, Information supplied by recruit Richard Simpson and statement of the services, accessed 18.02.2021 via Ancestry.co.uk.

105 *Irish Independent*, 08.05.1916, p. 4, www.irishnewsarchive.com.

106 Taylor, James W. (2016), *Guilty but Insane – J.C Bowen Colthurst: Villain or Victim?* Cork: Mercier Press, pp. 254–5.

107 Ibid.

108 Ibid.

109 *The Weekly Irish Times*, 1917, p. 264.

110 Morrissey, Conor (2016), 'Journalism: Scandal and Anti-Semitism in 1916: Thomas Dickson and "The Eye-Opener"', *History Ireland:* 24(4), pp. 30–3, p. 30.

111 Ibid., pp. 31–2.

112 O'Halpin, Eunan, and Ó Corráin, Daithí (2020), *The Dead of the Irish Revolution*, London: Yale University Press, pp. 42–3.

113 Ibid.

114 Taylor, *Guilty but Insane*, pp. 254–5.

115 O'Halpin and Ó Corráin, *The Dead of the Irish Revolution*, pp. 42–3.

116 Ibid.

117 Ibid.

118 O'Regan, Philip (2016), 'Gearóid O'Sullivan – in the fight for Irish Independence', illustrated talk given at the Skibbereen Credit Union Conference Room, available at www.michaelcollinshouse.ie/media/podcasts/ (accessed 1.04.2021).

119 *The Southern Star*, 22.05.1926, p. 4.

120 Scanlon, Joni (2020), *A Sacrifice of the Heart: The Biography of Irish Patriot Gearóid O'Sullivan*, Dublin: Kilmainham Tales, pp. 9–10.

121 Scanlon, Joni, 'Lecture 7: Adjutant General Gearóid O'Sullivan by author Joni Scanlon', available at www.youtube.com/watch?v=Xgf3grOB0aI (accessed 28.03.2021).

122 Wren, Jimmy (2015), *The GPO Garrison Easter Week: A Biographical Dictionary*, Dublin: Geography Publications, p. 284.

123 O'Regan, 'Gearóid O'Sullivan – in the fight for Irish Independence'.

124 Scanlon, *A Sacrifice of the Heart*, p. 11.

125 Ibid., p. 12.

126 Ibid., p. 13.

127 O'Regan, 'Gearóid O'Sullivan – in the fight for Irish Independence'.

128 Wren, *The GPO Garrison Easter Week*, p. 284.

129 Long, Patrick, 'Gearóid O'Sullivan', *Dictionary of Irish Biography*, available at dib.cambridge.org (https://dib.cambridge.org/viewReadPage.do?articleId=a7059&searchClicked=clicked&quickadvsearch=yes) (accessed 2.04.2021).

130 Ibid.

131 Scanlon, *A Sacrifice of the Heart*, p. 14.

132 *The Southern Star*, 03.04.1948, p. 6.

133 Military Archives of Ireland, File Reference No. W24SP1369 available at http://mspcsearch.militaryarchives.ie/docs/files//PDF_Pensions/R1/24SP1369GEAROIDOSUILLEAVAIN/W24SP1369GEAROIDOSUILLEAVAIN.pdf.

134 Scanlon, *A Sacrifice of the Heart*, p. 29.

135 Ibid.

136 Ibid., p. 37.

137 Ibid.

138 Ibid.

139 Military Archives of Ireland, File Reference No. W24SP1369.

140 O'Regan, 'Gearóid O'Sullivan – in the fight for Irish Independence'.

141 Ibid.

142 Ibid.

143 Scanlon, *A Sacrifice of the Heart*, p. 58.

144 Barton, Brian (2010), *The Secret Court Martial Records of the Easter Rising*, Stroud: The History Press, p. 34.

145 O'Connor, Batt (2019), *With Michael Collins in the Fight for Irish Independence*, Auckland: Pickle Partners Publishing (originally published 1929), pp. 70–1.

146 Scanlon, *A Sacrifice of the Heart*, p. 66.

147 Military Archives of Ireland, File Reference No. W24SP1369.

148 O'Malley, Ernie (2015), *The Men Will Talk to Me: West Cork Interviews*, Cork: Mercier Press, p. 38.

149 Ibid.

150 O'Mahony, Seán (1987), *Frongoch: University of Revolution*, Dublin: FDR Teoranta, p. 217.

151 Scanlon, *A Sacrifice of the Heart*, p. 83, quoting Denis Daly from his BMH WS.

152 Long, Patrick, 'Gearóid O'Sullivan', *Dictionary of Irish Biography*, available at dib.cambridge.org (accessed 2 April 2021).

153 Military Archives of Ireland, File Reference No. W24SP1369 available at http://mspcsearch.militaryarchives.ie/docs/files//PDF_Pensions/R1/24SP1369GEAROIDOSUILLEAVAIN/W24SP1369GEAROIDOSUILLEAVAIN.pdf.

154 Ibid., p. 86.

155 Cork County Gaol Register 1915–1924, available at www.findmypast.ie (accessed 29 March 2021).

156 Scanlon, *A Sacrifice of the Heart*, p. 90.

157 Cork County Gaol General Register 1915–24.

158 Ibid.

159 *Hue-and-Cry Police Gazette*, 13.02.1920.

160 Scanlon, *A Sacrifice of the Heart*, p. 93.

161 Ibid., p. 99.

162 Connell Jnr, Joseph E.A. (2017), *Michael Collins: Dublin 1916-22*, Dublin: Wordwell Ltd, p. 73.

163 Ibid., p. 332.

164 The National Archives, Kew, England, Ireland: Dublin Castle Records, CO 904/193-216; War Office: Army of Ireland, Administrative and Easter Rising Records, WO 35/206-207, p. 7.

165 Connell Jnr, *Michael Collins*, p. 290.

166 O'Regan, 'Gearóid O'Sullivan – in the fight for Irish Independence'.

167 Scanlon, *A Sacrifice of the Heart*, p. 120.

168 Ibid.

169 Dáil Debate, 06.01.1922, available at www.oireachtas.ie/en/debates/debate/dail/1922-01-06/3/#spk_220 (accessed 16 November 2020).

170 Scanlon, *A Sacrifice of the Heart*, p. 174.

171 Coogan, Pat Tim (1990), *Michael Collins A Biography*, London: Hutchinson, p. 415.

172 Kevin O'Shiel, BMH WS 1770.

173 *The Freeman's Journal*, 19.10.1922, p. 3, www.irishnewsarchive.com.

174 O'Sullivan, *Every Dark Hour: A History of Kilmainham Gaol.*

175 Price, Dominic (2017), *We Bled Together, Michael Collins, The Squad and the Dublin Brigade*, Dublin: The Collins Press, pp. 257–9.

176 Ibid.

177 Scanlon, *A Sacrifice of the Heart*, p. 270.

178 Ibid., p. 280.

179 Ibid., p. 281.

180 *The Irish Times*, 26.03.1948, p. 7.

181 *The Southern Star*, 03.04.1948.

182 Military Archives, File Reference No. W24SPE13, available at http://mspcsearch.militaryarchives.ie/docs/files//PDF_Pensions/R1/24SP1369GEAROIDOSUILLEAVAIN/W24SPE13GEAROIDOSUILLEAVAIN.pdf.

183 Ibid.

184 Boyne, Sean (2015), *Emmet Dalton: Somme Soldier, Irish General, Film Pioneer*, Dublin: Merrion Press, p. 261.

185 Ibid., p. 7.

186 RTÉ Archives (1978), 'I Don't Think That Today's Generation Could Survive It', available at www.rte.ie/archives/exhibitions/1011-ireland-and-the-great-war/1017-aftermath/315376-emmet-dalton-remembers/ (accessed 28 May 2022).

187 McDonagh, Michael (1917), *The Irish on The Somme*, London: Hodder and Stoughton, pp. 161–3.

188 Dempsey, Pauric J. and Boylan, Shaun (2009), 'Dalton, (James) Emmet', *Dictionary of Irish Biography*, available at www.dib.ie (accessed 29 May 2022).

189 Boyne, *Emmet Dalton*, pp. 38–54.

190 Dempsey and Boylan, 'Dalton, (James) Emmet'.

191 Ibid.

192 Boyne, *Emmet Dalton*, p. 127.

193 Dempsey and Boylan, 'Dalton, (James) Emmet'.

194 Boyne, *Emmet Dalton*, p. 219.

195 Dempsey and Boylan, 'Dalton, (James) Emmet'.

196 Ibid.

197 Boyne, *Emmet Dalton*, p. 259.

198 *Irish Independent*, 08.03.1978, p. 4

199 Boyne, *Emmet Dalton*, p. 259.

200 Ibid., p. 261.

201 George Cronin, National Archives UK, ADM 1123/117167 Royal Navy Ratings Service Papers.

202 Ibid.

203 US WWI Draft Registration Cards, Pennsylvania, Pittsburgh City.

204 Dodd, Conor (2018), *Glasnevin Cemetery and the First World War*, booklet, Dublin: Dublin Cemeteries Trust, pp. 15–16.

205 Dublin Cemeteries Committee General Minutes, Vol. 28, pp. 421–2.

206 *The Diary of Mary Martin*, available at https://dh.tcd.ie/martindiary/ (accessed 28 November 2020).

207 Ibid., pp. 1–2.

208 Ibid.

209 Ibid.

210 Ibid., p. 115.

211 Ibid., p. 117.

212 Ibid., p. 118.

213 Ibid., p. 119.

214 Ibid., p. 120.

215 *The Diary of Mary Martin*, available at http://catalogue.nli.ie/Record/vtls000172116#page/102/mode/1up (accessed 28 November 2020), p. 125.

216 Commonwealth War Graves Commission (CWGC), 'War Dead', available at www.cwgc.org/find-records/find-war-dead/casualty-details/1650961/CHARLES%20ANDREW%20MARTIN/ (accessed 20 December 2020).

217 *The Diary of Mary Martin*, available at https://dh.tcd.ie/martindiary/.

218 Colgan, Eibhlin, Archive Manager, *Guinness Archives*, William Coleman, GDB/PE01/013825.

219 Coleman, William, 'Active Service Form' W173_1408.

220 Lawlor, William, Copy of letter sent to Brompton Barracks in response to William Coleman's death' (Courtesy of Conor Dodd Historian Dublin Cemeteries Trust).

221 Dodd, Conor (Historian Dublin Cemeteries Trust), 'Copy of correspondence relating to death of William Coleman, Base Records R.E.'

222 *The Belfast Evening Telegraph*, 03.01.1916, p. 8.

223 Lawlor, William, Copy of letter sent to Brompton Barracks in response to William Colemans death'.

224 The War Office, Correspondence relating to Pension for William Coleman 10.04.1916, 7/Relatives C./1504. (F.31).

225 Abbott, Richard (2019), *Police Casualties in Ireland 1919–1922*, Cork: Mercier Press, pp. 52–3.

226 *The Freeman's Journal*, 31.07.1919, p. 3, www.irishnewsarchive.com.

227 Ibid.

228 *The Irish Times*, 23.09.1919, p. 2.

229 Price, *We Bled Together*, p. 60.

230 Dublin Metropolitan Police General Register, Patrick Smyth, 18 August 1893, available at https://digital.ucd.ie/view-media/ucdlib:53467/canvas/ucdlib:53728?manifest=https://data.ucd.ie/api/img/manifests/ucdlib:53467 (accessed 23 November 2020).

231 Price, *We Bled Together*, p. 61.

232 O'Halpin and Ó Corráin, *The Dead of the Irish Revolution*, p. 114.

233 Price, *We Bled Together*, p. 80.

234 Ibid., p. 81.

235 *Irish Independent*, 10.09.1919, p. 1, www.irishnewsarchive.com.

236 *Irish Independent*, 1.12.1919, p. 5, www.irishnewsarchive.com.

237 Hart, Peter (2019), 'Foreword', in Abbott, *Police Casualties in Ireland 1919–1922*.

238 O'Halpin and Ó Corráin, *The Dead of the Irish Revolution*, p. 275.

239 Ibid.

240 Ibid.

241 *Evening Echo*, 25.01.1921, p. 3, www.irishnewsarchive.com.

242 Ibid.

243 *The Gloucestershire Echo*, 25.10.1921.

DISASTER

1 Ferguson, Stephen (2018), 'RMS *Leinster* Centenary booklet', published by An Post, p. 3.

2 Lecane, Philip (2018), *Women and Children of the R.M.S Leinster*, Dublin: Elm Books, p. 25.

3 The Sinking of the RMS *Leinster*, www.rmsleinster.com/people/_people.htm (accessed 10 January 2021).

4 Ferguson, 'RMS *Leinster* Centenary booklet', p. 3.
5 Ibid.
6 Ó Caollaí, Breasal (2018), 'The Truth was also a casualty', *The Last Voyage of the Leinster: Remembering the Dún Laoghaire and Holyhead Mailboat*, Dublin: The Dún Laoghaire Holyhead Mail Boat Leinster Centenary Committee/Friends of the Leinster, p. 4.
7 Ibid., p. 5.
8 Lecane, *Women and Children of the R.M.S Leinster*, p. 28.
9 RMS Leinster.com, https://www.rmsleinster.com/people/_people.htm, accessed 10 January 2021).
10 Lecane, *Women and Children of the R.M.S Leinster*, p. 28.
11 Ibid., p. 164.
12 Ibid., pp. 164–5.
13 Ibid., p. 109.
14 Ibid., p. 167.
15 Ibid.
16 Ó Caollaí, 'The Truth was also a casualty', p. 4.
17 Lecane, *Women and Children of the R.M.S Leinster*, p. 33.
18 Ibid., p. 34.
19 Ferguson, 'RMS *Leinster* Centenary booklet', p. 5.
20 Lecane, *Women and Children of the R.M.S Leinster*, p. 36.
21 Ferguson, 'RMS *Leinster* Centenary booklet', p. 6.
22 *Belfast News-Letter*, 17.10.1918, p. 4, www.irishnewsarchive.com.
23 Ibid.
24 Lecane, *Women and Children of the R.M.S Leinster*, p. 95.
25 Ibid.
26 *The Freeman's Journal*, 16.10.1918, p. 4.
27 *The Irish Times*, 10.10.1919, p. 1.
28 *Belfast News-Letter*, 17.10.1918, p. 4, www.irishnewsarchive.com.
29 *The Irish Times*, 14.10.1918, p. 1.
30 Dodd, Conor (2018), *Remembering the R.M.S Leinster*, Online Exhibition, Glasnevin Cemetery Visitor Centre/Dublin Cemeteries Trust.
31 *The Freeman's Journal*, 11.10.1918, p. 4, www.irishnewsarchive.com.
32 *The Cork Examiner*, 12.10.1918, p. 7, www.irishnewsarchive.com.
33 *The New York Tribune*, 12.10.1918, p. 3.
34 Ferguson, 'RMS *Leinster* Centenary booklet', p. 6.
35 Dodd, *Remembering the R.M.S Leinster*.
36 Lecane, *Women and Children of the R.M.S Leinster*, p. 37.
37 Fallon, Donal (2014), *The Pillar, The Life and Afterlife of the Nelson Pillar*, Dublin: New Island Books, p. 38.
38 Ferguson, Stephen (2012), *GPO Staff in 1916*, Cork: Mercier Press, p. 14.
39 National Archives of Ireland, OPW 5 – 11497/19, GPO, Collapse of floor during demolition, death of two labourers.
40 *The Freeman's Journal*, 27.10.1919, p. 2, www.irishnewsarchive.com.

41 National Archives of Ireland, OPW 5 – 11497/19, GPO, Collapse of floor during demolition, death of two labourers.
42 *The Evening Mail*, 25.10.1919, p. 2.
43 National Archives of Ireland, OPW 5 – 11497/19, GPO, Collapse of floor during demolition, death of two labourers.
44 Pierce, Nicola (2021), *O'Connell Street: The History and Life of Dublin's Iconic Street*, Dublin: O'Brien Press, p. 140.
45 Harrington, Kevin (1982), 'A Dublin Tragedy of 1861', *Dublin Historical Record*, 35(2): 52–54, p. 52.
46 Ibid.
47 Harrington, 'A Dublin Tragedy of 1861', p. 52.
48 *The Freeman's Journal*, 8.04.1861, p. 3, www.irishnewsarchive.com.
49 *The Waterford News Star*, 12.04.1861, p. 3.
50 *The Freeman's Journal*, 08.04.1861, p. 3, www.irishnewsarchive.com.
51 *The Tuam Herald*, 13.04.1861, p. 4
52 *The Waterford News Star*, 12.04.1861, p. 3, www.irishnewsarchive.com.
53 Ibid.
54 Ibid.
55 *The Freeman's Journal*, 08.04.1861, p. 3, www.irishnewsarchive.com.
56 Dodd, Conor, from the exhibition 'Great Flu Pandemic in Ireland 1918–1919', Glasnevin Visitors Centre, October 2018–May 2019, in partnership with staff at the School of Histories and Humanities, Trinity College Dublin; Dublin Cemeteries Trust and Carlow College & Dr Ida Milne, Dr Georgina Laragy, Dr Francis Ludlow. Available at https://sway.office.com/xSi74wKxFeptCwrM (accessed 6 January 2021).
57 Milne, Ida (2018), *Stacking the Coffins: Influenza, War and Revolution in Ireland, 1918–1919*, Manchester: Manchester University Press, p. 30.
58 Ibid.
59 *The Irish Times*, 31.10.1918, p. 2.
60 Dodd, from the exhibition 'Great Flu Pandemic in Ireland 1918–1919'.
61 Milne, *Stacking the Coffins*, pp. 48–9.
62 Commonwealth War Graves Commission, 'Charles Heatley Lance Corporal', available at www.cwgc.org/find-records/find-war-dead/casualty-details/790890/CHARLES%20HEATLEY/ (accessed 8 January 2021).
63 Milne, *Stacking the Coffins*, p. 80.
64 RTÉ (2018), *Nationwide Spanish Flu in Ireland 2018*, available at www.youtube.com/watch?v=xvtoHumd4C8 (accessed 8 January 2021).
65 Ross, Peter (2020), *A Tomb with a View: The Stories & Glories of Graveyards*, London: Headline, p. 148.

POLITICS AND LAW

1 White, Trevor (2017), *Alfie: The Life and Times of Alfie Byrne*, London: Penguin Books, p. 196.

2 *The Evening Herald*, 15.03.1956, www.irishnewsarchive.com.
3 Keane, Ronan (2012), 'Kennedy, Hugh', *Dictionary of Irish Biography*, available at www.dib.ie (accessed 3 June 2023).
4 Towert, Thomas (1977), 'Hugh Kennedy and the Constitutional development of the Irish Free State, 1922–1923', *Irish Jurist*, 12(2): 355–70.
5 Keane, 'Kennedy, Hugh'.
6 Ibid.
7 Ó Corráin, Daithí (2006), '"Ireland in His Heart North and South": The Contribution of Ernest Blythe to the Partition Question', *Irish Historical Studies*, 35(137): 61–80, p. 61.
8 Fitzpatrick, David (2017), 'Ernest Blythe – Orangeman and Fenian', *History Ireland*, 25(3): 34–7, p. 34.
9 Ernest Blythe, BMH WS 939, pp. 2–3.
10 Ibid.
11 RTÉ (1966), 'Praying to God to Crown the German Eagles with Victory 1916', *Survivors*, available at www.rte.ie/archives/exhibitions/1993-easter-1916/2017-survivors/610313-the-survivors-earnn-de-blaghd/ (accessed 14 November 2020).
12 Fitzpatrick, 'Ernest Blythe', p. 35.
13 Ibid.
14 Ibid., pp. 35–6.
15 RTÉ, 'Praying to God to Crown the German Eagles with Victory 1916'.
16 *Irish Independent*, 21.05.1914, p. 6.
17 National Archives file, DE/2/368/001.
18 Ibid., p. 84.
19 National Archives file, DE/2/368/002.
20 Ernest Blythe, BMH WS 939, p. 108.
21 National Archives file, DE/4/3/14.
22 National Archives file, DE/2/119.
23 Dáil Debate, 22.12.1921, available at www.oireachtas.ie/en/debates/debate/dail/1921-12-22/2/#spk_76 (accessed 11 December 2020).
24 Dáil Debate 03.01.1922, available at www.oireachtas.ie/en/debates/debate/dail/1922-01-03/2/#spk_65 (accessed 11 December 2020).
25 Ibid.
26 Dáil Debate, 09.01.1922, available at www.oireachtas.ie/en/debates/debate/dail/1922-01-09/2/#spk_125 (accessed 10 December 2020).
27 Fitzpatrick, 'Ernest Blythe', p. 34.
28 Ibid.
29 *The Irish Press*, 03.07.1933, p. 9, www.irishnewsarchive.com.
30 Long, Patrick (2009), 'O'Duffy, Eoin', available at www.dib.ie (accessed 10 February 2023) .
31 *Donegal News*, 04.11.1950, p. 2, www.irishnewsarchive.com.
32 Ó Corráin, '"Ireland in His Heart North and South"', p. 79.
33 Ibid., pp. 79–80.
34 Ibid., p. 79.
35 *Irish Independent*, 15.02.1965, www.irishnewsarchive.com.

36 MacAnna, Tomas and Murray (1980), 'In Interview about the Later O'Casey Plays at the Abbey Theatre', *Irish University Review*, 10(1): 130–45, p. 131.
37 *The Cork Examiner*, 09.09.1972, p. 10, www.irishnewsarchive.com.
38 *The Cork Examiner*, 24.02.1975, p. 24, www.irishnewsarchive.com.
39 Ibid.
40 *Evening Herald*, 24.02.1975, p. 3, www.irishnewsarchive.com.
41 *The Cork Examiner*, 25.02.1975, p. 3, www.irishnewsarchive.com.
42 *The Southern Star*, 01.03.1975, p. 8.
43 Fitzpatrick, William J. (1900), *A History of the Dublin Cemeteries Committee*, Dublin: Dublin Cemeteries Committee, p. 135.
44 Pierce, Nicola (2021), *O'Connell Street: The History and Life of Dublin's Iconic Street*, Dublin: O'Brien Press, p. 49.
45 Woods, C.J. (2009), 'Gray, Sir John', *Dictionary of Irish Biography*, available at www.dib.ie (accessed 6 February 2023).
46 Pierce, *O'Connell Street*, p. 50.
47 Woods, 'Gray, Sir John'.
48 Ibid.
49 Ibid.
50 Dickson, David (2014), *Dublin: The Making of a Capital City*, London: Profile Books, p. 343.
51 Ibid., p. 344.
52 Ibid.
53 Woods, 'Gray, Sir John'.
54 *Dundalk Democrat*, 17.04.1875, p. 5.
55 Ibid.
56 Ibid.
57 *The Irish Times*, 16.04.1875, p. 5.
58 King, Carla (2013), '"A Whig Rebel"? The Parliamentary career of J.J. O'Kelly (1845–1916)', *Studia Hibernica*, 39(1): 103–35, p. 104.
59 Ibid.
60 Ibid.
61 McGee, Owen (2012), 'O'Kelly, James Joseph', *Dictionary of Irish Biography*, available at www.dib.ie (accessed 20 May 2023).
62 Ibid.
63 Ibid.
64 Ibid.
65 King, '"A Whig Rebel"?', p. 108.
66 McGee, 'O'Kelly, James Joseph'.
67 Ibid.
68 Ibid.
69 *The Ulster Herald*, 30.12.1916, p. 2.
70 *Irish Independent*, 29.12.1916, p. 2, www.irishnewsarchive.com.
71 King, '"A Whig Rebel"?', p. 135.

72 Maume, Patrick (2009), 'Sullivan, Alexander Martin', *Dictionary of Irish Biography*, available at www.dib.ie (accessed 10 March 2023).
73 Ibid.
74 Ibid.
75 *Kerry Sentinel*, 21.10.1884, p. 2, www.irishnewsarchive.com.
76 Ibid.
77 Maume, 'Sullivan, Alexander Martin'.
78 Ibid.
79 Ibid.
80 *Kerry Sentinel*, 21.10.1884, p. 2, www.irishnewsarchive.com.
81 Boyce, George. D. (2005), *Nineteenth Century Ireland*, Dublin: Gill & MacMillan, p. 160.
82 Maume, 'Sullivan, Alexander Martin'.
83 Ibid.
84 *The Nation*, 06.12.1884, p. 5, www.irishnewsarchive.com.
85 *Irish Independent*, 10.01.1959, p. 11, www.irishnewsarchive.com.
86 Callanan, Frank (2009), 'Sullivan, Alexander Martin, *Dictionary of Irish Biography*, available at www.dib.ie (accessed 10 May 2023).
87 Ibid.
88 Mitchell, Angus (2013), *16 Lives: Roger Casement*, Dublin: O'Brien Press, p. 293.
89 *Donegal News*, 17.01.1959, p. 6, www.irishnewsarchive.com.
90 *The New York Times*, 11.08.1900.
91 *Sunday Independent*, Looking Around, 1993.
92 Mitchell, *16 Lives: Roger Casement*, p. 293.
93 Ibid., pp. 293–6.
94 Callanan, 'Sullivan, Alexander Martin'.
95 Ibid.
96 Ibid.
97 *The Irish Times*, 16.04.1956.
98 Callanan, 'Sullivan, Alexander Martin'.
99 *Irish Independent*, 10.01.1959, p. 11, www.irishnewsarchive.com.
100 Ibid.

Acknowledgements

Working as a tour guide in Glasnevin Cemetery over the past eight years, I have had the privilege to bring many people to their heroes' gravesides and personally to learn about many people from history I had never heard about. I would like to thank all at Dublin Cemeteries Trust for the opportunity that they gave to me in 2016. I was at that point in time an undergraduate history and politics student at Maynooth University, with zero tour-guiding experience. Glasnevin and its history since then have become a significant part of my life.

I would like to sincerely thank Conor Graham and all those at Merrion Press who took a chance in believing in this project. To Patrick O'Donoghue, thank you for helping to guide me through the initial challenging stages as a first-time author. My thanks also to Wendy Logue for her constant advice and encouragement. Access to cultural institutions was a challenge in the initial stages of writing during the ongoing Covid-19 pandemic. Thankfully in the latter stages of editing things became easier. There is a high volume of accessible material online that made this book possible. I am indebted to the Royal Irish Academy and their online *Dictionary of Irish Biography*, to The National Archives of Ireland for their digitised census records, to the National Library of Ireland and their online catalogue, who have kindly given permission for me to make use of some images in this book, and to the Military Archives and the Bureau of Military History database, in particular their digitised witness statements. As a former student at Maynooth University, I quickly appreciated JSTOR as a handy way of accessing many scholarly journal articles online. Thanks also to The New York Public Library Digital Collections for permission to use images of old Fenians Hollywood and Duggan.

Dublin Cemeteries Trust can provide you with a record of where a loved one is buried in the cemetery. All records are digitised. This has allowed me to locate and record all of the individuals in this book. I would encourage anyone researching their family history to make use of this great resource. Subscription services including The Irish Newspapers Archive, *The Irish Times* Archives, Ancestry.com and Findmypast.com have all helped to further shape the people's stories in this book. Thank you to the Department of Tourism, Culture, Arts, Gaeltacht, Sport and Media and the

General Register Office for the freely accessible Irishgenealogy.ie website providing digitised birth, marriage and death certificates for many of those in this book.

My thanks to Lynn Brady for her unending passion for genealogy, grave locations, graveyards and Glasnevin. Thank you also to the Glasnevin Genealogy Group, which Lynn runs. I would like especially to thank Rod Dennison for bringing so many stories to me relating to Glasnevin, not all of which made it into this publication, to Fionnuala White for securing the birth and baptismal certificate for Fr Eugene McCarthy, and to John O'Grady for sharing his research into the graves of those who died in the RMS *Leinster* disaster. My thanks to all in the Michael Collins22 Society for their stories, anecdotes and encouragement in putting this book together. I have fond memories of my trip with the group to Clonakilty in August 2022 to commemorate the centenary of Collins' death at Béal na mBláth.

Within Glasnevin Cemetery there is a lengthy list of people whose previous work, internal research and passion for keeping the site's legacy alive have provided me with a good foundation for writing this book. Although this book is an independent work separate to Dublin Cemeteries Trust, I wish to thank Brendan Kavanagh, Visitor Centre Manager; Aoife Waters, CEO, Dublin Cemeteries Trust; Luke O'Toole, Director of Strategic Development; and David Bunworth, chairperson of the board at DC Trust. A special thank you to Conor Dodd, the resident historian in Glasnevin. He has researched and written extensively on the cemetery in all its guises. His research for tour content, exhibitions, pamphlets and commemorations has been referenced extensively in this book. It was an invaluable source of information that has helped to shape some of the stories here. Thank you to Anne-Marie Smith, Bridget Sheerin and Paddy Gleeson, who saw fit to give me the position as tour guide in January 2016, and to all guides, past and present, for their enthusiasm in re-telling the stories of Glasnevin, especially Paddy Gleeson, Bridget Sheerin, Alan Cleary, Daniel Eglington-Carey, Dr Caitlin White, Ultan Moran, Niall Bracken, Niall Oman, Irial O'Connell, Grainne Nolan, John Scanlon, Sean Hayes and Michelle O'Brien. I would also like to thank Michele O'Connor who, during her time as Education Officer, brought the story of Ally Sloper and Lady Margaret Nelson to my attention. Thank you to all I have worked alongside in Glasnevin and for the many pints of Guinness purchased for me in the Gravediggers/Kavanaghs Pub after our shifts.

To those no longer with us, I wish to express my thanks and appreciation to the late Shane MacThomáis, who did much to bring many of the stories in Glasnevin, both famous and forgotten, to light. To his family I want to acknowledge that 2024 sadly marks the tenth anniversary of his untimely death. It was seeing Shane in the award-winning documentary *One Million Dubliners* that inspired me to apply for a tour-guiding position. Also thank you to the late Dr Shane Kenna and his research into the Fenians and their many links with Glasnevin. His work on the centenary of the burial of O'Donovan Rossa in 2015 also played its part in inspiring me to become more interested in the cemetery. To his mother, Olive, thank you for your conversations at events and book launches and for encouraging me to write myself.

Away from Glasnevin I work full-time with Trinity Access Programmes (TAP) as their Primary and Junior Cycle Coordinator. Since 1993, TAP has been working tirelessly in partnership across the education sector with students, teachers, families, communities and businesses to widen access and participation at third level for under-represented groups. It is a job I am very proud to have. Those within the Schools Outreach Team will know it does not take much to get me talking about history and the cemetery. A common office game to play between colleagues is 'How long will it take Warren to mention that he works in Glasnevin?' I want to thank all in TAP for the work they do and for the support they have given me throughout this process. Thanks especially to Dr Kevin Sullivan, Fiona O'Reilly, Wendy Crampton, Professor Brendan Tangney and Georgia Spooner. Also thank you to colleagues who have since moved to new positions: Dr Becky Long, Niamh Ellis and Carly Elston for listening to my cemetery rants.

To the historians, history enthusiasts, archivists and curators who have generously given up their time in sending me sources, images, documents and in replying to my many emails, thank you. There are far too many people to name here, but I want to particularly mention Brian Crowley and Ciara Scott at the OPW; author Joni Scanlon; Sean Scaife and John Callanan from Wanderers FC rugby club; Robert McNicol, the Club Historian at The All England Lawn Tennis Club; author John Pinfold, Darina Wade and William Phelan in the houses of the Oireachtais; Billy Smith and the Everton FC Heritage Society; Darren Smith, the Broadcast and Liaison Manager at Everton FC; James Grange Osborne, Research Assistant at Mediahuis Ireland; Martin Byrne and the Fr O'Flanagan Memorial Group; Noelle Dowling, Archivist for the Dublin Dioceses; Jennie Ryan and John Scanlon from MoLI; Steven Kerr, College Librarian at The Royal College of Surgeons of Edinburgh; Rob Twamley for his activism in raising awareness about Peggy Dell's unmarked grave; Stephen Ferguson, Assistant Secretary & Museum Curator, An Post; author Catherine De Courcy; Dublin Zoo; the Board of Trinity College Dublin; Aisling Lockhart, Servives Executive in TCD Reading Room; Gill (Gillian) Whelan, Senior Digital Photographer, TCD Archives; the Digital Collections at Trinity College; Andrew Martin from the Irish Newspaper Archives; Sarah Timmins, Archivist at the Royal College of Surgeons Ireland; 'Mairead Delaney Archivist at the Abbey

Theatre Archive; and the National Gallery of Ireland, for permission to use portrait of Dora Sigerson Shorter.

Thanks also to my good historian pals Lorcan Collins, Donal Fallon and Gerard Shannon for their advice, friendship, support and countless history conversations at various places around the city. Dublin is lucky to have such talented and passionate historians keeping the heritage of our capital city alive. Special thanks to Lorcan for agreeing to write the foreword. To my best friend Thomas Maguire, thanks for accompanying me on my many historical walks about the city and especially for your company at Richmond Park to watch our beloved football team St Pat's; this has been a nice distraction from writing the book. During my time as a secondary school student at Drimnagh Castle there were many teachers who inspired me greatly. Two I would like to thank in helping to ignite my love of history are Dominic Price and Fergal Kelleher. Also thank you to Michelle Nolan O'Driscoll, my past drama teacher for continuing to support and encourage me to this day.

On a personal note, I wish to thank my partner, Loren Sinclair, for her unending patience in putting up with me whilst writing this book and for also accepting my ongoing obsession with Glasnevin. I am eternally grateful to you for always saying yes to visiting museums and going on tours with me, and for being my biggest champion. I love you very much.

To my parents Kim and David Farrell, I love you both and am indebted to you both for providing me with the education I have today. My love of the arts, heritage and reading comes from you both. To my dad, thank you for introducing me to Irish history with my first visit to Kilmainham Gaol in 1999. To my brother, Emmet, thanks for your companionship and for always keeping me on my toes. Thank you to Elizabeth my godmother, Gerald my godfather, Paul, Paula, John and Hannah Regan, Hajrija Nurkic and all close family friends who have always been there for me. I would especially like to pay tribute to my late grandfather Leo Farrell to whom I have dedicated this book. I wish you could have held a copy of it in your hand. To my grandmother Kathleen, your guidance and love continues to push me forward every single day. Thanks also to my grandmother for allowing me to re-tell the story of her descendants, the Lackens, in this publication.

Finally, I am very grateful to everyone who granted me permission to re-use and make use of material contained within this book. It has not been possible to contact the surviving relatives of everyone written about within. If you are a relative of someone included in this book and you feel something has been omitted, I would encourage you to contact the publisher and/or myself. I hope I have done their stories justice.

Index

Note: Page numbers in bold refer to photographs.